RESEARCH HANDBOOK ON THE WTO AGRICULTURE AGREEMENT

RESEARCH HANDBOOKS ON THE WTO

This timely series of *Research Handbooks* analyses the interface between international economic law and other disciplines at the centre of current debate about the role and impact of the WTO. Each volume is edited by a prominent expert at the heart of this debate and brings together original contributions from an internationally recognisable cast of leading scholars and practitioners.

These *Handbooks* will be essential reference tools for academic researchers and doctoral students as well as for policymakers and practicing lawyers.

Titles in this series include:

Research Handbook on the Protection of Intellectual Property under WTO Rules
Intellectual Property in the WTO, Volume I
Edited by Carlos M. Correa

Research Handbook on the Interpretation and Enforcement of Intellectual Property under WTO Rules
Intellectual Property in the WTO, Volume II
Edited by Carlos M. Correa

Research Handbook on the WTO Agriculture Agreement
New and Emerging Issues in International Agricultural Trade Law
Edited by Joseph A. McMahon and Melaku Geboye Desta

Research Handbook on the WTO Agriculture Agreement

New and Emerging Issues in International Agricultural Trade Law

Edited by

Joseph A. McMahon

*Professor of Commercial Law,
University College Dublin*

Melaku Geboye Desta

*Reader in International Economic Law,
CEPMLP, University of Dundee*

RESEARCH HANDBOOKS ON THE WTO

Edward Elgar
Cheltenham, UK • Northampton, MA, USA

Published by
Edward Elgar Publishing Limited
The Lypiatts
15 Lansdown Road
Cheltenham
Glos GL50 2JA
UK

Edward Elgar Publishing, Inc.
William Pratt House
9 Dewey Court
Northampton
Massachusetts 01060
USA

A catalogue record for this book
is available from the British Library

Library of Congress Control Number: 2011932879

ISBN 978 1 84844 116 3 (cased)

Printed and bound by MPG Books Group, UK

Contents

Contributors

Kym Anderson is George Gollin Professor of Economics and Foundation Executive Director of the Centre for International Economic Studies (CIES) at the University of Adelaide in Australia, where he has been affiliated since 1984 following six years as a Research Fellow at the Australian National University's Institute for Advanced Studies. In 2004–07 he was on extended leave at the World Bank's Development Economics Research Group in Washington DC as Lead Economist (Trade Policy). Before that he spent 1990–92 in the Research Division of the GATT Secretariat in Geneva. He has also served as a Panellist in WTO dispute settlement cases.

David Blandford is Professor of Agricultural and Environmental Economics, and former department head, in the Department of Agricultural Economics and Rural Sociology at the Pennsylvania State University. He was formerly a division director at the Organisation for Economic Co-operation and Development (OECD) in Paris and a Professor at Cornell University. Blandford was the president of the Agricultural Economics Society of the United Kingdom in 2010/11. He teaches courses in agri-business at Penn State and conducts research into food and agricultural policies, including their environmental, trade and rural development aspects.

Michael Cardwell is Professor of Agricultural Law at the University of Leeds. After working in legal practice with Burges Salmon, Bristol, he joined the School of Law, University of Leeds, in 1990. His early research was directed towards agricultural tenancies and European Community quota regimes. More recently, he has also addressed the broader legal issues generated by the reform of the EU's Common Agricultural Policy and, in particular, its compatibility with world trade obligations. His publications include *The European Model of Agriculture* (OUP, 2004).

Ignacio Carreño is a lawyer for the International Trade and Food Law team of FratiniVergano, a law firm based in Brussels, where he is responsible for internal market, agriculture and food law. He holds a Master's degree in EU law from the University Carlos III Madrid. He graduated in law at the University Bielefeld and has been practising in Brussels since 2000. He specialises in EU food and agricultural law and has worked on a number of court cases at the General Court of the EU and on issues such as the free movement of agricultural products and foodstuffs within the EU, WTO market access, sanitary and phytosanitary regulation and technical barriers to trade. Ignacio is a member of the Düsseldorf and Brussels Bars.

Melaku Geboye Desta is a Reader in International Economic Law and director of the PhD Programme at the Centre for Energy, Petroleum and Mineral Law and Policy at the University of Dundee. His research and teaching interests include WTO law, agriculture, energy, trade and development, international business transactions and international arbitration. Melaku has published widely in the areas of WTO and agriculture, trade and energy, and regional trade agreements. He also consults for governments, law firms and international organisations on international trade law and policy issues.

Graham Dutfield is Professor of International Governance at Leeds University School of Law. He has a keen scholarly interest in the law, science and the business of bio-technical innovation from the Enlightenment to the present. Other research areas include intellectual property and health, agriculture, and traditional knowledge. Recent books include *Intellectual Property Rights and the Life Science Industries: Past, Present and Future* (2nd edn), *Global Intellectual Property Law* (with U. Suthersanen), and *Intellectual Property and Human Development: Current Trends and Future Scenarios* (edited with T. Wong).

Christian Häberli is a Senior Research Fellow at the World Trade Institute, University of Bern (Switzerland). Christian's professional career in development, trade and agriculture has included postings in Madagascar, Thailand, Nepal and Switzerland. From 1978 to 1982 he worked for the International Labour Organisation (ILO) and from 1983 to 2007 for the Swiss Government. He completed his legal studies with a PhD on the subject of African Investment Law (1979); he also obtained a degree at the Institut Universitaire d'Etudes du Développement in Geneva (1975) and another in theology (Bern, 2009). As a representative for Switzerland at the WTO, he has chaired the Committee on Agriculture (Regular Session) and since 1996 has also served in five dispute settlement panels, namely *EC – Bananas III, Japan – Apples, EC – Biotech (GMO), China – Trading Rights*

(Audiovisual Services) and *United States – Country of Origin Labelling (COOL)*.

Lee Ann Jackson is a Counsellor in the Agriculture and Commodities Division at the World Trade Organization, where she has been involved in the Doha Development Round agricultural negotiations as well as implementation of the SPS Agreement, including WTO dispute settlement activities. Prior to joining the WTO, she held positions at the School of Economics at the University of Adelaide in South Australia and at the International Food Policy Research Institute. She has a PhD in applied economics, a joint Master's degree in public policy and environmental studies, and a degree in biology.

Tim Josling is Professor Emeritus at the (former) Food Research Institute at Stanford University; a Senior Fellow at the Freeman Spogli Institute for International Studies; and a faculty member at FSI's Europe Center. His research focuses on agricultural policy and food policy in industrialised nations; international trade in agricultural and food products; and the development of the multilateral trade regime. He is currently studying the reform of the agricultural trading system in the World Trade Organization; the use of geographical indications; the role of health and safety regulations in trade; the impact of climate change legislation on agricultural trade policies; and the treatment of biofuel subsidies in the WTO.

Eugenia Laurenza is a lawyer for the International Trade and Food Law team of FratiniVergano, a law firm based in Brussels, where she is responsible for EU and international trade law and food law. Eugenia graduated in law from the University of Rome, La Sapienza, and holds an LLM in European and International Trade Law from the Universiteit van Amsterdam. She has been practising in Brussels since 2005. Eugenia's main practice areas are WTO law and dispute settlement procedures, trade negotiations (bilateral and multilateral) in the areas of agriculture and services, market access, sanitary and phytosanitary standards, technical barriers to trade, subsidies, and regional integration. Eugenia is also a member of the Rome and Brussels Bars ('E' list).

Alan Matthews is Professor Emeritus of European Agricultural Policy in the Department of Economics, Trinity College Dublin, Ireland, where he was formerly Head of the Department of Economics and Director of the Institute for International Integration Studies. His major research interests include agricultural policy analysis, the impact of EU policies on developing countries, and the design of WTO trade rules for agriculture. He has worked as a consultant to the OECD, the Food and Agriculture Organisation of the United Nations, the World Bank and the European Commission, and has also been a panel member in a number of WTO dispute settlement cases.

Joseph A. McMahon is Professor of Commercial Law in the School of Law at University College Dublin, Ireland. His research interests include agriculture, both within the WTO and the EU, as well as the Development Cooperation Policies of the EU. He has also acted as a consultant on the SPS and TBT Agreements to projects in Mauritius and Indonesia. His recent works include *The Agreement on Agriculture* (Oxford University Press, 2006) and *The Negotiations for a New Agreement on Agriculture* (Brill USA, 2011).

Fiona Smith is Senior Lecturer in the Faculty of Laws, University College London (UCL). Her research principally focuses on agriculture and the WTO. She is particularly interested in how philosophical thought can reveal new dimensions to the problem of international agricultural trade regulation. She has spoken about her work throughout the world and has published a number of articles, as well as being the author of *Agriculture and the WTO: Towards a New Theory of International Agricultural Trade Regulation* (2009, Edward Elgar). Fiona is also co-Director of the WTO Scholars' Forum, Sidley Austin, Geneva.

Stephanie Switzer is a Lecturer in Law at the University of Dundee, Scotland. She was recently awarded her PhD in Law from University College Dublin and is interested in trade and development as well as the broader question of how the trade regime should respond to the challenges posed by the increased trade in biofuels.

Preface

When we were approached to edit a collection on International Agricultural Trade Law, we eschewed an approach which would have examined the existing provisions of the Agreement on Agriculture (AoA) and the agriculture negotiations in the Doha Round. A major factor in this decision was that a significant body of commentary and literature already exists on the rules of the AoA, a significant proportion of it authored by the contributors to this volume. We did not wish to repeat or reproduce that literature here. Instead, we have chosen to focus on the 'new' issues that are closely linked to the international regulation of agricultural production and trade, but that have neither been sufficiently covered by the rules of the AoA nor adequately addressed in the literature. Many of these issues are either left to some other non-WTO instruments and systems (e.g. climate change under the UNFCCC system, etc.), raising the issue of relations with the WTO regime as a key question, or simply fall in the cracks between the WTO and those other regimes (as the food security issue appears to be). This volume focuses on these borderline issues. At the same time, we also needed to put these issues within the context of the existing legal terrain. We use the Introduction chapter to provide the necessary background information, where we examine the provisions of the AoA, as informed by the jurisprudence of WTO Panels and the Appellate Body. This introduction also offers a very brief synopsis of the Doha negotiations, which concentrates on the content of the latest version of the Modalities issued by the Chair of the Special Session of the Committee on Agriculture in December 2008. Progress since then has been slow and, as one of our contributors concludes, also 'fruitless.'

In Chapter 2, Fiona Smith addresses food security, one of the most sensitive and least-understood issues in the field of international law. Dr Smith argues that what is needed is to address old problems from new perspectives. For her, changing all the international agricultural trade rules on food security does not necessarily imply improving them and, even if they were to be changed, this could result in consequential effects which might adversely impact on different aspects of international agricultural trade regulation. She concludes that the temptation to overload the rules addressing food security should be resisted and argues that the existing rules may be more than able to accommodate some contemporary food security concerns through small, incremental changes that may also maintain the integrity of the existing rules.

In Chapter 3, Christian Häberli picks up the argument and asks, rather provocatively, if WTO rules improve or impair the Right to Food. After demonstrating that this still lacks an adequate response under the present multilateral regime applying to food production and trade, Dr Häberli presents the issue as a systemic challenge of how to end the fragmentation between international humanitarian law and international trade law. He argues that such fragmentation cannot excuse WTO inaction and there is a need for a better regulatory framework in the WTO. This framework would enshrine the Right to Food within the WTO whilst also allowing food-insecure developing countries the necessary policy space to address the many aspects of this problem.

It is this issue of policy space that Alan Matthews discusses in Chapter 4. Professor Matthews examines the subject of policy space, focusing mainly on the so-called 'development box' issues of special products and the SSM, two areas of the Doha negotiations that are essentially about developing countries' ability to take certain measures for food security and other reasons. Examining the difficult negotiations on these instruments, reflecting as they do different conceptions of the Agreement on Agriculture and various views on what these instruments are intended to achieve, although there is room for compromise, he argues that developing countries do not require permanent exceptions to WTO rules to promote their food security, livelihood security and rural development goals. Matthews concludes that what is needed is an investment in agricultural production, infrastructure and institutions by both the developing countries themselves and donors.

One potential area for investment in the service of food security and overall development relates to the protection of intellectual property in plant varieties, a subject that Graham Dutfield addresses in Chapter 5. Outlining the scope of this intellectual property right, Professor Dutfield examines the International Convention for the Protection of New Varieties of Plants (UPOV) and asks whether this system is the most optimal legal system given the variety of conditions around the world. Dutfield argues that UPOV provides a one-size-fits-all solution for everything, making it insufficiently sensitive to the specific needs and realities of a diverse range of countries. He concludes that there is a huge lack of awareness about plant variety protection and, given the implications of such protection for issues such as biodiversity and rural development, this should be addressed either within or outside of UPOV.

A further aspect of agricultural investment relates to the use of new technology, in particular that of Genetically Modified Organisms (GMOs), which is addressed in Chapter 6 by Kym Anderson and Lee Ann Jackson. After examining the economic consequences of the diverse policy approaches by the enthusiasts and sceptics of GMOs, the chapter examines the evolving EU policy landscape in this area, including the developments after the WTO dispute on biotech products in 2007. The authors argue that the uncertainty about the EU regulatory environment operates as a major disincentive to further research in this area and the adoption of GMOs by other countries. They conclude that by investing in this technology developing countries would stand to gain in terms of alleviating poverty and adapting to the problems posed by climate change.

Whether conventional or biotech-based, everyone agrees that engaging in international trade is good for the participants in terms of general welfare as well as specific cases of food security. Agricultural trade liberalisation is being pursued today exactly for that reason. However, agricultural trade can also pose risks to human, animal and plant life or health and all liberalisation efforts have to be tempered with national regulation that is intended to eliminate or minimise such risks. There is therefore a balance that has to be struck at any point in time between these interests. Add to this the many other requirements that are set by supermarket chains and other private players and the issue of standards is bound to be controversial. These very issues are addressed in Chapter 7 and Chapter 8 which deal, respectively, with governmental or regulatory standards and private standards.

In Chapter 7, Eugenia Laurenza and Ignacio Carreño argue that in order to ensure that the benefits of tariff liberalisation and commercial concessions on agricultural products are not unduly impaired by trade concerns arising from the application of regulatory measures, negotiations and commercially meaningful results on regulations, standards and requirements affecting agricultural trade and falling within the scope of WTO Agreements should be factored into the ongoing multilateral trade negotiations, and accompany negotiations on agricultural tariff liberalisation and market access concessions. This novel approach to regulatory problems, the authors argue, could allow for technical and financial assistance to be offered to developing countries to ensure their compliance with the standards for products that are of particular interest to them. Tim Josling then addresses, in Chapter 8, the rapid growth in the number and scope of private standards, which is seen as a response to the evolution of public standards. Professor Josling assesses whether private standards facilitate or restrict trade, whether they conflict with public standards, and whether they pose problems for the WTO. Although there has been no major conflict with multilateral trade rules and a limited trade impact, Josling concludes that future conflict could be defused by the clarification of the place of private standards in the SPS Agreement, the use of codes of best practice for private standard-setting bodies, and a simplification of the task facing producers to comply with multiple standards.

The challenges posed by regulatory and private standards to agricultural trade and their implications for such issues as food security and overall welfare can be, and indeed are, negotiable between WTO member states or in other fora. The challenges posed to agricultural trade by climate change are of a different type; adaptation rather than negotiation will be the option. David Blandford addresses this issue in Chapter 9. This issue extends across the GATT and a number of WTO Agreements and Professor Blandford examines the interactions between climate change and agriculture policies. Blandford's discussion on biofuels highlights this interaction very clearly, and concludes that the WTO framework was not set up to deal with issues that have broad international implications such as climate change and that the preferential treatment afforded to agriculture may be a source of future conflict. Such conflict will be complicated as agriculture is a significant contributor to global greenhouse gas emissions but could also contribute to mitigation activities.

In Chapter 10, Stephanie Switzer takes the issue of biofuels further and addresses the challenges arising from increased use of biofuels, which include the potential impact that the use of agricultural products as feedstocks for biofuels could have on the availability and price of food and problems concerning environmental protection. Dr Switzer argues that both of these are recognised in the AoA as non-trade concerns. Echoing Smith's discussion in Chapter 2, Switzer argues that whilst leaving certain issues incompletely theorised may at times be both necessary and desirable there are occasions when more complete theorisation may be required to guard against the risk of inconsistency. Using the example of biofuels, she argues that communicative space is required within the trade regime to offer new understandings of non-trade concerns.

For now all issues that are related to agriculture, but that are not fully or directly addressed by the AoA, are loosely called non-trade concerns. It is this more general concept that Michael Cardwell addresses in the last chapter of this volume. Professor Cardwell examines this concept under the title of multifunctionality, a term often associated with the EU's efforts to broaden the scope of agriculture-related discussions and negotiations particularly in the WTO context so that the implication of agricultural production and trade policies for such issues as the environment, climate change, food security etc. would be taken into account. Having examined the boundaries of multifunctionality, the contestation of the concept within the WTO and its continued prominent position within the EU, Cardwell concludes that it is not easy to determine whether food security and climate change fit within conventional notions of multifunctionality. He suggests further analytical work exploring how to avert clashes between potentially conflicting multifunctional public goods so that the major policy challenges of food security and climate change may be simultaneously achieved.

As editors, we are delighted and honoured to bring together the excellent contributions in this volume; it was a privilege to work with each of our contributors – by responding with good grace and timeliness to all our requests for changes to their work, they made our work enjoyable. We thank them all. Our thanks also go to all at Edward Elgar Press, in particular Ben Booth and John-Paul McDonald, for their patience with us as editors. However, the largest thanks must go to our respective wives and families for their constant support and encouragement.

Abbreviations

AoA	Agreement on Agriculture
AFSI	Aquila Food Security Initiative
AIE	Analysis and Information Exchange
AIPPI	International Association for the Protection of Intellectual Property
AMS	Aggregate Measurement of Support
API	Agreement on Pre-shipment Inspection
APREBES	Association of Plant Breeding for the Benefit of Society
ASSINEL	International Association of Plant Breeders
BIRPI	Bureaux Internationaux Réunis de la Protection de la Propriété Intellectuelle
BRC	British Retail Consortium
CAJ	Administrative and Legal Committee
CBD	Convention on Biological Diversity
CFA	Comprehensive Framework for Action
CFS	Committee on World Food Security
CIOPORA	Communauté Internationale des Obtenteurs de Plantes Ornementales et fruitières de Reproduction Asexuée
CT	cap and trade
DDA	Doha Development Agenda
DSB	Dispute Settlement Body
DSU	Dispute Settlement Understanding
DUS	distinct, uniform and stable
EC	European Community
ECVC	European Coordination of Via Campesina
EFSA	European Food Safety Authority
EU	European Union
FAO	Food and Agriculture Organisation
FDI	Foreign Direct Investment
FIS	Fédération Internationale du Commerce des Semences
FMI	Food Marketing Institute
GATT	General Agreement on Tariffs and Trade
GDP	Gross Domestic Product
GHG	greenhouse gases

GM	Genetically Modified
GMOs	Genetically Modified Organisms
HLPE	High Level Panel of Experts
HLTF	High-Level Task Force
ICESCR	International Covenant on Economic, Social and Cultural Rights
IFS	International Featured Standards
IMF	International Monetary Fund
ISO	International Standards Organisation
MDGs	Millennium Development Goals
MFN	most-favoured-nation
MRL	Maximum Residue Levels
NAMA	Non-agricultural market access
NFIDCs	Net-Food Importing Developing Countries
NGO	Non-Governmental Organisation
OAPI	Organisation Africaine de la Propriété Intellectuelle
OAU	Organisation of African Unity
OECD	Organisation for Economic Cooperation and Development
OTDS	Overall Trade Distorting Support
PVP	Plant Variety Protection
RAM	Recently Acceded Member
R2F	Right to Food
SACU	Southern African Customs Union
SADC	Southern African Development Community
SCM	Agreement on Subsidies and Countervailing Measures
SDT	Special and Differential Treatment
SP	Special Products
SPS	Sanitary and Phytosanitary Measures
SSA	Sub-Saharan African
SSG	Special Agricultural Safeguard
SSM	Special Safeguard Mechanism
TBT	Technical Barriers to Trade
TC	Technical Committee
TRIPS	Trade-related Aspects of Intellectual Property Rights
TWP	Technical Working Parties
UDHR	Universal Declaration of Human Rights
UN	United Nations
UPOV	Union pour la Protection des Obtentions Végétales
US	United States
VCLT	Vienna Convention on the Law of Treaties

WFP	World Food Programme
WIPO	World Intellectual Property Organisation
WTO	World Trade Organization

1 The Agreement on Agriculture: setting the scene

Joseph A. McMahon and Melaku Geboye Desta

I. INTRODUCTION

This volume brings together views and analyses by leading scholars and practitioners around the world on some of the most pressing issues of international agricultural trade law, policy and regulation, including the implication of national and international trade policies on national food security, global climate change, and biotechnology. While the WTO system occupies a central role in all matters of agricultural production and trade policy, many of these new challenges remain on the fringes of the WTO system. In this introductory chapter we provide an overview of the WTO system as it applies to agricultural trade, with the object of putting the new and emerging issues into their broader analytical and conceptual context.

The Uruguay Round Agreement on Agriculture (AoA) marked a systemic shift in the international regulation of agricultural production and trade. The AoA put an end to an era of exceptionalism in which agriculture was excluded from key principles of the General Agreement on Tariffs and Trade (GATT), particularly those on quantitative import restrictions under Article XI and export subsidies under Section B of Article XVI, while the remaining parts of the GATT were largely ignored by the major contracting parties. The AoA has now brought this to an end. But even the AoA does not subject agricultural products to the same rules as other products. Indeed, we have the AoA as a sector-specific agreement precisely because members of the WTO are not yet ready to treat agriculture in the same way as other products. In the words of the Preamble, the AoA aims only to 'establish a basis for initiating a process of reform of trade in agriculture', while the long-term objective of that process is to 'establish a fair and market-oriented agricultural trading system'.

With these short- and long-term objectives in view, the AoA has: (1) defined what agricultural products are – i.e. all products listed in Chapters 1 to 24 of the Harmonised System except fish and fish products, plus certain other specified items;[1] and (2) established a framework for the regulation of agricultural trade around three pillars – market access, domestic support, and export competition. This design was chosen in order to realize the mandate given to the Uruguay Round under the Punta del Este Declaration to 'bring more discipline and predictability to world agricultural trade by correcting and preventing restrictions and distortions including those related to structural surpluses so as to reduce the uncertainty, imbalances and instability in world agricultural markets' (GATT, 1987).

This chapter provides a brief introduction to the three pillars of the agreement and an assessment of the provisions of the AoA on the basis of the available jurisprudence on the subject. This will then be followed by an overview of the Doha round of negotiations for the revision of the Agriculture Agreement and the national commitments in each of its three pillars. The main purpose of this chapter is to outline the major contours of the territory of the WTO regime on agriculture, which serves as a preface to the closer examination of the borderlines issues that follow in the rest of the volume.

II.   THE THREE PILLARS OF THE AGREEMENT

The reform programme launched by the AoA was made up of some degree of rule-making and the adoption of specific commitments to increase market access and to reduce domestic support and export subsidies, which would, in the words of the Preamble, lead to 'substantial reductions in agricultural support and protection sustained over an agreed period of time'. The agreed implementation period for the specific commitments undertaken as part of the Uruguay Round negotiations was six years (ten years for developing countries), save in the case of Article 13, the 'Peace Clause', which limited the possibility of disputes for a period of nine years (AoA Article 1(f)). This is, however, only the first of a series of such commitments. Article 20 of the AoA has already built an agenda for further negotiations so as to achieve the long-term objective of 'substantial progressive reductions in support and protection'. Stuart Harbinson (2009: 5), chairman of the agriculture negotiations in the early days of the Doha process, wrote that the main accomplishment of the AoA was 'to bring the trade within the scope of GATT/WTO disciplines for the first time. But, as a price for that, little was achieved in terms of liberalization through Uruguay Round commitments, and rule-making was basic.' The current negotiations are thus intended to bring about an improvement in the rules as well as further deepen the level of liberalization in agricultural trade.

A. Market Access

In terms of rule-making, a major achievement of the AoA on market access was the elimination of nearly all types of non-tariff barriers, which were to be converted into tariff equivalents, under a process known as 'tariffication'. Under Article 4.2: 'Members shall not maintain, resort to, or revert to any measures of the kind which have been required to be converted into ordinary customs duties, except as otherwise provided for in Article 5 and Annex 5'.[2] This is perhaps the most significant aspect of the entire Agreement, since it means that virtually all agricultural protection is now in the form of tariffs, which are more transparent and easier to negotiate than non-tariff measures. The Panel in *Chile – Price Band System* described Article 4.2 as central to 'the establishment and protection of a fair and market-oriented agricultural trading system in the area of market access' (DS207/R, 7.15). It went on to indicate that the list of measures in footnote 1 was not exhaustive, but merely illustrative.[3] The Appellate Body in the same dispute noted that Article 4.2 recorded the intention of the negotiators of the Agreement that in principle customs duties would become the only form of border protection (DS207/AB/R, 200).

Moreover, members also undertook specific commitments in the area of agricultural market access, which included the binding and reduction of tariffs and other commitments (AoA Article 4.1). The reduction commitments apply to both traditional tariffs and new tariffs (i.e. tariffs resulting from the process of tariffication). For developed members the average reduction was to be 36 per cent over six years (1995–2000), whereas for developing members the average reduction was to be 24 per cent to be implemented over a ten-year period (1995–2004). Least-developed members were required to bind their tariffs but not to undertake any reduction commitments. Both developing countries and LDCs were allowed the flexibility to offer ceiling bindings for those products that were subject to unbound ordinary customs duties (1993 Agriculture Modalities, para. 14). To reflect the comprehensive nature of the market-access negotiations, all participating members were required to make minimum reductions on each tariff line, 15 per cent per tariff line for developed countries and 10 per cent for developing countries.

The process of converting quotas (and other non-tariff barriers) into tariffs could of course reduce market access where the quota had been large and tariffication produced a high tariff. To ameliorate this effect each Member was required to include minimum and current access commitments, through a tariff rate quota (TRQ) system, for all tariffied products in its Schedules. Minimum access opportunities were to be established in those situations where the historic level of imports was below 3 per cent of domestic consumption, with the accompanying TRQs rising to at least 5 per cent by the end of the six-year implementation period. In cases where historic import levels were above this minimum, there was a requirement to maintain those current access opportunities and increase them further over the implementation period.

i.   Special treatment

Annex 5 to the Agreement contains two exceptions to the tariffication requirement. These exceptions are designed to deal with concerns raised during the negotiations relating to the tariffication of non-tariff barriers on particularly sensitive products. Annex 5A covers products that have been designated as subject to special treatment based on non-trade concerns such as food security and environmental protection and it was introduced at the request of Japan and Korea. Annex 5B exempts from the tariffication requirement primary agricultural products that are the predominant staple in the traditional diet of a developing country. A total of four countries used the Special Treatment provisions of Annex 5 in 1995: Japan, Korea and the Philippines for rice (hence, the expression 'rice clause' to refer to special treatment under Annex 5) and Israel for sheep and goat meat and dairy products. However, Israel and Japan converted their non-tariff measures as from 1999 and 2001 respectively, while the Philippines has renewed it for another seven years (until 2012; see Schedule LXXV – Philippines, effective 27 December 2006) and Korea for another ten years (until 2014, G/AG/W/71). We shall see later on that two related concepts have been introduced in the Doha agriculture negotiations in order to address product-specific interests in member states – sensitive products for all members and special products for developing countries only. However, while the Uruguay Round Special Treatment provision was introduced in order to exempt particular products from the tariffication requirement (i.e. so as to keep non-tariff barriers in place after the conclusion of the Uruguay Round), the two Doha concepts of special treatment are intended only to selectively protect these products from the otherwise high tariff reductions, i.e. to subject these products to tariff reductions below that required for all other tariff lines.

ii.   Special agricultural safeguard

While the exceptions to the tariffication requirement provided in Annex 5 were tailored to specific concerns raised by specific countries during the Uruguay Round, Article 5 of the Agreement provides a more widely-used special safeguard mechanism particularly for agricultural products that were subject to the tariffication process. Switzerland, the Member who urged the adoption of such an exception, viewed it as necessary to promote acceptance of the market access commitments and this was intended to remain in force for the duration of the reform process.

Under Article 5 two preconditions must be met before a special safeguard measure may be taken: firstly, it can only be taken with respect to tariffied products and, secondly, the Member must have designated the product in question with the symbol 'SSG' in its Schedule. If these two preconditions are met Article 5.1 creates two types of special safeguard measures that may be taken, one based on the volume of imports (volume-based) and the other based on the price of imports (price-based). A Member may take either type of special safeguard measure but not both at the same time. Article 5.8 prohibits the use of general safeguards, that is, those taken under Article XIX of the GATT and the Agreement on Safeguards, together with special safeguards measures under AoA Article 5.

The volume-based safeguard may only remain in effect until the end of the year in which it was imposed, and it may not exceed one third of the regular tariff. The trigger level is defined in Article 5.4 on the basis of market access opportunities, i.e., imports as a percentage of domestic consumption for the last three years of available data. Base trigger levels of 125 per cent, 110 per cent and 105 per cent are set where the market access opportunities for a product are respectively less than or equal to 10 per cent, between 10 and 30 per cent, and greater than 30 per cent. A special safeguard duty may be imposed whenever imports of the product in question exceed the sum of (a) the base trigger level multiplied by the average quantity of imports in the three preceding years and (b) the absolute volume change in domestic consumption of the product in the most recent year for which data are available compared with the preceding year. The trigger level must be at least 105 per cent of the average quantity of imports in the preceding three years.

The additional duty that may be imposed in the case of price-based safeguards is established according to a sliding scale schedule set out in Article 5.5. It is based on the difference between the import price and the trigger price, which is defined as the average reference price during the period 1986-88. If the difference is less than 10 per cent no special safeguard duty may be imposed. As the difference increases so too does the amount of the additional duty permitted. It is worth noting that Article 5.1(b) does not define the import price but instead provides that it is to be 'determined on the basis of the c.i.f. import price'. The

Appellate Body interpreted the c.i.f. import price to mean the 'price that does not include customs duties and internal charges' (*EC Poultry*, WT/DS69/AB/R, 145). Members are encouraged not to use price-based safeguards whenever import volumes are declining. In the case of perishable and seasonal products, Article 5.6 allows for shorter time periods to be used in the case of a volume-based safeguard and for different reference prices for different periods in the case of a price-based safeguard. Other Members must be given the opportunity to consult with the Member introducing the measures on the conditions giving rise to the measure (Desta, 2002: 86–92; McMahon, 2006: 56).

iii.   Summary

In summary, the market access provisions of the AoA represent a significant achievement with import protection now limited to tariffs, but they have had a limited concrete impact on the market. One of the reasons for this is that the reduction commitments were expressed as an average reduction in tariffs rather than a reduction in the average tariff (de Gorter *et al.*, 2003a). In addition, it is asserted that a number of Members engaged in what is referred to as 'dirty tariffication' as in the process of tariffication Members chose data that would allow the highest possible tariffs (Ingco, 1996). The resulting high tariffs were not always applied in practice; however, they reduced the impact of the reform process since a reduction of the tariff from the nominal amount counted towards the tariff reductions required by the Agreement. Increasing market access was one of the objectives of the negotiations but the process of tariffication was sufficiently flexible, for example, in the definition of the external price and by the use of various mechanisms to increase the internal price, to allow Members, such as the US and the EC, not to significantly increase access to their markets (OECD, 1999). In addition, under the terms of the Agreement, those countries that had undertaken the process of tariffication were allowed to use special safeguards under AoA Article 5 as an additional means of protection for the tariffied products. Although the minimum and current access commitments were introduced to mitigate the adverse impact of the inflated tariffs that resulted from the tariffication process, the tariff rate quotas (TRQs) that were introduced in order to administer those commitments ended up being another source of uncertainty as members put in place complex and unpredictable TRQ administration systems along with high in-quota tariffs. As of 2005, 45 WTO members had TRQ commitments on 1,434 tariff lines shown in their Schedules (TN/AG/S/20). The AoA did not offer specific rules on the administration of such quotas and tariff quotas were rarely filled during the implementation period. Issues have also arisen about the extent of tariff escalation in developed countries and an associated problem of the proliferation of standards (Desta and Hirsch, 2011).

B. Domestic Support to Agriculture

If international trade in agricultural products is subject to a different set of rules and regulations, it is mainly because many WTO member countries provide different types of support to their farmers for a variety of social, economic and other reasons. When such support or subsidy results in domestic agricultural production that is higher than would otherwise be the case, producers in other countries worry about its impact on their trade opportunities – either because it reduces their ability to export to the subsidising country or because the excess supplies from that country will unfairly compete with theirs in third country markets. It is because of this trade-distortion potential of agricultural domestic support that an international agreement on trade has ended up regulating what are purely domestic policy instruments. At the same time, it is also worth bearing in mind that the WTO is not too concerned about the amount of support a government provides to its farmers; this support matters only to the extent that it affects, directly or indirectly, international trade in the sector. The rules of the AoA on domestic support reflect the delicate balance that has to be struck between the desire to leave governments free to support their agricultural sectors as they see fit and the need to reduce or eliminate the trade-distortive effects of those otherwise domestic measures. The AoA thus distinguishes between domestic support measures that are deemed to be trade-neutral and those that are deemed to be trade-distorting. The AoA leaves countries free to provide domestic support measures that are considered trade-neutral, known as Green Box measures, while it prohibits or restricts the use of those measures that are deemed trade-distorting, known as Amber Box measures. The detailed disciplines contained in the AoA and the national schedules are of course much messier than this, but an appreciation of this binary classification remains critical for a proper understanding of the AoA discipline on domestic agricultural support.

i. Amber Box domestic support

On Amber Box measures, the AoA stipulates that those countries that provided such support during the base period will establish a base level of support and undertake specific reduction commitments in their Schedules, which will be carried out over the agreed implementation period; those countries that did not provide such measures during the base period will not be allowed to maintain or introduce them in the future except within the terms of a few narrowly defined exceptions (AoA Article 7.2(b)). The centrepiece of the commitments in the area of domestic support is the concept of the Aggregate Measurement of Support (AMS), which is defined in Article 1(a) as 'the annual level of support, expressed in monetary terms, provided for an agricultural product in favour of the producers of the basic agricultural product or non-product-specific support provided in favour of agricultural producers in general ...'[4] Annex 3 to the Agreement gives detailed guidance on the calculation of the AMS by requiring a calculation of the value of market price support, non-exempt direct payments and other non-exempt policies. According to the provisions of this Annex, the AMS is to be calculated on a product-specific basis for each product receiving any type of non-exempt support. Paragraph 1 of Annex 3 provides that non product-specific support is to be aggregated into one number, which is to be included in the total AMS. By virtue of paragraph 7 of Annex 3 the AMS is to be calculated as close as practicable to the point of first sale of the basic agricultural product concerned, although measures directed at agricultural processors are to be included only to the extent that a benefit accrues to the producers of the basic agricultural product.

Market price support, a method of supporting agriculture by direct governmental or regulatory intervention in the workings of the market, usually by setting minimum or guaranteed prices, is a classic example of a trade-distorting domestic support device that belongs to the Amber Box. The AMS for market price support is to be calculated according to paragraph 8 of Annex 3 by 'using the gap between a fixed external reference price and the applied administrative price multiplied by the quantity of production eligible to receive the applied administrative price'. Payments made to maintain the gap are to be excluded and these cover such payments as storage costs. Annex 3 goes on to define what the fixed external reference price, which is based on the years 1986 to 1988, is to be for a net exporting country, generally the average f.o.b. value for the product and for a net importing country generally the average c.i.f. value for the product, adjusted if necessary for quality differences. In those situations where a fixed external reference price cannot be calculated, Annex 4 of the Agreement provides for the calculation of an Equivalent Measurement of Support, to be based on the applied administrative price and the quantity of the product benefiting from this price or, if this is not possible, on budgetary outlays, which under Article 1(c) of the Agreement would include foregone revenues. The applied administrative price is the price that the government determines producers should receive.

Non-exempt direct payments are defined in paragraph 10 of Annex 3 as payments that are dependent on a 'price gap' which is to be calculated on the difference between a fixed external reference price and the applied administrative price multiplied by the quantity of production that is eligible to receive the applied administrative price. If the direct payments are not dependent on a price gap, the AMS calculation will be based on budgetary outlays. As for other non-exempt measures, such as input subsidies and marketing-cost reduction measures, these are to be valued based on budgetary outlays. Where budgetary outlays do not reflect the full extent of the subsidy, provision is made for calculating the difference between the price of the product benefiting from the measure and a representative market price for a similar product, which is then multiplied by the quantity of the product benefiting from the measure. Levies or fees paid by producers are to be deducted from the AMS and the Equivalent Measurement of Support.

Having calculated the AMS by product, the next step is to calculate the Total AMS. This is defined in Article 1(h) as being the sum of all non-exempt domestic support provided to agricultural producers. It includes all aggregate measurements of support for basic agricultural products, all non-product-specific aggregate measurements of support, and all equivalent measurements of support for agricultural products. By virtue of Article 6.1 of the Agreement, the domestic support reduction commitments are to be expressed in terms of Total Aggregate Measurement of Support and Annual and Final Bound Commitment Levels. In Part IV of each Member's Schedules, a table can be found which consists of several columns. The first column specifies a Base Total AMS, which represents the level of support provided during the 1986–88 base period. The final column in the table is the Final Bound Commitments, which represent the effect of the implementation of the reduction commitment on the Base Total AMS. Between these two figures are the Annual Bound Commitments, which represent the AMS commitments for each year of the implementation period. Under the Uruguay Round Modalities Agreement, each developed country Member is committed to reducing its Base Total AMS by 20 per cent during the six-year implementation period. Developing countries are committed to a 13.3 per cent reduction over ten years, while no reduction is required in the case of the least-developed countries. In order to comply with the reduction commitments, the Current Total AMS in any given year must not exceed the corresponding annual or final bound commitments specified in Part IV of the Member's Schedule. In *Korea–Beef* (DS62/AB/R,

112) the Appellate Body noted that two elements were required to calculate the Current AMS, namely 'in accordance with the methodology in Annex 3 and taking into account the constituent data and methodology used in the tables incorporated into a Member's Schedule'. By virtue of Article 3.1 the domestic support commitments made in Part IV of each Member's Schedule are an integral part of GATT 1994.

Article 6 of the Agreement exempts a number of domestic support measures from the reduction commitment. The first of these reflects the agreement reached at the Mid-Term Review of the Uruguay Round that certain government measures to encourage agricultural and rural development programmes in developing countries would not have to be included in the calculation of a Member's Current Total AMS. Article 6.2 of the Agreement lists the three measures as being generally available agricultural investment subsidies, agricultural input subsidies generally available to low-income and resource-poor producers, and domestic support to encourage diversification from growing illicit narcotic crops. The second exemption is provided for in Article 6.4 of the Agreement under which members are not required to include either product-specific or non-product specific domestic support that falls below a certain percentage of the total value of production of a basic agricultural product during the relevant year. The level of *de minimis* support is set at 5 per cent for developed countries and 10 per cent for developing countries. By virtue of Article 7.2(b), where a Member's Schedule does not include a Total AMS commitment, the level of support must not exceed the relevant *de minimis* level. Article 6.5 of the Agreement exempts from the reduction commitment direct payments under production-limiting programmes provided that they are based on fixed areas and yields, or on 85 per cent or less of the base level of production, or in the case of livestock payments, on a fixed number of head. Payments under such programmes need not be decoupled from production. This is the notorious Blue Box.

ii.   Green Box domestic support
As noted earlier, the Green Box contains measures that are deemed trade-neutral. Annex 2, paragraph 1, of the AoA states that Green Box domestic support policies 'shall meet the fundamental requirement that they have no, or at most minimal, trade distortion effects or effects on production'. Furthermore, such policies must conform to two basic criteria:

(i)   the support in question shall be provided through a publicly-funded government programme (including government revenue foregone) not involving transfers from consumers; and,

(ii)   the support in question shall not have the effect of providing price support to producers.

If specific measures are excluded on the basis that they are Green Box measures, it is up to the Member to ensure that such policies remain consistent with the requirements of Annex 2. Article 7.2(a) of the Agreement makes it clear that in the event that they do not, they will be included in future calculations of the current total AMS.

Paragraphs 2 to 13 of Annex 2 go on to list 12 specific types of policies, the so-called Green Box policies. First on this list are general services, i.e. measures providing services or benefits to agriculture or the rural community that do not involve direct payments to producers or processors. Measures such as pest and disease control and training services would be included in this category. Also exempt is public stockholding for food security purposes provided purchases are made at current domestic market prices and sales at no less than current domestic market prices. Food purchases by the Government at current market prices for use as domestic food aid are also exempt provided eligibility to receive such aid is subject to clearly defined criteria relating to nutritional objectives.

Paragraphs 6 to 13 allow for various forms of direct payments to producers to be exempt from the reduction commitment, provided the basic criteria laid down in paragraph 1 plus the specific criteria applicable to the individual payment are satisfied. These paragraphs cover decoupled income support (paragraph 6); government financial participation in income insurance and income safety-net programmes (paragraph 7); payments for relief from natural disasters (paragraph 8); structural adjustment assistance provided through producer retirement programmes (paragraph 9); structural adjustment assistance provided through resource retirement programmes (paragraph 10); structural adjustment assistance provided through investment aids (paragraph 11); payments under environmental programmes (paragraph 12); and payments under regional assistance programmes (paragraph 13).[5]

iii.   Summary

In summary, it is notable that the AoA allows a lot of room for different ways of supporting the agricultural sector, and it is only when the domestic support affects international trade, actually or potentially, that the AoA becomes relevant. Moreover, a WTO Member that provides domestic support, and as we shall see below, export subsidies, in accordance with the AoA rules, is unlikely to be successfully challenged on the basis of the more generic rules of the WTO Agreement on Subsidies and Countervailing Measures (the SCM Agreement). This is not to say that the SCM Agreement is completely irrelevant to agricultural subsidies; on the contrary, as the Panel in *US – FSC* observed in the context of the definition of subsidies for purposes of the AoA, 'Article 1 of the SCM Agreement, which defines the term "subsidy" for the purposes of the SCM Agreement, represents highly relevant context for the interpretation of the word "subsidy" within the meaning of the Agreement on Agriculture, as it is the only article in the WTO Agreement that provides a definition of that term' (WT/DS108/R, 7.150). Likewise, in *US – Upland Cotton* (DS267/R, 7.1058), the Panel in its discussion of the Green Box maintained that 'the operation of Article 6.3 AoA does not pre-empt or exclude the operation of the obligations under Article 3.1(b) of the SCM Agreement', thus raising the possibility that claims could be made under both the AoA and the Subsidies Agreement. AoA Article 13 on due restraint, usually known as the peace clause, was intended to reduce the likelihood of agricultural subsidies being challenged under the SCM Agreement, and its expiry at the end of 2003 was a cause for concern in this respect. Seven years after this event, we can say that this concern was overstated.

The discipline on domestic support provided by the provisions of the AoA may be viewed as relatively weak, although separate pillars, elements of market access and export subsidies are included within the calculation of the AMS, which itself could be manipulated (Baffes and de Gorter, 2005). While a mechanism was found to reduce border protection and export subsidisation, the level of domestic support has remained largely unchanged. Blandford (2001: 42) ascribes this to the reduction in AMS support rather than total support, the existence of the Green Box, and the flexibility accorded to members in managing the reduction. Various defects in Annex 3 to the AoA can be highlighted –for example, the AMS calculation was not based on actual prices but on administered prices. Moreover, the effect of the reduction commitments was limited by the aggregation of all policies and commodity sectors and the flexibility accorded to members to increase support in some sectors whilst decreasing it in others. Additional flexibility is provided by the *de minimis* exception. As a final example, support provided through the Blue Box is included in the calculation of the Base Total AMS but is not included in the calculation of the Current Total AMS which was used to determine whether a Member had complied with its reduction commitments for a particular year during the implementation period or afterwards.

Increasing use of the Green Box by the EC and other members may necessitate a fundamental revision of the provisions of Annex 2 to ensure that members do not use the box as a way to evade their reduction commitments on domestic support. It is to be regretted that in *US – Upland Cotton* the Panel eschewed a definition of the fundamental requirement in Annex 2 of 'no, or at most minimal, trade-distorting effects or effects on production' as not being necessary given its finding that there was a breach of paragraph 6. One area of concern is that this definition combines two contrasting definitions of decoupled payments, i.e. those that refer to payment impact in contrast to policy design. A policy is fully decoupled, with reference to payment impact, if it 'does not influence production decisions of farmers receiving payments, and if it permits free market determination of prices' (OECD, 2000). As for policy design, Burfisher and Hopkins (2003: 4) note 'only subsidies that do not depend on current prices, factor use, or production can be considered fully decoupled from farm production decisions'. If the disciplines of the domestic support pillar are to be respected, it is important to have an agreed definition of decoupling so that members cannot frustrate the process of reform by transferring payments into the Green Box and thus maintaining the overall level of support for agriculture without reducing the trade-distorting effects of such payments. Such an agreed definition could apply to all direct payments made under the Green Box with policies that have a trade-distorting effect being transferred into the Amber Box.

C.   Agricultural Export Subsidies

Article 1(e) of the AoA defines export subsidies as 'subsidies contingent upon export performance, including the export subsidies listed in Article 9 of this Agreement'. Article 9.1 lists the six types of export subsidy that are subject to the reduction commitments and under Article 3.1 the export subsidy commitments in each Member's Schedules are made an integral part of GATT 1994. In contrast to the domestic support commitments, this part of the national Schedules contains disaggregated, product-specific commitments expressed in terms of maximum annual budgetary expenditures and volumes for 22 product categories.[6] Over the six-year implementation period, developed country Members were required to reduce their expenditure on export subsidies to a level that was 36 per cent below the levels existing in the 1986–1990 base period and the quantities benefiting from export subsidies by 21 per cent. The equivalent figures for developing countries are 24 per cent and 14 per cent, and Article 15.2 of the Agreement provides them with a ten-year period over which to make these reductions.[7] Least-developed country Members are not required to undertake any reduction commitments. The burden of proof is on the exporting party to show that any quantities exported in excess of the scheduled commitments have not benefited from the subsidies listed in Article 9.1.

Products that are unscheduled cannot benefit from any export subsidies. Under Article 10.1 non-listed subsidies can be granted to scheduled products, but they 'shall not be applied in a manner which results in, or which threatens to leads to, circumvention of export subsidy commitments ...'. Under Article 10.2 Members undertake to work toward developing disciplines governing the provision of export credits, export credit guarantees and insurance programmes. The meaning and relevance of this programmatic provision has come under question since the AB said, in *US – Upland Cotton*, just like the Panel that the anti-circumvention provision of Article 10.1 already applies to export credits, export credit guarantees and insurance programmes (WT/DS267/AB/R, 609–616). In a relatively rare event in WTO Appellate Body practice, one member wrote a separate opinion in which he underlined that 'pursuant to Article 10.2, export credit guarantees, export credits and insurance programs are not currently subject to export subsidy disciplines under the *Agreement on Agriculture*, including the disciplines found in Article 10.1' (WT/DS267/AB/R, 636). Article 10.4 extends disciplines to the food aid operations of donor countries.

Beyond the disciplines on export subsidies imposed by the AoA, the Subsidies Agreement also contains provisions on export subsidies. For example, Article 3.1(a) of the Subsidies Agreement provides: 'Except as provided in the Agreement on Agriculture, the following subsidies, within the meaning of Article 1 shall be prohibited (a) subsidies contingent, in law or in fact, whether solely or as one of several other conditions, upon export performance ...'. The Panel in *Canada – Dairy (Recourse to Article 21.5 by New Zealand and the US I)* declared that Article 9.1 of the AoA and Articles 1.1 and 3.1 of the Subsidies Agreement 'can be said to be "closely related" and "part of a logical continuum"' (DS103/RW and DS113/RW, 6.92). As an example, the requirement of contingency on export performance is essential for an export subsidy under both agreements. However, there are important differences between the two agreements. Article 4 of the Subsidies Agreement on remedies provides special or additional rules and procedures on dispute settlement that are absent from the AoA. This article also establishes a stricter timeframe for the settlement of disputes than that generally available under the Dispute Settlement Understanding; indeed, Article 4.2 goes further and provides that the request for consultations should 'include a statement of available evidence with regard to the existence and nature of the subsidy in question'. Finally, Article 4.7 obliges a panel to recommend that a subsidy found to be contrary to Article 3 of the SCM Agreement be withdrawn without delay and to specify the time period for such a withdrawal.

The provisions of the AoA on export competition are perhaps the most successful part of the Agreement. While several factors may be mentioned for this, the following are particularly notable: (1) unlike the commitments in domestic support, those on export subsidies are expressed at a product-specific level, thereby eliminating the possibility for Member countries to meet an overall target while freely increasing the export subsidies for particular products; (2) the duality of commitments in export subsidies is another factor, i.e. the fact that the commitments constrain both the quantity of the specific product that can benefit from export subsidies and the maximum amount of money that could be spent subsidising the exportation of particular products; (3) the anti-circumvention provision of Article 10 of the AoA makes it impossible for countries to use measures with an export subsidisation effect, including such measures as export credits and export credit guarantees for the provision of which a new agreement was supposed to be concluded; and (4) as a result of the approach taken by the AoA, only 25 WTO members (counting EU-15 as one) have the right to use export subsidies today, i.e. agricultural export subsidies are already illegal for all WTO members except these 25.[8]

However, the export subsidies provisions can still be criticised. For example, the commitments have proved to be fairly easy to meet possibly because of the generous base period chosen to establish the budgetary and volume commitment thresholds. The agreed base period to establish the threshold for both market access and domestic support commitments was 1986–88, while that for export subsidies was 1986–90. Moreover, a 'front-loading' option was allowed for those countries whose export subsidies increased in 1991 and 1992, i.e. soon after the agreed base period, so they would start their reductions from those higher levels while the commitment for the end of the implementation period remains that which was based on the 1986–90 average (Desta, 2002: 250). Disciplines on implicit export subsidies were arguably weaker for example, on food aid, and until *US – Upland Cotton* on export credits, and no disciplines were imposed on the activities of state trading enterprises.

The inescapable conclusion therefore is that the AoA has not led to a significant liberalization of agricultural trade but the rules have taken the first and most important step on the road towards a fundamental reform of the way agricultural trade has been conducted for generations. Members recognized that they had only just done so and in Article 20 of the Agreement they provided for the next step, promising negotiations for a further stage in the reform process that would build on the achievements of the first agreement and thus advance the objective identified in the Preamble of establishing a fair and market-oriented agricultural trading system.

D.   Special and Differential Treatment

The Preamble to the Agreement establishing the WTO recognizes the need for positive efforts to ensure that developing and least-developed countries secure a share in the growth of international trade commensurate with the needs of their economic development. The AoA provides some flexibility for developing countries in each of the three pillars. For example, as noted earlier, developing countries were given an option with respect to Article 4 of the AoA to go for ceiling bindings instead of tariffication. On the down side, those countries that went for this option were denied the right to introduce special safeguard measures under the AoA's Article 5 while they were still required to offer minimum access commitments. In the area of domestic support developing countries were allowed a number of flexibilities, including generally available investment subsidies, input subsidies to low-income farmers, and subsidies to support diversification away from the growing of illicit crops. These flexibilities were further supplemented by lower reduction commitments in Amber Box measures that could be implemented over a longer period and *de minimis* levels of support that were twice those allowed for developed countries. Finally, in respect of export subsidies, developing countries were allowed lower reduction commitments implemented over longer periods while LDCs were exempted altogether from the reduction commitments. The LDCs of course did not provide any export subsidies during the base period, which left their base levels at zero and thereby made the special and differential treatment gesture in this area have no effect.

Under Article 16.1 of the AoA developed country Members are required to take the action provided for in the Decision on Measures Concerning the Possible Negative Effects of the Reform Program on Least-Developed and Net Food-Importing Developing Countries (NFIDC), which was reached at the conclusion of the Uruguay Round.

By virtue of Article 16.2, the Committee on Agriculture is to monitor the follow-up to the Decision. The Decision itself recognizes that implementation of the reform package in agriculture may have negative effects on these countries in relation to the supply of food imports on reasonable terms and conditions, which would arise as a result of reductions in the level of domestic production and the restrictions on the use of export subsidies. To ameliorate these negative effects and improve the level of food security in these countries, during the reform programme it was agreed that the level of food aid would be reviewed periodically and that a level of food aid commitments would be set that was sufficient to meet the legitimate needs of developing countries. Paragraph 3 of the Decision goes on to urge the adoption of guidelines that would ensure that an increasing proportion of such aid be in grant form and/or supplied under appropriate concessional terms. In addition, greater consideration would be given to providing technical and financial assistance for agricultural development and infrastructure projects in these countries. Under paragraph 4 of the Decision any future agreement on agricultural export credits would make appropriate provisions for the differential treatment of the least developed and net food-importing countries. Finally, under paragraph 5 those developing countries experiencing short-term difficulties in financing their normal level of commercial imports could draw on the resources available from international financial institutions, the IMF and World Bank, that were either existing or had been specially created to deal with this problem. As for the beneficiaries of the Decision this was left to the Committee on Agriculture (Desta, 2002).

E.   Institutional Provisions

In the AoA Article 18 has established a Committee on Agriculture with the power to review progress in the implementation of the commitments that resulted from the Uruguay Round negotiations. To that end, Members are required to submit periodic reports to the Committee on how they have complied with the Agreement. These reports are to be made 'at such intervals as shall be determined', though usually on an annual basis. Article 18.3 provides that 'any new domestic support measure, or modification of an existing measure, for which exemption from reduction is claimed shall be notified promptly'. The notification is to contain details on how the measure notified meets the criteria set out in either Article 6 or Annex 2. Trying to assess whether a Member has complied with its commitments as a result of these reports and notifications is not a simple matter, especially when one considers the complexity of the Schedules. Article 18 also provides for annual consultations on 'normal growth in world trade in agricultural products within the framework of the commitments on export subsidies' and paragraph 6 allows Members the opportunity to raise concerns about the implementation of commitments, including those concerning developments in the agricultural policy of another Member.

F.   The AoA and Its Relationship to GATT and other Multilateral Trade Agreements

Under Article 21.1 of the AoA the GATT and other agreements would apply subject to the provisions of the AoA, and as the Panel indicated in *EC – Bananas III* (DS27/R, 7.122) 'there must be a provision of the Agreement on Agriculture that is relevant in order for this priority provision to apply'. The Appellate Body in *US – Upland Cotton* agreed with the Panel's assessment of the three situations in which Article 21.1 could apply:

> ... where, for example, the domestic support provisions of the Agreement on Agriculture would prevail in the event that an explicit carve-out or exemption from the disciplines in Article 3.1(b) of the SCM Agreement existed in the text of the Agreement on Agriculture. Another situation would be where it would be impossible for a Member to comply with its domestic support obligations under the Agreement on Agriculture and the Article 3.1(b) prohibition simultaneously. Another situation might be where there is an explicit authorization in the text of the Agreement on Agriculture that would authorize a measure that, in the absence of such an express authorization, would be prohibited by Article 3.1(b) of the SCM Agreement. (DS267/AB/R, 532 citing para 7.1038 of the Panel Report)

However, the Appellate Body did acknowledge that there could be situations other than those identified by the Panel where Article 21.1 may also be applicable.

III. CONTINUATION OF THE REFORM PROCESS

A.   The In-built Agenda

We have seen that the AoA's short-term mission is 'to establish a basis for initiating a process of reform of trade in agriculture', while its long-term goal is 'to establish a fair and market-oriented agricultural trading system'. Article 20 of the AoA provided the so-called in-built agenda for further negotiations in order to ensure that the effort to reach the long-term goal of the AoA would continue after the Uruguay Round. Indeed, it was this in-built agenda that rescued agriculture from the Seattle debacle in 1999. Article 20 provided that one year before the end of the implementation period in 2000, negotiations would begin to continue the process of reform. These would take into account the experience of implementing the reduction commitments, the effects of the reduction commitments on world trade in agriculture, non-trade concerns and special and differential treatment. To lay the groundwork for these negotiations two steps were taken: firstly, the 1996 Singapore Ministerial Declaration initiated a process of analysis and information exchange (AIE) on agriculture between the Members (WTO, 1996: para 10); and secondly, the 1998 Geneva Ministerial Declaration established a work programme for the General Council that would allow it to issue recommendations concerning, inter alia, 'the issues, including those brought forward by members, relating to the implementation of existing agreements ... [and] the negotiations already mandated at Marrakesh, to ensure that such negotiations begin on time' (WTO, 1998: para 9).

The AIE process began in 1998 and was undertaken through informal open-ended meetings on the basis of papers submitted by the Members and factual and analytical background papers prepared by the WTO Secretariat. Over the course of these meetings, which lasted up to the Seattle Ministerial in 1999, 74 informal papers were submitted by 36 Members and although no conclusions were drawn from the meetings, summary reports were issued by the Chairman under his own responsibility. The AIE process revealed considerable differences between the Members on the future shape of the AoA, not the least of which was over the interpretation of non-trade concerns in Article 20(c). Concerns such as food security, environmental protection (biodiversity), rural development and consumer protection issues relating to the quality and safety of food were identified as falling within this concept. Whilst there were differences between the Members on how to recognize such concerns there was an agreement that a difference existed between the non-trade concerns that were of interest to developed countries and those that were of interest to developing countries with food security being identified as an urgent issue for the latter (other issues included rural development and poverty alleviation). Developing Members insisted that given the variation in development needs between developing countries flexibility would be a key element in the new agreement, but the exact contours of that flexibility would depend on the progress of the negotiations. The AIE process gave some indications of the changes that would be required in each of the three pillars of the agreement. For example in market access, new rules were proposed on tariff quota administration, tariff escalation, and the problem of tariff peaks.

At the final meeting under the AIE process the Chairman reported that it had met the objectives set for it, namely, a better understanding of the issues involved and an identification of the Members' interests before embarking on the pre-agreed negotiations (G/AG/R/20, Annex III, para 8). The process also revealed considerable dissatisfaction among developing countries about the liberalization that had occurred under the Agreement and underlined the need for a new one to be more sympathetic to their demands. Within the developed country group, a divergence was obvious between those who wished to pursue a further liberalization of agricultural trade and those who wanted to attenuate the requirements of the Agreement so as to continue to afford some degree of support and/or protection to their agricultural producers. Although it may have met the objectives set for it, the AIE process also gave an early warning of the difficulties ahead in the negotiations for a new Agreement.

In the aftermath of the AIE process, members moved on to fulfil the mandate of the Geneva Ministerial Declaration and submitted communications on the future of the Agreement. In its communication on behalf of the Cairns Group, Australia indicated the resolve of the Group 'to ensure that the next WTO agriculture negotiations achieve fundamental reform which will put trade in agricultural goods on the same basis as trade in other goods' (WT/GC/W/156, para 1). Other Members naturally disagreed with the idea of radically changing the Agreement, arguing that its basic framework should be maintained so that reform could progress consistently. Such progress would allow for a recognition of the multifunctional nature of agriculture, thus continuing the debate initiated in the AIE process about how to accommodate non-trade concerns. Whilst developed Members continued to propose that special and differential treatment would be provided to developing Members, for their part developing Members were beginning to demand a new type of Agreement that would be more responsive to their needs. For example, India noted the need:

> ... to address both trade and non-trade concerns, as mandated in the Preamble, has not been fully reflected in the provisions of the Agreement and consequently in its implementation. The major thrust of the Agreement appears to be based on the hypothesis that liberalization is the panacea of all ills in the agricultural sector. While this may be tenable from a conventional economic view point, such reasoning does not take into

account the problems faced by developing countries, which because of underlying constraints, have to necessarily take into account non-trade concerns such as food security and rural employment while formulating their domestic policies. (WT/GC/W/342, para 1)

In recognition of the needs for flexibility, a proposal was made for a Development Box to meet the development and food security needs of developing countries (WT/GC/W/374).

The range of issues raised in the communications indicated that the proposed Article 20 negotiations would be problematic and this was subsequently confirmed as Members began working on a process of reaching the compromises necessary to agree a Ministerial Declaration to launch a new round of trade negotiations at the ministerial meeting in Seattle in December 1999. The Ministerial ended without agreement on a new round. Although reaching an agreement on agriculture was relatively close in Seattle, in its aftermath Members returned to the mandate provided by Article 20. Using this mandate, a new round of agricultural negotiations was launched on 23 March 2000, in Geneva, to be held in Special Sessions of the Committee on Agriculture. Phase One of the negotiations ended in early 2001 after proposals had been submitted on behalf of 126 Members, which were discussed in seven Special Sessions of the Committee on Agriculture. Phase Two concentrated on in-depth work on the options for reform set forth in these proposals in an attempt to reach a consensus on changes to the AoA.

What emerged from the pre-Doha agriculture negotiations was a general acceptance that there would be another AoA but the nature and scope of that agreement was uncertain. Three different ideas of the Agreement emerged from three different groups and within these groups it was also possible to see the beginnings of further differentiation. The first idea belongs to the Cairns Group and the United States. For them the agreement is a stepping stone to the incorporation of agriculture within the disciplines of the GATT, with the next agreement on agriculture paving the way for full integration. Existing mechanisms within the Agreement are either transitional, for example the Blue Box or the Special Agricultural Safeguard, or must be drafted in such a way that their operation has minimal or no impact on trade, for example, the Green Box. As a group of agricultural exporters, these Members view the Agreement as an exercise in liberalization so that market forces alone will predominantly determine the state of their agricultural sector.

The second idea of the AoA belongs to the EU and the other Members of the so-called Friends of Multifunctionality group. These

Members may be seen to have reluctantly accepted the need for an AoA but are seeking in their own agricultural policies to recognize that agriculture promotes certain public goods which are not adequately recompensed through the operation of the market. As reluctant liberalizers, they seek an agreement that allows them to continue to support their agriculture and to limit access to their market by competing products from other members. The existing disciplines of the Agreement are the right mix for them and the process of liberalization will be slow, necessitating a succession of agreements on agriculture. Within this group there are some who are more liberal than others (for example, the EC) whilst others are inherently conservative (such as Japan and Norway), but the overall philosophy is one of promoting a balance between imports and exports, between intervention and a free market, and between trade and non-trade concerns as they understand them.

The third idea of the AoA belongs to a group of developing Members who see the agreement as an exercise that is driven by developed Members which fails to account for the particular characteristics of developing country agriculture. In itself this is not surprising as this group had only been marginally involved in the discussions in the Uruguay Round which led to the AoA. For this group, the idea for a future agreement is one which re-balances the existing agreement in order to promote greater equity through either flexibility in obligations or even different obligations. For them what is missing from the existing Agreement is a development dimension and the existing mechanisms of special and differential treatment are not sufficient to promote development. This is exemplified by the NFIDC Decision and particularly the failure to implement that decision effectively. In this idea of the agreement all developed Members, whether they are enthusiastic or reluctant liberalizers, are the sources of the problem and disciplines should be imposed on them that would allow developing Members to develop.

In one sense the emergence of these three groups (and further groups within these groups) could have been predicted. Article 20 required Members to reflect on their experience to date in the implementation of the Agreement and the reduction commitments – it would have been remarkable if those experiences had all been positive. It also encouraged them to consider non-trade concerns and again Members have done this in a way that is reflective of their domestic agricultural interests. Traditional developed country supporters of agriculture fashioned the concept of multifunctionality as an expression of concerns that had been addressed domestically which should also be addressed internationally as part of the establishment of a 'fair' agricultural trading system. Equally, developing Members' experience of the special and differential treatment provisions of the Agreement convinced them that it needed rebalancing. The long-term objective is substantial progressive reductions in support and protection but developing Members are not in a position to offer as significant an amount of support to their agricultural community as the major developed Members. The mechanisms of the agreement are not therefore as relevant to them and thus there has been the call for a development dimension. Finally, the objective was to be realized over the longer term, but without any indication of how long that term should be.

Article 20 in a sense completed its mission with the launching of an agriculture-specific negotiation process in March 2000, but the negotiations soon clearly indicated that the progress in agriculture would be achieved only in the context of a broader round of multilateral trade negotiations that would allow for trade-offs between different sectors and interests. With the launch of the Doha Development Agenda in 2001, agriculture once again found itself at the centre of such a comprehensive negotiation process in which everything is on the table, anything is possible, and nothing is agreed until everything is agreed.

B. Agriculture and the Doha Development Agenda

i. Agriculture in the Doha Declaration
Having failed to launch the round in Seattle, Members could not fail again as they met for the fourth Ministerial Conference in Doha. Paragraph 13 of the resulting Declaration notes:

> We recognize the work already undertaken in the negotiations initiated in early 2000 under Article 20 of the Agreement on Agriculture, including the large number of negotiating proposals submitted on behalf of a total of 121 Members. We recall the long-term objective referred to in the Agreement to establish a fair and market-oriented trading system through a programme of fundamental reform encompassing strengthened rules and specific commitments on support and protection in order to correct and prevent restrictions and distortions in world agricultural markets. We reconfirm our commitment to this programme. Building on the work carried out to date and without prejudging the outcome of the negotiations we commit ourselves to comprehensive negotiations aimed at: substantial improvements in market access; reductions of, with a view to phasing out, all forms of export subsidies; and substantial reductions in trade-distorting domestic support. We agree that special and differential treatment for developing countries shall be an integral part of all elements of the negotiations and

shall be embodied in the schedules of concessions and commitments and as appropriate in the rules and disciplines to be negotiated, so as to be operationally effective and to enable developing countries to effectively take account of their development needs, including food security and rural development. We take note of the non-trade concerns reflected in the negotiating proposals submitted by Members and confirm that non-trade concerns will be taken into account in the negotiations as provided for in the Agreement on Agriculture. (WTO, 2001a)

Paragraph 14 of this Declaration envisaged that the modalities for the further commitments would be established no later than 31 March 2003, with draft Schedules being submitted in time for the fifth Ministerial Conference. These modalities, just like their Uruguay Round predecessors, would provide 'instructions regarding the scheduling of commitments and amendments that will be required to the Agreement on Agriculture' (TN/AG/26, 46).

The Doha Declaration clearly moves beyond Article 20. Both recognize the long-term objective of establishing a fair and market-oriented trading system through a programme of fundamental reform. However, the Declaration is ambiguous with respect to how non-trade concerns are to be treated just as Article 20 itself does not indicate how such concerns are to be taken into account. Unlike Article 20, the Declaration specifies the nature of the specific commitments on support and protection by calling for substantial improvements in market access, substantial reductions in trade-distorting domestic support, and most encouraging of all, the reduction, with a view to phasing out, of all forms of export subsidies. It must be noted that paragraph 13 does state the objectives in these three areas 'without prejudging the outcome of the negotiations'. Likewise, the wording on special and differential treatment is stronger in the Declaration, which offers members two ways in which to incorporate such preferences. It could be 'embodied in the schedules of concessions and commitments' and it could be an element of 'the rules and disciplines to be negotiated, so as to be operationally effective and to enable developing countries to effectively take account of their development needs'. Whilst the latter speaks to the idea of a Doha Development Agenda especially if those rules and disciplines are conceived of from a development point of view, the former is more consistent with what developed Members would expect from the negotiations as their sense of special and differential treatment relates mostly to granting developing Members more flexibility in terms of specific commitments and longer periods for their implementation. There is an obvious tension between these two approaches and to the extent that the development aspect is stressed above the trade aspect the prospects for a development-oriented round would be high.

Another element of the single undertaking that would constitute the Doha Development Agenda was the issue of Market Access for Non-Agricultural Products (NAMA). In contrast to the substantial improvements in market access mandated by paragraph 13 of the Declaration for agricultural products, paragraph 16 on NAMA mandates negotiations to reduce (or eliminate) tariffs and to reduce (or eliminate) tariff peaks, high tariffs and tariff escalation, as well as non-tariff barriers especially on products of export interest to developing Members, who along with least-developed countries would not be expected to offer full reciprocity in reduction commitments. Product coverage is to be comprehensive with no *a priori* exclusions. The Doha Declaration also mandated discussions in four new areas: trade and investment, trade and competition policy, transparency in government procurement, and trade facilitation. The final substantive paragraph of the Declaration ends with an agreement to review all special and differential treatment provisions 'with a view to strengthening them and making them more precise, effective and operational'. Paragraph 44 of the Declaration concludes by endorsing the work programme on special and differential treatment set out in the Decision on Implementation-Related Issues and Concerns (WTO, 2001b).

Unlike previous rounds of multilateral trade negotiations, which had been launched with only a Ministerial Declaration establishing a work programme for the negotiations, the Doha Declaration was accompanied by a Decision on Implementation-Related Issues and Concerns reflecting the determination of the Members 'to take concrete action to address issues and concerns that have been raised by many developing country Members regarding the implementation of some WTO Agreements and Decisions, including the difficulties and resource constraints that have been encountered in the implementation of obligations in various areas'. Eleven WTO Agreements, including the AoA, were listed in the Implementation Decision and it concludes by instructing the Committee on Trade and Development to address a number of cross-cutting issues. Recommendations for decisions were to be made by July 2002 by the committee in their report to the General Council on:

(i) ... those special and differential treatment provisions that are already mandatory in nature and those that are non-binding in character, to consider the legal and practical implications for developed and developing Members of converting special and differential treatment measures into mandatory provisions, ...

(ii) ... additional ways in which special and differential treatment provisions can be made more effective, to consider ways, including improved information flows, in which developing countries, in particular the least-developed countries, may be assisted to make best use of special and differential treatment provisions ...

In the context of the work programme, the committee was also asked to consider how special and differential treatment could be incorporated into the architecture of WTO rules. No date was set for this report.

With respect to the AoA the Implementation Decision identifies three issues (WTO, 2001b: 2). The first of these is a request that Members exercise restraint when challenging measures notified by developing Members as Green Box measures promoting rural development and addressing food security concerns. This was to be implemented with immediate effect, whereas the remaining two concerns were to be followed up and their outcomes reported to the General Council. The first of these two issues related to the implementation of Article 10.2 of the Agreement on the development of internationally agreed disciplines on export credits, export credit guarantees or insurance programmes. Implementation of the NFIDC decision was the final issue identified in the Doha Implementation Decision. However, the development of disciplines on export credits and specific mechanisms to address the lack of implementation of the NFIDC Decision through a more principled approach to the issue of food security (and the associated problem of the use of food aid) has become intertwined with the negotiations for a new AoA and is no longer seen primarily as an Implementation Issue and Concern.

ii.   Agriculture on the road to Cancun

The Doha negotiations on agriculture would be held in the Special Session of the Committee on Agriculture, building on the work that had been done in Phases One and Two of the Article 20 negotiations. The negotiations on the Modalities were to be completed by March 2003, well in advance of the Ministerial scheduled for the late summer of 2003 in Cancun, Mexico. To realize this goal the Chair of the Special Session, Stuart Harbinson from Hong Kong, China, was to produce an Overview Paper before the end of 2002 with negotiations in the early months of 2003 being devoted to the Modalities. The dynamics of the negotiations were to be affected by the passage of a new US Farm Bill, which led to a new negotiating proposal and the on-going reform of the EU's Common Agricultural Policy, which delayed a proposal from the EC until January 2003.

By this time the Overview Paper had been produced and it noted that although there had been substantial progress in some areas, a substantial number of important issues had still to be agreed (WTO, 2002). Included in the latter category was the level of ambition for the negotiations, disagreements among Members, including the developing Members, on the appropriate provisions for special and differential treatment, and deciding how to accommodate non-trade concerns within the revised Agreement. The Annex to the Overview Paper goes through each of the issues across all the pillars, looking not only at the working hypothesis in that area but also proposed variations or additions. Running to 75 pages, the Annex reveals the importance, if not the necessity, of the Members addressing the questions asked by the Chair. Decisions of some significance were needed to progress the negotiations towards an agreement on Modalities and the first draft of the Modalities recognized the lack of guidance from Members on possible answers to the questions posed in the Overview Paper. The result was that the first draft had numerous square brackets indicating a lack of agreement, with the cautious additional reminder that the non-bracketed text did 'not convey any degree of acceptance' (WTO, 2003a). Discussions of the first draft of Modalities gave more focus to the negotiations but did not promote greater consensus on the way forward. With the end of March deadline looming, a revision of the draft Modalities emerged but only a limited number of changes were made.

The failure to agree the Modalities for agriculture by 31 March 2003 was not to be the only missed deadline across the negotiations as a whole. Members had also missed the deadlines for the negotiations on TRIPs and access to essential medicines, implementation issues and special and differential treatment. Two other deadlines falling before the Cancun Ministerial also proved problematic, namely, on non-agricultural market access and reform of the Dispute Settlement Understanding. The negotiations on agriculture took a new, but not unexpected, turn on 13 August with the release of an EC–US Joint Text on Agriculture, prompting a series of responses from other Members in the run-up to Cancun, including one from a group that would become known as the G20 and another from a group that would later become known as the G10. This flurry of activity led to the production by the Chair of the General Council of a draft Ministerial Declaration setting out a framework approach to the Modalities.

The Cancun Ministerial was held from 10 to 14 September 2003 and it was clear that agreeing on agriculture would be a touchstone for the success of the conference. As if to emphasize this, on the eve of the conference a new grouping was formed to promote Special Products (SP) and the Special Safeguard Mechanism (SSM) so that the AoA would respond positively to the needs of food security and rural development – this group would later become known as the G33. At the conference itself divisions over agriculture, cotton and the possible launch of negotiations on the Singapore issues (e.g. competition) were among the factors that led the Chair of the Conference to decide to end the discussions without an agreement on a Declaration. The Ministerial Statement that ended the conference instructed officials to continue work on outstanding issues and decisions would be taken at a General Council meeting that would take place before 15 December 2003 on how to complete the negotiations (WTO, 2003c: para 3).

With the collapse of the Cancun Ministerial Conference, the negotiations entered a waiting phase as Members considered the best way to maintain the degree of convergence referred to in the Ministerial Statement. Work on agriculture would begin again with the election of a new Chair of the Special Session of the Committee on Agriculture, Ambassador Tim Groser from New Zealand, who would organize a series of agriculture weeks for the Members to negotiate a framework agreement by July 2004. On 1 August the General Council adopted a decision that set out a framework for establishing Modalities in agriculture (Annex A) and NAMA (Annex B), recorded the recommendations of the Special Session of the Council for Trade in Services (Annex C), and launched negotiations on trade facilitation on the basis of Modalities contained in Annex D (WTO, 2004a).

iii.   The July 2004 Framework

Annex A on Agriculture begins by recalling paragraph 13 of the Doha Declaration (including the reference to non-trade concerns) and reiterating the level of ambition in that paragraph as the basis for the negotiations. It also recalls the objective of the AoA to establish a fair and market-oriented trading system, which is presented as the long-term objective. Also recognized is the importance of special and differential treatment and the need for developing countries to be able to pursue 'agricultural policies that are supportive of their development goals, poverty reduction strategies, food security and livelihood concerns'. Recalling the Doha Declaration's call for substantial reductions in trade-distorting domestic support, the Framework indicated that in achieving this result the Modalities would offer special and differential treatment to developing countries through longer implementation periods and lower reduction commitments alongside the continuation of the flexibilities under the AoA's Article 6.2. For developed Members there would be a strong element of harmonisation in the reductions made across the Amber Box, the Blue Box and *de minimis* with higher levels of support subject to deeper cuts. This would be achieved through the use of a tiered formula. Product-specific AMS would be capped according to a methodology to be agreed to prevent circumvention through transfers of unchanged domestic support between different support categories. There would be a review of the Green Box, which would take due account of non-trade concerns.

The Framework is particularly notable for what it says on export competition: 'Members agree to establish detailed modalities ensuring the parallel elimination of all forms of export subsidies and disciplines on all export measures with equivalent effect by a credible end date'. The measures having equivalent effect to export subsidies included export credits; export credit guarantees or insurance programmes; the trade distorting practices of state trading enterprises; and food aid not provided in accordance with disciplines to be agreed. In addition to longer implementation periods, developing countries would benefit from the continued availability of Article 9.4 (which initially exempted, for the duration of the implementation period, subsidies to reduce marketing and internal transport costs on export shipments from the discipline applying to export subsidies) and the implementation of paragraph 4 of the NFIDC Decision. The Framework Agreement also promised that state trading enterprises in developing countries which enjoyed special privileges to preserve domestic consumer price stability and to ensure food security would receive special consideration for maintaining a monopoly status. Finally, disciplines on export prohibitions and restrictions in Article 12.1 of the Agreement on Agriculture would be strengthened.

The Framework Agreement also endorsed a tiered formula to achieve the substantial improvements in market access promised by the Doha Declaration. Under paragraph 29 tariff reductions would be made from bound rates, each Member except LDCs would make a contribution, and there would be deeper cuts in higher tariffs with flexibilities for sensitive products. The number of bands, the thresholds for each band, the reduction in each band, and the role of a tariff cap were all left for future negotiations. Members would also be able to designate an appropriate number of tariff lines to be treated as sensitive (the exact percentage would be the subject of negotiation) and there would be a 'substantial improvement' in the market access for such products, which could be achieved through a combination of tariff reductions and tariff quota commitments. Other issues to be negotiated included the reduction or elimination of in-quota tariff rates to enable Members, particularly developing Members, to benefit from market access opportunities, improvements in tariff quota administration, tariff escalation, and the special agricultural safeguard.

The Framework Agreement also contained a number of special and differential treatment provisions for the benefit of developing countries. For example, in recognition of their food security, livelihood security and rural development needs, developing countries would be able to designate an appropriate number of products as Special Products, which would be eligible for more flexible treatment subject to further negotiations. Further negotiations would also be necessary on the Special Safeguard Mechanism and on the liberalization of tropical products and preferences. The Framework added that developed countries and developing countries in a position to do so would provide duty-free and quota-free market access for products originating from LDCs, while LDCs themselves would not be required to undertake any reduction commitments. Finally, the Framework Agreement provided that Article 18 of the Agreement on Agriculture would be amended with a view to enhancing monitoring and transparency across all three pillars. On the Cotton Initiative the Annex recognized that the trade aspects of this issue would be 'addressed ambitiously, expeditiously, and specifically, within the agriculture negotiations'. A Sub-Committee on Cotton would be established which would report to the Special Session of the Committee on Agriculture who would review progress.

iv.   Agriculture on the road to Hong Kong

The plan at the time was that work would resume after the summer break to translate the political commitment contained in the Framework into detailed modalities in time for the Hong Kong Ministerial of December 2005. But progress was slow and on 1 August 2005 the Chairman of the negotiations admitted that 'the agriculture negotiations are stalled – there is no way to conceal that reality' (TN/AG/19, 4). Several new proposals soon followed, including from the G20, the US, the EC and the G10, so as to energize the negotiations. Moreover, convergence also seemed to be emerging in the domestic support and export competition pillars, but Members remained too far apart particularly on market access in order for a real breakthrough to happen. The category of sensitive products was also fast becoming a problem issue, so much so that part of the preparation for the Hong Kong Ministerial focused on how to manage expectations by scaling back its ambitions to well short of the original plan in order to reach agreement on a modalities text for agriculture.

In his report to the Trade Negotiations Committee at the end of

November the Chair of the agriculture negotiations attempted to provide an objective summary of the state of the negotiations and this report was reproduced as Annex A of the Hong Kong Declaration (WTO, 2005). Paragraphs 4 to 12 of the Declaration noted the elements of convergence. For example, on domestic support paragraph 5 provided that there would be three bands for reductions in Final Bound Total AMS and in the overall cut in trade-distorting domestic support, with higher linear cuts in higher bands. The EC would be in the highest band, with the US and Japan in the next band and all other developed Members in the lower band; Members in this band with high relative levels of AMS would make additional reductions. Developing country Members with no AMS commitments would be exempt from reductions in *de minimis* and the overall cut in trade-distorting domestic support.

The most eye-catching achievement of the Conference on agriculture was contained in paragraph 6 which set the date of 2013 for the parallel elimination of all forms of export subsidies and disciplines on all export measures with equivalent effect. This date would be confirmed on completion of the Modalities. On state trading enterprises, disciplines would be developed on the use of monopoly powers, government financing, and the underwriting of losses. On food aid, a 'safe box' would be developed for *bona fide* food aid, which would contain disciplines on in-kind food aid, monetization and re-exports. Special and differential treatment in this pillar would include the ability to use Article 9.4 of the AoA for five years after the date set for the elimination of export subsidies.

All that could be agreed in the market access pillar was that there would be four bands for structuring tariff cuts. Agreement had yet to be reached on thresholds and sensitive products. Developing countries would self-designate an appropriate number of products as Special Products on the basis of criteria based on food security, livelihood security and rural development. Further agreement would be necessary on the precise import quantity and price triggers for a Special Safeguard Mechanism. Paragraph 24 of the Declaration provided:

> We recognize that it is important to advance the development objectives of this Round through enhanced market access for developing countries in both Agriculture and NAMA. To that end, we instruct our negotiators to ensure that there is a comparably high level of ambition in market access for Agriculture and NAMA. This ambition is to be achieved in a balanced and proportionate manner consistent with the principle of special and differential treatment.

Progress was also made on cotton. Paragraph 12 reflected an agreement that developed countries would eliminate all forms of export subsidies by 2006, grant duty-free and quota-free access for cotton exports from least developed Members from the beginning of the implementation period, and that trade-distorting domestic subsidies for cotton producers would be reduced under the agreed formula over a shorter implementation period. The Hong Kong Declaration, after reaffirming the Doha Declaration and the July 2004 Framework, recommitted Members to make the development dimension a 'meaningful reality, in terms both of the results of the negotiations on market access and rule-making'. A new deadline of 30 April 2006 was set for agreement on the full Modalities, with comprehensive draft schedules to be submitted by 31 July 2006.

v.   The July 2008 package

However, the timeline for April 2006 was not met and negotiations were suspended in all areas in July of that year. When these resumed in 2007 the Chair issued a number of 'challenges' papers which re-ignited the negotiations, leading to the first version of the draft Modalities. On 17 July 2007 the Chair issued the long-awaited draft Modalities for agriculture as a restricted document (JOB(07)/128), which was later released as TN/AG/W/4 on 1 August 2007.[9] A series of Working Documents were released afterwards by the Chair to capture progress which led to a revision of the Modalities. These were discussed at a mini-Ministerial in July 2008 which looked promising but there were still too many difficult issues to be resolved to conclude the negotiations. The Director General chaired a meeting of the group of seven members (Australia, Brazil, China, EC, India, Japan and the US – the G7), whilst consultations between other Members were chaired by the Chair of the Special Session of the Committee on Agriculture. This meeting proved to be a failure and the proximate cause was disagreement among the G7 about the operation of the Special Safeguard Mechanism, especially in relation to pre-Doha bound rates. It is worth noting, however, that any compromise agreed on this issue within the G7, even if there had been one, would still have had to be accepted by the rest of the membership. Equally one issue had still not been discussed when the negotiations ended – cotton.

Efforts to build on the progress made at the mini-Ministerial were to begin again in October and a further revision of the Modalities was issued on 8 December 2008, capturing the progress made at the July mini-Ministerial (TN/AG/4/Rev.4). This version of the Modalities draft was the only thing we had to work from by the time the manuscript for this book went to press in June 2011.

vi.   The December 2008 Modalities Draft

In Domestic Support the starting point was setting the base level for reductions in Overall Trade Distorting Support (OTDS). This was to be the sum of the final Bound Total AMS plus, for developed Members, 10 per cent of the average total value of agricultural production in the 1995–2000 base period plus the higher of average blue box payments as notified to the Committee on Agriculture, or 5 per cent of the average total value of agricultural production, in the 1995–2000 base period. Developing members could choose either 20 per cent of the average total value of agricultural production in the 1995–2000 or the 1995–2004 period. For OTDS greater than $60 billion the reduction would be 80 per cent; for OTDS between $10 billion and $60 billion the reduction would be 70 per cent; and for OTDS less than or equal to $10 billion the reduction would be 55 per cent. Developed Members with at least 40 per cent of the average total value of agricultural production in the 1995–2000 period would undertake an additional effort equivalent to one half of the difference between the top two reduction rates. The reduction rate for developing Members would be two-thirds of the relevant rate; those developing Members with no Final Bound Total AMS commitments and NFIDCs would not be required to undertake reduction commitments. Special arrangements were also made for Recently Acceded Members (RAMs). The implementation period would be five years (six instalments) for developed Members and eight years (nine instalments) for developing Members.

There are three tiers for the reduction of the Final Bound Total AMS (FBTAMS), which once again differentiates between developed and developing countries. For developed countries, the reduction formula would be as follows: 70 per cent where the FBTAMS was greater than $40 billion; 60 per cent for FBTAMS between $15 billion and $40 billion; and 45 per cent for the bottom tier. Developed Members with high relative levels of FBTAMS (defined in the same way as in OTDS) would undertake an additional effort, equal to the differences between the relevant reduction rates. The six steps in the reductions for developed Members would be a down-payment of 25 per cent reduction on entry into force, followed by five equal instalments over five years. The reduction rate for developing countries would be implemented in nine equal annual instalments over eight years, but Members with a FBTAMS level at or below $100 million would not be required to undertake reductions. Also not undertaking reduction commitments in this area would be NFIDCs while special arrangements were also made for RAMs.

The Modalities also provide for product-specific AMS limits: for all developed Members except the US this would be the average of the product-specific AMS during the Uruguay Round implementation period; for the US this would be 'the resultant of applying proportionately the average product-specific AMS in the 1995–2004 period to the average product-specific total AMS support for the Uruguay Round implementation period (1995–2000) as notified to the Committee on Agriculture' (TN/AG/W/4/Rev.4, 23). In both cases the figures used would be those notified to the Committee on Agriculture. Succeeding paragraphs make provision for cases in which product-specific AMS support above (and below) the *de minimis* level was introduced after the implementation period. The limits are to be implemented in full on the first day of the implementation period and if notifications reveal higher product-specific AMS limits would be implemented in three equal annual instalments. Developing Members would be offered a choice of three methods for the calculation of their product-specific AMS limits. The *de minimis* levels for developed Members would be reduced by no less than 50 per cent effective on the first day of the implementation period and for developing Members the reduction would be two-thirds of that for developed Members to be implemented over three years. Once again special arrangements are made for RAMs and NFIDCs.

Reflecting the negotiations the Blue Box would be amended to allow for the inclusion of direct payment programmes that do not require production and an overall limit on expenditure of 2.5 per cent of the average total value of agricultural production in the 1995–2000 base period. A Member would have to decide which Blue Box to use. For those Members with an exceptionally large percentage of their trade-distorting support (defined as 40 per cent during the 1995–2000 base period) in the Blue Box, the limit is to be established by application of a percentage reduction equal to that used by the Member in its Final Bound Total AMS to be implemented in not more than two years. Blue Box product-specific limits are also to be introduced (separate rules would apply to the US – Annex A). For developing Members, the maximum permitted value of Blue Box support would be 5 per cent of the average total value of agricultural production in the 1995–2000 or the 1995–2004 base period, with the choice being left to the Members concerned. Special arrangements are again made for RAMs. Annex B of the Modalities sets out changes to the Green Box which are directed, for example, towards ensuring that income support programmes are truly decoupled and that developing Members have greater flexibility on food stock-piling.

The draft Modalities establish a formula for the reduction of trade-distorting domestic support for cotton and a Blue Box limit of one-third of the otherwise applicable rate. The reductions would be implemented over one-third of the usual implementation period. The reduction rate for developing Members with AMS and Blue Box commitments on cotton would be two-thirds of that which was applicable to developed Members. Developed Members and developing Members declaring themselves to be in a position to do so would give duty- and quota-free access for cotton exports from least-developed Members as from the first day of the implementation period. For those developing Members not offering such treatment, they are required to examine the possibilities for increased import opportunities for cotton from least-developed Members. Export subsidies for cotton would be prohibited with immediate effect for developed Members, while developing Members are given one year to implement this prohibition.

On export competition the Modalities confirm that developed Members will eliminate their remaining scheduled export subsidy entitlements (both budgetary outlay and quantity reduction commitments) by the end of 2013. The equivalent date for developing Members would be the end of 2016, but they would be allowed to continue to use Article 9.4 of the AoA for five years after the end-date for the elimination of export subsidies, which comes to the end of 2021. Existing commitments to NFIDCs would remain unaffected. New disciplines would be established for export credit, export credit guarantees or insurance programmes (Annex J), agricultural exporting state trading enterprises (Annex K), and international food aid (Annex L). In each case the disciplines seek to ensure that there is an equivalence between the obligations on export subsidies and other forms of export competition and that the latter do not lead to the circumvention of export subsidy commitments. For example, export credits programmes would be self-financing and repayment periods would be limited to up to 180 days. In food aid a distinction was drawn between emergency food aid which would be placed in a Safe Box and other aid which would be subject to disciplines to prevent it from replacing commercial trade. Differences over the monetization of food aid continued to be a problem. Disciplines would also be tightened for introducing new export restrictions.

The most problematic area of the negotiations was market access and the Modalities here reveal continuing disagreements. An agreement has been reached to simplify the agricultural market access regime by converting all non-*ad valorem* tariffs into *ad valorem* equivalents. Keeping the lessons of the Uruguay Round tariffication process and the consequent claims of dirty tariffication, a number of countries have been concerned that the current process of tariff simplification could also lead to what has come to be known as 'dirty simplification', i.e. a situation where the resulting *ad valorem* tariffs would be higher than the specific and complex tariffs they replace (G-20 communication, JOB(09)/174, para. 19).

Once the AVEs have been agreed, the reductions would be made according to the following formula for developed Members: for tariffs greater than 75 per cent, the reduction would be 70 per cent; for tariffs greater than 50 per cent but less than 75 per cent, the reduction would be 64 per cent; for tariffs greater than 20 per cent but less than 50 per cent, the reduction would be 57 per cent; and for all remaining tariffs, the reduction would be 50 per cent. The minimum average cut would be 54 per cent. The reduction rate for developing Members would be two-thirds of the reduction rate for developed Members and the bands would be 0 – 30, 30 – 80, 80 – 130 and above 130 per cent, with a minimum average cut of 36 per cent. Special concessions are accorded to LDCs, RAMs and small and vulnerable economies (SVEs) in the form of either no or limited reduction requirements. The implementation periods are five years for developed Members and ten years for developing Members. The formula will not apply to all products as flexibility is built in for Sensitive Products and Special Products.

Each developed Member would have the right to designate up to 4 per cent of tariff lines as Sensitive Products, but Canada and Japan have resisted this; Canada appears to want a 6 per cent flexibility while Japan goes for 8 per cent (TN/AG/W/5). The Chairman of the agriculture negotiations reported as recently as April 2011 that Japan and Canada have not relented on their demands (TN/AG/26, 13). The Members have not agreed on which products would qualify as sensitive – for example, would it be those that are currently subject to a TRQ commitment (which might be taken as indicator of sensitivity) or would any product qualify? The answer to this is not as yet known (TN/AG/W/6). Agreement was reached on the treatment of such products, namely there would be a deviation of one-third, half or two-thirds from the tariff reduction that would otherwise have been required, with compensation being offered through tariff quotas, whose size will depend on the deviation – 3, 3.5 or 4 per cent of domestic consumption. The Modalities also allow up to 6 per cent of products to be designated as sensitive if the Member has more than 30 per cent of products in the top band of the tariff reduction formula; compensation is offered in this case by an additional tariff quota constituting 0.5 per cent of domestic consumption. Considerable detail is provided in the Modalities on the calculation of domestic consumption (Attachments a – d). Flexibility is accorded to developing Members in terms of quota expansion (two-thirds the amounts for developed members) and domestic consumption data need not include the consumption of produce by subsistence farmers. As for Special Products developing Members would be entitled to self-designate such products guided by indicators based on the criteria of food security, livelihood security and rural development which are laid out in Annex F. The Modalities provide that there would be 12 per cent of tariff lines available for self-designation as Special Products, with up to 5 per cent of lines having no cut and an overall average cut of 11 per cent. However, a number of developing Members have indicated that their agreement on the percentages is dependent on decisions in other areas of the Modalities. Special provisions will apply to small vulnerable economies who moderate the tariff reduction formula and to RAMs.

The Modalities also provide for a mechanism to address tariff escalation on a list of products enumerated in Annex D. This mechanism would not apply if a product was declared sensitive and the formula for reduction would not apply to tropical products if that resulted in a greater reduction. In such cases the tropical products reduction would apply. The Modalities offered Members a choice between two options for this latter reduction. Either a reduction to zero for tariffs less than or equal to 25 per cent and an 85 per cent reduction for all other tariffs, or a reduction to zero for tariffs less than 10 per cent and a reduction of 75 per cent for other tariffs, with tariffs in the top band being reduced by the tariff escalation tariff cut for that band increased by two points. The Modalities also include the solution proposed by the EC, ACP and banana-producing Members to the problem of preference erosion, with a choice being offered between no tariff reductions on Annex H products for ten years and reductions then implemented over five years or an extended implementation period accompanied by technical assistance. The Modalities also provide for consultations with commodity-dependent commodity-producing Members.

The Modalities also provide for new rules on tariff quotas and tariff quota administration and the future of the special agricultural safeguard, which for developed Members shall be reduced to 1 per cent of scheduled tariff lines and eliminated by the end of the seventh year of implementation. Options are proposed for the new Special Safeguard Mechanism that would impose disciplines to ensure that it would not be triggered unnecessarily and that if it were applied the duty increases would not exceed pre-Doha bound levels. A separate paper offers a negotiating text on the issue of raising tariffs above the pre-Doha bound rates – the issue that was the proximate cause for the failure of the July mini-Ministerial (TN/AG/W/7). However, the paper also reveals that a significant amount of detail is needed to complete the Modalities on this issue.

IV. CONCLUSION

In the aftermath of the publication of the December 2008 Modalities, there has been a change in the political climate affecting the overall negotiations, particularly from the US. On 27 February 2009, US President Barack Obama released a document outlining US trade policy which on the Doha negotiations identified the need 'to correct the imbalance in the current negotiations in which the value of what the United States would be expected to give is well-known and easily calculable, whereas the broad flexibilities available to others leaves unclear the value of new opportunities for our workers, farmers, ranchers, and businesses'. According to the US, this concern would have to be addressed in the form of 'meaningful market access commitments in agriculture, non-agricultural market access and services, particularly from key advanced developing countries that have been the fastest growing economies and are increasingly key players in the global economy' (USTR, 2009: 2–4). This move by the US appears to have brought about a change in the structure of the negotiations, as in addition to work on the Modalities Members would engage in 'outcome testing' that would provide them with information on how others would use the flexibilities and thus allow for an assessment on the overall outcome of the Round.

In his report to the Trade Negotiations Committee submitted on 21 April 2011, which incorporated the 2010 Report, the Chair of the Special Session of the Committee on Agriculture indicated that four broad streams of work have been undertaken since 2009 (WTO, 2011a WTO, 2010). Work has been undertaken on the highly technical area of the development of templates, data requirements and data verification to promote 'outcome-testing' of the commitments that would be undertaken on the basis of the December 2008 Modalities. The Template Development work has been undertaken in two steps in each of the three pillars of the Agreement: the identification and development of templates for the presentation of base data and, secondly, for the presentation of the final Doha commitments. Whilst work on Step 1 is well-advanced, since April 2010 most of the effort has focused on Step 2: however, this remains incomplete. An essential objective of template development is to facilitate the collection and verification of the relevant data which has been on-going since the process was initiated, but this also remains incomplete with a number of questions on data provision still to be addressed.

Work on the templates, data collection and verification will not be complete until an agreement has been reached on the Modalities. This work has been on-going, focusing particularly on issues that were bracketed in the December Modalities. Summarizing the discussion since 2009, the Chair lamented that Members 'have not been in a position to substantively resolve matters nor is there any discernable progress on these issues that can be captured in text' (WTO, 2011a: para 6). The Chair's report goes on to list the areas in which there have been consultations and the progress that has been made. On product-specific limits to Blue Box domestic support, for example, consultations have reached a stage where a decision is needed on the bracketed numbers. On cotton, although there have been no new contributions, Members have yet to agree on a text despite reaffirming the Hong Kong Declaration's commitment in this area. As noted earlier, Japan and Canada continue to insist on additional flexibilities on the designation of sensitive products but whether other Members will agree, and at what cost, remain open questions. The Chair reported sharp divisions on the proposed tariff cap while divisions persisted on tariff quotas. Consultations on tariff simplification are also on-going, especially on how it would work in practice, and the Report suggests that a possible alternative to the Modalities' text on this point is being developed. On Special Products the consultations reveal that the annotation to paragraph 129 remains factually accurate, with some members suggesting that the paragraph should be seen as 'stabilised'. The Report confirms that the most problematic area remains the Special Safeguard Mechanism. Despite the Chair's invitation in October 2010 to move to engage in problem solving, Members have continued to engage in technical discussions on aspects of the mechanism. The Report lists only one area in which there has been relatively significant development – tropical and diversification products. This development is a result of the letter from the EU, the ACP countries and Latin American banana producers outlining a Modality for the treatment of tropical products and preference erosion. Consultations have been on-going on how the interests of Members who are not party to the proposal would be affected and further clarification of the proposal is still awaited from its proponents.

Beyond these specific issues, the submission of proposals from Members in 2011 points to continuing problems on reaching agreement on the Modalities. It is worth noting that in concluding his April 2011 report the Chair considered it 'regrettable that Members did not feel able, at this point in the process of negotiations, to present more of that activity in a way that could be captured in agreed or otherwise visible text' (WTO, 2011a: para 71).

The stalemate facing the negotiations on agriculture is matched by an equal lack of progress across all aspects of the Doha negotiations, giving rise to the question as to what should be the next step for the Doha Round. Many have already written Doha's obituary, their concern apparently shifting from using Doha to enhance the WTO to rescuing the WTO from Doha. Three possibilities have been widely spoken about. First, the negotiations would continue in their current format but after ten years the omens are not good for a positive outcome. Second, the Members could decide to stop the negotiations and admit to their failure which may have negative consequences on the credibility of the WTO. The third option would be to try to rescue whatever is possible from the negotiations in the form of stand-alone agreements.

On 31 May 2011, the WTO Director-General, Pascal Lamy, outlined a 'three-speed search for Doha outcome in December' (WTO, 2011b). Before outlining his proposal, the Director General made it clear that dropping the Doha negotiations was not on the table, nor was he prepared to see the Single Undertaking formula abandoned in any way. At the same time, the 8th WTO Ministerial Conference will be taking place in December 2011 and the ministers will want to send a clear signal about Doha. It was in the context of the December Ministerial that Lamy outlined his three-speed search, which he described as a three-lane highway with fast, medium, and slow tracks. Lamy thinks there are some important decisions that can be taken in December 2011, and he sees development as 'the common thread running through the issues which could be mature by the end of the year, and in particular LDC-related issues'. Ready for the fast lane would be such LDC issues as Duty-Free, Quota-Free, including Rules of Origin, the LDC Services Waiver, and a step forward on cotton. But the Director General also wants 'an LDC–plus outcome with a significant development component', with a number of issues that are 'candidates for adding in to the LDCs specific issues'. These candidate issues will be put on the middle lane but he does not specify what they are, leaving them instead for the Members to bring them to the table through their 'on-going deliberative process'. The major issues of the Doha negotiations, including not only agriculture but also market access in NAMA, Services, trade remedies and TRIPS are all left for the slow lane, with no outcomes expected by December 2011 but on which work will continue from 2012 (WTO, 2011b).

The proposed approach promises a number of virtues particularly for the poorest Members of the Organization, but the fact that agriculture is not included in the list of issues on the fast lane is to be regretted. At the same time, Lamy's medium track is also meant for the inclusion of new issues that will be part of the package in December 2011, and the issues for this category will emerge from the negotiations between now and December. Looking back through the negotiations and bearing in mind the development of the AoA, perhaps the most obvious agriculture issue that qualifies for the medium track is that of export competition. Such a decision would seek to implement paragraph 6 of the Hong Kong Declaration under which Members agreed to ensure the parallel elimination of all forms of export subsidies and disciplines with equivalent effect by the end of 2013. The decision here would in effect be paragraphs 160 to 169 (along with Annexes J, K and L) of the December 2008 Modalities. Although this could contribute to operationalising the NFIDC Decision, a problem with this approach is that it will require concessions from some Members for which there will be no 'compensation' offered in the other two pillars of the Agreement. A decision avoiding this problem would be one implementing Annex M of the Modalities on the Monitoring and Surveillance of existing commitments. Although this would need to be amended to reflect the lack of agreement on the Modalities, it would, in the words of Annex M, 'give an opportunity to Members to assess the contribution of these obligations to the long-term objective of establishing a fair and market-oriented agricultural trading system'. It would also offer Members a forum on which to reflect, as part of the slow-track items, on a range of issues, closely linked to international regulation of agricultural production and trade, which are either left to some other non-WTO instruments and systems (e.g. climate change), thus raising the issue of relations with the WTO as a key question, or will simply fall in the cracks between the WTO and other regimes (as the food security issue appears to have done).

In the end, however, we believe that agriculture remains the weakest link in the WTO system, with the most basic rules and the least-meaningful constraints on national trade distortive practices. For that reason alone, we remain optimistic that the Doha Round will reach the end of the highway, irrespective of the speed at which it travels; that a new AoA will be agreed; and that a new agreement will bring agricultural trade much closer to the mainstream WTO rules than ever before.

NOTES

1. The additional products outside Chapters 1-24 are mannital, sorbitol, essential oils, albuminoidal substances, modified starches, glues, finishing agents, sorbitol n.e.p., hides and skins, raw furskins, raw silk and silk waste, wool and animal hair, raw cotton, waster and cotton carded or combed, raw flax and raw hemp.
2. The measures to be converted are listed in footnote 1 as 'quantitative import restrictions, variable import levies, minimum import prices, discretionary import licensing, voluntary export restraints, and similar border measures other than ordinary customs duties, whether or not the measures are maintained under country-specific derogations for the provisions of GATT 1947, but not measures maintained under balance-of-payments provisions or under other general, non-agricultural-specific provisions of GATT 1994 or of the other Multilateral Trade Agreement in Annex 1A to the WTO Agreement'.
3. The Panel also noted 'In our view the object and purpose of Article 4.2 is to bring measures whose definitive legal status had long remained unresolved, including price-related border restrictions, under more effective GATT disciplines on the basis of an explicit prohibition, in order to protect a regime for agricultural products based on the use of ordinary customs duties which resulted from the Uruguay Round negotiations' (WT/DS207/R, para 7.32).
4. 'Basic agricultural product' is defined as 'the product as close as practicable to the point of first sale'.
5. If a particular payment is not specified in these paragraphs, it can still be exempt from the reduction commitment provided the general criteria of paragraph 1 are satisfied and the criteria of paragraph 6 (b) through to (e) are also satisfied.
6. These 22 categories are: wheat and wheat flour, coarse grains, rice, oilseeds, vegetable oils, oilcakes, sugar, butter and butter oil, skimmed milk powder, cheese, other milk products, bovine meat, pig meat, poultry meat, sheep meat, live animals, eggs, wine, fruit, vegetables, tobacco and cotton.
7. Under Article 9.4, during the six-year implementation period, developing countries do not have to reduce two categories of subsidy: those designed to reduce the cost of export marketing and preferential internal transport and freight charges; provided that they are not applied in a manner that circumvents the reduction commitment.
8. They are, Australia, Brazil, Bulgaria, Canada, Colombia, Costa Rica, Cyprus, the Czech Republic, the EU, Hungary, Iceland, Indonesia, Israel, Mexico, New Zealand, Norway, Panama, Poland, Romania, the Slovak Republic, South Africa, Switzerland, Turkey, the US, Uruguay and Venezuela (TN/AG/S/8/Rev.1, 31 January 2005).
9. This Modalities text has undergone four major revisions: TN/AG/W/4/Rev.1 (8 February 2008), TN/AG/W/4/Rev.2 (19 May 2008), TN/AG/W/4/Rev.3 (10 July 2008) and TN/AG/W/4/Rev.4 (6 December 2008). Despite several attempts to further refine this document and conclude the process, the fourth revision from December 2008 remains unchanged at the time of writing this chapter (June 2011).

BIBLIOGRAPHY

Baffes, J. and de Gorter, H. (2005) 'Disciplining Agricultural Support through Decoupling', *World Bank Policy Research Working Paper* 3533. Washington, DC: World Bank.

Blandford, D. (2001) 'Are Disciplines Required on Domestic Support?', 2 *Estey Centre Journal of International Law and Trade Policy,* **35**.

Burfisher, M. and Hopkins, J. (2003) 'Decoupled Payments: Household income transfers in contemporary US agriculture', *USDA Agricultural Economic Report no. 822*. Washington, DC: USDA.

Cho, S. (2007) 'Doha's Development', *Berkeley Journal of International Law,* **25***:* 164.

de Gorter, H., Ingco, M., Ignacio, L. and Hraniova, J. (2003a) 'Market Access: Agricultural policy reform and developing countries', *Trade Note 6*. Washington, DC: World Bank (available at http://www.worldbank.org/trade/tradenote).

de Gorter, H., Ingco, M. and Ignacio, L. (2003b) 'Domestic Support for Agriculture: Agricultural Policy Reform and Developing Countries', *Trade Note 7*. Washington, DC: World Bank.

Desta, M. G. (2002) *The Law of International Trade in Agricultural Products: from GATT 1947 to the WTO Agreement on Agriculture*. Amsterdam: Kluwer.

Desta, M. G. and Hirsch, M. (2011) 'African Countries in the World Trading System: International Trade, Domestic Institutions and the Role of International Law', *forthcoming in ICLQ*.

GATT (1987) Basic Instruments and Selected Document 33rd Supp/19.

Harbinson, S. (2009) 'The Doha Round: "Death-Defying Agenda" or "Don't Do it Again"?', *ECIPE Working Paper No. 10/2009*, available at http://www.ecipe.org/publications/ecipe-working-papers/the-doha-round-a-death-defying-act/PDF

Ingco, M. (1996) 'Tariffication in the Uruguay Round: How much liberalisation?', *The World Economy,* **19**(4): 425.

Ismail, F. (2005a) 'Mainstreaming Development in the World Trade Organisation', *Journal of World Trade,* **39**: 11.

Ismail, F. (2005b) 'A Development Perspective on the WTO July 2004 General Council Decision', *Journal of International Economic Law,* **8**: 377.

McMahon, J. A. (2006) *The Agreement on Agriculture*. Oxford: Oxford University Press.

Mitchell, A. D. and Voon, T. (2009) 'Operationalising Special And Differential Treatment in the World Trade Organization: Game over?', *Global Governance: A Review of Multilateralism and International Organisations,* **15**: 343.

OECD (1999) *Preliminary Report on Market Access Aspects of Uruguay Round Implementation* COM/AGR/APM/TD/WP(99). Paris: OECD.

OECD (2000) Decoupling*: A Conceptual Overview* COM/AGR/APM/TD/WP(2000)14/FINAL. Paris: OECD.

OECD (2003) *Evolution of Agricultural Support in Real Terms in OECD Countries from 1986 to 2002*. Paris: OECD.

Panagariya, A. (2002) 'Developing Countries at Doha: A Political Economy Analysis', *World Economy,* **25**: 1205.

Swinbank, A. and Tranter, R. (2005) 'Decoupling EU Farm Support: Does the new single farm payment scheme fit within the green box?', *Estey Centre Journal of International Law and Trade Policy,* **6**: 47.

USTR (2009) *2009 Trade Policy Agenda and 2008 Annual Report of the President of the US on the Trade Agreements Program*. Washington: USTR.

Wha Chang, S. (2007) 'WTO Trade and Development post Doha', *Journal of International Economic Law,* **10**: 553.

WTO (1996) *Singapore Declaration*, WT/MIN(96)/Dec.

WTO (1998) *Geneva Ministerial Declaration*, WT/MIN(98)/Dec.

WTO (2001a) *Doha Ministerial Declaration*, WT/MIN(01)/DEC/1.

WTO (2001b) *Decision on Implementation-Related Issues and Concerns*, WT/MIN(01)/17.

WTO (2002) *Overview Paper*, TN/AG/6.

WTO (2003a) *First Draft of the Agricultural Modalities*, TN/AG/W/1.

WTO (2003b) *Report of the Chair of the Special Session of the Committee on Agriculture to the TNC*, TN/AG/10.

WTO (2003c) *Cancun Ministerial Statement*, WT/MIN(03)/W/20.

WTO (2004a) *August Decision*, WT/L/579.

WTO (2004b) *Report of Committee on Agriculture*, G/AG/R/40.

WTO (2005) *Hong Kong Ministerial Declaration*, WT/MIN(05)/DEC.

WTO (2010) *Negotiating Group on Agriculture: Report by the Chairman*, HE Mr David Walker, to the Trade Negotiations Committee (TN/AG/25).

WTO (2011a) *Negotiating Group on Agriculture: Report by the Chairman*, HE Mr David Walker, to the Trade Negotiations Committee (TN/AG/26).

WTO (2011b) 'Lamy outlines three-speed search for Doha outcome in December', *WTO News Item*, 31 May.

Young, C. E. and Westcott, P. (2000) 'How Decoupled is US Agricultural Support for Major Crops?', *American Journal of Agricultural Economics*, **82**: 762.

2 Food security and international agricultural trade regulation: old problems, new perspectives
Fiona Smith

I. INTRODUCTION

How can the World Trade Organization's (WTO) rules on international agricultural trade address food security more effectively? This is a question taxing trade negotiators, policy officials outside the WTO and many eminent academic commentators. There is such a wealth of institutional literature and academic commentary advocating changes to the WTO's international agricultural trade rules beyond those in the Doha Draft Modalities for Agriculture that it is easy to get swept along with the strong impetus for fundamental change (WTO, 2008b). Recent events have ensured that food security is high on the political agenda too.

The 2010 Russian wheat export ban is putting pressure on international wheat supplies. Russia is the world's fourth largest wheat exporter and its export ban means supply problems for many WTO Members. Argentina also retains long-term restrictions on the export of agricultural products. In 2008 the Argentinean government introduced further higher variable export taxes on beef, soybeans and oilseeds, together with slightly lower rates for maize and wheat, on domestic food security grounds (Nogués, 2008). The effectiveness of this policy is questionable. Argentina suffered a severe social and economic crisis in 2002. Export taxes were introduced as a very quick way to generate crucial income to alleviate the severe poverty rates. Whilst this policy alleviated the worst problems in the short term, the long-term effects were surprising. The Nogués study shows these taxes actually led to a *reduction* in agricultural production and an *increase* in rural unemployment and consumer prices for food. The high export taxes operated as a disincentive to produce. Farmers were unable to compete effectively on export markets as the export price was artificially inflated by the tax, so their production was either diverted straight onto the domestic consumer market or the domestic processing industry. The price farmers received for their products was kept artificially low by the tax, so as some of the revenue from the tax was not diverted to farmers as compensation they received less income over time. As a consequence, the farmers switched production to other non-taxed agricultural products or, more often, left farming completely. The result was a decline in the food supply and an increase in unemployment as farms closed. Whilst consumers benefited from artificially depressed food prices in the short term as the farmers had no incentive other than to supply the domestic market, in the long term farmers adjusted their production and consumer prices increased as domestic supplies food was sourced from outside the country (*Financial Times*, 2011 Special Report on Commodities, 24 May). As rural unemployment increased with the decline in farms, so consumers became less able to afford to buy the food that was produced. The policy resulted in significant civil unrest in Argentina itself as agricultural producers staged a blockade of major routes as a protest against their ability to export and thus gain a higher revenue for their products. The decline in Argentinean exports also contributed to the overall decline in the volume of food available on world markets, thereby putting further upward pressure on world food prices.

The Food and Agriculture Organisation (FAO) met in September 2010 to highlight the rise in food prices caused by supply problems and discuss what measures could be put in place to prevent another major food crisis like that of 2008. Pressure will inevitably be brought to bear on trade negotiators in order to ensure the new international agricultural trade rules will also adequately address food security. But before the trade negotiators rush to change the rules and the current Draft Modalities in line with these ideas on food security, a word of caution should be sounded. A commonly held view is that changing all the international agricultural trade rules on food security necessarily implies improving them and, as a corollary, that retaining the existing rules unchanged is a retrograde step. Therefore, it is thought, unless great changes occur the existing rules will remain stagnant and unresponsive to contemporary political problems, and as a result will be unable to fully address contemporary problems such as food security. Change is not inevitably an improvement, rather, it is more synonymous with disturbance: for good and bad. Even when it seems obvious that the existing international agricultural rules should be changed to more fully accommodate all aspects of food security, there will be other effects that may have been overlooked. And these other consequential effects could, in fact, adversely impact on different aspects of international agricultural trade regulation in a profound way.

This point is best illustrated with an example that has already been referred to above. Argentina's export tax on agricultural products appeared to be an excellent way to address its domestic food supply problems and rural poverty. Amending the rules was thought to only ever lead to positive effects for its farmers, the rural population and consumers. However, the reality of doing so was much more complex: farmers and consumers did gain in the short term, but the long-term effects were much less predictable: food production declined; farmers moved out of agricultural production; and domestic food prices increased. Therefore changes to the existing international agricultural trade rules do not only lead to positive improvements in the way the international agricultural trade rules deal with food security; they also create an entire new regulatory environment for international agricultural trade where the 'better' rules on food security are only one dimension. Thus change is always more extensive than is originally anticipated. Whilst it may be true ultimately that alterations to the rules do mean food security problems are more successfully resolved by the international agricultural trade rules, equally it may also mean that this innovation simultaneously causes a significant modification in the nature of international agricultural trade regulation as a whole. The WTO's international agricultural trade rules may address food security; however, the temptation to overload the WTO's international agricultural trade for those rules to address all dimensions of food security should be resisted. It is important to fully understand the richness of the current international agricultural trade rules' treatment of the problem of food security and the proposals for change before trade negotiators move ahead and make changes, since contrary to current thinking it may be that the existing rules are more able to accommodate some contemporary food security concerns and a small, incremental change is all that is required.

The discussion here is in three parts. To begin with Part II will look at the way the existing international agricultural trade rules' and Draft Modalities' relationship with food security is traditionally described, how problems are identified and solutions crafted. Part III will then show how this is not the only way to look at this relationship; that it is possible to adopt a different perspective and so discover new truths about the interaction of the rules, the Draft Modalities and food security. I shall also show the ways in which this new perspective changes how the international agricultural trade rules' impact on food security is thought to happen and what the appropriate solution is. Finally, Part IV will draw some conclusions and illustrate why it is not necessarily inevitable that the existing international agricultural trade rules' treatment of food security should be fundamentally changed.

II. INTERNATIONAL AGRICULTURAL TRADE REGULATION AND FOOD SECURITY: OLD PROBLEMS, TRADITIONAL PERSPECTIVES

How do the existing international agricultural trade rules affect food security? Where are the problems with the rules' coverage and effects and how can these problems be resolved? Do the Draft Modalities help, or merely add new problems to an already complex and difficult symbiotic relationship? A common way to analyse these questions in the context of international agricultural trade regulation is to focus on whether the existing rules address food security effectively and how the Draft Modalities improve that effectiveness. This effectiveness is explored in two overlapping ways. First, how the rules strike the balance between trade and food security and what practical effect this balance has for Members' domestic agricultural policies and international agricultural trade in general. Second, the ways the rules cause food insecurity, either by their internal deficiencies (i.e. in the way they are drafted or the values they represent and promote) or because Members have not fully implemented them.

In each instance of effectiveness, a common starting point from which the rules are analysed is a definition of food security. The most commonly used definition is the Rome Declaration on World Food Security from the 1996 World Food Summit (WFS, 1996). Under paragraph 1, food security is said to exist 'when all people, at all times, have physical and economic access to sufficient, safe and nutritious food to meet their dietary needs and food preferences for an active and healthy life'.[1] It is thought that assessing the international agricultural trade rules to the Rome Declaration in this way is the key to showing how effective the rules are, how they impact on food security, and where the problems are. Once the problems with the existing rules are fully articulated in this way, the effectiveness of the Draft Modalities can be properly assessed and appropriate proposals for changes to the rules can be framed.

So, for example, Christian Häberli predicates his critique of the international agricultural trade rules and the Doha proposals' inability to address food security on a particular version of the Rome Declaration. For Häberli (2010: 298), food security is 'continuing access, by way of either domestic production or trade to quantitatively and qualitatively adequate food, including for the poorest segments'. From this beginning, he then shows how Members' domestic agricultural policies, like subsidies on biofuels, export bans and declines in levels of food aid, all contribute to food insecurity; how these policies adversely impact on net-food importing developing countries (NFIDCs) through high commodity prices, reduce cheap imports of food and lead to growing balance of payments problems; and, finally, how the international agricultural trade rules are unable to prevent such distortions and in fact exacerbate them (Häberli, 2010: 302–308).

From his perspective, the current market access rules do not give full access to developing country agricultural exports because developed countries retained high tariffs despite Members' market access reduction commitments. Domestic support reduction commitments did not fully rein in subsidised agricultural production and food dumping remained prevalent, even through food aid (2010: 304). In addition, the export subsidy commitments in the Agreement on Agriculture (AoA) did not fully address the needs of net-food importing nations that were heavily dependent on food aid for their food security needs. The existing international agricultural trade rules do not fully anticipate that whilst food aid is an important part of famine relief, it has the power in the long term to displace domestic production (Desta, 2001: 457). Developed country Members also use food aid, sometimes perniciously, as a way to dump excess food production (irrespective of the recipient country's needs) and to avoid their export subsidy reduction commitments (Häberli, 2010: 307). The conclusion is, therefore, that the existing rules do not as yet fully address this aspect of food security, but they should.

Other commentators focus on the Rome Declaration to critique the WTO's impact on the problem of food security and climate change. For example, a 2006 UK government report showed how temperatures are predicted to rise by 2–3 per cent globally over the next 50 years and how this will have negative impacts on agricultural yields, particularly in Africa. Water will cease to be so readily available and, as a consequence, agricultural yields will drop. World cereals' yields will also be hit (DEFRA, 2006; Stern, 2006). Climatic variations, paradoxically, will also cause severe flooding with consequential adverse effects on production (Keleman *et al.*, 2010). Pressure on food supplies as a result of growing demand for food will be inevitable. When assessing the international agricultural trade rules against the Rome Declaration in the context of climate change, the commentators found the rules only exacerbate food supply problems in such cases in two linked ways: first, the flexibility in Article XI GATT and Article 12 AoA allow major wheat exporters, like the Ukraine, to impose export bans as a way of managing its own population's food demands, thereby causing even greater restrictions on available food for net-food importers (DEFRA, 2010). The rules also encourage countries to develop trade in sectors where they have a comparative advantage. If a country's comparative advantage is not in agriculture, it becomes increasingly dependent on trade and may not remain self-sufficient in food production. As the WTO encourages liberalised trade in agricultural products, the rules are then thought to effectively restrict the availability of nutritious foods: that is, they make a Member's food *in*secure. From a climate change perspective, it may be better to discourage an over-dependence on trade to meet domestic food needs and, as a corollary, to suggest greater political flexibility be put into the WTO rules to enable Members to encourage domestic production (DEFRA, 2006: 35–50).

Other commentators consider the relationship between the international agricultural trade rules, food security and sustainable farming techniques. Here, the emphasis is on the availability of land on which to grow food. 'Land grabs' in areas of sub-Saharan Africa by countries like China, Saudi Arabia, South Korea and Kuwait for the purposes of alleviating their food supply problems are thought to put severe stress on sub-Saharan food supplies (BBC, 2009). These reduce the amount of land available for cultivation domestically and thereby also reduce the available income generated from the land (Coula *et al.*, 2009). The Rome Declaration's definition of food security makes it clear that people should have 'physical and economic access' to food. Clearly land grabs severely impede that access. Neither of these issues is addressed in the existing international agricultural trade rules and commentators argue that they should.

It is clear from the discussion so far that one way of exploring the relationship between the international agricultural trade rules and food security is to use a definition such as that found in the Rome Declaration as a fixed determinant of what food security *should be* and then assess the international agricultural trade rules and Draft Modalities against it. Where the rules and Modalities address the same issue or they have no adverse impact, the rules and Modalities are thought to address food security adequately. However, where the rules and Draft Modalities do not address the same dimensions of food security in the Rome Declaration or impede them, then they are thought to be deficient. Accordingly, the existing rules and the emphasis in the Draft Modalities must be adjusted in such a way that this ensures the final body of rules will allow international agricultural trade (at least under the WTO rules) to attain every dimension of the food security definition in the Rome Declaration.[2] But a different picture emerges if the starting point for analysis is shifted away from a definition of food security that is in a different legal instrument to the WTO rules and is instead shifted towards the rules themselves. In other words, once an analysis of the rules, the Draft Modalities and food security focuses on what the rules and Draft Modalities *themselves* say about food security, then it is possible to see what food security is in international agricultural trade regulation and why changing the rules to accommodate a wider, more nuanced understanding of food security based on a definition like the Rome Declaration is more problematic than it first appears. This new approach looks at all the same problems as existing commentators, but it also brings new perspectives on these problems into contact with new ideas about how to view changes to the rules.

In one sense this new form of analysis describes what the rules and Draft Modalities say about food security, for it proceeds by analysing the wording of the existing international agricultural trade rules and the Draft Modalities in order to show which problems surrounding food security the current rules are designed to address and how the Draft Modalities can modify that picture. At the same time, this description reveals deeper truths about the fundamental nature of international agricultural trade regulation and the place that food security occupies within it (Smith, 2010). Adopting this new viewpoint, rules are more than just 'container[s] for the transmission of messages' to direct Members to formulate their domestic agricultural policies on food security in a certain way (White, 1990: ix). Instead, the existing international agricultural trade rules and Draft Modalities are also the embodiment of a political choice to regulate some aspects of food security and not others and to regulate those chosen aspects in certain ways. This political choice is, in turn, part of a larger vision about how international agricultural trade should be regulated in the WTO: specifically, which problems should be regulated; how they should be regulated; who should be subject to the rules; who should be the target of the rules; what the non-trade concerns are; which non-trade concerns are relevant to the regulation of international agricultural trade in the WTO and how the balance between trade and non-trade concerns should be struck; and, finally, what the scope of the rules' impact should be (OECD, 2010: 9).

It would be disingenuous to describe these choices about food security and agricultural trade regulation as being wholly detached from Members' domestic political imperatives and trade negotiators' need to make political trade-offs in the Uruguay Round multilateral trade talks and the Doha Development Round. What can be said though is that, irrespective of the motivation for the choices, only certain problems of food security are regulated in the existing international agricultural trade rules and these are regulated in a certain way. When the existing international agricultural trade rules and Draft Modalities are understood in this deeper way, it becomes apparent that changing them to address every dimension of food security highlighted in the current literature is not only a question of adding in extra, 'better' language, it is also about changing the fundamental nature of the political vision for international agricultural trade in the WTO as a whole. In the next section, the discussion describes how the existing international agricultural trade rules address food security as a way of also revealing which dimensions of food security the rules will focus on and the political choices that underpin that regulation. It will then show how the Draft Modalities adjust that picture and what the implications of that adjustment are. The final section of this article addresses the tricky issue of reform.

III. INTERNATIONAL AGRICULTURAL TRADE REGULATION AND FOOD SECURITY: OLD PROBLEMS, NEW PERSPECTIVES

The existing international agricultural trade rules in the AoA and the Decision on Measures Concerning the Possible Negative Effects of the Reform Programme on Least-Developed and Net Food-Importing Developing Countries (the NFIDC Decision) are designed to address one particular problem of food security: that is, that as food becomes more expensive as a consequence of the removal of price support mechanisms in Members' domestic agricultural policies under the WTO rules on international agricultural trade so some countries may find it difficult to maintain their food supply, since it is implicit in liberal market economics that price support mechanisms used in domestic agricultural policies in the period before the WTO rules artificially kept the costs of agricultural production low by off-setting the true costs of production through the payment of domestic subsidies to farmers (Anderson and Martin, 2006: 31). These subsidies allowed farmers to sell their products cheaply on domestic and international markets to gain a market share without any substantial loss of revenue. Export subsidies to domestic farmers further supported that production model by keeping the export price of the domestically produced product artificially low, as the difference between the low export price and the true costs of production were met by the export subsidy; and, finally, various import barriers insulated domestic farmers from competition imports of agricultural products from countries like Kenya that enjoy a comparative advantage in agricultural production. Reducing these price support mechanisms causes price rises in the short term because the true costs of agricultural production will now feed directly into the export price of agricultural products; food aid supplies will also be vulnerable (Clapp, 2004).

The NFIDC Decision specifically acknowledges in paragraph 2 that the relevant countries, in particular, may experience food supply problems as a consequence of this liberalisation programme in the WTO rules on international agricultural trade, but paragraph 6 of the Preamble of the AoA also makes it clear that the rules will provide some relief from the price support reduction commitments in the Agreement for *any* Member that suffers from food supply problems as a result of the implementation of the reforms to their domestic agricultural policies.

The existing international agricultural trade rules are all orientated towards ameliorating this food supply problem as a result. Relief from the reduction commitments on food security (i.e. food supply) grounds is provided in each of the three pillars of the Agreement: market access, domestic support, and export competition commitments. In terms of market access, generally the rules require all non-tariff barriers to be converted into tariffs under Article 4.2 of the AoA. However, the rules do provide Members with some temporary and very limited relief from the conversion process on food security grounds.[3] Annex 5A of the AoA potentially allows all Members to exclude border measures on '*any* primary product and its worked and/or prepared products' where the product, *inter alia,* has been designated in the Member's tariff schedule for special treatment that reflects 'factors of non-trade concerns such as food security ...' (Annex 5A, para1(d)), whereas under Annex 5B developing country Members can exclude non-tariff measures from tariffication where the measure concerned relates to a primary agricultural product that is the 'predominant staple in the traditional diet' and where it complies with Annex 5A, paras 1(a)-(d). Retention of non-tariff barriers under these circumstances seems to allow more targeted protection of domestically sensitive agricultural products from the import of cheap agricultural products produced with the benefit of large domestic subsidies. However, the Annex 5 exemption was time limited and only available if the specific narrow circumstances specified in Annex 5 were complied with, including a minimum market access commitment which exceeded that which was required under Article 4.2. In reality, only Japan, Korea, the

Philippines and Israel made such reservations in their Schedules and Japan suspended its use of the provision in 1998 (Desta, 2002).

Concerns that domestic agricultural production would be overwhelmed by the flood of cheap agricultural imports following the tariffication of non-tariff barriers and the new tariff bindings was also alleviated by the inclusion of the special safeguard provision in Article 5. Article 5 allows a Member to impose additional import duties on products it designates as particularly vulnerable in its Schedule (i.e. by using the symbol SSG in their Schedule for the product in question) when either there is an increase in the volume of imports in excess of a pre-determined trigger level or a decrease in the import price below the trigger level (Article 5.1(a) and (b)). Article 5 allows countries, who have so designated their 'tariffied' products, to respond to such import surges if there is a genuine threat to the domestic food supply or where there is only a perceived threat, as the Article 5 does not require the Member to show there is actually injury or the threat of injury to their food supplies (Desta, 2002).

The rules on domestic support also provide an exemption from the reduction commitments in Part IV of the AoA where Members want to maintain food supplies, but do not wish to be dependent on external sources of food. Annex 2 of the AoA allows Members to exclude payments to their domestic farmers, either because they are stockpiling important foodstuffs (paragraph 3) or because they wish to give food aid to a sector of their population (paragraph 4). The former allows Members to claim exemption if the money is given to their farmers for the purchase and accumulation of essential food stocks as part of an 'integral part of a *food security* programme identified in national legislation'. This exemption also extends to government payments made to private contractors who store the goods on behalf of the government. In both cases, the exemption is only available if certain prescribed criteria are met, notably that the volume and accumulation of the stocks must not exceed certain 'predetermined targets' that relate solely to food security, that the accumulation and purchase process is fully transparent, and that purchases and sales of the accumulated products are made at current market prices. For Members to claim exemption from their domestic support commitments for their food aid programmes under paragraph 4, each Member must show that the food aid programme has clearly defined nutritional objectives; that the food is either to be given in kind or in subsidised food to eligible individuals; and that any purchase of food made by the Member for these purposes must be made at commercial rates. This exemption is available, according to the first paragraph of Annex 2, to all Members irrespective of their status and is subject to the general over-riding proviso that such support has 'no, or at most minimal effects on production'. The NFIDC Decision does recognise that forcing Members to buy food at market prices for their domestic food aid programmes to gain the advantage of the exemption in paragraph 4 may be particularly problematic for NFIDCs as the high costs may mean access to adequate foodstuffs is difficult. Paragraph 3 of the NFIDC Decision therefore seeks to off-set that food supply problem: Members agree to 'establish appropriate mechanisms to ensure that the implementation of the ... [reform programme] does not adversely affect the *availability* of food aid at a level which is sufficient to continue to provide assistance in meeting the needs of developing countries ...'.

In the context of the export subsidy reduction commitments, the food supply problem is understood in a different way. Members are required to make specific reduction commitments for their use of export subsidies (Part V of the AoA). Only those existing export subsidies which meet the criteria in Article 9 are permitted (subject to reduction commitments); Article 10 contains anti-circumvention provisions. Articles 8–10 do impact on the exporting Member's agricultural policies as the reduction commitments mean the amount of agricultural products subsidised reduces, with the result that the dumping of excess agricultural production on to third countries' markets should reduce too. Article 10 specifically limits the circumstances where an exporting Member can claim exemption from its export subsidy reduction commitments on the grounds it is exporting products as food aid. The rules are therefore also protecting the importing country's food supply in two ways: first, they attempt to prevent the dumping of agricultural produce well below the cost of production in the importing country which then drives domestic producers out of the market; second, when food is exported as food aid 'in kind' Article 10 seeks to ensure the food supplied to the ultimate consumer is in fact nutritious and in accordance with the dietary needs of the local population. Article 10.4 therefore requires donors of international food aid to make certain that their provision of aid is 'not tied to ... commercial exports' of agricultural products to the donee country; that the food aid is provided in accordance with recognised requirements in the FAO's Principles of Surplus Disposal and Consultative Obligations; and that it is given in grant form wherever possible or at least under the terms of the Food Aid Convention. The move towards genuine food aid is also recognised in paragraph 3 of the NFIDC Decision.

Members who are net-food exporters are also able to address food supply problems. In the case of such Members problems occur when domestic food production is significantly curtailed due to production conditions, such as bad weather for example. In these circumstances Members in this position fear that there will be insufficient food for their domestic population if the usual levels of export trade in the agricultural products concerned are maintained. Article XI:2(a) of GATT allows Members to impose temporary export restrictions on key domestic agricultural products 'to prevent or relieve *critical shortages of foodstuffs* ...'. This provision was modified by Article 12 of the AoA which makes it clear that, prior to implementing an export ban, the Member is required to 'give due consideration' to the food security needs of importing Members. Full details of the measure, particularly its general nature and its duration, must be given to the Committee on Agriculture. There is also a duty to consult other Members who may have a substantial interest in the export ban, like NFIDCs who are reliant on those exports (Hermann and Peters, 2010). In addition Article 12 imposes a duty to provide further detailed information to those Members if a request is made. Different arrangements apply to export bans imposed by developing countries, although these special arrangements do not apply if the developing country concerned is a net-exporter of the specific agricultural product which is subject to the export restriction.

It is evident that the current international agricultural trade rules are focused on solving one particular problem in the context of food security: that is, the adverse effect of the liberalisation programme on food supplies for WTO Members, particularly the NFIDCs. What do the policy choices made in the rules reveal about the way food security is addressed in the existing international agricultural trade rules?

Food security is not an end in itself for the existing rules. Rather, as paragraph 3 of the AoA's Preamble states, the rules' objectives are in fact to liberalise international agricultural trade and push WTO Members towards policy choices that are more market-oriented and less focused on short-term domestic political imperatives. Food security's relevance to the rules is then reduced to a factor that must be weighed against the market liberalisation objective. As paragraph 6 of the Preamble specifically states, Members' agricultural support reduction commitments 'under the reform programme, should be made in an equitable way among Members, having regard to non-trade concerns *including food security*'. Food security is not the only non-trade concern listed in the AoA, but is one of a number of non-trade objectives listed, together with environmental preservation, special and differential treatment, and the potential adverse effects on NFIDCs of the reforms instituted by the Agreement. The balance envisaged by the Agreement is one between the market liberalisation objective and each non-trade concern that is considered as a distinct challenge for the liberalisation agenda. The relationship and balance between competing non-trade concerns in the context of agriculture, like maximising food security but on sustainable land-use principles or not maximising production in ways that exacerbate climate change, are irrelevant considerations for the existing rules (FAO, 2008). This balance is something for each Member to decide within its own domestic agricultural policy. Whilst a Member may have undertaken international commitments on climate change and development which will influence how its domestic agricultural policy may be constructed, it is not for the WTO to force that Member into acceding to these international commitments through the 'back door' by prescribing how the balance between non-trade concerns should be addressed under the current international agricultural trade rules; the policy choice therefore remains largely under the control of the Member.

Food security is not defined at any point in the AoA or in the NFIDC Decision. Article 1 of the AoA which defines the terms used in the Agreement as a whole is a substantial provision and contains over nine definitions of the terms used in the rules. Some of the definitions are utilised to calculate the level of a Member's domestic support for the purposes of the reduction commitments in the AoA and each runs to more than one paragraph. It is clear therefore that the trade negotiators' attention was drawn to the need to include a definition section in the rules and that they understood its importance for these rules' effectiveness. The omission of a definition of food security appears to be deliberate and implies that food security is not a matter for the rules *per se*, but is something separate which is to be determined by other international agreements and/or by the WTO Member. It is then for the Member to decide what is most appropriate for the needs of its domestic population in food security terms. Whether the policies work and the Members' population benefits are not relevant considerations for the current international agricultural trade rules.

As a corollary to this, an individual's right to nutritious, safe food that meets their dietary needs, or whether the needs of different sections of the population are addressed, such as those of women, within the Member's food security policy is also outside the rules. Even when the NFIDC Decision notes the importance of recognising the negative impact of the reform programme on food security, this is described only in terms of the problems the *Member* has in terms of its food security policy. Paragraph 2 states that Members must recognise that 'least-developed and net-food importing developing *countries*' might feel the effect, not that their populations must suffer as a result of the reform programme before the Member can rely on the more liberal regime in the Decision. Each Member has considerable autonomy to determine whether it is experiencing food security problems or not, and when it can react to those problems.

The current rules also only recognise food supply difficulties for four homogeneous types of Member: the developed country, the developing country, the least developed country, and the NFIDC. The NFIDC Decision highlights particular difficulties in terms of access to food aid for NFIDCs, but beyond this rather crude division between the four categories of state in the rules, there is no recognition about the actual food security challenges for each Member and the fact that a range of policy choices may be better for those states at different times. Some Members might be particularly vulnerable either because their agricultural production is erratic or their climate unpredictable, thereby causing food supply problems in some years and not others (WFP, 2010), or even because food aid supplies to them are unpredictable and domestic production is unable to cope with the unpredictable shortfalls in supply (Stevens *et al.*, 2000: 14–15). Such Members are not part of a homogeneous group and their Membership fluctuates over time just as their needs do. These complex and ever-changing needs are not relevant considerations for the current rules. Rather, these difficulties fall outside the WTO framework and are covered by other organisations and legal regimes and/or the Members themselves are thought to be best placed to formulate the most appropriate solutions for their domestic situation. In either case, the WTO's rules only purport to offer a framework to increase the market orientation of existing rules and their fairness and increased trade may be an incidental effect of these rules. The final resolution of the other dimensions of food security suffered by these countries is not thought to lie with the WTO.

Thus the focus in the balance between food security and the market liberalisation objective in the existing international agricultural rules is not a balance between the need to keep markets open and having food security policies that actually *work*. Rather it is a balance between allowing a Member to pursue its own food security policy without any external regulatory constraints and having a situation where certain limitations on Members' policy space are necessarily imposed.

Both the AoA and the NFIDC Decision do place some distinct limits on Members' autonomy, but these limits are mainly focused only along one dimension of their food security policies. For it is the measures Members use to achieve food security that are the subject of the rules, not their policy as such; and it is primarily those measures which restrict the inflow of agricultural products into Members' domestic markets that the existing rules concentrate on. Therefore the rules are principally import-focused. Measures regarded as prohibited restrictions for the purposes of the rules are those taking the form of non-transparent quantitative restrictions, as these directly impede the free-flow of imports at the border. Although Article 5 of the AoA allows Members some relief from the adverse effects of the reduction of import barriers on food security grounds, this is generally only in the form of additional duties and is not a return to the use of highly distortive quotas or other non-tariff barriers. It is also only available on a temporary basis. Annex 5's exemption on food security grounds from the tariffication commitment only applies in a very limited range of circumstances; most notably where imports of the product were at historically very low levels, where effective production-limiting measures are applied to the primary product, and where export subsidies have not been imposed on the product in question. Minimum access commitments must still be given in accordance with the explicit provisions of Annex 5A. Even where a Member is able to restrict imports on food security grounds because the product is also the 'predominant staple in the traditional diet of a developing country', imports of the product must still be historically low and the minimum access commitments must be given. The emphasis is solely on keeping markets open and import restrictions are only permitted in very limited circumstances.

In addition, payments or other forms of support given to farmers, outside permitted levels, that directly stimulate specific types of domestic agricultural production are restricted by the AoA because these are thought to distort the market for agricultural products by artificially depressing the costs of agricultural production and reducing the price to consumers of domestic agricultural products compared with imported ones. As noted above, it is possible for Members to gain exemption from payments to domestic farmers on food security grounds if a Member is purchasing food as part of a public stockholding programme or they are providing food aid to its population. However, in both cases the nature of the food aid and stockholding programmes is not a matter for the rules: it does not matter what food the Member is purchasing, or whether the food truly meets the nutritional needs of its population. Rather, the concern is about the transparency of the measure, the price at which the Member buys the food, and also, most importantly, whether the measure has 'no, or at most minimal effects on domestic production' and is not an indirect subsidy to its domestic agricultural producers. These three concerns all relate to the measure's potential effect on the market for the product in question: that is, whether domestic farmers are gaining a financial advantage as a result of the food security policy which will enable them to sell their products cheaply on the international markets. Food security is not a concern *per se*, it is the measure's potential to create cheap exports which might flood international markets which is the real worry.

Finally, payments to farmers that off-set the costs of domestic agricultural production are severely restricted by the existing rules on the grounds that such export subsidies enable them to sell their products at more competitive prices on international markets to the detriment of those farmers who have not had the advantage of the export subsidy. It is the relationship between export subsidies and food aid which lies at the heart of the AoA's provisions on export subsidies and food security. As noted, Article 10.4 is designed to address a particular problem: to prevent Members circumventing the export subsidy commitments by heavily subsidising commercial exports under the guise of food aid. What food aid is and whether Members' policies meet the food security needs of developing and least-developed nations is not covered by the existing rules, but is instead pushed towards the FAO under their Principles for Surplus Disposal and Consultative Obligations and the Food Aid Convention 1986. Whilst it is not inconceivable that the panels and Appellate Body might be called upon to interpret whether Members' provision of food aid does in fact accord with these provisions, the over-riding objective in Article 10 is to determine whether a Member is circumventing the export subsidy commitments. Even the NFIDC Decision only requires Members to agree to put appropriate mechanisms in place to maintain food aid flows, rather than to undertake any substantive commitment to strengthen food aid *per se*.

The existing international agricultural trade rules focus on food security as a problem of food supply for four homogeneous groups of WTO Member rather than an end in itself. The relationship between food security and other non-trade concerns, like preservation of the environment, is not a matter for the rules. Instead, the rules are unconcerned with whether a Member's policies solve food security problems for that Member or whether individuals become more food secure. The rules address food supply problem in specific ways without distorting international agricultural trade markets any more than is necessary. All the other policy choices lie with the Member concerned.

The rules should not be thought to regard food security as an unimportant consideration simply because they do not address all its dimensions. Rather, the rules see food security as a domestic problem which is best addressed at a national level. Understood in this way, the rules give more power to each Member to address food security rather than less. So how is this picture changed by the Draft Modalities?

Paragraph 13 of the Doha Ministerial Declaration sets out the negotiating objectives for the reform of international agricultural trade regulation (WTO, 2001). It reiterates that the long-term objective of international agricultural trade regulation in the WTO remains to 'establish a fair and market-oriented trading system' by reducing distortions in the market and eliminating export subsidies. The Draft Modalities still focus heavily on opening markets, reducing domestic support and eliminating export subsidies in ways that have been designed to cut the levels of price support for international agricultural trade more effectively than the existing international agricultural trade rules (WTO, 2008c). However, there are subtle changes in the way food security is understood, which in turn suggest a small change in the political vision of international agricultural trade regulation for the WTO.

Food security is still one of the factors that should be balanced against the liberalisation objective, together with preservation of the environment and special and differential treatment. The balance between individual non-trade concerns is still not to be addressed and food security will not be an end in itself for the reformed rules if they are based on the December 2008 Draft Modalities. This means the rules should not address the problem of 'land grab', the adverse impact on the environment caused by intensive farming production techniques, and the impact of climate change on food supply. So the problem of the environment must still be understood in terms of access to food rather than as a need to rectify any of the underlying environmental causes of food insecurity. The role of the international agricultural trade rules is still not to rectify the tensions between non-trade concerns in the trade context; this is for each Member to determine.

The Draft Modalities continue to be heavily focused on each Member's attempts to alleviate food security difficulties rather than on individuals' needs *per se*. However, unlike the current international agricultural trade rules, food security is now set within a more nuanced conception of special and differential treatment in the Draft Modalities that concentrates on the needs of a wider range of developing countries. As a result food security problems in recently acceded

Members (RAMs), including a sub-category of small and vulnerable recently acceded Members, small and vulnerable economies more broadly, and developing, least developed countries and NFIDCs, are targeted throughout the Draft Modalities. For example, paragraphs 7 and 17 regarding the calculation of the levels of domestic support are designed to address the fact that NFIDCs are particularly vulnerable to price rises in agricultural commodities as a result of the required reductions in tariff levels in the reform programme. Both paragraphs exclude NFIDCs from the need to reduce their domestic support, however; thereby allowing them to maintain enough support to bolster their domestic agricultural production. Likewise, the Draft Modalities in paragraphs 66 to 69 also identify small low-income recently acceded Members, especially those with economies in transition, as experiencing particular difficulties because the reduction in tariff revenue from imports of agricultural products significantly reduces the revenue available to them for their broader food security policies. The Draft Modalities therefore allow a slower implementation of market access commitments for these countries.

Whilst it is clear in the Draft Modalities that the problem of food security remains one of food supply, there is a subtle shift to recognising that countries, in reality, experience food security problems in different ways. These are closely tied to the needs of their domestic population, how agricultural trade is organised domestically, and how it is best financed. However, this connection does not mean that the Draft Modalities require Members to show that their policies directly correct food insecurity for vulnerable sectors of their populations, or that the way they choose to organise and finance their domestic agricultural sectors is necessarily effective at bolstering domestic agricultural production. Rather, it is more a question of further expanding Members' policy space so that each Member is able to use more appropriate measures which *it* believes can guarantee the food supply more effectively. For example, in the context of market access commitments, the Draft Modalities still recognise that some developing country Members, especially NFIDCs, will be particularly vulnerable and may need the valuable income gained from high tariffs on the import of agricultural products to alleviate food supply problems and rural poverty which can lead to vulnerable sectors of the population becoming food insecure. However, rather than simply suggesting these problems can be alleviated through temporary exclusion of certain key foodstuffs from the tariff bindings and meeting any deficit with food aid, the Draft Modalities in paragraphs 129 to 131 go further and expand each Member's power in order to enable it to exclude specific food products from its reduction commitments on food security grounds. An illustrative list of these grounds is found in Annex F. This includes factors that relate a foodstuff directly to the nutritional needs of individuals; how vulnerable sectors of the population such as women are dependent on certain foods; how many domestic farmers are producing a particular food; and how many people are employed in a food's production.

The Draft Modalities in Annex L acknowledge that the issue of food aid is a more complex problem than envisaged in the current international agricultural trade rules. They suggest that the amended rules should not simply concentrate on how Members might disguise export subsidies as food aid, which is essentially a supply-side problem, but should instead focus on the demand side of food aid. Food aid should therefore involve the provision of food that is nutritious for a Member's domestic population and it should not lead to greater food insecurity. In particular, the donor must be aware that the market conditions of the donee state may mean the provision of food aid in a particular form is inadequate and, if given in that form, may actually displace domestic production and lead to greater food insecurity. The Draft Modalities further recognise that food aid should not just take the form of dumped produce from the donor Member, but should be more attuned to the actual needs of the recipient country. There *is* therefore a deepening recognition of the appropriate nature of food aid in the Draft Modalities. However, it is *not* an acknowledgment that food aid must be given, nor that the WTO is the appropriate regulatory environment in which to determine whether food aid *per se* is the most appropriate way to alleviate the food security problems of the receiving Member.

The Draft Modalities do move the AoA towards a more nuanced and complex recognition of the problems developing countries face, especially in the context of food security. It is clear from the discussion that the Draft Modalities create even greater policy space for Members to adjust their policies in ways that will be targeted towards their own particular domestic needs. Nevertheless, the Draft Modalities indicate that actually *achieving* food security remains an issue for each Member. It is not within the WTO's competence to regulate food security directly, to force Members to address particular food security objectives within their domestic agricultural policies, nor to adjudicate on when a Member's food security policies are working and when they are not. The needs of the individual, whilst relevant to allowing the Member greater flexibility in the choice of policy instrument, are not directly relevant to the rules. Non-trade food security objectives like the provision of micro-financing in domestic agricultural production, supporting the role of women in agriculture and labour migration to the cities away from farms are all outside the consideration of the rules. Should the existing international agricultural trade rules and the Draft Modalities be changed to accommodate more complex notions of food security?

IV. AMENDING THE RULES: A STEP TOO FAR?

It is tempting to believe that the existing international agricultural trade rules and Draft Modalities fail to strike the right balance between reducing protectionism in international agricultural trade and food security for the reasons highlighted in the first part of this discussion. Such a view sees the current regulatory framework as being out of touch with the contemporary reality of food security problems; as being blind to the suffering of people with insufficient access to food; as being too wedded to free market economics as the instrument of change; and as being too reluctant to expand the WTO's scope when it seems obvious that its dispute settlement system makes the WTO one of the most effective international regimes with the potential to successfully regulate many controversial areas of international relations. Changing the WTO to accommodate all the dimensions of food security, by adding extra rules to the existing framework on international agricultural trade that can be upheld through the dispute settlement system, seems to be the obvious way forward. But wide-ranging innovation can have unexpected consequences.

The Rome Declaration on World Food Security's definition of food security has been referred to earlier in this discussion. The existing international agricultural trade rules could be changed in line with the definition and objectives in the Rome Declaration. The Declaration regards food security not only as a problem for the individual and their household, but also as a problem at national, regional and global levels. It defines food security as 'when all people, at all times, have physical and economic access to sufficient, safe and nutritious food to meet their dietary needs and food preferences for an active and healthy life'. The problem which the Declaration is designed to address is whether an individual has access to food: not only in terms of having food to eat, but also in terms of an individual's financial capacity to buy the right food. This right food is not merely that which provides a basic calorie intake, but is also food that the individual actually wants (either for their dietary needs, or because they enjoy it). In paragraphs

1 to 7 of the Rome Declaration there is a role not only for national action but also for regional and international co-operation to ensure poverty eradication, economic stability, and ultimately to guarantee food security. Food security imperatives should also take into account the complex balance between agricultural production, the 'sustainable management of natural resources', food aid, variations in climate, and the specific problems of certain developing countries, notably those in sub-Saharan Africa (FAO, 2010).

Changing the way the existing international agricultural trade rules deal with food security and the emphasis in the Draft Modalities on the ways suggested in the Rome Declaration seems therefore to be only a positive move. Such innovation gives a clear indication that the WTO is moving towards greater recognition of its role in the implementation of the Millennium Development Goals and also understands its impact on vulnerable individuals. However, the Rome Declaration is predicated on resolving different problems of food security to that of the WTO: it is the difficulty of eradicating hunger which is the focus for the Rome Declaration, whereas the WTO rules concentrate on ameliorating the adverse effects on food supply of price rises caused by agricultural liberalisation; these issues are distinct. Whilst the individual might benefit as a result of the WTO's action, this is not an obligatory consequence of the WTO's rules. Rather, for the WTO the Member is thought to be best placed to address food security concerns in ways which are most appropriate for its domestic population. Thus the WTO rules' emphasis is on keeping the Members' domestic policy space as open as possible so Members can pursue food security issues through their domestic agricultural policies, whilst only limiting Members' use of trade measures where they exacerbate trade tensions. Moving the WTO away from this pro-autonomy stance towards a recognition of the food security rights of the individual has profound ripple effects.

There is a power shift away from the Members towards the WTO as an organisation: it would be for the WTO (through dispute settlement) to determine whether an individual in the Member's territory had actually benefited from the Member's food security policies or not rather than the Member itself as in the current rules. This new assessment would involve the WTO assessing various policy options against one of several possible benchmarks to decide whether that Member's policies were successful or not. This is a significant incursion into the autonomy of the Member and a constraint on its ability to act in the best interests of its population. This change to the existing rules would in fact narrow the Member's policy space in regard to food security with the consequence that it would be less able to react to the needs of its domestic population. However, given the fact that many Members have made commitments to human rights treaties, a broadly conceived 'right to food' may be thought to be a necessary constraint on Member autonomy as the WTO matures as an organisation.

How, then, should international trade negotiators proceed in the face of growing global food insecurity? The way forward is to re-evaluate the richness of the existing international agricultural trade rules in each context in which change is mooted and to re-think what change should look like in this highly politicised environment. It is important to remember that the international agricultural trade rules do not purport to be a panacea to all the world's ills in every aspect of food security. Rather, they balance the need to liberalise international agricultural trade with the potential adverse effects on food supplies. The absence of a fuller recognition of all the dimensions of food security within the existing rules (and the Draft Modalities) does not mean that food security is being ignored by the international trade regulation. Instead, it means that the power to control food security lies elsewhere. Specifically, it is the Member who retains the right to address food security through its agricultural policies in the ways that are best suited to its domestic circumstances. It is also for the Member to make important trade-offs between the various non-trade concerns. Contrary to some accounts of the relationship between the international agricultural trade rules and food security, my view of the function of the rules is that they are designed to keep each Member's policy space as wide open as possible, whilst also trying to maximise the trade liberalisation objective. As this can only ever be a balance, inevitably, there will be times when greater power is held by the WTO – for example, when specifying that food aid cannot be used as a disguised export subsidy – and other times when greater power remains with the Member – for example, in relation to export prohibitions on food security grounds. The international agricultural trade rules' function then is not to impose any particular 'correct' way of achieving food security upon its various Members in all instances. To do so would be to impose a single vision of food security on all Members that disregards the fact that their food security needs are widely diverse and fluctuate over time. It would disregard the fact also that Members' policy responses have to change and adapt to their own domestic circumstances. Whilst it might be held it is for the WTO rules to require Members to guarantee a brighter future where their domestic populations are adequately fed, this view assumes that the Members do not share this goal and so need some external stimulus to pressure them into addressing the needs of their populations; in reality the converse is more likely.

To see the existing international agricultural trade rules' treatment of food security as striking a balance between state power and the need to liberalise international agricultural trade is also to ascribe a different function to the rules: they act as a stable point in an otherwise highly volatile and ever-changing environment, mediating between the need for stability and the desire for change as the problems of food security alter and evolve. The rules' very stability is what makes them useful as Members know what their obligations are, and, over time, they can adapt and change their domestic agricultural policies in line with them. Radically changing a regulatory framework just because the political environment is ever-changing is to misunderstand what it is that makes rules effective in international agricultural trade.

Instead, changes to the rules should be made in small and incremental ways that will slightly refine the balance between trade liberalisation and the adverse impact of the liberalisation programme on food supply problems. This change should *reflect* the consensus of state practice when it has had time to settle into a particular pattern. Change should not be at the expense of the existing rules' integrity. It is clear that the rules have not achieved a full liberalisation of international agricultural trade as yet, and nor have they made huge inroads into alleviating food security, but they have stabilised the legal landscape for agricultural trade. The Draft Modalities can therefore be seen as a reflection of what the current state practice is in the context of how food security will need to be regulated in international agricultural trade regulation at this point in time and what the power balance should be between Members and the WTO. The Draft Modalities also reflect how Members believe food security fits into the larger picture of international agricultural trade regulation: for food security is only one dimension of the highly complex and intricate balance that the current rules strike between many diverse trade and non-trade issues. To advocate a fundamental change to the international agricultural trade rules' treatment of food security would be to undermine the current rules' success in stabilising the legal environment. In the words of Oakeshott, we should see innovation as '... an activity in which a valuable set of tools is renovated from time to time and kept in trim rather than as an opportunity for perpetual re-equipment' (1991: 431). Change should be small, slow, incremental, and in line with state practice. Not drastic, revolutionary, and bold.

NOTES

I would like to thank Dr Christian Häberli, Professor Sean Coyle, Professor Maria Lee, colleagues at the UCL Centre for Law and the Environment and the editors of this collection for comments on an earlier draft of this article. Any errors remain my own.

1.   The 2002 Declaration adds 'social needs' to the various needs which must be met for food security to exist.
2.   This discussion focuses on the Rome Declaration's definition on food security but the same point is equally relevant to other definitions of food security.

BIBLIOGRAPHY

Anderson, K. and Martin, W. (2006) 'Scenarios for Global Trade Reform', in T. W. Hertel and L. A. Winters (eds), *Poverty and the WTO: Impacts of the Doha Development Agenda*. Washington, DC: World Bank/Basingstoke: Palgrave.

BBC (2009) 'Africa Investment Sparks Land-Grab Fear', 5 August, available at http://news.bbc.co.uk/1/hi/business/8150241.stm (accessed 17 December 2010).

Clapp, J. (2004) 'WTO agricultural trade battles and food aid', *Third World Quarterly*, **25**(8): 1439–1452.

Coula, L., Vermeulen, S., Leonard, R. and Keeley, R. (2009), *Land Grab or Development Opportunity? Agricultural investment and international land deals in Africa* (FAO, IIED & IFAD).

DEFRA (2006) 'Food Security and the UK: An Evidence and Analysis Paper'. (Food Chain Analysis Group, DEFRA). London: DEFRA.

DEFRA (2010) *Policy Narrative on Global Food Security and Sustainable Agriculture*. London: DEFRA.

Desta, M. G. (2001) 'Food Security and International Trade Law: An appraisal of the World Trade Organization's approach', *Journal of World Trade*, **35**: 449–468.

Desta, M. G. (2002) *The Law of International Trade in Agricultural Products: from GATT 1947 to the WTO Agreement on Agriculture*. Amsterdam: Kluwer.

FAO (2008) *Climate Change and Food Security: A Framework Document*. Rome: FAO.

FAO (2010) Follow-up reports, available at http://www.fao.org/wfs/index_en.htm (accessed 17 December 2010).

Guardian (2010) 'UN Calls Special Meeting to Address Food Shortages Amid Predictions of Riots', 5 September.

Häberli, C. (2010) 'Food Security and the WTO Rules', in B. Karapinar and C. Häberli (eds), *Food Crises and the WTO: World Trade Forum*. Cambridge: Cambridge University Press, pp. 297–322.

Hermann, M. and Peters, R. H.(2010) 'Impact of the Food crisis on Developing Countries and Implications for Agricultural Policy', in B. Karapinar and C. Häberli (eds), *Food Crises and the WTO: World Trade Forum*. Cambridge: Cambridge University Press, pp. 242–296.

Keleman, A., Goodale, U.M. and Dooley, K. (2010) 'Conservation and the Agricultural Frontier: Collapsing the boundaries', *Journal of Sustainable Forestry*, **29**: 539–559.

McMahon, J. A. (2007) *The WTO Agreement on Agriculture: A Commentary*. Oxford: Oxford University Press.

Nogués, J. J. (2008) *The Domestic Impact of Export Restrictions: the Case of Argentina*, IPC Position Paper–Agricultural and Rural Development Policy Series.

Oakeshott, M. (1991) 'On Being Conservative' in *Rationalism in Politics*. Indianapolis: Liberty Fund, pp. 407–437.

OECD (2010) *Agricultural Policies in OECD Countries 2010*. Paris: OECD.

Reuters (2010), 'World Bank Urges Nations to Avoid Export Bans', 10 August, available at http://www.guardian.co.uk/business/2010/sep/05/commodities-food-drink-industry (accessed 17 December 2010).

Smith, F. (2010) 'Law, Language and International Agricultural Trade in the WTO', *Current Legal Problems:* 448–474.

Stern, N. (2006) *Stern Review on the Economics of Climate Change.* Cambridge: Cambridge University Press.

Stevens, C. *et al.* (2000) 'The WTO Agreement on Agriculture and Food Security', *Economic Paper 42*, Commonwealth Secretariat.

UNGA (2009) Report of the Special Rapporteur on the right to food (Oliver De Schutter), *Large-Scale Land Acquisitions and Leases: A Set of Minimum Principles and Measures to Address the Human Rights Challenge,* A/HRC/13/33/Add.2, United Nations General Assembly Human Rights Council, 28 December.

USDA/ERS (2008) *US Rice Industry: Background Statistics and Information,* available at http://www.ers.usda.gov/news/ricecoverage.htm

WFP (2010) *Fighting Hunger Worldwide* (WFP).

WFS (1996) *World Food Summit Plan of Action 1996* (13 November 1996) (FAO).

White, J. B. (1990) *Justice as Translation: An Essay in Cultural and Legal Criticism.* Chicago: University of Chicago Press.

WTO Reporter (2010) 'Ukraine Establishes Grain Export Quotas of 2.7 million tonnes for Corn, Wheat and Barley', 19 October.

WTO (2001) *Ministerial Declaration,* WT/MIN(01)/DEC/1, 20 November.

WTO (2005) *European Communities–Export Subsidies on Sugar,* WT/DS265/AB/R, WT/DS266/AB/R, WT/DS283/AB/R, 28 April.

WTO (2006) *European Communities–Measures Affecting the Approval and Marketing of Biotech Products*, WT/DS291, 292 & 293/R, 29 September.

WTO (2008a) *Working Document No.10 Market Access: Sensitive Products* (January). Geneva: WTO.

WTO (2008b) *Working Document No.15 Market Access: Special Products* (January). Geneva: WTO.

WTO (2008c) *Draft Agriculture Modalities* – TN/AG/W/4/Rev.5 (6 December).

Yusuf, G. (2009) 'Marginalization of African Trade and Development: A Case Study of the WTO's Efforts to Cater to African Agricultural Trading Interests Particularly Cotton and Sugar', *African Journal of International and Comparative Law,* **17**(2): 213-239.

3 Do WTO rules improve or impair the right to food?

Christian Häberli

I. INTRODUCTION

The global food crisis of 2007–08 seems to have been forgotten. Media attention at the time focused on food riots in Haiti and Mozambique, while world leaders and more than a dozen international organizations gathered for several food summits, calling for immediate relief measures. All in all, however, the governmental and inter-governmental response was sadly limited to a few high-profile conferences and action plans with no follow-up at the regulatory and institutional level. The attention of the mighty and wealthy focused on the subsequent financial and economic crises. What is really alarming, however, is that apparently no lessons were learned when for the first time in history the number of hungry people exceeded 1 billion (FAO Press Release, 2009a). Interestingly this ominous record was reached in mid-2009 – at a time when food prices had already dropped by 40 per cent. By 2010 'only' 925 million people were still undernourished – yet this number was still higher than before the food crisis (FAO, 2010). In November 2010 the World Food Programme (WFP) warned that prices could rise again in 2011 (WFP, 2010). And so they did.[1] Moreover, the IMF expected this rise to continue with non-oil commodity prices expected to increase by 11 per cent in 2011 (IMF, 2011: 6). Again, this seemed to matter only where the angry poor rioted in the Middle East and elsewhere.

But not a single government seems to remember its obligations under the Right to Food (R2F) which the United Nations (UN) had enshrined back in 1948. In 1976 this most basic of all human rights acquired treaty power and on 8 September 2000 it was reaffirmed as the first Millennium Development Goal (MDG) 'to eradicate extreme poverty and hunger'. In 2004 the Food and Agriculture Organization (FAO) Council adopted voluntary R2F implementation guidelines (UN, 2000; FAO, 2006).

Why is it that in the twenty-first century hunger – which Jean Drèze and Amartya Sen (1989: 15) had called a 'many-headed monster' – has raised these ugly heads higher than ever before? Why do high food prices not translate into higher incomes and increased production by poor farmers? Can we really classify hunger as a regrettable by-product of poverty and adopt a couple of stop-gap measures like food aid?

The good news is that the first MDG of halving hunger between 1990 and 2015 might actually be reached in many countries. However, the global figures disguise large regional differences and there is no evidence that this estimate reflects a definitive trend. As pointed out in Chapter 2, the structural causes of food insecurity persist: the situation remains fragile both for the hungry and for food aid which instead of calories is often pledged in dollars and in kind (and sometimes still of the wrong type to fit with local dietary habits). Perversely, and tellingly, food aid volumes decrease when food prices increase (Häberli, 2010: 300).[2] Despite some statistical progress the prospects for global food security remain dim especially in view of the new challenges ahead. To name only three global issues, there is climate change and water, 'peak oil'[3] and 'peak phosphorus',[4] and subsidies and other incentives to foreign direct investment (FDI) in agriculture. This third issue I call an 'under-regulated and over-protected' topic, because both national and international rules fail to take the agricultural specifics of FDI into account and also because they tend to prefer the interests of the investor over those of the public. From a regulatory perspective investment in agriculture is a largely unaddressed issue. But the cardinal question remains of how on earth the world's farmers are going to feed 9.1 billion people by 2050 (FAO Press Release, 2009b). As for some of the natural causes of food insecurity, in the year 2010 alone there were huge floods, droughts and fires. These events, along with fluctuations in oil prices, currencies and stocks and other cyclical causes of food insecurity, caused not only substantial price volatility. Some of these also led to new export restrictions, including in Russia, India, and China, with new buffer stocks and speculative hoarding in both exporting and importing countries.

Today we have to acknowledge that the R2F still lacks an adequate response under the present multilateral rules and disciplines applying to food production and trade. Yet for the lack and inadequacy of multilateral trade rules no remedies were available to enforce the R2F. As for the other problems on which national and global interests seem to clash, policy-makers, intergovernmental agencies, stakeholders and pundits continue to disagree on how to ensure the R2F and through which regulatory mechanisms it should be done.

This book is an enquiry into a number of issues that are either incompletely addressed or not addressed at all by the WTO Agreement on Agriculture (AoA). In this chapter on the R2F the focus is on the role played by the agricultural trade rules in the fight against hunger. We ask whether and how these rules contribute to the R2F to which virtually the whole WTO membership is committed. We start in Part II by recalling the foundations of the R2F in public international law. The responses of the international community to the latest food crisis are used as an example of how the R2F really works – or does not work – in times of crisis. The record so far, to put it mildly, is poor. Moreover, the fragmentation between codified humanitarian law and codified trade law is likely to continue despite the strikingly similar objectives of both treaties.[5] Part III provides an overview of the well-researched debate on the general applicability of such rights in the multilateral trading system. Part IV examines the present rules and disciplines under the AoA and of those contemplated in the Doha Development Round. Here we find that despite claims to the contrary they contribute precious little to the R2F. Our analysis from a legal perspective in Part V shows that some of the present rules, or the lack thereof, can act as disincentives for global food security. The lack of real agricultural trade liberalization amounts to a violation of their R2F obligations by many WTO Members.

As things stand, WTO Members have done little, and they are still not ready, to live up to their commitments in the relevant UN treaties and to improve the R2F by way of better trade rules. Despite the common objective of the two legal regimes there seems to be a misalignment in terms of instruments. This is partly due to the fundamental differences between global, national and household food security. In the solutions suggested in Part VI, I will try to show not only the possibilities and the limits for trade rule improvements, but also that the R2F obligations do not allow stopping at facile claims of 'mutual supportiveness'. Some of the proposals go beyond the Doha Development Agenda (DDA). Nonetheless, it is high time to go beyond exhortatory rhetoric and provide the R2F with concrete regulatory content – preferably before another and even bigger food crisis hits the headlines. Three avenues requiring an increasing degree of ambition and systemic rules change are available. First, as a minimum, there is an obligation for clear 'do no harm' commitments and disciplines. Second, there is room for legal interpretation that is more in line with the R2F obligations of the international community, even though I see more of such room being created by way of General Council and Ministerial Conference decisions than through dispute settlement. Finally, I propose some more substantial and institutional changes that might pave the way for a better R2F as a human and social right across the whole WTO membership.

II. THE INTERNATIONAL FRAMEWORK FOR A 'RIGHT TO FOOD' AND RESPONSES AT THE POLITICAL LEVEL

The R2F was first recognized in 1948, in Article 25(1) of the Universal Declaration of Human Rights (UDHR):

> Everyone has the *right to a standard of living adequate for the health and well-being of himself and of his family, including food, clothing, housing and medical care and necessary social services*, and the right to security in the event of unemployment, sickness, disability, widowhood, old age or other lack of livelihood in circumstances beyond his control.

Ever since, governments, international organizations, advocacy groups and scholars have been grappling with the legal nature of the R2F and trying to give this right concrete meaning at the national and international levels, including through rules and obligations (for good overviews of these developments see Vasak, 1977; Tomuschat, 2008; Kaufmann and Ehlert, 2009). The UN further substantiated the R2F in the first of its two International Human Rights Covenants. Article 11(2) of the International Covenant on Economic, Social and Cultural Rights (ICESCR) which came into force in 1976 is regarded as the most explicit international human rights provision in respect of the R2F:

> The States Parties to the present Covenant, recognizing the *fundamental* right of everyone to be free from hunger, *shall take, individually and through international co-operation, the measures*, including specific programmes, which are needed:
> (a) To improve methods of production, conservation and distribution of food by making full use of technical and scientific knowledge, by disseminating knowledge of the principles of nutrition and by developing or reforming agrarian systems in such a way as to achieve the most efficient development and utilization of natural resources;
> (b) Taking into account the problems of both food-importing and food-exporting countries, *to ensure an equitable distribution of world food supplies in relation to need.*

A further development to this provision is found in the General Comment No 12 on the right to adequate food, adopted in 1999 by the UN Committee on Economic, Social, and Cultural Rights (CESCR). This legally binding instrument divides the rights under the ICESCR into an *obligation to respect* (liberal citizen rights), an *obligation to protect* (access to activities protected by economic and social rights), and an *obligation to fulfil* (i.e. the obligation of states to provide individuals with the benefits of the rights accruing to them under the Covenant) (Tomuschat, 2008: 43).

Together with the UDHR and the International Covenant on Civil and Political Rights, the ICESCR forms the so-called *International Bill of Human Rights*. As such it is part of the second generation (better, 'dimension') of human rights (Riedel, 1989). Whether or not it also belongs to the so-called third dimension – comprising the right to development,[6] to peace,[7] and to a clean environment[8] – is a matter for debate (Tomuschat, 2008: 54). The ICESCR and a multitude of other, related international treaties also enshrine many individual and even collective human rights (Kaufmann and Heri, 2007). Perhaps significantly, the R2F is the only right in the Covenant designated as 'fundamental'. However, this fact and the legal uncertainties surrounding the 'third dimension of human rights' are not directly relevant to our enquiry into the R2F. In addition, this chapter cannot address in detail the legal nature of the R2F under public international law.

We shall now have a precursory look at the question of judicial enforcement of the R2F. Here we have to distinguish between national and international obligations, and between the various remedies for governments and for private actors available in national and in international courts.

A recent survey by the UN shows numerous and generally rather recent explicit references to the R2F in national constitutions (UN, 2009).[9] Yet access to national courts for hungry citizens and under national law looks like a rather remote possibility. Interestingly, social rights also lag behind environmental issues for access to justice questions (Hartling, 2007). Looking at the obligations of ICESCR signatories both at home and abroad, one could hope for access to and enforcement by courts under international treaty rights. Here too, however, there seems to have been no case in which the ICESCR was ever invoked at a national level let alone in an international judiciary forum. This leaves us with the question of whether there are any R2F enforcement cases at the intergovernmental level. For instance, there have been instances where food exports enforced by undemocratic governments caused local hunger – a clear violation of the R2F. But even here, no government has ever lodged a complaint in an international court arguing that the R2F of another country's citizens was ignored.

Even though the ICESCR compels governments to take certain actions this lack of judicial action at all levels is not really surprising. From a WTO perspective these obligations resemble the way regulators have to follow international food standards: as such,

ICESCR obligations are of a procedural nature and not open to complaints by individuals. In addition, unlike food standards, the right to food is not even mentioned in any of the WTO Agreements. Admittedly, although violations of trade rules can of course be addressed in WTO dispute settlement, cases of R2F violations would be much more difficult to argue on the basis of WTO obligations. Moreover, private actors or non-governmental organizations have no access to courts under either the ICESCR or the WTO, arguably because this would raise important and difficult sovereignty issues. So does this mean no court will ever hear a claim under the R2F?

Interestingly, all WTO Members have an obligation under WTO rules to allow their own as well as foreign citizens and companies access to national courts in certain cases. So-called 'access to justice' obligations are found in the Agreement on Trade-Related Aspects of Intellectual Property Rights (TRIPS) and in the (plurilateral) Agreement on Government Procurement. Guzmann and Meyer note that this right can extend to complaints brought by individuals (2010: 206). In respect of the R2F, as defined in the ICESCR, Courtis (2007: 319) also calls for a qualified access to justice mainly in national courts; unfortunately he refrains from addressing the question of how to ensure justiciability in international courts, let alone under the WTO dispute settlement system. There are intrinsic differences between the aforementioned intellectual property and procurement issues on the one side, and the collective nature of the R2F obligations each state has not only for its own nationals but also in respect of its own policies and the acts of its investors abroad on the other. Obviously, the establishment of a clear causal link between the R2F, be it for an individual or a community, and an act or an omission by a state or an investor is likely to be difficult. Furthermore, it is by no means clear that non-economic human rights can be guaranteed let alone enforced via WTO rules and procedures. The idea that the WTO could become an arbiter of R2F-policies certainly seems far-fetched. The question of whether any WTO Member would want to bring a complaint to the WTO for cases where another Member is denying access to justice for R2F claims in its national courts is another matter. As will be shown below, there is no dearth of candidates as respondents in a R2F violation claim. There can be no case without a complainant. At the same time, the progressive liberalization of trade and investment may well increase the present imbalance in rights and obligations at the expense of the socially weak. This imbalance between social and economic rights, and the potentially negative impact which free trade might have on economically frail structures without the means for compensation for trade-induced welfare losses, would seem to warrant further changes to the rules including in the multilateral trading system. As for enforcement, I see no reason not to examine the 'access to justice' pathways established by the WTO for the enforcement of 'economic rights' with a view to using them also for 'social rights' like the R2F.

According to the ICESCR implementing the R2F means more than guaranteeing it as a right of individuals under national legislation. It also implies obligations for states in their relations with each other, for instance by avoiding subsidies and food dumping which negatively impact on food security in poor developing countries (FAO, 2006: para. 53). A direct causal link for specific cases of famine or food riots might be difficult to establish. However, it is easy to see that trade-distorting agricultural support artificially lowers market prices (Anderson, 2009). Such support also acts as a disincentive for investment because it reduces the profitability for foreign investors and domestic entrepreneurs alike and it can drive otherwise competitive local farmers without subsidies out of business. For these farmers, 'agro-dumping' impairs the R2F and thus constitutes a violation by the subsidizing country of its general obligation to 'do no harm' and of Article 11(2b) ICESCR. But there is more. Many scholars have pointed out that international human rights law establishes the obligations of all signatory states 'to respect, to protect and to fulfil' (Kong, 2009), or to 'protect, respect, and remedy' according to the 'Ruggie Framework' (Ruggie, 2009). Smith (2009: 66) has argued that the principle of equality needs to be broadened if food security for all is to be achieved. Johnston (2010: 71) also cautions against out-of-context technical solutions. The crux of the matter addressed in this chapter lies in the question of whether and how the trade- and investment-related aspects of the R2F can be improved through better trade and investment regulation.

A sober look at the responses to the food crisis at the political level reveals that the international community continues to confine the official discourse to the embryonic state in which it has remained since 1948. On 10 July 2009, the G-8 and a large number of countries, organizations and research institutions endorsed the 'Aquila Food Security Initiative' (AFSI) at their meeting in the Italian city of that name. They pledged *inter alia* 'to act with the scale and urgency needed to achieve sustainable global food security'. Sadly, besides a fleeting reference at the Africa Partnership Forum in Toronto, Canada, on 30 April 2010, no follow-up to the AFSI has been reported (Muskoka, 2010).

Concrete regulatory action in the appropriate institutions seems to remain as elusive as ever. There have been attempts, however. In 2004 the FAO developed voluntary guidelines on food aid. While insisting that these guidelines did not create new obligations, the FAO experts have nevertheless examined a number of avenues on their 'justiciability' – without reaching a final conclusion (FAO, 2006). Similarly Olivier de Schoutter, the current Special Rapporteur on the right to food, considers that the R2F must be regarded as a 'global common good' and calls for 'accountability mechanisms' for R2F violations (de Schoutter, 2009c: 11 and 41). In 2008 the United Nations Secretary General established a High-Level Task Force (HLTF) on the Global Food Security Crisis composed of 21 international agencies. The HLTF produced a Comprehensive Framework for Action (CFA) which blandly just called for more of the same: 'It is necessary to immediately scale up public spending and private investment' (UN, 2008: para 12 and page 34). But no proposals were made for rule reforms, and nobody seemed to consider the reasons and the remedies for under-investment in food production. The first HLTF report produced by 21 international agencies confirmed this approach to economic planning without addressing the question of implementation.[10] Moreover, it contained not a shadow of an explanation of system failures, let alone any institutional self-criticism. Nevertheless, in the field of trade the report demanded 'adjustments of distorting trade practices' and courageously pinpointed some of the real trade issues impacting on the R2F: 'some policies – such as direct price controls, export restrictions, or generalized subsidies or wage increases – can further distort markets, or be ineffective over time, or be fiscally unsustainable' (UN, 2008: section 1.3).

At the Madrid High Level Conference on Food Security in January 2009, the UN Secretary General called for a third track to the CFA and proposed to add the R2F 'as a basis for analysis, action and accountability' (UN, 2009). Unfortunately, in terms of trade policy developments, the second 200 page-long HLTF Progress Report from October 2009 was even less substantive than the first. It emphasized that 'local, regional and international trade is a key component of solutions to food insecurity' and repeated its criticism of export restrictions and extraordinary taxes. It courageously added that these measures were 'particularly detrimental when it comes to humanitarian food aid' (UN, 2009: 4). However, besides recalling the still ongoing Doha Round negotiations and the Aid for Trade activities in the WTO, and listing several regional food-related trade initiatives in Africa and elsewhere, the HLTF had nothing new to report on the international trade dimension of the R2F.

Yet another inter-agency body is the Committee on World Food

Security (CFS). It was established by the UN back in 1974 as a result of the food crisis of the 1970s, with a rather insipid mandate to review and follow up on policies concerning world food security. After a drawn-out period of conspicuous inactivity behind a forest of bureaucratic briars the 2007–08 food crisis brought new life to the CFS. An ambitious institutional reform plan was adopted at its Thirty-fifth (CFS, 2009) and Thirty-sixth (CFS, 2010) Sessions. A new feature is the involvement of non-governmental organisations and a High Level Panel of Experts (HLPE) on food security and nutrition. The FAO expects the CFS henceforth to constitute 'a better home for global food security including governments, international institutions, researchers, civil society and the private sector' (FAO, 2009c). One of the first mandates given to the 'new' CFS was to contribute to the ongoing and inclusive process in respect of agricultural FDI, resulting in the 'Voluntary Guidelines on the Responsible Governance of Tenure of Land and Other Natural Resources', and the 'Principles for Responsible Agricultural Investments that Respect Rights, Liveli-hoods and Resources' (CFS, 2010: para. 26).

International support to agricultural investment has so far followed a similar trend. In late 2008 the World Bank had finally admitted to under-investment in agricultural production, despite its umpteen mission statements and strategic action plans: 'For most of the past two decades, both governments and donors, including the World Bank, have neglected the sector' (IBRD, 2008a: 16). Perhaps to its own surprise, two years later it reported a 'rising global interest in farmland' – but this apparently made (local) food security even worse. Indeed, this new wave of FDI, instead of producing food crops, was largely going into export cash crops like palm oil, biofuels, and feed grains. Still worse, the Bank noted that in many instances land was acquired or leased by foreign investors with a complete disregard for local land rights along with the connivance of host governments ('land grab'). Possibly for the first time ever the World Bank realized that FDI in agriculture was no longer inherently good for everybody but raised serious concerns about whether it could yield sustainable and equitable benefits (IBRD, 2010).

Advocacy groups like Vía Campesina associate the R2F with the emotionally loaded notion of 'Food Sovereignty'. In her history of this first global agricultural grassroots movement Annette Desmarais describes how food sovereignty became a symbol of the struggle against the negotiations on agriculture in the WTO, and how this notion differs from the concept of food security (Desmarais, 2007: 34, 184). On this question I can offer only two remarks here. It is true that quite a few countries pursue a policy of self-reliance and, clearly, neither China nor India could be fed by Brazil and Australia. However, while many countries produce more calories than they consume, even a food giant like Brazil still has hungry citizens and not a single country is entirely self-sufficient in food production and has no need for imports of food, feed, seeds, capital and know-how. Taken together these facts demonstrate that trade in agricultural products remains a constitutive component of food security which self-sufficiency cannot guarantee.

Economists seem to differ in their analysis of the 2007–08 global food crisis. For instance, Kappel, Pfeiffer and Werner (2010) see three reasons why the number of hungry people was still higher in 2009 than before the food crisis: the financial and economic crises, the subsequent reduction in FDI which also reduced incomes in poor countries, and the fact that food prices remained between 50 and 100 per cent higher than before the price boom. Lang (2010: 95) considers that 'the crisis in 2005–08 was not a blip, but creeping normality'. Baldwin (2009: 184) found only a small impact of the 'great trade collapse' on global food trade, while also underlining that Africa''s food exports amount to only 2.7 per cent of its total exports, with the rising import prices partly mitigated by increased export receipts.

It is not difficult to foresee that the international community is very likely to revert to the R2F when the pictures of the next food crisis appear on our television screens. This now leads us on to the question of whether and how public international law such as the ICESCR may be applied to – or, rather, reconciled with – the relevant WTO norms.

III. APPLICABILITY OF PUBLIC INTERNATIONAL LAW IN THE MULTILATERAL TRADING SYSTEM: INTERPRETATION THROUGH DISPUTE SETTLEMENT, COUNCIL DECISIONS, OR RULES CHANGE?

The thinking of the orthodox trade lawyers is generally unreceptive to the suggestion of a general applicability of public international law to the rules and disciplines enshrined in the multilateral trading system. The argument seems to be simple: *lex specialis derogat legi generali*, meaning that specific trade rules enjoy priority over principles of general international human rights law. Some would also question whether the WTO as an inter-governmental body can, or even should, guarantee human rights. Incidentally, the presently defunct general exception in GATT Article XX(h) for commodity agreements might be remembered, as well as an attempt by then Agriculture Committee Chair Crawford Falconer to revive such 'managed economy' provisions, which he formulated in the Doha Round Modalities dated 6 December 2008 (WTO, 2008: paras 95–102). Clearly all endeavours to introduce trade restrictions into the multilateral trading system would have far-reaching institutional implications for the WTO as well as for Members' rights and obligations.

The present reality seems to limit all reform ambitions without even needing to look at differences in the form and substance of international legal norms. Trade diplomats love to call the relationship with other international law regimes 'mutually supportive'. At the same time the WTO membership has always made it clear that no provisions or decisions outside the WTO legal framework could alter the rights and obligations of the Members under the WTO Agreements. This limitation also applies to treaty interpretation by the judiciary. Article 3.2 of the Dispute Settlement Understanding (DSU) insists that the 'recommendations and rulings of the [DSB] cannot add to or diminish the rights and obligations provided in the covered agreements'. Are these provisions the firewall behind which WTO shields itself from non-trade issues and their impact? And can the WTO afford to rule out all trade sanctions against human rights violations in a country like Myanmar? Will the trade in 'blood diamonds' remain the only one against which the WTO allows for certain trade restrictions by way of a waiver?[11] And can the WTO turn a blind eye on trade relations with the Libyan Arab Jamahiriya when the UN Security Council deplores 'the gross and systematic violation of human rights' and decides on an arms embargo, a travel ban, an asset freeze and other trade-relevant measures, and refers the matter to the Prosecutor of the International Criminal Court?[12] Given its importance on the human rights priority scale, might the trade dimension of the R2F become a pioneer in breaking through this firewall?

For sure, trade barriers erected against human rights violations would more easily pass the intent test under the non-discrimination obligation than measures taken to directly protect domestic producers. Seen from this angle, and on the assumption that the R2F is in fact *ius cogens,* the question of whether WTO rules secure or impair the R2F cannot be avoided. It could also be argued that under the Vienna Convention on the Law of Treaties (VCLT) the R2F must guide WTO rules as 'context', regardless of the *ius cogens* question, *inter alia* because as mentioned above the Preambles to the WTO and ICESCR are almost identical. Further research and development of rules along these lines may find that the present institutional and regulatory structure of the WTO leaves little space for addressing the trade- and investment-related dimensions raised by the R2F. At the same time, use of the policy space left open by the WTO may, or may not, be furthering the R2F at global and national levels. In both cases, however, such policy space escapes justiciability under WTO dispute settlement. On the other hand, and probably more promising for R2F-related action in the WTO, there could be a mechanism by which violations of the general 'do no harm' obligation may also be pursued in a trade organization like the WTO.

The question of whether the R2F is enforceable under international trade law basically follows the same lines as the scientific debate on other social rights or environmental concerns. Some scholars make a distinction between rules interpretation, jurisprudence, and rules development. As will be argued below such distinctions also matter for the R2F. The discussion of the human rights dimension of international trade law has been an area of great academic interest.

Among the most explicit advocates for an activist law and policy development has been Robert Howse for whom human rights enjoy primacy over trade liberalization (Mutua and Howse, 2001: 81). Together with Trebilcock he argues that human rights constrain national sovereignty in important ways and that 'human rights norms now vest sovereignty in the people' (Trebilcock and Howse, 2005: 579). In his reply to Petersmann and including for the R2F, he also describes 'international human rights law enhancing the purported function of WTO legal norms as protections for private economic actors against the activist state' (Howse, 2008: 948). In this light even soft law provisions 'appear less polyannish (sic) when one considers that, through interpretation, they can have important normative effects on international economic relations' – under the condition that 'the norms to be applied in interpretation reflect recognized universal values (human rights and humanitarian principles for example) that are expressed in custom or *ius cogens* (even if the specific norm itself does not have the status of custom or *ius cogens*)'. Whether the R2F has actually reached the status of *ius cogens* is a question which Howse and the other authors seem not to have decided.

Joost Pauwelyn on the other hand sees clear limits for a general application of public international law (which he considers 'decentralized') in the multilateral trading system. Even so, and because for him WTO law for non-trade agreements merely constitutes a *lex generalis*, he finds that for other issues 'non-WTO rules may actually apply before a WTO panel and overrule WTO rule' (2001: 577). Isabelle Van Damme considers that the WTO Appellate Body 'has probably developed one of the most intensive interpretative practices in the history of international dispute settlement' (2009: 383). That may be the case. Actually, efforts at 'harmonious interpretation' guided by the Vienna Convention on the Law of Treaties seem to have been limited to issues where WTO agreements explicitly refer to other rules of international law, like in Art.1.1 of the Agreement on Technical Barriers to Trade (TBT Agreement) and in the Preamble to the Agreement on the Application of Sanitary and Phytosanitary Measures (SPS Agreement). Other, vaguer references in various other WTO agreements were not found sufficient (Van Damme, 2009: 358, 363). Van Damme considers that in cases where the WTO-covered agreements are incomplete, it could be necessary to use non-WTO law by way of treaty interpretation. She nonetheless concludes that, while international relations can be understood in terms of regimes, this is not the case for international law which therefore 'just like any other field of law, can be explained in workable legal-technical terms' (2009: 31). Also following this line of 'development by interpretation' Gabrielle Marceau (2002: 756) considers that a good faith interpretation of WTO rules will allow for a 'coherent reading' with human rights, depending on their relevance in specific cases. She quotes from a Doha Round submission by Mauritius arguing that the evolutionary clause in Article 20 of the AoA should be interpreted in a way that is consistent with relevant international conventions on the R2F and, for that reason, should take into account the rights and needs of both food-importing and exporting developing countries. However, she rightly emphasizes that it is not sufficient merely to identify such provisions.

In a very recent contribution, Mary Footer takes this debate a step further. She posits a return to soft law as a means to reconcile the antinomies in WTO law, and even for a conclusion of the Doha Round negotiations (Footer, 2010). Quoting numerous examples of soft law provisions which allow for regulatory and policy progress, such as the Trade Facilitation programme initiated in 2005, she makes five propositions to solve various antinomies or paradoxes in WTO law. The limits of 'soft international law' (defined here as all forms of non-binding law in the WTO legal order) are of course recognized, but her 'idea of variable normativitiy and its responsiveness to the antinomies in WTO law' certainly deserves attention. In particular, her first proposition for an 'elaborative soft law' providing guidance in rules interpretation could also be used for sources of public international law exogenous to the WTO such as human rights and environmental treaties. Her third proposition then develops this approach, which in both private and public international law is known as 'rule referencing' or 'rule sourcing', to include external institutional fora with a view to a greater harmonisation of regulatory systems. An interesting example given is that of *Brazil – Aircraft*, a WTO case where an indirect reference in the WTO Subsidies and Countervailing Measures Agreement to the (non-binding) *OECD Export Credits Arrangement* was used by the Appellate Body as a benchmark to determine 'material advantage' in the field of export credit terms. Finally, there is an interesting reference to state liability arising out of acts not prohibited by international law – a situation which Footer describes as an example of 'soft responsibility' – and which of course could be equally interesting in a R2F context.

As an intermediate conclusion on the question of a general application of public international law to WTO economic law overlapping with social issues, it appears that many scholars see both the antinomies between the two regimes as well as several possibilities to address them. However, for different reasons most of them are reluctant to see an overarching obligation to reach the safe haven of coherence.

In dispute settlement, the challenge looks even more difficult to me. The above-quoted Article 3.2 DSU prevents rule-making by panels and the Appellate Body. So far, there has not even been a case of 'interpretation by deference' (for instance to the ICESCR). Indeed, despite the calls for further development of WTO rules, panels and the Appellate Body have generally taken a very cautious approach. Oft-quoted examples are international norms for the protection of the environment which could inform the legal situation of national measures under international trade law (Stoll, 2003: 446). The most prominent example of evolutionary interpretation, also referred to by Van Damme, is of course the *US – Shrimp* case where the Appellate Body found that various international conventions and general principles of international law, such as good faith, justified an evolutionary interpretation of the concept of 'natural resources' in Article XX(g) GATT (Van Damme, 2009: 369; WTO, 1998, Footer, 2010: 262). Remarkably, Van Damme has also noted that of all the WTO disputes so far only *EC – Biotech* has actually discussed Article 31(3)(c) of the Vienna Convention as the single codified interpretation principle explicitly referring to other rules of international law. In that case the Panel recognized that treaties and general principles of law could constitute 'rules of international law' as per Article 31(3)(c) and ruled that the Panel had the discretion to consider such rules as 'context' to determine the 'ordinary meaning' under Article 31(1). Nonetheless, that Panel then applied a 'narrow' interpretation of this provision in respect of the applicability of the Convention on Biodiversity and of the Biosafety Protocol to the precautionary principle in Article 5.7 of the SPS Agreement (WTO, 2006).

When it comes to human rights there is simply no example where a WTO dispute settlement case used public international law to interpret a trade rule, be it as *ius cogens* or by way of a contextual interpretation based on Art.31(3)(c) VCLT. Such pusillanimity may be justified in a 'Member-driven' trade organization which, as pointed out above, forbids any alteration of rights and obligations through dispute settlement. It is true that a few courageous panellists and Appellate Body members have found comfort in reading further down in Article 3.7 DSU that 'the aim of the dispute settlement mechanism is to secure a positive solution to a dispute'. However, so far there are few signs of progress along the jurisprudential track. To put it flippantly, sea turtles seem to enjoy better protection in WTO courts than hungry people. Similarly, it would be difficult to find a panel ruling out international food aid under the provisions of AoA Article 10.4 when that 'aid' was actually a case of food aid donors overreacting to a projected 600,000 ton food deficit in Malawi, and sending close to that amount to that country, thereby causing estimated losses to the Malawian economy of reportedly 15 million US Dollars (Zunckel, 2010: 21). Incidentally, even the Doha Round has so far failed to produce more stringent disciplines in this respect (Heri and Häberli, 2011). WTO rules may one day effectively prevent non-genuine food aid from displacing the commercial supplies of third countries. However, unless a more coherent and less fragmented approach can be agreed upon the WTO will continue to turn a blind eye when such 'aid' destroys the livelihood of local farmers.

This is clearly an unsatisfactory situation when one contemplates the hierarchy of policy objectives between, say, the elimination of hunger and the promotion of global economic welfare on the still stubbornly uneven 'level-playing field'. Quite possibly the challenge to address what are basically the rights of individuals (and groups of individuals) in an inter-state framework of rules and obligations such as the WTO is a root cause for this fragmentation between social and human rights and international trade rules. The same goes for rights and obligations at the national level. Apart from the above-mentioned obligations to protect individual intellectual property rights, and to provide access to domestic courts in cases such as government procurement disputes, there are very few instances where WTO rules directly shape the jurisdictional leeway of its Members at the domestic level.

Proposals to expand WTO obligations by bringing in 'rights' for the individual are likely to meet with resistance from national governments, even when such obligations are already enshrined under public international law commitments, as is the case with the R2F. This of course does not mean that there could be no negotiated solution, with 'rules of international law' drawn upon to modify, say, the AoA so as to better integrate the R2F in applicable trade rules and disciplines. With this in mind we now turn to the WTO rules and their role in the protection of the R2F.

IV. TRADE RULES AND THE R2F: IS WTO PART OF THE SOLUTION OR PART OF THE PROBLEM?

The extent of real improvements in market access and in effective limitations of trade-distorting domestic support and export subsidies as a result of the Uruguay Round (1986–1994) is generally considered to be limited. After 1995 some export market share transfers in favour of less-subsidizing and more competitive countries did take place. But the causal link for such developments is difficult to establish. The biggest merit of the AoA and other legal texts is the systemic change they brought about in agricultural trade (McMahon, 2005: 202). Basically, border protection is now limited to tariffs and there are disciplines applying to all forms of subsidies and caps on all trade-distorting measures.

Before looking at the multilateral trade rules with respect to the R2F, a few remarks are necessary on how the substantive public international law provisions of the R2F impact on specific commitments in the field of trade. As shown above, ICESCR signatories are committed to take multilateral and individual action in order 'to ensure an equitable distribution of world food supplies in relation to need'. Kaufmann and Grosz regard 'poverty as a violation of human rights' (2008: 107). This line was further developed by Olivier de Schoutter when he proposed new trade disciplines to ensure the R2F. For instance, on the subject of agricultural FDI he insisted on 'a clause providing that a certain minimum percentage of the crops produced shall be sold on local markets, and that this percentage may increase, in proportions to be agreed in advance, if the prices of food commodities on international markets reach certain levels' (de Schoutter, 2009b: 15). He also considered food price speculation to be detrimental to the R2F and postulated international regulation and market intervention to reduce the risks of price volatility (2010: 8). The question of course is whether or not the inter-governmental WTO should even attempt to go down such a road which impacts heavily on private operators and farmers and which potentially even discourages 'good' FDI. Indeed the proponents of new trade rules would have to convincingly argue a causal link between famines and agro-dumping or trade liberalization. Others might on the contrary consider the R2F as implying a right to cheap and subsidized food for the poor.

A case in point showing both the complexity and a regulatory way out for specific problems is irrigation subsidies. Under the AoA all price support measures belong in principle to the so-called Amber Box where reduction commitments apply. There are general exemptions available to all countries under two Green Box provisions (i.e. without reduction commitments). Under the first provision, irrigation subsidies may not involve direct payments to producers and processors and they would only be allowed for infrastructural investments ('the expenditure shall be directed to the provision or construction of capital works only, and shall exclude the subsidized provision of on-farm facilities'). In other words, preferential user charges and running costs are not allowed under this provision (AoA Annex 2, para 2(g)). The same restriction would apply under the investment aids provision in paragraph11, the second exemption for irrigation subsidies in the Green Box: such aids can only be provided under structural adjustment assistance programmes, they shall be given 'only for the period of time necessary for the realization of the investment in respect of which they are provided' and 'be limited to the amount required to compensate for the structural disadvantage'. Interestingly, this issue has so far been carefully avoided and has never been the subject of dispute settlement – perhaps because almost every government provides such subsidies to its producers. In a R2F context it might be argued that irrigation subsidies should be allowed for basic crops without the potential to distort trade. As a matter of fact, the so-called *Developing Country Green Box* defined in Article 6.2 of the AoA goes somewhat beyond the general Green Box. It exempts two types of support from reduction commitments: (i) investment subsidies 'generally available to agriculture in developing country Members' and (ii) 'agricultural input subsidies generally available to low-income or resource-poor producers in developing country Members'.[13] The second provision can be read as a careful additional carve-out from production support disciplines for poor farmers in developing countries: while generally available investment subsidies in agricultural and rural development programmes would be exempt from reduction commitments for all (developing country) farmers, input subsidies such as preferential electricity or fuel rates would only be exempt from reduction commitments if they are exclusively available to *low-income or resource-poor producers*. Even though this provision only addresses the producer side of the R2F equation, without looking at the situation of poor consumers, it may show the way for similar issues where WTO and other international rules have so far been absent.

On the negative side, as shown by the example of surplus disposal in the form of food aid, even WTO-legal measures can displace local farmers. Such measures would thus constitute a violation of the donor country's obligations under Article11(2) of the ICESCR. Taking this line of thought further one could argue that such R2F violations could occur through all types of domestic support instruments. The trade-distorting effect of these measures might also cause a displacement of food production in other countries – even when these measures remain within the limits of the WTO caps on domestic support. The FAO remains conspicuously prudent in its assessment of the impact of the present rules on non-subsidised production in developing countries (Sharma and Konandreas, 2008). But many economists today would agree with the trade- and investment-distorting nature of rich country subsidies and some would also contend that even so-called Green Box support instruments may have a negative impact on farmers in developing countries (Anderson, 2006; IBRD, 2007; ICTSD, 2009).

The question which matters most here is what rights and needs give rise to which obligations and measures. For instance, it has not been established whether the R2F justifies export restrictions under Article XI:2 GATT and Article 12 of the AoA (supposedly protecting domestic consumers). Likewise, it is unclear whether the public morals clause in Article XX(a) GATT might allow restrictions of commercial imports under the R2F (arguably protecting small farmers' livelihoods). Export restrictions are often introduced when politically influential groups of citizens risk having to pay more for their food than the government considers appropriate, regardless of the impact this may have on their own farmers let alone on net food-importing developing countries (NFIDCs). Clearly, given that such restrictions always act as disincentives to increase production, they cannot and will not improve food security in any lasting manner. One could also discuss whether a WTO Member can use GATT Article XXI (security exceptions) to intervene in the market as a matter of national security: at a certain level gross violations of human rights, including the R2F, may indeed become a matter of world peace.

International trade disciplines, and trade liberalization, are generally recognized as a contribution to better food security, even though it is also recognized that increased liberalization also carries significant risks for countries dependent on food imports (Wager, 2009). The UN High Commissioner on Human Rights noted that 'without the introduction of appropriate safeguards and transitional measures, trade rules and policies could have adverse effects on the right to food, workers' rights and other rights of small farmers and the rural poor' (2005: 2). Similarly Belete Hailu (2010: 22), while supporting trade liberalization in the long run, argues that 'The short run implication of the rules [...] may create problems for many net food importing African countries, as food may become economically unavailable to the majority of the population'. Again, the cardinal question seems to be whether we can afford to embark on a new round of trade liberalization without an adequate regulatory framework ensuring the R2F.

Many scholars including Anderson (2009), Desta (2002: 240) and Kaufmann and Ehlert (2009) would agree that the Uruguay Round results and in particular the AoA have brought about few real market openings for developing countries. They consider that the limits on domestic and export subsidies are insufficient to prevent a continuation of food dumping to the detriment of food producers in developing importing countries. One could even argue that the failure of the AoA to establish more stringent domestic support disciplines, more market access, and fewer export restrictions may have contributed to the recent food crisis. In this context it is worth recalling the so-called 'tariff overhang' whereby countries will refrain from scheduling their unilateral market openings and raise their applied tariffs back to MFN levels in times of lower world food prices (Anderson, 2010). An equally pernicious fact is the 'subsidy overhang' allowing many countries to return to their scheduled export and domestic subsidy ceilings as and when they see fit (Anderson, 2009). For Mechlem (2006: 165) the AoA is thus both 'a significant achievement and a failure' for the R2F. Desta (2002: 415) also makes a general case for stricter disciplines, for instance in order to guarantee a genuine use of food aid and food stockholdings.

V.   THE NEED FOR A WIDER REGULATORY R2F FRAMEWORK

Article 20 of the AoA describes liberalization of agricultural trade as a continuous 'reform process'. It is understood – and the DDA encompasses all these elements – that this process has to address the 'three pillars': market access, domestic support, and export competition. As for the R2F, additional elements are contained in the so-called NFIDC Decision and, debatably, in other provisions including GATT Articles XI (import quotas and export restrictions) and XX (exceptions) (Stoll and Strack, 2007; UN Commissioner on Human Rights, 2005; Bartels, 2002).

In Chapter 2 Smith has shown that the 'reform program' cannot so far be said to have yielded a result leading to more food security and by which the commitments under the R2F are respected. It is true that the policy space available to developing countries, for example under the already mentioned Article 6.2 of the AoA, allows for a number of measures in support of local farmers. Nonetheless, in many countries the resources necessary for implementing such policies are simply not available – or their use might be constrained by the international financial institutions. For example, Mechlem (2006: 153) sees structural imbalances and incoherence between World Bank and International Monetary Fund (IMF) policies and WTO disciplines. However, more worrying from an R2F perspective is that rich countries still have the right to subsidise domestic production and exports (including through export credits and state trading). I would consider this to be the biggest impediment to agricultural development in poor countries – whether or not the right is being used in a given year. All forms of price support will depress food prices – which might be good for the urban poor – but, more importantly, they unfairly compete with farming in poorer countries and discourage investment in their agriculture, both for local production and for exports of cash crops which could in turn finance food imports. Innovation, induced through private research and development efforts, also tends to follow the more remunerative markets and neglect non-subsidised farmers and their needs. Land flight, out-migration and a general neglect of rural development will often complete this not unrealistic 'food dumping' impact scenario.

It can thus be generally assumed that trade and investment distortions, whether legal or not under the present multilateral rules, will negatively affect the competitive position of poor developing countries. Moreover, excessive reliance on imported food at artificially depressed prices increases food insecurity because both structural and cyclical imbalances may reduce imports for those countries and households that are unable to pay higher food bills. In this sense what might be called import food 'addiction' will also reduce price shock resilience. Africa is today the world's biggest importer of cereals. Perhaps, among other reasons, this could be due to artificially cheap cereal imports having displaced local production and forcing non-subsistence farmers to produce food for non-distorted markets. In many developing countries' farm-gate prices are way below world market and local consumer prices, with intermediaries earning the difference regardless of the value of the services they provide. At any rate, the food crisis of 2007–08 and some of the food riots have shown that poor farmers were often unable to respond to price hikes and to external supply interruptions by increasing their saleable production.

The Doha Round results, if and when they are achieved somewhere near the modalities of 2008, will definitely improve the situation by further restricting the policy space of developed countries. The case is less clear for some of the flexibilities which typically come along with over-ambitious reduction formulas. The two main instruments already agreed in 2005 will be the so-called Special Products (SP) and the Special Safeguard Mechanism (SSM). These flexibilities could be used as tools to protect small and vulnerable producers, even though this may imply more expensive food for their own consumers, including the large number of subsistence farmers who are net food consumers rather than surplus producers. From a perspective of food security ensured by local production as well as imports, the question arises of whether these flexibilities, especially for developing countries, will increase their food security by tilting the balance towards economically sustainable local production. This is probably where we will find the biggest clash of interests and of opinions in respect of the R2F. Moon (2009: 639) argues that 'possible methodologies do exist for Special and Differential Treatment (SDT) which would allow real needs to be targeted and, hence, which would support the justifiability of S&DT as a substantive equality initiative'. At the same time she also notes a consensus in the WTO membership that the so-called SDT has failed to take the fundamental inequalities sufficiently into account and she correctly demonstrates that the case for extensive flexibilities for developing countries is far from being clear, even for the SP envisaged under the DDA.

Other trade-related problems in a R2F perspective are waiting for solutions which even the Doha Round will not provide. The 2008 Modalities foresee more open borders and less price support but they do not adequately address the potential of export restrictions, non-genuine food aid, and they preserve loopholes in export credit instruments and export state trading which can continue to undermine local production. Small and not yet competitive farmers especially could be driven out of the market by the artificially cheap imports still allowed under post-Doha disciplines. The R2F and the contribution of these farmers to food security in the longer term would thus be curtailed by a job half-done, i.e. a lack of comprehensive trade rules and disciplines as well as adequate accompanying measures. Emergencies and acute hunger in populations without purchasing power aside, it is the resilience of local production structures which contributes most to sustainable food production and to food security for the poor. Seen in this light both the SP and the SSM appear like stop-gap measures rather than instruments for ensuring long-term and sustainable agricultural production. Until now, however, no regulatory solution has been proposed to sustainably enhance local farmers' resilience in a context of trade liberalization. Finally, further discussion is needed on the perhaps mostly short- versus long-term usefulness of the DDA flexibilities.

Perhaps the reasons for the lack of progress in the DDA negotiations lie in the nature of WTO commitments. Basically, WTO rules deal with market access and a level playing field for competition between different suppliers. While the objective of enhanced welfare is certainly in line with R2F obligations we have to acknowledge that the implementation tool-kit envisaged under the WTO agreements is only partially congruent with R2F instruments. While the former is mainly to address trade, production, circumvention and competition-distortion at the expense of other suppliers, the latter deal with an obligation to protect, respect and remedy (Ruggie, 2009). Clearly, rich country obligations involve more than food aid to real hunger situations. This is the gap where the role of trade in ensuring the R2F for all remains unaddressed, as long as the WTO stops short of formulating a general obligation to cooperate in the sense of Article 11(2) ICESCR. As already pointed out the WTO today allows measures which are prohibited under codified international humanitarian law, such as food dumping. Similarly, attempts to discipline international food aid are limited to the prevention of market displacement at the expense of third countries, whereas the negative impact on local production escapes WTO disciplines.

This assessment of the WTO rules applicable to trade in agriculture leads us to conclude that the present subsidy and regulatory leeway available to rich countries prevents a level playing field for the trade in food. This 'freedom to dump' violates the R2F obligation to which each signatory of the ICESCR is committed. The Uruguay Round has brought little more than a systemic change by limiting but not preventing the rights to distort trade and investment. Even if over time the Doha Round results do no more than significantly curtail the present so-called tariff and subsidy overhang (Anderson, 2010), they will at least reduce some of the present entitlements and discipline some of the tools used to distort trade. This would clearly be good for NFIDC producers *and* for 'food security through cash crops', even though the end of subsidies is bad for poor consumers at least in the short term. Nonetheless, the present state of the negotiations makes it clear that the first but timid caps foreseen in paragraphs 21–26 of the December 2008 Modalities on product-specific maximum levels of domestic support will not be sufficient to prevent food dumping. Disciplines preventing a negative impact on local production are also unlikely to find acceptance. In particular, export restrictions limiting the global food supply and surplus disposal through food aid will probably continue unhindered. In other words, the WTO framework does not and will not even follow the 'do no harm' principle of public international law.

These seem to be the limits to multilateral trade rules from a R2F perspective at this stage. Besides, even if the WTO could guarantee individual or collective human rights should it really do so and in what way? We have seen the various dilemmas and conflicting interests involved here, for instance between food-exporting and importing developing countries, or between poor urban consumers and small farmers. The biggest problems in this regard are faced by subsistence farmers not meeting their own dietary needs because artificially cheap food is both good and bad for them. Even 'food sovereignty' advocates have failed to propose concrete disciplines to solve such conflicts at a multilateral level. Are we thus reduced to preambular language-type appeals for 'mutual supportiveness' and letting the WTO return to (trade) business as usual?

As this book went to press, renewed attempts at concluding the Doha Round were being made. We have shown here how such a conclusion would improve the R2F. At the same time and from a poor country perspective 'Doha', even if it does succeed, would not amount to more than a job half done. Considerable literature is already available to show the limited or even negative impact on the poorest countries and, in particular, the net food importers. Polaski (2006), later supported by Berisha-Krasniqi *et al.* (2008) and Von Braun (2008), predicted that the poorest countries will lose their market shares and export revenues unless alternative scenarios are implemented. And even the World Bank admitted that poverty in NFIDCs would increase as a result of higher food prices resulting from trade liberalization (IBRD, 2008b).

These rather dire forecasts did provoke counter-arguments. For instance, Margulis (2009) argues that in the absence of a Doha Round conclusion regional trade agreements will lead to an even worse impact on NFIDCs and on the R2F because of a lack of multilateral domestic support disciplines including on biofuels. Besides, the present policy space in terms of food security is clearly in need of clarification for all but the LDCs and not only for the envisaged new instruments of SP and the SSM. On the positive side tariff and subsidy reductions will enhance market access security *and* help to level the playing field for competitive producers.

This brief overview shows that the overall results for both global and national food security are still largely unclear (Wager, 2009). By way of a tentative assessment the following observations could be made:

1. The WTO objective to promote economic development through freer trade appears to be inherently cash crop and 'export biased', without any regard for small farmers and food crop producers (Hailu, 2010; Kaufmann and Heri, 2007). Indeed, presently applicable disciplines for agricultural production and trade are mainly attempts to combat import protectionism and export dumping; however, in times of rapidly rising commodity prices many countries will reduce import tariffs and surpluses will disappear. The reductions of many trade distortions envisaged in the Doha negotiations would contribute to more food security in the sense that food will be produced more efficiently and more competitively and it will flow to those countries with the greatest purchasing needs (and capacities). But under both present and future trade rules and disciplines a large policy space remains for both rich and poor countries. This does not necessarily represent an improvement of the R2F.

2. The WTO does not and is unlikely ever to discipline at least three key elements of food security: domestic support for specific food crops by way of effective maximum ceilings, abuse of food aid to the detriment of producers in beneficiary countries, and export restrictions reducing food availability on world markets (OECD, 2010; Zunckel, 2010).

3. Trade liberalization would favour food security strategies relying on (agricultural) exports rather than on domestic production. But it could also hamper food-insecure countries without such export capacities.[14]

4. R2F as a legitimate public policy issue has yet to be recognized as a principle and to be operationally reflected in the multilateral trading system.

This leaves the question of how the R2F could be improved by way of better WTO rules.

Mechlem (2006) discusses four possibilities for taking the R2F into account at the level of the WTO negotiations and rule-setting: (i) inserting an explicit reference to human rights into the AoA; (ii) interpreting the R2F 'into' the AoA and Article XX GATT – along the lines also proposed by Howse and also by Footer; (iii) recognizing the R2F as inalienable rights pre-existing laws and treaties (*ius cogens* to be recognized as a general exception to trade rules), and which therefore must take precedence in case of conflicts; (iv) adopting a new trade rule recognizing that the ICESCR implies the obligation not to conclude treaties that harm the R2F. In the aftermath of the 2007–08 food crisis these proposals deserve further consideration. As discussed above, and in line with Van Damme and Marceau, I would consider simple references by way of preambular language as clearly insufficient. Equally unlikely would be a judicial interpretation in a (difficult to imagine) case of dispute settlement where a party invokes the R2F as a general defence for a GATT/AoA violation. Nevertheless, a solution somewhere along the lines of Mechlem's proposals (iii) and (iv) could contribute to clarifying the relation between the R2F and AoA rules and disciplines. For instance, the WTO General Council could adopt a decision by which obligations under the ICESCR would prevent food dumping, or might warrant certain measures to promote local agriculture, or preclude restrictions applying to food crop exports to poorer countries. Such a rule-making scenario – even in the form of 'primary soft law' as suggested by Footer – is currently not very realistic. However, new food crises may occur at almost any time in the future, lending a new sense of priority and urgency for new rules.

VI. CONCLUSIONS AND RECOMMENDATIONS

At least from a moral high ground, the R2F thus appears like a valuable test case for the international community to better solve the fragmentation between social and economic treaties, and policies. Clearly the WTO can only offer very partial solutions because we cannot fail to see the challenge of reinforcing trade disciplines and liberalizing trade while maintaining the policy space which food-insecure countries demand in order to ensure the R2F in their own countries.

As of November 2010 the ICESCR had been ratified by 160 countries. The 125 WTO Members that have ratified this treaty have human rights obligations applying to their trade relations (Kaufmann and Heri, 2007: 157). This obligation includes the R2F (Mechlem, 2006: 164). The objectives under the WTO (raising standards of living) and the ICESCR (providing an adequate standard of living) are strikingly similar. The situation changes when it comes to rules and disciplines. The R2F focuses on the hungriest and poorest, both as individuals and as a group. The WTO more vaguely aims at aggregate 'standards of living' at the national level. Global inequality is recognized but largely unaddressed despite a plethora of SDT measures. Moreover, the uneven distribution of welfare gains at the national level resulting from trade liberalization is an issue that is entirely left to the WTO's Member governments.

In my view, the fragmentation of international law cannot be an excuse for inaction at the WTO. As pointed out by Hangzo (2010: 15) who describes the various food safety nets in place in Asia, global food security is not brought about just by producing enough food. Beyond availability there is the question of access and for virtually all countries food security comprises trade and investment. Admittedly trade cannot bring food to people in emergency situations and to those without any purchasing power. But any food imported on concessional terms can destroy the livelihood of fragile rural communities that are unable to compete with 'gifts' financed by foreign taxpayers. Likewise depressed world food prices and non-genuine food aid may benefit poor consumers, but they also deprive non-subsidized farmers of their legitimate income expectations. Trade distortions (as well as insufficient genuine food aid) can act as poverty traps. In 1981 Amartya Sen proposed his famous *entitlement approach* as a way out of starvation and famines:

> The entitlement approach to starvation and famines concentrates on the ability of people to command food through the legal means available in the society, including the use of production possibilities, trade opportunities, entitlements vis-à-vis the state, and other methods of acquiring food.... Ownership of food is one of the most primitive property rights, and in each society there are rules governing this right. The entitlement approach concentrates on each person's entitlements to commodity bundles including food, and views starvation as resulting from a failure to be entitled to any bundle with enough food. (Sen, 1981)[15]

It is true that the 'entitlement approach' has been hotly debated and sometimes misunderstood (Devereux, 2001: 246). Nevertheless, this is where the R2F obligation and responsibility of the WTO membership are at stake. On this basis I would submit that five problematic aspects of the R2F need to be re-evaluated for a better food security outcome and assessment of the present WTO rules and of the DDA.

1. There is a need for a better multilateral regulatory framework in the WTO, first and foremost for trade rules. The conundrum is that food importing countries and countries whose own food security can only be ensured through market access-guaranteed exports are taking opposite positions in the ongoing Doha negotiations: Brazil and Costa Rica, for example, are arguing that their food exports should benefit from increased opportunities to also access other developing country markets. This directly conflicts with the views of the 'Small and Vulnerable Economies' and of recently acceding Members like Ukraine, which are calling for a Special Safeguard Mechanism with protective duties above pre-Doha levels (ICONE, 2009: 19). Unsurprisingly, these countries require different policy tool-kits, and sometimes even mutually exclusive policy space.

    i. Importers and small and vulnerable farmers need to adapt to increased competition, even though freer and less distorted markets contribute to better global food security. The R2F responsibility of the WTO membership is to ensure that a policy space remains for food-insecure developing countries. This depends not only on market access limitations such as the future SP treatment and the SSM. A number of additional special provisions for food-insecure NFIDCs have been called for, including for food crop production, with some of them proposing waivers for GATT Articles I and XIII (preferential access and tariff-rate quotas for exports to developed country markets) and II (scheduling SDT) (Bartels and Häberli, 2010). At the same time, in order not to perpetuate unsustainable farming practices, precise eligibility thresholds and automatic exit criteria are also needed (Desta, 2001: 50).

    ii. On the other hand, the policy space claimed by many food exporting developing countries includes export restrictions, albeit for sometimes problematic domestic reasons. This once again raises the dilemma of national and household food security ensured by local production versus global food security achieved through open borders. It would indeed be difficult to argue that export restrictions can sustainably protect hungry (urban) consumers and at the same time not reduce global food security.

    iii. The ambiguities in the vast but unsecured food security policy tool-kit become particularly evident when one considers the conflicting interests between different developing countries. Food-exporting countries ensure their food security through exports and thus need maximum market access, while NFIDCs claim full policy space for all matters relating to food production regardless of the competitiveness of their producers. At the same time, it is acknowledged that the biggest agricultural trade potential existing in the Doha Round is in the so-called South–South trade. To say the least, there are no easy solutions here.

2. A second problem is the lack of comprehensive investment rules addressing the food security issues which unqualified FDI protection may involve. Attempts at safeguarding public interest and regulating trade distorting effects of investment policies, in the WTO and elsewhere, have mostly failed. This is also regrettable from a R2F perspective. Sustainable food production clearly has an international investment dimension: Olivier de Schoutter (2009a) rightly claims that the R2F implies obligations not only for host states but also for investors and their home states.

3. Thirdly, as shown above, access to justice is today an avenue that is increasingly available to the R2F in a number of national jurisdictions around the world. Some WTO agreements have mandated such access for certain economic rights (intellectual property, government procurement) so why should this not be so for the most basic of all human rights?

4. Awareness of trade negotiators is a fourth issue. De Schoutter (2009a: 16, 18) convincingly argues that 'trade negotiators either are not aware of the human rights obligations of the Governments they represent, or they do not identify the implications for their position in trade negotiations'; he also calls for an assessment of the impact of trade agreements on the right to food 'based on the normative requirements of the human right to adequate food, and the corresponding indicators'. This issue reflects the problem of inter-ministerial dialogue and co-operation which the national line agencies in charge of WTO matters need to address in order to achieve better policy coherence.

5. Finally, there is the intrinsic link between trade liberalization and the R2F. The Doha Final Act adopting the negotiation results by way of a 'single undertaking' should do better than the present NFIDC Decision in the Marrakesh Agreement which was found to be useless and toothless even at the height of the last food crisis. There are at least four possibilities by which the possible negative impact of the negotiation results (or the lack thereof)

should and could be mitigated from a R2F perspective:

i. By enshrining the R2F in the WTO regulatory framework. Given its exogenous origin and the potential conflict with the NFIDC Decision, a simple reference to Article 11(2) ICESCR, for instance by a General Council decision, or a reference in the Doha Round Final Act, would perhaps not be sufficient. A clarification of its meaning in a WTO context, either in the Marrakesh Agreement itself or in the AoA, would be preferable.

ii. By a formal commitment by food aid donors not to reduce food aid volumes in times of food price increases.

iii. By a commitment to exempt food supplies to NFIDCs from export restrictions.

iv. By a decision on a mandatory and quantified Aid for Trade Programme by which the 'Doha winners' contribute to more and more efficient food crop production in NFIDCs.

Some of these recommendations may at present appear to be far-fetched, over-ambitious or downright impossible. Not one of them would be simple, easy to adopt and to implement, and without its own drawbacks. The R2F, however, is not a matter of political will and domestic policy space (only). It implies a legal obligation under codified humanitarian law to improve multilateral trade rules so as to ensure that, as a minimum, they do no more harm and, better still, that they contribute to making food available in a sufficient quantity and quality to all people in need. The bottom line is this: because public international law cannot be divided in separate regimes, WTO compatibility cannot make right what codified humanitarian law prohibits.

NOTES

I am grateful to Fiona Smith (University College London), Simona Stirling-Zanda (University of Edinburgh) and Peter-Tobias Stoll (Georg-August-Universität Göttingen) for their advice and comments. Research for this chapter was funded by the Swiss National Science Foundation under a grant to the National Centre of Competence in Research on Trade Regulation, based at the University of Bern's World Trade Institute in Bern, Switzerland.

1. For the month of February 2011 the FAO reported an average Food Price Index of 236, which was up 2.2 per cent from January, the highest rise in real and nominal terms since the FAO started monitoring prices in 1990. See http://www.fao.org/worldfoodsituation/wfs-home/foodpricesindex/en/ (accessed 4 March 2011).

2. The World Food Programme (WFP) reports that '[g]lobal food aid deliveries of 5.7 million mt in 2009 were the lowest since 1961: programme food aid declined by 25 percent, emergency food aid by 12 percent and project food aid by 6 percent.' (cf. Food Aid Flows 2009, Report available on http://documents.wfp. org/stellent/groups/public/documents/newsroom/wfp223562.pdf, accessed 4 March 2011).
3. '*Peak Oil*' is of particular importance for agriculture, because most farmers depend on oil for fertilisers, production and transport. Overall, the importance of fossil fuels is higher for agriculture than for most other industries.
4. For a good introduction to '*peak phosphorus*' see Cordell *et al.* (2009).
5. The WTO aims at 'raising standards of living' while the ICESCR is to ensure an 'adequate standard of living'.
6. Cf. Kéba MBaye (1972), Le droit au développement comme un droit de l'homme. 2-3 Revue des droits de l'homme (1972) 503. Cf. Barsh, Russel Lawrence (1991), The right to development as a human right: Results of the Global Consultation, *in* 13 *Human Rights Quarterly* (August): 322–38. Cf. Res.5(XXXV) dated 2 March 1979 of the Human Rights Commission. Cf. UNGA Res.36/133 dated 14 December 1981 and 41/128 dated 4 December 1986.
7. Cf. UNGA Res.33/73 dated 15 December 1978 and 39/11 dated 14 December 1981. Art.1 of UNGA 41/128 dated 4 December 1986 also refers.
8. Cf. Principle 1 of the Declaration adopted by the UN Conference on Human Environment, 1972, Stockholm. Cf. UNGA Res.45/94 dated 14 December 1990. Cf. Rio Declaration on Environment and Development dated 14 June 1992 *in* 31 ILM (1992) 876. Cf. UNGA Res.37/7 dated 28 October 1982 ('World Charter for Nature').
9. The latest example is Article 43 of the 2010 Kenyan Constitution: '(1) Every person has the right [...] (c) to be free from hunger, and to have adequate food of acceptable quality' cf. http://www.fao.org/righttofood/news42_en.htm (accessed 19 November 2010).
10. The UN's Special Representative on the subject, David Nabarro, confirmed this quantitative focus on aid by the HLTF in his presentation to the WTO Committee on Agriculture on 18 November 2010 ('more 'aid for trade' and for better trade financing infrastructure'). At the same time he also emphasized the wider context of the R2F (cf. http://www.wto.org/english/news_e/news10_e/agri_18nov10_e.htm accessed 23 November 2010).
11. 'Kimberley Process Certification Scheme for Rough Diamonds' General Council Waiver Decision of 15 December 2006, Document WT/L/676 dated 19 December 2006. For Footer (2010: 274) this case has the 'exceptive character of a waiver decision' which provides a remedy (against nullification and impairment of benefits) in the absence of a right.
12. Resolution 1970 (2011) adopted by the Security Council on 26 February 2011 (S/RES/1970 (2011).
13. A third exemption which is not relevant in this context is for 'domestic support to producers in developing country Members to encourage diversification from growing illicit narcotic crops' (Art.6.2/2).
14. As an example see McMillan *et al.* (2003) discussing the privatization and liberalization of the cashew nut sector in Mozambique.
15. Quoted in Robinson (2010: 3).

BIBLIOGRAPHY

Anderson, K. (2006) 'Reducing Distortions to Agricultural Incentives: Progress, pitfalls and prospects', *World Bank Policy Research Working Paper 4092*. Washington, DC:

World Bank.

Anderson, K. (2009) 'Five Decades of Distortions to Agricultural Incentives', *Agricultural Distortions Working Paper 76*. Washington, DC: World Bank.

Anderson, K. (2010) 'Krueger/Schiff/Valdés Revisited: Agricultural price and trade policy reform in developing countries since 1960', *IBRD Policy Research Working Paper 5165*. Washington, DC: World Bank

Baldwin, R. (ed) (2009) *The Great Trade Collapse: Causes, Consequences and Prospects.* London: Centre for Economic Policy Research.

Bartels, L. (2002) 'Article XX of the GATT and the Problem of Extraterritorial Jurisdiction – The Case of Trade Measures for the Protection of Human Rights', *Journal of World Trade*, **36**: 353.

Bartels, L. and Häberli, C. (2010) 'Binding Tariff Preferences for Developing Countries under Article II GATT', *Journal of International Economic Law*, **13** (4): 969–995.

Berisha-Krasniqi, V., Bouët, A., Laborde, D. and Mevel, S. (2008) *The Development Promise: Can the Doha Development Agenda Deliver for Least Developed Countries?* Washington, DC: IFPRI Briefing Note.

Committee on World Food Security (CFS) (2009) *Final Report*, Thirty-fifth Session, 14, 15 and 17 October. Rome: FAO.

Committee on World Food Security (CFS) (2010) *Final Report*, Thirty-sixth Session, 11–14 October and 16 October. Rome: FAO.

Cordell, D., Drangert, J-O. and White, S. (2009) 'The Story of Phosphorus: Global food security and food for thought', *Global Environmental Change*, **19**: 292–305.

Courtis, C. (2007) 'The Right to Food as a Justiciable Right: Challenges and strategies', *Max Planck Yearbook of United Nations Law*, **11**: 317.

de Schoutter, O. (2009a) 'Report of the Special Rapporteur on the Right to Food, Addendum, Mission to the World Trade Organization (25 June 2008)', *Human Rights Council, Promotion of and Protection of All Human Rights, Civil, Political, Economic, Social and Cultural Rights, Including the Right to Development*, Document A/HRC/10/5/Add.2, 4 February.

de Schoutter, O. (2009b), 'Large-scale Land Acquisitions and Leases: A set of core principles and measures to address the human rights challenge', *Report of the Special Rapporteur on the Right to Food*, 11 June.

de Schoutter, O. (2009c) *Report of the Special Rapporteur on the Right to Food, Crisis into Opportunity: Reinforcing multilateralism*. United Nations General Assembly, Human Rights Council, Document A/HRC/12/31, 21 July, Geneva.

de Schoutter, O. (2010) 'Food Commodities Speculation and Food Price Crises: Regulation to reduce the risks of price volatility', *Briefing Note No 2*, September.

Desmarais, A. (2007), *La Vía Campesina, Globalization and the Power of Peasants.* Halifax/Ann Arbor: Fernwood Publishing /Pluto Press.

Desta, M. G. (2001) 'Food Security and International Trade Law: An appraisal of the WTO approach', *Journal of World Trade*, **35** (3): 449–468.

Desta, M. G. (2002) *The Law of International Trade in Agricultural Products: From GATT 1947 to the WTO Agreement on Agriculture*. The Hague: Kluwer Law International.

Devereux, S. (2001) 'Sen's Entitlement Approach: Critiques and counter-critiques', *Oxford Development Studies*, **29** (3).

Drèze, J. and Sen, A. K. (1989) *Hunger and Public Action* (reprinted in 2002). Oxford: OUP.

FAO (2006) *The Right to Food Guidelines, Information Papers and Case Studies*. Rome: FAO.

FAO (2009a) *Declaration of the World Summit on Food Security*, 18 November. Rome: FAO.

FAO (2009b) Statement by Hafez Ghanem, Assistant Director-General of FAO, *FAO Press Release*, 20 October (available at http://www.fao.org/news/story/en/item/ 36446/icode/ accessed 8 December 2010).

FAO (2010) *The State of Food Insecurity in the World: Addressing Food Insecurity in*

Protracted Crises. Rome: FAO.

FAO Press Release (2009a), '1.02 billion people hungry: One sixth of humanity undernourished – more than ever before', 19 June (available at http://www.fao.org/news/story/0/item/20568/icode/en/ accessed 16 November 2010).

FAO Press Release (2009b) '2050: A third more mouths to feed', 23 September, (available at http://www.fao.org/news/story/0/item/35571/icode/en/ accessed 22 November 2010).

Footer, M. (2010) 'The (Re-)turn to Soft Law in Reconciling the Antinomies in WTO Law', *Melbourne Journal of International Law,* **11**(2): 241–276.

Guzman, A. and Meyer, T. (2010) 'International Soft Law', *Journal of Legal Analysis,* **2**(1) (online publication available at http://jla.hup.harvard.edu).

Häberli, C. (2010) 'Food Security and WTO Rules', in B. Karapinar and C. Häberli (eds), *Food Crises and the WTO*. Cambridge: Cambridge University Press.

Hailu, M. (2010) 'Food Security and Agricultural Trade Liberalization', Conference Paper, SIEL Second Biennial Global Conference, Barcelona.

Hangzo, P. K. K. (2010) 'Comprehensive Food Security: An approach to sustainably address food insecurity', *NTS Perspectives,* **3.** Singapore: NSIS Centre for Non-Traditional Security (NTS) Studies.

Hartling, A. (ed) (2007) *Access to Environmental Justice: A Comparative Study*. Leiden: Nijhoff.

Heri, S. and Häberli, C. (2011) 'Can the World Trade Organization Ensure that International Food Aid is Genuine?', *Developing World Review on Trade and Competition,* **1**(1) (forthcoming).

Howse, R. (2008) 'Human Rights, International Economic Law and Constitutional Justice: A reply', *European Journal of International Law,* **19**: 945–953.

IBRD (2007) A McCalla and J Nash (eds). *Reforming Agricultural Trade for Developing Countries.*

IBRD (2008a) *The World Bank Annual Report 2008: Year in Review.* Washington, DC: IBRD.

IBRD (2008b), 'Potential Impact of Higher Food Prices on Poverty', *Policy Research Working Paper 4745.* Washington, DC: IBRD.

IBRD (2010) *Rising Global Interest in Farmland: Can it Yield Sustainable and Equitable Benefits?* Washington, DC, 7 September.

Institute for International Trade Negotiations (ICONE) (2009) *How Current Proposals on the SSM in the Doha Impasse Matter for Developing Country Exporters.* Available at http://ictsd.net/downloads/2009/02/ssm-paper_icone-format_13jan2009.pdf (accessed 14 December 2010), Sao Paolo, January.

International Centre for Trade and Sustainable Development (ICTSD) (2009), *Agricultural Subsidies in the WTO Green Box* (R. Meléndez-Ortiz, C. Bellmann and J. Hepburn, eds). Cambridge: ICTSD/ Cambridge University Press.

International Monetary Fund (IMF) (2011) *World Economic Outlook Update*, 25 January.

Johnston, D. (2010) 'Introduction to a Symposium on the 2007–8 World Food Crisis', *Journal of Agrarian Change,* **10**/1: 69–71.

Kappel, R., Pfeiffer, R. and Werner, J. (2010) 'What Became of the Food Crisis in 2008?', *Aussenwirtschaft,* **65**(1): 36.

Kaufmann, C. and Ehlert, C. (2009) 'International and Domestic Trade regulations to Secure the Food Supply', *Deakin Law Review,* **14** (2): 233.

Kaufmann, C. and Grosz, M. (2008) 'Poverty, Hunger and International Trade: What's law got to do with it? Current mechanisms and the Doha development agenda', *German Yearbook of International Law,* **51**: 75–109.

Kaufmann, C. and Heri, S. (2007) 'Liberalizing Trade in Agriculture and Food Security – Mission Impossible?', *Vanderbilt Journal of Transnational Law,* **40**: 1039.

Kong, K. (2009) 'The Right to Food for All: A rights-based approach to hunger and social inequality', *Suffolk Transnational Law Review,* **32**: 525–566.

Lang, T. (2010) 'Crisis? What Crisis? The normality of the current food crisis', *Journal of*

Agrarian Change, **10**/1: 87–97.

Marceau, G. (2002) 'WTO Dispute Settlement and Human Rights', *European Journal of International Law*, **13**: 753-814.

Margulis, M. (2009) 'Multilateral Responses to the Global Food Crisis', available at http://www.cababstractsplus.org/cabreviews. Hamilton, Ontario: McMaster University.

McMahon, J. A. (2005) 'The Agreement on Agriculture', in P. Macrory, A. Appleton and M. Plummer (eds), *The World Trade Organization: Legal, Economic and Political Analysis* Volume I. New York: Springer, pp.187–229.

McMillan, M. S., Welch, K. H. and Rodrik, D. (2003) 'When Economic Reform Goes Wrong: Cashew in Mozambique', Brookings Trade Forum: 97–151.

Mechlem, K. (2006) 'Harmonizing Trade in Agriculture and Human Rights: Options for the integration of the right to food into the Agreement on Agriculture', *Max Planck Yearbook of United Nations Law*, **10**: 127–190.

Moon, G. (2009) 'Trade and Equality: A relationship to discover', *Journal of International Economic Law*, **12** (3): 617–642.

Muskoka (2010) *Muskoka Accountability Report, available* at http://g8.gc.ca/wp-content/uploads/2010/06/mar_annex55.pdf (accessed 17 November 2010).

Mutua, M. and Howse, R. (2001) 'Protecting Human Rights in a Global Economy: Challenges for the World Trade Organization', in H. Stokke and A. Tostensen (eds), *Human Rights in Development Yearbook 1999/2000: The Millennium Edition*, pp. 510–82.

OECD (2010) *Export Restrictions* (TAD/TC/WP(2009)34/FINAL). Paris: OECD.

Pauwelyn, J. (2001) 'The Role of Public International Law in the WTO: How far can we go?', *American Journal of International Law*, **95**: 535.

Riedel, E. (1989) 'Menschenrechte der dritten Dimension', *Europäische Grundrechtzeitung*: 9-21.

Robinson, C. (2010) 'North Korea: Migration patterns and prospects' (CSIS Working Paper, August). Baltimore, MD: Center for Refugee and Disaster Response, Bloomberg School of Public Health, Johns Hopkins University.

Ruggie, J. (2009) 'Report of the Special Representative of the Secretary-General on the Issue of Human Rights and Transnational Corporations and Other Business Enterprises: Protect, respect, and remedy: a framework for business and human rights', *UN Doc. A/HRC/8/5*, dated 22 April.

Sen, A. K. (1981) *Poverty and Famines: An Essay on Entitlement and Deprivation*. Oxford: OUP.

Sharma, R. and Konandreas, P. (2008) 'WTO Provisions in the Context of Responding to Soaring Food Prices', *FAO Commodity and Trade Policy Research Working Paper No. 25*. Rome: FAO.

Smith, F. (2009) *Agriculture and the WTO: Towards a New Theory of International Agricultural Trade Regulation*. Cheltenham, UK and Northampton, MA, USA: Edward Elgar.

Stoll, P.-T. and Strack, C. (2007) 'Article XX GATT 1994' in R. Wolfrum, P.-T. Stoll and A. Seibert-Fohr (eds), *WTO-Technical Barriers and SPS Measures*. The Netherlands: Koninklijke Brill NV, pp. 96–120.

Stoll, P.-T. (2003) 'How to Overcome the Dichotomy Between WTO Rules and MEAs?', *Heidelberg Journal of International Law*, **63** (2): 439–458.

Tomuschat, C. (2008) *Human Rights*. Oxford: OUP.

Trebilcock, M. and Howse, R. (2005) *The Regulation of International Trade* (Third Edition). London: Routledge.

UN (2000) *United Nations Millennium Declaration* (General Assembly Resolution 55/2). (For an overview of all MDGs see the official UN site at http://www.un.org/millenniumgoals/index.shtml, accessed 8 December 2010.)

UN (2008) High-Level Task Force on the Global Food Security Crisis, *Comprehensive Framework for Action*. New York, July.

UN (2009) High-Level Task Force on the Global Food Security Crisis, *Progress Report*

(April 2008-October 2009). New York, November.

UN High Commissioner on Human Rights (2005) *Human Rights and World Trade Agreements: Using General Exception Clauses to Protect Human Rights*. New York and Geneva: United Nations.

van Damme, I. (2009) *Treaty Interpretation by the WTO Appellate Body*. Oxford: OUP.

Vasak, K. (1977) 'A 30-Year Struggle: The sustained efforts to give force of law to the Universal Declaration of Human Rights' *UNESCO Courier*, November: 29–32.

Volume One, *Key Issues For A Pro-Development Outcome Of The Doha Round*.

Volume Two, *Quantifying the impact of the multilateral trade reform*.

von Braun, J. (2008) *Food and Financial Crises – Implications for the Poor* (IFPRI Food Policy Report). Washington, DC: IFPRI.

Wager, S. (2009) 'International Agricultural Trade Liberalisation and Food Security: Risks associated with a fully liberalised global market place', *Aussenwirtschaft*: 139–165.

WFP (2009) *Food Aid Flows 2009*. Report available at http://documents.wfp.org/stellent/groups/public/documents/newsroom/wfp223562.pdf

World Food Programme (WFP) (2010) 'WFP Keeps Careful Watch On Food Prices'. Press Release, 17 November (available at http://www.wfp.org/stories/wfp-keeps-careful-watch-food-prices, accessed 23 November 2010).

WTO (1998) *United States - Import Prohibition of Certain Shrimp and Shrimp Products* (Report of the Appellate Body in WT/DS58/AB/R, dated 12 October).

WTO (2006) *European Communities – Measures affecting the Approval and Marketing of Biotech Products* (Reports of the Panel in WT/DS291/R, WT/DS292/R, and WT/DS293/R, dated 29 September).

WTO (2008) *Committee on Agriculture in Special Session, Revised Draft Modalities for Agriculture*, WTO Doc. TN/AG/W/4/Rev.4, 6 December.

Zunckel, H. (2010) 'Reforming the International Legal Regime for Food Aid', Conference Paper, SIEL Second Biennial Global Conference, Barcelona, 8–10 July.

4 The impact of WTO agricultural trade rules on food security and development: an examination of proposed additional flexibilities for developing countries
Alan Matthews

I. INTRODUCTION

Disciplines on agricultural trade measures and trade-distorting domestic subsidies to agriculture were included for the first time in the Uruguay Round Agreement on Agriculture (AoA) which came into force for WTO member countries in 1995. Since then, there has been a continuing debate over whether these disciplines are appropriate for developing countries seeking to promote their agricultural development and food security (De Schutter, 2009; Diaz-Bonilla and Ron, 2010; Gonzalez, 2002). Criticisms range from arguments that the AoA rules are lop-sided and essentially favour developed countries which can continue to heavily support their agricultural sectors, that they constrain the ability of developing countries to pursue their agricultural development and food security policies, and even that they undermine the right to food of developing countries. There is a widespread perception that developing countries got a raw deal in the AoA. It is certainly the case that the extent of the additional market access offered by developed countries was less than was hoped for (Ingco, 1995).

Based on their experience of the implementation of the WTO agreements, developing countries prepared a list of implementation issues in 1999 aimed at removing the serious imbalances and inequities they perceived in these agreements. When the Doha Round of trade negotiations was launched in 2001, all countries agreed that a primary objective was to foster development in poorer developing countries (WTO, 2001). Paragraph 3 of the Doha Declaration 'committed to addressing the marginalization of least-developed countries in international trade'. Paragraph 12 noted the separate decision taken on some implementation issues and that 'negotiations on outstanding implementation issues shall be an integral part of the Work

Programme' in the coming years. Paragraph 13 stated that Special and Differential Treatment (SDT) measures 'shall be an integral part of all elements in the negotiations on agriculture' and these measures should be 'operationally effective and enable developing countries to take account of their development needs, including food security and rural development'. As the negotiations continued, it became clear that the various participants interpreted this mandate in different fashions. For some, mainly developing countries, this was an opportunity to carve out special and distinct trade rules that would apply to developing countries given their particular structural characteristics and development needs. Other countries insisted that developing countries should continue to adhere to the long-term objective of 'strengthened rules and specific commitments on support and protection in order to correct and prevent restrictions and distortions in world agricultural markets', while also opening up the possibility for longer time periods to adapt to new rules, providing technical assistance, and permitting some exemptions and deferrals from WTO rules and other forms of preferential treatment. In this view, providing limited flexibility in some instances was a means to achieve greater ambition for the Round as a whole. This failure to agree on the ultimate objective of the negotiations helps explain why the agricultural negotiations in particular, during the Doha Round, have been so tortuous and thus far fruitless.

For many developing countries, safeguarding domestic food production capacity has become an essential component of their food security strategies. They fear that lowering protection to their agricultural sectors would negatively affect their large rural populations, which still contain the largest concentrations of poverty, and which often have limited access to employment alternatives. They also fear sudden negative trade impacts on poor producers whose vulnerable livelihoods may be severely disrupted by market instability and sudden import surges. During the Doha Round negotiations, they sought exemptions from tariff reductions for products that are important, *inter alia*, for their food security as well as the right to protect themselves from destabilising import competition.

These concerns initially found expression in the demand for a 'Development Box' to provide additional flexibilities for developing countries in WTO rules (WTO, 2000). Special Products (SPs) and the Special Safeguard Mechanism (SSM) emerged in that context as specific development box mechanisms (Mably, 2009). In the run-up to the Cancun Ministerial Council meeting in 2003 a coalition of developing countries known as the G-33 came together with the objective to secure SP flexibility for products which play an important role in food security, livelihood security and rural development as well as the introduction of a SSM for developing countries.[1] The WTO General Council Decision of 1 August 2004 (the Framework Agreement) stated that developing country Members 'must be able to pursue agricultural policies that are supportive of their development goals, poverty reduction strategies, food security and livelihood concerns' (WTO, 2004). It went on to specify that 'developing country Members will have the flexibility to designate an appropriate number of products as Special Products, based on criteria of food security, livelihood security and rural development needs. These products will be eligible for more flexible treatment.' The Framework Agreement further states that a 'Special Safeguard Mechanism will be established for use by developing country Members'. However, key aspects of these instruments – such as the selection and treatment of SPs, or the specific modalities for a new SSM, including product coverage, possible trigger mechanisms and remedies – were left for future negotiations.

Other voices urged caution in pursuing the Development Box proposals. In part, this reflected the inherent dilemma that increased flexibilities for those countries which emphasise their defensive interests in the negotiations mean fewer opportunities through increased market access for those countries, including other developing countries, which seek to promote their food security and rural development through agricultural export-led growth. But the caution also reflects the view that seeking to maintain protection may not, in fact, be an effective route to food security. As Eugenio Diaz-Bonilla noted some time ago: 'Developing countries should make sure that the greater flexibility they seek within the "development" or "food security" box will really help them meet their food security and economic goals. Some of the suggested changes could help, but others may well work against the poor and the hungry' (IFPRI, 2002: 1).

Low productivity in developing country agriculture is a serious problem and an important cause of poverty and hunger. Increasing agricultural productivity is an important goal for developing country policy. But whether more restrictive trade policies help to raise productivity and contribute to food security is contested. Raising food prices has the biggest negative impact on poor food consumers, many of whom are also small farmers who are the net purchasers of food staples. The benefits accrue to commercial farmers in proportion to their output, and thus higher prices benefit most of those larger farmers who have least need of it. Protection creates costs through stimulating inefficient production, without necessarily addressing the underlying problem of low productivity. Protection for food products leads to discrimination against other sectors which may also have the potential for increased employment and poverty reduction. Development-focused policies involving measures such as improved infrastructure, education, technology and improved property rights can be much more effective than trade protection in raising productivity (Ivanic and Martin, 2006).

With this debate in mind, the purpose of this chapter is to explore the value of the proposed SP designation and the SSM for development, food security and poverty alleviation. In each case, the rules set out in the latest Draft Modalities are described and their likely effectiveness is assessed. Suggestions on how to overcome the current impasse are set out in the concluding section.

II.   TRADE BACKGROUND

The case for increased flexibilities for developing countries must be assessed against the background of changing patterns of agricultural trade, and in particular the growing importance of South-South trade. While developed countries still account for the great majority of world imports of agri-food products, developing countries are rapidly growing in importance as import markets (see Figure 4.1). Developed countries accounted for 70 per cent of global agri-food imports in 1995, while developing countries accounted for 27 per cent (the remaining 3 per cent were absorbed by transition economies).[2] By 2009, the share of developed countries had fallen to 61 per cent and that of developing countries had risen to 34 per cent. The value of global agri-food imports was $411 billion in 1995 and $893 billion in 2009. Between 1995 and 2009, the value of global agri-food imports increased by $482 billion, of which developing country importers accounted for 41 per cent of the increase. For the five-year period 2004–2009, the developing country share of the growth of imports was 44 per cent. And in the two year period 2007–09, the period affected by the global recession, the developing country share of the growth of agri-food imports was 74 per cent. Developing country import demand is driven by rising incomes, urbanisation and the rapid diversification of diets, and in some countries by failures in agricultural policy. It is clear that developing country markets are the future growth markets for agri-food exporters, and this also includes other developing countries.

At the same time as developing countries now provide the largest increment to the global demand for food, developing country exporters

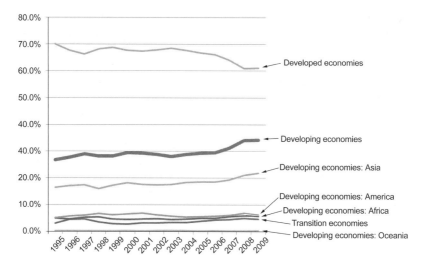

Source: Own calculations based on UNCTADStat

Figure 4. 1 Shares in world agricultural imports

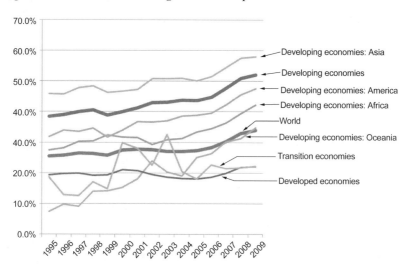

Source: Own calculations based on UNCTADStat

Figure 4.2 Share of developing country exports in destination markets

are capturing a larger share of these developing country imports (see Figure 4.2). Between 1995 and 2009, the developing country share of global exports increased from 26 per cent to 34 per cent. But their share of exports to other developing countries rose from 39 per cent to 52 per cent over the same period.[3] The figures differ relatively little across developing country regions; in 2009, developing country agricultural exporters accounted for 42 per cent of exports to Africa, 48 per cent of exports to Latin America, and 58 per cent of exports to Asia. Only in the case of the relatively small market in Oceania does the share fall to just 22 per cent. The share of South-South trade in total world trade of agri-food products, which was just 13 per cent in 1995, reached 20 per cent in 2009. These trends underline the fact that the most important domain for WTO trade rules, which are often seen as mainly governing North-North and North-South trade flows, will be to facilitate South-South trade flows in future. Empirical studies confirm that the significant exemption of developing countries from effective disciplines considerably reduces the potential gains from the Round for developing countries by substantially reducing the possibility to increase South-South trade flows (Anderson and Martin, 2005; Bouët, 2006).

III. SPECIAL PRODUCTS

a.   Doha Round Draft Modalities

The 2004 Framework Agreement proposed that 'Developing country Members will have the flexibility to designate an appropriate number of products as Special Products, based on criteria of food security, livelihood security and rural development needs. These products will be eligible for more flexible treatment. The criteria and treatment of these products will be further specified during the negotiation phase and will recognize the fundamental importance of Special Products to developing countries' (WTO, 2004). The key issues in the negotiations on SPs concern the number of products to be eligible for this status, the identification of these products, and their treatment.

At the 2005 Hong Kong Ministerial meeting WTO Members agreed to grant developing countries the 'flexibility to self-designate an appropriate number of tariff lines as Special Products guided by indicators based on the criteria of food security, livelihood security and rural development' (WTO, 2005a). Compared to the Framework Agreement the previous year, the main developments were greater flexibility (self-designation by developing countries), the limitation to an appropriate number, and the reference to indicators for the stated criteria.

The G-33 as the main demandeur for SPs initially sought maximum flexibility in their designation and treatment. There should be no restriction on the number of SPs, SPs should be exempt from any tariff reduction obligations and no *quid pro quo* in the form of increased TRQs (as for sensitive products) should be required (WTO, 2005b, c, d). Its position subsequently evolved to seeking up to 20 per cent of the tariff lines of developing countries to be designated as SPs, guided by a non-exhaustive list of indicators reflecting the three development criteria and based on at least one indicator at a national, regional or household level. No agricultural product would be *a priori* excluded. Fifty per cent of the tariff lines so designated would be exempt from any tariff reduction commitment. An additional 15 per cent of designated tariff lines would be exempted from tariff reductions if there were 'special circumstances' (e.g., low bound tariffs, high ceiling bindings, high proportion of low income or resource-poor producers). A further 25 per cent of designated SPs would be subject only to a 5 per cent reduction in bound tariff rates while the remaining tariff lines would be subject to cuts that would be no greater than 10 per cent (Mably, 2009)

Positions remained far apart during 2006. The United States issued a paper in May 2006 that proposed that SPs would be limited to five tariff lines and that the SP designation would be restricted to products meeting certain criteria (for example, that SPs would have to be products produced domestically but not exported). Some developing countries, such as Thailand, Malaysia and Costa Rica, also proposed a limited and restrictive approach to SP product designation, focusing particularly on products that were important in South-South trade. In his 'reference paper' on the SP negotiations in April 2006 the Chairman of the Special Session of the Committee on Agriculture noted three distinct approaches to SPs in the negotiations (WTO, 2006a). SP proponents sought the possibility to designate products guided by an 'illustrative, non-exhaustive, non-prescriptive, and non-cumulative list of indicators' without any limit on the overall percentage of tariff lines that could be selected. Another group of countries wanted agreement on a common set of indicators that could be used to 'filter' or 'screen' candidates for SP designation, possibly combined with a limit on the number of SPs that could be selected. A third option would be to start with a limit on the number or proportion of tariff lines that might be self-designated, possibly combined with indicators for the criteria. Not surprisingly, in the first draft of the agricultural modalities in July 2006, the section dealing with SPs appeared entirely in multiple square brackets, simply describing the positions put forward at that date (WTO, 2006b). As the Chair himself admitted, it was not an elegant document.

In the February 2008 version of the Draft Modalities, the text had evolved to propose that 'Developing country Members shall be entitled to self-designate Special Products guided by indicators based on the criteria of food security, livelihood security and rural development. There shall be a minimum entitlement of 8 per cent, and a maximum entitlement of [12] [20] per cent, of tariff lines available for self-designation as Special Products. Under this provision, there is an entitlement to [6] per cent of tariff lines which shall take a tariff cut of [8] [15] per cent. A further [6] per cent is available with a cut of [12] [25] per cent. [A further] [8 per cent of] [no] tariff lines shall be eligible for no cut.]' (WTO, 2008a, footnotes omitted).

The December 2008 Draft Modalities proposed that 'developing country Members shall be entitled to self-designate Special Products guided by indicators based on the criteria of food security, livelihood security and rural development. There shall be 12 per cent of tariff lines available for self-designation as Special Products. Up to 5 per cent of lines may have no cut. The overall average cut shall, in any case, be 11 percent' (WTO, 2008b). While the square brackets around the numbers (indicating disagreement) had disappeared, a footnote to the text noted that a number of developing country Members had continued to express some reservations concerning the numbers specified in this paragraph, noting also that this could be affected by what was decided upon in other areas of the text. More favourable treatment would be offered to small vulnerable economies (SVEs) and to recently acceded members (RAMs).[4] The former group of countries would have an alternative option not to apply the tiered formula but simply to meet an overall average cut of 24 per cent through having in effect opted to designate as many tariff lines as they choose as Special Products. The tariff lines so chosen need not be subject to any minimum tariff cut and need not be guided by the indicators. In the latter case, the maximum tariff line entitlements to SPs would be 13 per cent and the overall average cut to be achieved for the designated tariff lines may be further reduced to 10 per cent. Importantly, this flexibility would not be taken into account in assessing whether using the market access formula would result in a developing country exceeding the maximum overall average cut on final bound tariffs of 36 per cent.

b.   Assessment of the Special Products proposal

The December 2008 Draft Modalities can be assessed from two standpoints. From the G-33 perspective, the issue is whether the numbers in the Draft Modalities give them the flexibility they desire to avoid or limit reductions in bound tariffs in developing countries for products deemed important from a food security, livelihood security and rural development perspective. From a food security perspective, the issue is whether the Special Products designation will advance this objective or not.

An extensive literature drawing on studies commissioned by the FAO and ICTSD attempted to identify how many products might qualify as SPs in various developing countries under the Framework Agreement criteria and how many tariff lines these products would represent (FAO, 2007a; Ford *et al.*, 2006, 2007; ICTSD, 2007). These studies faced a number of challenges. The proposed criteria were very broad and extremely complex to define and measure. Appropriate indicators had to be defined to measure these impacts and appropriate thresholds chosen. Both the FAO and ICSTD proposed a wide set of relevant indicators, as did the G-33 (in part, drawing on the FAO/ICSTD work: see Mably, 2009). Annex F of the December 2008 Modalities also contains an illustrative list of indicators for the designation of SPs. These lists are very comprehensive and some of the indicators proposed would allow developing countries to essentially designate any product.

But the selection of indicators can only be an initial step. For example, if the proportion of calories per day contributed by a product to population nutrition were to be used as an indicator, what should be the cut-off point (10 per cent, 30 per cent?) above which a product would be eligible for SP status? Would an SP be required to meet just one of the criteria or all three? Would the evaluation be conducted at a national level or would products important at a regional or local level also be eligible to be designated? Are data available to allow countries to make a rigorous selection of this kind? The case studies commissioned by the FAO and ICTSD adopted a fairly flexible approach. In addition to a strict application of indicators, potential SPs were also identified through national stakeholder consultations allowing a role for political judgement and influence.

A series of 19 ICTSD country studies found that an appropriate number of SPs would probably range from six to 20. The most commonly identified potential SPs were rice, corn, wheat, beans, milk, dairy products, bovine meat, goat meat, sheep meat, pork, chicken, potatoes, tomatoes, onions, vegetable oils and sugar (ICTSD, 2007; 2008). On average, SPs represented around 10 per cent of agricultural tariff lines (although this varied widely from 3 to 20 per cent) in the ICTSD studies. In the nine country case studies conducted by the FAO, the average proportion of tariff lines selected for SP status was considerably higher at 17.8 per cent. These proportions ranged from 8.5 per cent to 18.6 per cent in the Caribbean countries, but from 16 per cent to 26.3 per cent in the African studies. From an exporter perspective, what matters is the proportion of tariff lines where trade is taking place or the value of imports likely to be designated as SPs. In the ICTSD studies, the proportion of agricultural trade covered by the potential SPs varied from 6 to 64 per cent.

From a developing country perspective, it would not necessarily make sense to designate every potential SP without taking into account the current trade and trade policy situation to identify those products that require increased flexibility (FAO, 2007a). The FAO/ICTSD methodology thus provides an additional set of 'filters' which take into consideration the trade dimension of SPs in order to help countries prioritise their lists for the purpose of WTO negotiations. This includes the extent to which imports could displace local production (such as rice or wheat imports displacing traditional crops like sorghum or cassava); the extent to which products face unfair competition from imports that are heavily subsidised; the extent to which tariffs and other measures currently protect the products in question and the likelihood of this being affected in the course of current trade negotiations; and the extent to which products may be able to withstand competition from low-cost imports. For example, under the market access draft modalities, developing countries can make use of sensitive product (SnP) designation, and many of the products likely to be selected as sensitive might also be justified by the criteria as Special Products.

In many developing countries bound tariffs are much higher than applied tariffs and this tariff overhang will persist even after applying the proposed Doha Round market access modalities.

Bernabe (2008) examined the extent of tariff overhang for the 16 products on the ICTSD's (2007) list for a sample of 30 developing country members of the G-33, excluding the least developed countries. Her objective was to calculate what percentage of SPs and tariff lines should be exempted from tariff cuts if applied tariffs on SPs were not to be reduced following a Doha Round agreement. Using as a threshold criterion countries and commodities that had no or minimal tariff overhangs (not exceeding 10 percentage points), she concluded that the percentage of potential SPs that should be excluded from tariff cuts varied widely, from 6.25 per cent of tariff lines designated as potential SPs in the cases of Grenada and Guyana, to as much as 100 per cent in the cases of China and Cote d'Ivoire. When country-specific SP lists are used these percentages increase, sometimes substantially. In terms of tariff lines the percentage of SPs requiring market access flexibility ranges from zero to 11 per cent of total HS (harmonised system) six-digit tariff lines, based on data from countries that identified their SPs at this level. However, she cautioned that the wide differences in the tariff structures of developing countries made these figures less meaningful. Unfortunately, this study did not estimate the proportion of trade that would be affected by these flexibilities.

Several agriculture-exporting developing countries argued that the selection and treatment of SPs should not undermine the food and livelihood security or rural development of their numerous poor and vulnerable farmers, whose welfare depends on improved market access for a few export products. There are wide differences in the estimates of the value of trade that might be affected by SP status. The Chair of the agricultural negotiations caused consternation among SP proponents when he included in his May 2006 reference paper calculations by the WTO Secretariat that designating 20 per cent of tariff lines as SPs could allow two unnamed developing countries to shield as much as 98.4 and 94 per cent of the total value of their respective farm imports from Doha Round tariff cuts (WTO, 2006a; ICTSD, 2006).

Given that developing country imports are often concentrated in a few tariff lines, it is not unusual that providing SP exemptions on even a small percentage of tariff lines could impact on a very large portion of the agricultural trade that occurs. Gillon & Associates (2008), writing on behalf of US farm organisations, calculated that approximately 90 per cent of agricultural imports into developing countries (by value) are concentrated in only 10 per cent of tariff lines, and that the 5 per cent exemption from any tariff cuts proposed in the December 2008 Draft Modalities would cover between 80–85 per cent of their agricultural imports. For China the proportion is 86 per cent, and for India it is 87 per cent. These figures assume that developing countries would designate as SPs those products with the highest import values. SP proponents point out that the choice of SPs will be limited to products which meet the qualifying criteria in the Draft Modalities. The ICTSD studies found that the SPs selected accounted for less than one-quarter of the value of total agricultural imports, though with a lot of variation between countries (see above). Clearly, a great deal depends on whether the qualifying criteria would, in practice, turn out to limit the discretion of developing countries to arbitrarily self-designate the products that might be eligible for SP status, and the extent to which developing countries would want to make use of the designation once the proposed 'trade' filter was taken into account. The extensive elasticity implicit in the wide range of indicators proposed adds to the uncertainty of exporters about the real degree of additional market access that they would obtain. The fact that SPs would be in addition to sensitive product designation (albeit that the latter would require compensatory increases in tariff rate quota access) also needs to be borne in mind when evaluating the overall change in market access from a Doha Round agreement.

IV. THE SPECIAL SAFEGUARD MECHANISM (SSM)

a. Doha Round Draft Modalities

The July 2004 Framework Agreement noted that 'A Special Safeguard Mechanism will be established for use by developing country Members'. Safeguards are designed to protect against the adverse consequences of domestic market disruption caused either by unduly low-priced imports or import surges. However, it appears there was never a broad agreement on the purpose of the SSM, which complicated and eventually poisoned discussion on the design of the instrument to the point where divisions over the SSM were blamed for the breakdown in the Doha Round talks in 2008 (Wolfe, 2009). The principal difference underlying the debate about the SSM was whether it was intended to deal with the market disruption resulting from the Doha Round liberalisation, or whether it was supposed to address market disruption more broadly. Differences over the design of the mechanism, including its product coverage, triggers, remedies and duration, all flowed from differences over its fundamental objective.

Proponents of the SSM argued that developing countries needed access to an SSM because of the vulnerability of their producers, and especially low-income and resource-poor producers, to a sharp drop in market prices caused either by unexpectedly low world market prices or a surge in imports, because of the growing exposure of countries to external market instability and to import surges as trade barriers are reduced, and due to the absence of alternative risk management and safety net instruments. They argued that they did not have and could not afford the policies that supported farmers in developed countries and therefore needed access to a general stabilisation mechanism.

The alternative view, put forward not only by the United States but also by developing country exporters (see the communication from Argentina, Paraguay and Uruguay; WTO 2006c), insisted that the SSM should be a trade policy instrument, an exceptional measure, to be used under exceptional circumstances resulting from the liberalisation process. It should not imply 'a unilateral modification of schedules without any due compensation'. In this view, the purpose of a new safeguard measure should be to support a more ambitious market opening by providing for the possibility of a temporary withdrawal of tariff reduction offers in strictly defined circumstances. Supporters of this narrower view of the SSM wanted to confine it to staple food products, to products necessary for food security, or to products that already had low tariffs in order to facilitate the overall liberalisation process.

The debate on the SSM revolved around three main issues: the eligible products, the conditions to be met to invoke the mechanism, and the remedies once the mechanism was invoked. The SSM under discussion is broadly based on the Special Agricultural Safeguard (SSG) under Article 5 of the AoA which includes two triggers – one based on the price of imports and one on the volume of imports. There are a number of published accounts of the SSM negotiations to date (Montemayor, 2007; Wolfe, 2009; WTO, 2008c). Here we summarise the state of play as incorporated in the December 2008 draft modalities (WTO, 2008b), together with a separate document that the Chair circulated at the same time in which he put forward his interpretation of where discussions had reached on the contentious issue of whether the remedies could breach existing pre-Doha tariff bindings (WTO, 2008d). Neither document was endorsed by the WTO membership and subsequent interventions made clear there was no agreement on either text (for G-33 views, see WTO (2010a, b, c, d) and also the paper circulated by Australia and Canada (ICTSD, 2010). The Agriculture Chair's report in April 2011 confirmed that, despite extensive technical and analytical discussions, no compromise text had yet been presented to the negotiating group (WTO, 2011).

The December 2008 Draft Modalities would allow countries to impose specified additional duties when the total volume of imports of an agricultural product exceeded a specified trigger level, or when import prices from a particular supplier fell below a trigger price. The price-based SSM uses a reference price based on a three-year moving average of import prices from all sources. When the price of an individual shipment falls below 85 per cent of the reference price, a duty can be used to remove 85 per cent of the shortfall. There is a market test or cross-check that developing countries should not normally take recourse to the price-based SSM where the volume of imports of the products concerned in the current year is manifestly declining or is at a manifestly negligible level incapable of undermining the domestic price level.

The volume-based SSM can be used when imports in a year exceed 'base imports' – a rolling average of imports in the preceding three year period. The additional duty that can be applied increases as imports exceed this base (the triggers and remedies are discussed in the following paragraphs). The volume-based safeguard can only be imposed for two years and if it is used twice in succession cannot be used for another two years. If a safeguard duty is imposed, and imports are lower than in the period before imposition, the trigger level is not reduced – thus avoiding a potential outcome where use of the duty itself causes the trigger to decline. Countries are allowed to use just one of the price-based and volume-based measures per tariff line in any given year.

The December 2008 Modalities set out the trigger points and remedies for the volume trigger as follows:

(a) where the volume of imports during any year exceeds 110 per cent but does not exceed 115 per cent of base imports, the maximum additional duty that may be imposed on applied tariffs shall not exceed 25 per cent of the current bound tariff or 25 percentage points, whichever is higher;

(b) where the volume of imports during any year exceeds 115 per cent but does not exceed 135 per cent of base imports, the maximum additional duty that may be imposed on applied tariffs shall not exceed 40 per cent of the current bound tariff or 40 percentage points, whichever is higher;

(c) where the volume of imports during any year exceeds 135 per cent of base imports, the maximum additional duty that may be imposed on applied tariffs shall not exceed 50 per cent of the current bound tariff or 50 percentage points, whichever is higher.

Unlike the February 2008 Draft Modalities, there is no limit on the number of tariff lines for which the normal SSM might be invoked in the December draft. The major flexibility of the SSM is that it would allow developing countries to raise applied tariffs (including the SSM remedy) above their post-Doha bound rate if the trigger conditions are met. Indeed, it may also give comfort to those countries that continued to have a significant gap between bound and applied tariffs even after the Doha Round modalities were applied, and which might not otherwise be expected to need the SSM given their ability to raise applied tariffs up to the bound ceiling. The result of the *Chile–Price Bands* case showed that varying applied tariffs even within the bound ceiling could be found illegal if the way that they are applied is inconsistent with the footnote to Article 4 of the AoA (Gifford and Montemayor, 2008).

However, the major sticking point in the discussions on the SSM has been whether countries should be allowed to raise tariffs above their pre-Doha level and, if so, under what conditions. The Draft Modalities stated that the applied duty plus the safeguard remedy should not exceed the pre-Doha tariff binding, but in the case of the volume-based SSM they provided for exceptions for three country groups – least developed countries, SVEs, and for all other developing countries under particular conditions. For the least developed countries, the maximum remedy allowed for could be applied provided that the maximum increase over a pre-Doha bound tariff did not exceed 40 *ad valorem* percentage points or 40 per cent of the current bound tariff, whichever was higher. In the case of SVEs, the text (in square brackets, indicating no agreement) limited the maximum increase over a pre-Doha binding to 20 *ad valorem* percentage points or 20 per cent of the current bound tariff, whichever was the higher, but for a maximum of 10-15 (in square brackets) of tariff lines in a given period. For all other developing countries, the maximum pre-Doha tariff could be exceeded by up to 15 percentage points or 15 per cent of the initial tariff binding for 2–6 six-digit tariff lines.

The Chair's proposal in December 2008 for triggers in the case of remedies which would bring tariffs above the pre-Doha bound rate in the case of the volume-based SSM was significantly different (WTO, 2008d).[5]

(i)   where the volume of imports during any period exceeds 120 per cent but does not exceed 140 per cent, the maximum additional duty that may be imposed shall not exceed one-third of the current bound tariff or eight percentage points, whichever is the higher;

(ii)   where the volume of imports during any period exceeds 140 per cent, the maximum additional duty that may be imposed shall not exceed one-half of the current bound tariff or 12 percentage points, whichever is higher.

SSM remedies above the pre-Doha bound tariff should not be applied to more than 2.5 per cent of tariff lines in any 12 month period.

Compared with the Draft Modalities, for developing countries not in the LDC or SVE categories the allowed excess over the pre-Doha bound rate is calculated differently (for countries with higher bound tariffs there is greater flexibility, but for countries with low bound tariffs the flexibility is slightly reduced) and an additional trigger threshold is introduced, but the number of products for which the pre-Doha cap could be exceeded in any period is increased (from 2–6 to 2.5 per cent of total tariff lines). Also this document did not make any reference to exceeding pre-Doha tariffs in the case of the price-based SSM.

b.   Frequency of Import Surges

For the G-33, the key question regarding the SSM is its accessibility (the frequency with which it can be invoked to address import surges and price depressions) and the effectiveness of the remedies (whether they provide an effective means of stabilising domestic prices in the face of import surges and price depressions or not).

Early studies focused on simulations to calculate the minimum triggers that were necessary to allow safeguards to be invoked. A small cottage industry developed for assessing the threat posed by import surges where the focus was placed on the volume-based trigger (Sharma, 2005). There is no single definition of what constitutes an import surge. The definition used by the FAO in their set of conceptual and empirical studies was a 30 per cent positive deviation from a three-year moving average of import data (de Nigris, 2005). The choice of 30 per cent is, of course, arbitrary, and alternative numbers give very different incidences of import surges. An alternative definition is that which is provided in Article 5 of the AoA dealing with the SSG. This is based not only on the total volume of imports but also on their share in total domestic consumption and on the growth in domestic consumption.

What is clear is that, as a statistical phenomenon, import surges are very frequent (ActionAid International, 2008; FAO, 2003; de Nigris, 2005, South Centre, 2009a). For example, defining an import surge as a 20 per cent positive deviation from a five-year moving average, the FAO (2003) showed that import surges occurred on average in about one-third of the years for each product in each country over the period 1984–2000. The South Centre (2009a) examined import surges in 56 developing countries (using a more stringent definition of imports more than 110 per cent over the preceding three-year average) and concluded that these countries imported around 16 per cent of their agricultural products under an import surge (23 per cent in the case of LDCs). In their analysis, they concluded that 29 per cent of HS six-digit tariff lines in each country in any year experienced an import surge, while 56 per cent of tariff lines in each country on average experienced an import surge in at least one year during the 2004–07 period.

The FAO analysis highlighted that import surges appeared to become more frequent in the period following the implementation of the trade liberalisation measures agreed in the AoA (de Nigris, 2005). The belief that the implementation of WTO commitments has been accompanied by increased import surges and the displacement of domestic production in some developing countries has been part of the motivation for strengthened safeguard instruments in the Doha Round (ActionAid International, 2008). However, while the frequency of surges in the post-Uruguay Round period has increased, the FAO concluded that the resulting market liberalisation was only a contributory factor and not their main cause. The gradual implementation of tariff reductions under multilateral trade commitments did not appear to have been a direct cause of sudden import surges. Rather, in the more open market environment fostered by trade liberalisation the effects of other causal factors, including structural constraints on domestic production, have been accentuated (FAO, 2007b).

While the incidence of surges may have risen, and surges appear to be a fairly common phenomenon in developing countries, these figures tell us nothing about their impact. It is important to underline that there is nothing either inherently 'good' or 'bad' about an import surge. Rising imports are not necessarily a negative thing for developing countries, as they add to food availability and to the reduction of hunger. It is often presumed that an import surge of a particular commodity disrupts local markets and pushes down prices, negatively affecting the livelihoods of people relying on the production of that commodity (ActionAid International, 2008). De Nigris (2005) examined correlations between import surges (measured in per caput terms) and production per caput. He found many examples of negative correlations indicating an inverse relationship between imports and domestic production, suggesting that imports were needed to compensate for domestic shortfalls. He also found positive correlations for other products where imports increased at the same time as domestic production and which probably reflected increasing demand for these products generated by economic growth. In neither instance is it obvious that the import surge is associated with the displacement of domestic production and injury to the domestic sector. The South Centre (2009b: 22) concludes that over 85 per cent of import surges are not accompanied by declines in import prices, suggesting that most import surges are driven by domestic shocks such as declines in domestic production. Furthermore, not all import surges in a statistical sense are economically meaningful. Import surges may have a different impact on domestic agricultural and processing industries depending not only on their absolute levels but also on their share of total domestic production or consumption. The impact of an import surge, both on the general economy and on the specific commodity sector, will be influenced by its relative share of production and consumption.

Sharma (2005) criticised much of the evidence presented on the importance of import surges. Drawing on the framework set out in the WTO Safeguards Agreement, he argued that a good study should meet four requirements: statistical evidence that an import surge has occurred; a negative correlation with some performance indicator of the domestic sector (e.g. production, area planted, market share, employment); evidence of a causal link between imports and the negative performance; and non-attribution, i.e. properly identifying and accounting for the role of other factors that might affect domestic performance. He instanced cases where an import surge occurred even while domestic prices had continued to rise. Such cases suggest that imports have been 'pulled in' through prior shortfalls in domestic production rather than higher imports causing domestic production to fall. Few of the studies he examined met the analytic standards he described.

While a certain scepticism may be justified about using the evidence on import surges to support the need for additional safeguards for developing countries, the link between trade liberalisation and greater domestic price volatility is much more plausible but also much less researched. Trade policy reforms enhance the transmission to domestic markets of international price movements and thus introduce a further source of domestic price instability (Valdés and Foster, 2005), although there is very little evidence on the importance of this effect. The excessive focus on import surges and the volume SSM may have distracted attention from the necessary analysis of the price SSM, despite the fact that import prices have a more direct impact on domestic markets in the importing country than the volume of imports and calculating the necessary remedy is a more straightforward task.

c.   **Impact of a Potential SSM**

Three recent studies shed light on the likely use and impact of the SSM. Montemayor (2010) examined the accessibility and effectiveness of the

SSM using the triggers set out in the December 2008 Draft Modalities (previous versions of this study using earlier versions of the Modalities are Montemayor, 2007; 2008). His simulations covered 27 products from six developing countries. Accessibility was defined as the frequency with which the SSM could be invoked to address import surges and price depressions, given the rules set out in the Modalities. Effectiveness was defined through a three-step procedure. First, the number of months (or 'shipments', where the average monthly price is assumed to be the shipment price) during which average import prices (converted to local currency) plus bound tariffs fell below corresponding domestic wholesale prices by more than 10 per cent were counted. These were called 'problematic' months in which additional safeguard duties would be needed. He then assessed whether additional safeguard duties could be invoked during these problematic months under the proposed SSM rules. Finally, he calculated the additional SSM duty that would be permitted and calculated whether this would be sufficient to bring the duty-inclusive import price to within 90 per cent of the domestic price or higher. In such instances, the SSM was deemed to be effective. The strong normative assumption behind this approach was that the SSM had been designed to offset all destabilising impulses from lower import prices beyond the 10 per cent threshold.

He estimated that the volume SSM could be accessed in one-third of total months and the price SSM for 18 per cent of all months (this latter figure underestimates the likely use of the price-based SSM because it ignores differences in shipment prices across different suppliers within a month). Not surprisingly, he calculated that an SSM duty would be required in about half of the total months in which import prices inclusive of bound tariffs would be at least 10 per cent lower than domestic prices. The volume SSM would be available in about one-third and effective in one out of every four of these 'problematic' months, provided that the Chair's more flexible rules for breaching the pre-Doha tariff bindings were allowed. Its effectiveness would drop to 2 per cent if pre-Doha starting tariffs could not be exceeded when imposing SSM duties. The price SSM would be less effective. It would be available in only one-quarter of the problematic months and only be effective in remedying the price gap in 6 per cent of these months. The value of trade affected by these measures was not reported.

Finger (2010) provided a different twist on Montemayor's results. He believed that the proposed SSM formulas would provide a poor guide for policy because they would frequently prescribe action when it is not needed and also frequently fail to prescribe action when it was appropriate. Using the results from Montemayor's (2008) simulation exercise, he showed that in more than half of the periods of serious price undercutting the SSM would not have triggered an additional duty, while more than half of the additional duties triggered would not be in periods of serious price undercutting (these were periods when the SSM would be accessible but the month was not problematic). The implicit assumption behind such calculations was that developing countries, if given the opportunity, would always apply a safeguard remedy. This is disputed by SSM proponents who would argue that the limited use made of existing safeguards by those developing countries which in principle had access to them shows that recourse to safeguard duties is likely to be much more limited than these figures suggest (WTO, 2010a).[6]

The second study by De Gorter *et al.* (2009) investigated the frequency of use of both the price-based and volume-based triggers as set out in the December 2008 Draft Modalities for four developing countries (India, China, Korea and Indonesia) based on trade data for 1998–2003. Unlike the Montemayor study, they proxied the shipment-by-shipment basis for the price-based trigger by using bilateral unit values. The price-based safeguard would have been triggered on between 25–33 per cent of all bilateral trade tariff lines. In total 8.6 per cent of trade by value would have been affected. The average remedy would have been equivalent to an additional tariff of around 13 per cent for India and Indonesia (15–17 per cent if the pre-Doha tariff cap were lifted on a limited number of tariff lines). The equivalent figures for China and Korea would have been an average remedy of an additional 2–6 per cent with a cap or 6–10 per cent without a cap. The volume-based safeguard would have been triggered on a far greater value of trade (more than four times as much or more than 40 per cent of total imports), and the additional tariff remedy would have averaged 11–19 per cent allowing for the exceptions to the cap.[7] These results suggest that the proposed safeguards would indeed be of considerable value to developing countries. Whether they would be effective in stabilising domestic markets is not an issue that this chapter set out to answer.

An important finding of this study was that both the volume- and price-based triggers would hit developing country imports to these markets much more than developed countries. This was because the shipment-by-shipment price-based SSM would impose higher duties on exports of relatively lower-priced products, which typically originated in developing countries. Based on the same insight, Finger (2010) calculated that, in a given year, unit values from specific countries were sufficiently below aggregate monthly unit values to trigger restrictions on 59 per cent of agricultural tariff lines regardless of the trend in domestic prices.

The third study by Hertel *et al.* (2010) used a stochastic model of the world wheat market to investigate the stabilising effect of the SSM on domestic prices. Their model again assumed that countries would always use safeguards when the rules allowed these. With this extreme assumption, it is perhaps not surprising that they found that both the quantity-based and price-based safeguards would destabilise domestic producer prices (by restricting imports when domestic output was low and prices were high). In future work as the authors themselves noted, it would be important to consider the actual impacts of safeguard duties on domestic outcomes and not simply mechanically implement the duties provided for under the SSM proposal. However, the difficulty would be that the SSM proposal as drafted leaves huge uncertainty about when and how often it might be used, thereby leaving exporters to entertain their worst fears.

Although the SSM is justified by the need to stabilise domestic markets for poor and vulnerable producers, it does nothing to assist the producers of agricultural exports who are widely exposed to price shocks and have little ability to cope with them. Indeed, it could even make their position worse. If a significant number of developing countries make use of the SSM to protect against depressed world market prices the volatility of world prices will be greater than would otherwise be the case, thus making exporters dependent on these world prices worse off (Hertel *et al.*, 2010). This suggests that eligibility to use the SSM should be confined to the minimum number of developing countries. This is not only for the standard argument about SDT measures that significant exemptions from the normal WTO rules are only likely to be acceptable when the trade-distorting effects are not large. All countries are concerned about price instability, but by definition not all can simultaneously insulate themselves against this. The efficacy of a widely-applicable measure will be eroded if a large number of countries resort to it when international prices are low.

There is also the issue of the vulnerability of low-income consumers to periods of unexpectedly high prices brought about by short conditions on world markets. The importance of this issue has been underlined by the recent spikes in global food prices, which in a number of countries have led to riots and social unrest. A safeguard clause would not address this particular consumer issue; however, to the extent that developing countries continue to have tariff protection they may have the option to lower applied tariffs to offset the impact of unexpectedly high prices on world markets. These limitations do not mean that developing countries should forgo opportunities to stabilise markets for import-competing commodities, but it does suggest the merit of looking for more comprehensive measures that can address the consequences of instability regardless of its source.

V.   CONCLUSIONS

WTO rules constraining the protection developing countries can provide for their agricultural sectors have been a controversial element of the emerging regime governing agricultural trade. Developing countries with largely defensive interests, grouped together within the G-33, have sought maximum flexibility to maintain tariff protection both for use as a development strategy, to promote their food security, and for short-term market stabilisation. To this end they have sought the introduction of SP designation as an additional way to limit tariff reductions in any Doha Round agreement, as well as seeking the introduction of an SSM which would allow additional duties in the event of particularly depressed world prices or a sudden import surge.

These proposals have been accepted in principle by all WTO members. However, the design of these instruments has been among the most difficult issues in the agricultural negotiations. Countries with defensive interests in the negotiations, such as the G-33, fear that a lack of sufficient flexibilities in the current and proposed WTO rules could lead to economic and social disruption if tariffs on sensitive commodities are substantially reduced and if they are prevented from taking action to offset a sudden surge in imports or unusually low world market prices. Countries with offensive interests, including some developing countries, fear that too much flexibility would limit their market access gains and thus their ability to use agricultural exports as a route to greater food security and rural development through raising the per capita incomes of their food-insecure farmers.

The negotiations have been complicated by the very different views adopted regarding the context in which these can take place. For developed country exporters, these limits on market access by developing countries are used to justify holding back on more ambitious offers to reduce tariff peaks or trade-distorting domestic support. Developing countries, on the other hand, perceive the continued high protection for developed country farmers after the AoA as unfair and unreasonable and would argue that SPs and the SSM are merely levelling the playing field and not demands for which they should have to pay in negotiating terms. Indeed, many of the complications in agreeing modalities arise from the fact that the starting point is the historical and uneven pattern of tariff bindings, which are very different even for countries at the same level of development, rather than a more logical structure in which countries' overall tariff bindings reflect objective development criteria. The fact that countries differ over whether the negotiations are intended solely to pursue trade liberalisation or should also provide the opportunity to redress historically uneven entitlements to agricultural protection explains to a large extent the intensity of the disagreement over these issues.

The negotiations have also been complicated by the very different views expressed on what these instruments are intended to achieve. For some countries, mainly but not only developed countries, safeguards have a role in providing some flexibility as countries must undertake a long-run commitment to liberalisation. For the proponents of SPs and the SSM, they are mechanisms to legitimise protection as a permanent feature of the global trade regime. In much of the discourse on the impact of WTO trade rules on food security, there is a presumption that greater policy space is synonymous with greater food security. WTO rules are criticised because they limit the policy space of developing countries, although often without any analysis of the link between policy space and food security. The fact that, increasingly, developing country imports are supplied by developing country exporters is just one pointer to the need for a more balanced discussion. Developing countries now supply more than one-half of all developing country food imports and thus will be most affected by the continued protection of developing country markets.

Of the two instruments reviewed in this chapter, the Draft Modalities on SPs appear to be more settled, although this apparent agreement may be misleading and could simply reflect the negotiators' focus on the SSM and other issues since 2008. The December 2008 Modalities propose that developing countries could self-designate up to 12 per cent of their tariff lines as SPs (13 per cent in the case of SVEs and RAMs), guided by indicators based on the criteria of food security, livelihood security and rural development. This proportion is closer to the G-33 proposal of 20 per cent than to the more restrictive alternatives on the table. Further, a proportion (5 per cent) would be exempt from tariff cuts, although the overall average cut would have to be 11 per cent (10 per cent for SVEs and RAMs). The proposed indicators appear to be so broad that they are unlikely to constrain developing countries in their choice of tariff lines to designate as SPs. Taking into account that the majority of developing countries have a substantial tariff overhang between bound and applied tariffs, and also taking into account the possibility to avoid formula tariff cuts through designating sensitive products, these SP Modalities mean only a few developing countries would be required to reduce applied tariffs as a result of the Doha Round.

The situation with respect to the SSM is different. A 2010 G-33 paper noted that discussions on the SSM have highlighted the gulf that persists in perceptions on the rationale, structure and design of this instrument (WTO, 2010a). The proponents of the SSM want an effective, easy to operate instrument which addresses their development needs. They thus reject the current texts which impose conditions on its use, limiting when it can be invoked and the extent of the remedies. According to the South Centre, which has substantial influence with the G-33, 'Developing country proposals have become so drastically watered down during the horsetrading of negotiations that the mechanism would be practically useless to developing countries if the current draft negotiating texts (December 2008) are agreed upon' (South Centre, 2009c: 1).

However, for a successful outcome the SSM Modalities must be acceptable to agricultural exporters as well as to importers. The previous analysis indicated some possible room for compromise. Applying the existing Draft Modalities, and particularly the volume-based SSM, would seem potentially to expose a high proportion of trade with developing countries to the risk of supplementary safeguard duties. SSM proponents protest that, in practice, developing countries are unlikely to use more than a fraction of these opportunities. Indeed, it is clear that many so-called import surges contribute to food availability when domestic production suffers a setback. But an agreement cannot be based on such vague uncertainty. If, indeed, SSM proponents envisage using the mechanism on relatively few occasions, then there would seem to be scope to construct rules which could clarify when these occasions would occur. Whether these rules would involve limits on the number of tariff lines for which the SSM could be invoked at any one time, more rigorous trigger conditions or a strengthened cross-check condition would be for negotiators to decide.

The SSM would allow developing countries to impose tariffs which would breach their post-Doha tariff bindings. A second nettle which must be grasped here is the circumstances in which pre-Doha Round bound tariffs could be exceeded. The reason why this is such an issue is because of the huge variability in bound tariffs between developing countries, depending in part on the choices they made at the conclusion of the Uruguay Round negotiations in 1994 or the timing of their subsequent accession. Those countries which opted for ceiling bindings in 1994 often have high bound tariffs, while RAMs were required to offer much lower bound rates. The remedies available to the latter group if the pre-Doha bound tariff is retained as a cap are severely curtailed. When additional SSM duties are tied to bound tariffs as in the December 2008 Modalities, countries with low pre-Doha bound tariffs would very frequently exceed these tariffs with the SSM. This would automatically be the case for all countries which designated SPs with the zero tariff cut option. These products would not be eligible for the volume SSM remedy under the December 2008 Draft Modalities because there would be no difference between bound and pre-Doha starting tariffs in any year. However, the bigger problem is China. Some countries see removing the pre-Doha cap as allowing China to reverse the disciplines it accepted when it became a WTO member. But not allowing China to exceed its bound tariff level would effectively eliminate its use of the SSM altogether. This issue needs to be addressed as part of a successful outcome, possibly by varying the number of tariff lines for which the pre-Doha ceilings could be breached according to the size of the bound MFN tariff.

This chapter takes the view that developing countries do not require a permanent exception to WTO market access rules in order to promote their food security, livelihood security and rural development goals. By far the more important issue to address in that context is the continued under-investment in agricultural production, infrastructure and institutions by both developing countries themselves and donors. WTO disciplines do not constrain such investments in any way. If safeguards are justified as permitting temporary protection from import surges above and beyond that provided by their tariff schedules, then the compromise proposal of Hufbauer and Adler (2008) is worth considering. In their proposal, consistent with the spirit of progressive liberalisation, trigger levels would initially be set at a low level and then gradually raised while remedies would be set at a high level and then gradually lowered. What is distinctive in their proposal is that the phasing-out of the safeguard would take place at different rates for different country groupings. They distinguish between four country groupings on the basis of their 'need' for safeguard remedies (least developed countries, small and vulnerable economies, recently acceded members, and other developing countries). Setting a sufficiently long period for such a phasing-out might provide importing countries with the comfort they are seeking while also reassuring exporters that liberalisation would occur (in this context, if the Doha Draft Modalities came into force in 2013, the SSG would be available to those countries, mainly developed countries, that would have access to it for 25 years). In any case, over the next two decades, it seems likely that developing countries will find agricultural shortfalls and rising food prices more painful than gluts and falling food prices.

NOTES

I am grateful to the editors of this volume and to Jonathan Hepburn for helpful comments on earlier drafts but the views expressed and any remaining errors are my responsibility.

1.   The G-33 now has 46 members. The full membership can be found on the WTO website at http://www.wto.org/english/tratop_e/agric_e/negoti_groups_e.htm
2.   There are different definitions of what is meant by agricultural trade. A relatively restricted definition is used in this section, referred to as Basic Food in UNCTADStat, and defined as SITC Sections 0, 22 and 4. Excluded from this definition are beverages and tobacco (SITC Section 1) as well as agricultural raw materials in SITC sections 2 less 22, 27 and 28. The overall trends described for basic food also hold for a wider definition of agri-food products.
3.   This is not a new observation. A WTO Secretariat note on agricultural trade performance by developing countries observed that South/South trade, as a share of developing countries' total agricultural export trade, increased from 32 to 46 per cent over the 1990-2003 period (WTO, 2005f). Their analysis was confined to goods covered by the AoA.
4.   A list of the countries in these two groups is also given in the WTO internet page referenced in endnote 2.
5.   These proposals built on the Lamy package proposed on 25 July 2008 and the G-33 response on 27 July 2008. The Lamy package allowed for a volume-based remedy that exceeded pre-Doha bound rates when import volumes were 40 per cent above a three-year rolling average. Developing countries could then impose remedies that were 15 percentage points or 15 per cent of the current bound tariff, whichever was higher, on up to 2.5 per cent of tariff lines. The G-33 proposal would allow safeguard duties to exceed bound rates when import volumes were 10 per cent greater than the three-year rolling average. With this proviso, safeguard duties could be up to 30 percentage points or 30 per cent of the bound tariff, for up to 7 per cent of tariff lines. See WTO (2008c) for a discussion of these proposals.
6.   Hertel *et al.* (2010) discuss some of the reasons why developing countries do not use agricultural safeguards to which they are otherwise entitled.
7.   The average remedies quoted in this paragraph are simple averages. The weighted average remedies would be slightly lower under the price-based trigger but considerably higher under the volume-based trigger. Hertel *et al.* (2010) in their simulation of the use of the SSM in the world wheat market also conclude that the quantity-based safeguard is an order of magnitude more damaging to world trade than the price-based safeguard.

BIBLIOGRAPHY

ActionAid International (2008) *Impact of Agro-Import Surges in Developing Countries*, South Africa.

Anderson, K. and Martin, W. (2005) 'Agricultural Trade Reform and the Doha Development Agenda', *World Economy,* **28** (9): 1301–1327.

Bernabe, R. (2008) *Treatment of Special Products: Implications of the Chair's May 2008 Draft Modalities Text,* ICTSD Project on Special Products and a Special Safeguard Mechanism, Issue Paper No.14, International Centre for Trade and Sustainable Development, Geneva, Switzerland.

Bernal, L. (2005) *Methodology for the Identification of Special Products (SP) and Products for Eligibility Under the Special Safeguard Mechanism (SSM) by Developing Countries,* International Centre for Trade and Sustainable Development, Geneva, Switzerland.

Bouët, A. (2006) *What Can the Poor Expect from Trade Liberalization? Opening the 'Black Box' of Trade Modeling,* MTID Discussion Paper No. 93, Washington, DC, International Food Policy Research Institute.

De Gorter, H., Kliauga, E. and Nassar, A. (2009) *How Current Proposals on the SSM in the Doha Round Matter for Developing Country Exporters,* Institute for International Trade Negotiations.

De Nigris, M. (2005) *Defining and Quantifying the Extent of Import Surges: Data and Methodologies,* FAO Import Surge Project Working Paper No. 2, Rome.

De Schutter, O. (2009) *Report of the Special Rapporteur on the Right to Food, Mission to the World Trade Organization,* presented to the Human Rights Council in March (UN doc. A/HRC/10/005/Add.2), New York.

Diaz-Bonilla, E. and Ron, J. (2010) *Food Security, Price Volatility and Trade,* ICTSD Programme on Agricultural Trade and Sustainable Development, International Centre for Trade and Sustainable Development, Geneva, Switzerland.

FAO (2003) *Some Trade Policy Issues Relating to Trends in Agricultural Imports in The Context of Food Security,* CCP 03/10, Committee on Commodity Problems, Sixty-fourth Session, Rome, 18–21 March, available at http://www.fao.org/docrep/meeting/005/Y8319e/Y8319e00.htm (accessed 14 May 2011).

FAO (2007a) *Indicators for the Selection of Agricultural Special Products: Some Empirical Evidence, FAO Trade Policy Briefs on Issues related to the WTO Negotiations on Agriculture* No. 15, Rome, Food and Agriculture Organization.

FAO (2007b) *Import Surges: Analysis, Preliminary Findings and Lessons Learned, Committee on Commodity Problems,* Sixty-sixth Session, CCP 07/11, Rome.

Finger M. (2010) 'A Special Safeguard Mechanism for Agricultural Imports: What experience with other GATT/WTO safeguards tells us about what might work', *World Trade Review,* **9** (2): 289–318.

Ford, J. R. D., Koroma, S., Yanoma, Y. and Khaira, H. (2006) 'Identifying 'Special Products' – Developing Country Flexibility in the Doha Round', in FAO, *Commodity Market Review 2005–2006,* Rome.

Ford, J. R. D., Koroma, S., Yanoma, Y. and Khaira, H. (2007) 'Special Products: A comprehensive approach to identification and treatment for development' in J. Morrison and A. Sarris. (eds), *WTO Rules for Agriculture Compatible with Development,* Rome, FAO.

Gifford, M. and Montemayor, R. (2008) *An Overview Assessment of the Revised Draft WTO Modalities for Agriculture,* International Centre on Trade and Sustainable Development, Geneva, Switzerland.

Gillon & Associates (2008) *Special Products Exemption Sharply Reduces Market Access Gains,* Doha Round Discussion Paper, available at http://www.farmpolicyfacts.org/word/08Special_Products_Lamy_Nov08.pdf (accessed 14 May 2011).

Gonzalez, C. (2002) 'Institutionalizing Inequality: The WTO Agreement on Agriculture, Food Security, and Developing Countries', *Columbia Journal of Environmental Law,* **27** (2): 431–487.

Hertel, T., Martin, W. and Leister, A. (2010) 'Potential Implications of a Special Safeguard Mechanism in the World Trade Organization: The case of wheat', *World Bank Economic Review,* **24** (2): 330–359.

Hufbauer, G. and Adler, M. (2008) *The Special Safeguard Mechanism: Possible Solutions to the Impasse*, note prepared for the World Bank, 28 October, available at http://ictsd.org/downloads/2008/11/ssm-paper-oct282-with-tables.pdf (accessed 14 May 2011).

ICTSD (2006) 'Falconer Paper On Special Products Splits G-33, Farm Exporters', *Bridges Weekly Trade News Digest*, **10** (16): 10 May.

ICTSD (2007) *Indicators for the Selection of Agricultural Special Products: Some Empirical Evidence*, Information Note, Number 1, July, Geneva.

ICTSD (2008) *Implications of the Chair's May 2008 Draft Modalities for Agricultural Special Products*, Information Note Number 7, Geneva.

ICTSD (2010) 'Special Safeguard Mechanism Could "Seriously Impede" Normal Farm Trade, Say Exporters', *Bridges Weekly Trade News Digest*, **14** (19): 26 May.

IFPRI (2002) 'Thinking Inside the Boxes', *IFPRI Perspectives*, **25**: August, Washington, DC, International Food Policy Research Institute.

Ingco, M. (1995) *Agricultural Trade Liberalization in the Uruguay Round: One Step Forward, One Step Back?,* Policy Research Working Paper 1500, Washington, DC, World Bank.

Ivanic, M. and Martin, W. (2006) *Potential Implications of Agricultural Special Products for Poverty in Low-Income Countries.* Washington, DC: World Bank (mimeo), available at http://www.tradeobservatory.org/library.cfm?refID = 89834 (accessed 14 May 2011).

Ivanic, M. and Martin, W. (2008) 'Implications of Higher Global Food Prices for Poverty in Low-income Countries', *Agricultural Economics,* **39**: 405–416.

Jales, M. (2005) *Tariff Reduction, Special Products and Special Safeguards: An Analysis of the Agricultural Tariff Structures of G-33 Countries*, International Centre for Trade and Sustainable Development, Geneva, Switzerland.

Mably, P. (2009) 'Centralized Production: The Group of 33', in D. Tussie (ed), *The Politics of Trade: The Role of Research in Trade Policy and Negotiation*, Boston: Republic of Letters Publishing.

Montemayor, R. (2007) *Implications of Proposed Modalities for the Special Safeguard Mechanism: A Simulation Exercise,* ICTSD Agricultural Trade and Sustainable Development Series, Issue Paper 10, International Centre for Trade and Sustainable Development, Geneva, Switzerland.

Montemayor, R. (2008), *How Will the May 2008 'Modalities' Text Affect Access to the Special Safeguard Mechanism, and the Effectiveness of Additional Safeguard Duties?* International Centre for Trade and Sustainable Development, Geneva, Switzerland.

Montemayor, R. (2010) *Simulations on the Special Safeguard Mechanism: A Look at the December 2008 Draft Agriculture Modalities*, ICTSD Programme on Agricultural Trade and Sustainable Development Issue Paper No.25, International Centre for Trade and Sustainable Development, Geneva, Switzerland.

Sharma, R. (2005) *Overview of Reported Cases of Import Surges from the Standpoint of Analytical Content*, FAO Import Surge Project Working Paper No. 1, Rome, Food and Agriculture Organization.

South Centre (2009a) *The Extent of Agriculture Import Surges in Developing Countries: What are the Trends?* Analytical Note SC/TDP/AN/AG/8, Geneva.

South Centre (2009b) *The Volume-based Special Safeguard Mechanism (SSM): Analysis of the Conditionalities in the December 2008 WTO Agriculture Chair's Texts* , Analytical Note SC/TDP/AN/AG/9, Geneva.

South Centre (2009c) *The Proposed Special Safeguard Mechanism (SSM) in the WTO: Is it still 'Special'?,* Policy Brief (draft), Geneva.

Valdés, A. and Foster, W. (2005) *The New SSM: A Price Floor Mechanism for Developing Countries*, International Centre for Trade and Sustainable Development, Information Note No. 7, April.

Wolfe, R. (2009) 'The special safeguard fiasco in the WTO: the perils of inadequate analysis and negotiation' *World Trade Review,* **8** (4): 517–544.

WTO (2000) *Proposal to the June 2000 Special Session of the Committee on Agriculture* by Cuba, Dominican Republic, Honduras, Pakistan, Haiti, Nicaragua, Kenya, Uganda, Zimbabwe, Sri Lanka and El Salvador, Committee on Agriculture Special Session, G/AG/NG/W/13, 23 June, Geneva.

WTO (2001) *Ministerial Declaration adopted on 14 November 2001*, Ministerial Conference Fourth Session Doha, 9–14 November, WT/MIN(01)/DEC/1, 20 November 2001, Geneva.

WTO (2004) *Doha Work Programme, Decision Adopted by the General Council on 1 August*, WT/L/579, Geneva.

WTO (2005a) *Doha Work Programme, Ministerial Declaration adopted on 18 December 2005*, WT/MIN(05)/DEC, Geneva.

WTO (2005b) *G-33 Proposal on the Modalities for the Designation and Treatment of any Agricultural Product as a Special Product by any Developing Country Member*, WTO JOB (05)/304, 22 November, Geneva.

WTO (2005c) *G-33 Communication on Special Products*, WTO JOB(05)/230, 12 October, Geneva.

WTO (2005d) *G-33 Proposal on Special Products*, WTO JOB(05)/ 91, 3 June, Geneva.

WTO (2005e) *G-33 Proposal on Special Safeguard Measures*, WTO JOB(05)/ 92, 3 June, Geneva.

WTO (2005f) *Agricultural Trade Performance of Developing Countries 1990-2003*, TN/AG/S/19, Geneva.

WTO (2006a) *Chairman's Reference Paper on Special Products*, Committee on Agriculture, Special Session Market Access, 4 May, Geneva.

WTO (2006b) Draft Possible Modalities on Agriculture, Committee on Agriculture Special Session, TN/AG/W/3 12 July 2006, Geneva.

WTO (2006c) Revised Consolidated Reference Paper on Possible Modalities on Market Access – SSM: Some Unanswered Technical Issues [Argentina, Paraguay and Uruguay], Committee on Agriculture, Special Session, JOB(06)/197/Rev.1, 21 June 2006, Geneva.

WTO (2008a) Draft Possible Modalities on Agriculture, Committee on Agriculture Special Session, TN/AG/W/4/Rev.1 8 February 2008, Geneva.

WTO (2008b) Draft Possible Modalities on Agriculture, Committee on Agriculture Special Session, TN/AG/W/4/Rev.4 6 December 2008, Geneva.

WTO (2008c) An Unofficial Guide to Agricultural Safeguards, http://www.**wto**.org/english/tratop_e/agric_e/ssm_explained_4aug08_e.doc, corrected 5 August 2008, accessed 14 May 2011.

WTO (2008d) Revised Draft Modalities For Agriculture Special Safeguard Mechanism, Committee on Agriculture Special Session, TN/AG/W/7, 6 December 2008, Geneva.

WTO (2010a) G-33 Submission on Refocusing Discussions on the Special Safeguard Mechanism (SSM): Outstanding Issues and Concerns on its Design and Structure, Committee on Agriculture Special Session, TN/AG/GEN/30, 28 January 2010, Geneva.

WTO (2010b) G-33 Communication on Issues and Concerns on the Price-Based Special Safeguard Mechanism: Some Analysis and Technical Contributions for the Design and Structure, Committee on Agriculture Special Session JOB/AG/5, Geneva.

WTO (2010bc) G-33 Submission on the SSM: Seasonality, Committee on Agriculture Special Session, JOB/AG/4 5 February 2010, Geneva.

WTO (2010d) G-33 Submission on the SSM: Price and Volume Cross-Check Conditionalities, Committee on Agriculture Special Session, JOB/AG/3 5 February 2010, Geneva.

WTO (2011) Negotiating Group on Agriculture, Report by the Chairman, H.E. Mr. David Walker, to the Trade Negotiations Committee, TN/AG/26, 21 April 2011, Geneva.

5 Plant intellectual property, food security and human development: institutional and legal considerations, and the need for reform
Graham Dutfield

I. INTRODUCTION

Plant variety protection (PVP) is a type of intellectual property right, like patents, copyright and trademarks. As an intellectual property right specifically for protecting new plant varieties, PVP has important implications for crop improvement. But its significance goes far beyond this. PVP relates also to agricultural and food policy, food security, rural development, biodiversity and genetic resource conservation, and human rights. To date, the only PVP system with international recognition is the one defined under the International Convention for the Protection of New Varieties of Plants whose contracting parties form an association known in the original French as the *Union pour la Protection des Obtentions Végétales* (UPOV). Officially, UPOV's mission is 'to provide and promote an effective system of plant variety protection, with the aim of encouraging the development of new varieties of plants, for the benefit of society'. UPOV is legally separate from, but has a close relationship with, the World Intellectual Property Organization (WIPO) which houses the secretariat (the UPOV Office) in its Geneva headquarters.

UPOV started off as very much a West European club. The Convention was largely conceived and designed by and for European breeding interests in a way that balanced these interests with those of farmers. Agriculture ministries were also involved. In its early years the Convention applied exclusively to European countries. These same European breeding interests continue to be intimately involved in the operations of the Convention and of the Union and have also played important roles in encouraging more and more countries to join UPOV. By the end of 1995, the year that the World Trade Organization (WTO) was established, there were still only 29 members, mostly developed countries. However, many developing countries are now members of the Union and parties to the Convention. Today,

UPOV has 68 members including the European Union (EU) with the majority of the membership now comprising developing countries or former communist nations. The Convention was last revised in 1991 and there are no plans for further revisions. Consequently this quite radical change in the membership profile has had no effect on the text, which continues to be one that has been designed primarily by and for plant breeders.

Who needs plant intellectual property anyway? Crop improvement has gone on for at least 10,000 years and almost entirely before there had ever been patents or plant variety protection and when open access regimes are assumed to have been the norm.[1] Even the advent of scientific breeding methods, which has dramatically increased the pace of crop improvement, preceded the availability of plant intellectual property. Thus, this is a perfectly reasonable question to pose. Advocates of intellectual property rights over plant varieties claim that such legal protection can contribute to food security and to the transfer of high-value and high-yielding field and horticultural varieties, including fruits, vegetables and ornamentals.

UPOV is in fact only one element of a genetic resource property 'regime complex' that includes a number of instruments and thus cannot be considered in total isolation. The World Trade Organization's (WTO) Agreement on Trade-related Aspects of Intellectual Property Rights (TRIPS) requires Member states to provide 'effective intellectual property protection for plant varieties'. The WTO allows governments a significant amount of choice in how they put this requirement into effect: TRIPS negotiators elected *not* to mention the UPOV Convention, allowing for possibilities other than joining UPOV. WTO Members may extend patent protection to cover plant varieties and provide no other form of intellectual property protection (Dutfield *et al.*, 2010: 540–588). Alternatively, they may choose to keep conventional plant breeding out of the patent system, as in Europe. In the latter case, though, TRIPS requires a specific ('*sui generis*') intellectual property regime for plant varieties. Another important agreement is the FAO International Treaty on Plant Genetic Resources for Food and Agriculture, which contains important provisions relating to the rights of farmers that should be taken into account when governments draw up their PVP rules. The Convention on Biological Diversity (CBD) is also important. The CBD requires that access to genetic resources be conducted on the basis of terms that have been mutually agreed between the user and authorities representing the provider country and that benefits arising from their use should be shared fairly and equitably. Similar requirements apply to the knowledge, innovations and practices of indigenous and local communities embodying traditional lifestyles.

This chapter makes no effort to assess the evidence for or against intellectual property and offers no new empirical evidence to what others have provided (Jaffé and van Wijk, 1995; Louwaars *et al.*, 2005; UPOV, 2005). What it does consider is whether it is safe to assume automatically that the UPOV system is ideal for all countries of the world whose conditions vary considerably, and what policy and diplomatic implications arise from the likelihood that it is *not* the most optimal legal system for all countries in all circumstances that could be conceived of. History tells us that national or regional patent and copyright rules and regulations should ideally be carefully designed and tailored to the specific conditions of each country or region (Dutfield and Suthersanen, 2005). The same is likely to be true for other intellectual property rights. Arguably, the UPOV Convention provides little scope for this and the situation is likely to be exacerbated by the expansion of patentability into plant-related subject matter.

An ideal plant variety intellectual property regime needs to provide incentives and attract research investment in at least two directions: first, and most importantly, towards supporting breeding targeted towards the nutritional needs of the whole populace without unduly disrupting existing traditions and farming systems; secondly, to support the development of non-food or luxury food crops for sale on national and international markets that can generate wealth which to the greatest extent possible is captured at local and national levels. How far is the UPOV system able to support such aspirations? It would go too far to suggest that to design legal regimes capable of promoting both these goals in an optimal fashion is impossible. However, we must remember that the UPOV Convention is detailed and substantive to the extent that compatible PVP regimes must unavoidably be very similar. Accordingly, there are reasonable concerns that the UPOV system fails to provide sufficient flexibilities for developing countries to fashion optimal PVP regimes that will accommodate their own plant improvement needs which are likely to vary quite widely. Unfortunately, the Union and its institutional set-up appear to inhibit debate on appropriate rules for an increasingly diverse membership that includes developed, developing, and least-developed countries. Indeed, there is evidence to suggest a lack of transparency and accountability in the way the Union operates.

Even in Europe the benefits of plant intellectual property should not entirely be taken for granted, especially given that patenting and PVP are both available for plant innovation there and may not operate together in a harmonious fashion. A recent study by Louwaars *et al.* (2009: 56) is broadly uncritical regarding the effects of PVP *in the European context*, stating that PVP 'makes a positive contribution to innovation and hardly causes restrictions'. But it does raise concerns about the dangers of patents (i) accelerating corporate concentration with few new market entrants to counter this; (ii) encouraging strategic behaviour contrary to the public interest; and (iii) restricting access to breeding material and eliminating farmers' privilege, thereby undermining the effective workings of PVP. It is noteworthy that this study was conducted in the Netherlands, which has had long experience of providing intellectual property protection for plant varieties, has resident breeding institutions that are major users of foreign PVP systems and thus benefit from the globalization of UPOV's norms, and that as a European Union member state is subject to rules that to some extent at least have sought to maintain a separate but cooperative relationship between the patent and PVP systems.

The existence of the UPOV system does not preclude non-UPOV members adopting other PVP regimes as long as these are 'effective' according to Article 27.3(b) of the TRIPS Agreement. But while some non-UPOV *sui generis* systems have been established in recent years (e.g. in India and Thailand) developing countries are more often opting for UPOV membership than exploring other approaches. Frequently, developing countries agree to apply for UPOV membership – or adopt UPOV 1991 compatible legislation – in their trade agreements with the United States, the European Union, Japan and the European Free Trade Association. The decision to do this is part of the 'price' to be paid for enhanced access for other goods to developed world markets. Given the increasing competition among developing countries to access these markets, meaning the share of access is spread among more and more countries (or a few dominant ones like China), it is uncertain as to whether this price is worth paying. In addition, technical assistance programmes funded or implemented by agencies representing or influenced by commercial breeders can result in PVP rules that may comply with the latest version of the UPOV Convention but are in no way tailored to the local conditions. Unfortunately, the direct recipients of technical assistance are sometimes inclined unquestioningly to accept advice, financial assistance and technical resources, and to adopt legal texts and regulations drawn up by their providers. Institutions responsible for administering PVP rules must be transparent in how they operate and democratically accountable. They should also seek a diversity of views. All stakeholders and interested parties should have a say in how the relevant institutions are run, including UPOV. This chapter argues that UPOV urgently needs institutional reforms in this respect and suggests some measures to achieve positive change.

II. PLANT INNOVATION AND INTELLECTUAL PROPERTY

The hyper-abundance of food products in the developed world and the reduction of mass poverty in a few developing countries are largely attributable to modern agriculture. Concerns about overconsumption should not be used to gainsay this important point. Despite its potential for huge social welfare enhancement, generating revenues from plant breeding is a challenge. For varieties that *breed true*, meaning they have consistent traits that persist generation by generation, farmers and even amateur gardeners can save, clean and replant or sell seeds. Asexually-reproducing species can be mass-copied through techniques such as cutting and grafting. In response, technology, intellectual property and utilizing contract law through the use of licences that purchasers must agree to (which may be more restrictive than PVP rules) may be deployed so that breeders can derive revenue from the plant varieties they have developed.

Plant innovation is inherently cumulative, based on incremental improvements on what already exists. Much of what exists goes back thousands of years and has generally been freely available for everyone's benefit. Admittedly, modern field-crop breeders are not usually reliant on traditional crop varieties (or 'landraces' as they are commonly referred to) on an everyday basis, except when they are starting up new breeding programmes. Even then this reliance is likely to diminish over time as they focus ever more on the recycling of modern varieties.[2] However, local landraces and the wild relatives of crops continue to be extremely important for breeding crop species in order to integrate new traits or new variants of known traits (e.g. disease resistance). Global food security can be enhanced by encouraging their use and also by ensuring that access to them be kept open, subject to the rules and principles of the FAO International Treaty on Plant Genetic Resources for Food and Agriculture, which establishes a multilateral system of access to plant genetic resources but respects national sovereignty and requires benefit sharing. The Treaty also provides certain safeguards for the rights of farmers.

So what of innovation in traditional agricultural systems, which persist in vast areas of the inhabited world, especially in the developing countries? It may well be true that these systems alone will never support today's global population of which more than half is urban dwelling, and that modern intensive agriculture based on high yielding varieties and large doses of chemical inputs is vital. Nonetheless, they should not be disparaged. So-called 'traditional farmers' can also be highly innovative in the face of fluctuating and unpredictable environmental conditions. Indeed, not all landraces are ancient; neither are they all 'traditional': sometimes there is cross-breeding with modern varieties (Kingsbury, 2009: 50). Anthropologist Paul Richards (1999: 315–316) explains, for example, how Mende farming communities in Sierra Leone continue effectively to manage agricultural genetic diversity, experiment on-farm with traditional *and modern* rice varieties and to produce their own varieties whose performance is often better than those provided by extension services.

There are very good reasons why such innovation should be allowed to persist and not be interfered with by inappropriate and monopolistic intellectual property laws and seed regulations. The intellectual property laws may have this effect if they narrow or eliminate the privilege of farmers to replant and exchange saved seed. Seed regulations may do so if they require that the only cultivated varieties sown by farmers be those on an official seed list and that landraces be mainly or entirely excluded from it for failing to meet strict, inflexible criteria. Unfortunately, in many parts of the world, workable local agricultural systems have been modified and distorted and thereby rendered ineffective (Brokensha, 1999: 309–312). One should not be romantic about traditional agriculture, if for no other reason than that many of these systems have been degraded through no fault of the local people themselves and no longer function as they did. Population increases, the spread of market economies with the introduction of export crops and Green Revolution technologies, all-too-prevalent assumptions that Western techniques and methods such as high-input monocultural agriculture are superior to local ones like intercropping, the imposition of inappropriate laws and regulations by governments, and war, are all factors in this.

Nonetheless, original agricultural systems are intact in many areas of the world. Moreover, some good results have been achieved by reviving the use of traditional crop species and introducing modern post-harvesting technologies that ironically can enhance the viability of 'old' varieties and species for the benefit of farmers and consumers (Cruz, 2004: 16–17). Clearly, we should not throw the baby out with the bathwater. On the other hand, some countries rely heavily on cultivating and exporting non-traditional crops and their produce. For example, Kenya greatly depends on the trade in tea, coffee, and horticultural produce including vegetables and cut flowers. These products are extremely important not just as sources of foreign exchange but also for employment and an income for rural people. Ornamental varieties are normally bred in Europe and the breeding firms may be insistent that these must be intellectual property protected in the developing country where they are planted and from where they are exported. Argentina and Brazil are also large exporters of agricultural produce such as soybean, wheat and coffee. Nonetheless, the interaction of traditional knowledge with agricultural techniques applied to local *or exotic* crops is fertile ground for innovation.

III. ORIGINS AND EVOLUTION OF THE UPOV CONVENTION

Before the 1960s intellectual property protection of plant varieties was uncommon. With very few national regimes European breeder associations were instrumental in UPOV's existence. Two organizations were deeply involved in the creation of the UPOV Convention: (i) the International Association for the Protection of Intellectual Property (AIPPI), which largely comprises lawyers with a pro-industry stance; and (ii) the International Association of Plant Breeders (ASSINSEL), the forerunner to today's International Seed Federation. Both took the strategic view that the lack of intellectual property norms specifically for plants needed to be resolved internationally.

In 1956, ASSINSEL's members called for a conference to consider the possibility of developing a new international instrument for protecting plant varieties and requested that the French government organize this (Heitz, 1987). That conference established the basic principles of plant variety protection as were later incorporated into the UPOV Convention. There were few existing models for drawing up a PVP system. However, it appears that the drafting of the Convention did draw in part on the German Law of 27 June 1953 on the Protection of Varieties and the Seeds of Cultivated Plants. This law offered legal protection for 'useful' new varieties that were 'individualised' (read: distinct) and 'stable' (Heitz, 1987). In turn this law was derived from non-intellectual property seed regulations. As explained by plant breeder Gregory Sage (2002), these 'began as consumer protection regulations specifying aspects such as germination capacity, freedom from disease, levels of admixture and trueness to type'. Indeed legally separate but complementary seed regulations continue to exist alongside PVP in many parts of the world and in some cases these require commercial farmers to use only registered seed.

Only European governments were invited, mainly the representatives of agriculture ministries. These agreed to set up a committee to draft the convention. A follow-up conference – in which 12 European countries participated – took place in November 1961. The *Bureaux Internationaux Réunis de la Protection de la Propriété Intellectuelle* (BIRPI), which subsequently became WIPO's International Bureau, and the Food and Agriculture Organization of the United Nations, attended as observers. AIPPI and several industry organisations participated: ASSINSEL, the *Communauté Internationale des Obtenteurs de Plantes Ornementales et fruitières de Reproduction Asexuée* (CIOPORA), and the *Fédération Internationale du Commerce des Semences* (FIS).[3] All of these were and remain organizations that headquartered in Europe.

The International Convention for the Protection of New Varieties of Plants was adopted in December 1961, coming into force in 1968 once it had been ratified by three countries which then formed the Union. It took so long to come into force as few countries already had PVP systems and ratification required a national PVP system already to be in place, as it still does. UPOV was revised in 1972, 1978, and 1991. The latter revision came into force in 1998. The Convention's provisions are extremely detailed and specific (Dutfield, 2008). *This point cannot be stressed strongly enough.* To be eligible for protection, plant varieties must be novel, distinct, uniform[4] and stable (the 'DUS criteria'). To be **novel**, the variety must not have been offered for sale or marketed, or if it has, it should not have been for a certain limited period according to the type of plant. To be **distinct**, the variety must be distinguishable by one or more characteristics from any other variety whose existence is a matter of common knowledge. To be considered as **stable**, the variety must remain true to its description after repeated reproduction or propagation. Unlike patents there is no disclosure requirement. Generally, applicants are required to submit the plant material, which may be used by a government institution (or a private institution authorized by the government to conduct this role) to demonstrate stability and homogeneity through planting trials, also known as 'DUS examinations'.

Some countries undertake no DUS examinations and benefit from the exchange of examination results among UPOV members. The Office of UPOV hopes this will become easier once there is a full harmonisation of examination procedures at the various national and regional PVP offices. It is by no means a simple matter for a country to set up a PVP system from scratch including running the field trials. The technical assistance available from the UPOV system may therefore be quite useful, although there are reasonable concerns that this harmonisation contributes to a creeping PVP rule uniformity that may not suit many developing countries. As with other intellectual property rights PVP defines the scope of protection. UPOV sets out the breeder's rights to authorize various acts in relation to the PVP-protected variety, such as production, reproduction, offering for sale, marketing, importing, and exporting. UPOV 1991 further extends the scope of the breeders' rights in certain ways including in respect of harvested material. However, the right of breeders both to use protected varieties as an initial source of variation for the creation of new varieties and to market these varieties without authorisation from the original breeder (the 'breeders' exemption') is upheld in both versions. In addition, in order to respond to new scientific developments UPOV 1991 extends rights to varieties which are *essentially derived* from the protected variety, meaning ones that have been subjected only to minor modifications such as through genetic engineering.

There is reference in UPOV 1978 to the right of farmers to use seed harvested from protected varieties for private and non-commercial purposes (often referred to as 'farmers' privilege' or 'farmers' rights'). Most parties to the UPOV 1978 uphold this right. UPOV 1991 upholds farmers' rights in that it specifies the breeder's right in relation to a variety may be restricted 'in order to permit farmers to use for propagating purposes, on their own holdings, the product of the harvest which they have obtained by planting ... the protected variety'. However under Article 15(2) of UPOV 1991, the state party must take necessary measures to safeguard 'the legitimate interests of the breeder'. Implicitly, the European Union, through its Regulation 2100/94 on Community Plant Variety Rights, links this requirement to Article 17(2) of UPOV 1991 so that safeguarding these interests entails ensuring 'that the breeder receives equitable remuneration'.[5] At present the strength of the 'farmers' privilege' varies quite widely. France has no farmers' privilege at all with the exception of tender wheat, while the USA until the 1990s allowed farmers even to sell protected seed to other farmers. The French approach is uncommon, though. Louwaars (2006) sums up the key changes introduced in UPOV 1991:

- the restriction of the farmers' privilege to the saving of seed of a restricted number of crops 'taking into account the interest of the breeder' instead of a broad interpretation of the 'non-commercial use' article. This outlaws the exchange of seed of protected varieties among farmers;

• a slight limitation of the breeder's exemption which allows for rights that go beyond the limits of an individual variety (but avoid the large-scale stacking of rights in the patent system) in the case of 'essentially derived varieties';

• possibilities to claim rights on the harvested product when the breeder has not had a reasonable opportunity to claim rights (read: royalties) on the harvested product, which deals with what is called 'parallel imports' in the patent systems.

While PVP is assumed to provide a weaker monopoly than do patents, one could also argue the opposite. TRIPS Article 28 lists five acts by third parties in relation to a patent that require the holder's authorisation: making, using, offering for sale, selling, or importing. The UPOV 1991 list of acts requiring such authorisation includes not just importing but also exporting. Thus, in the early 1990s, Argentinean strawberry plant growers could not export their plantlets to Europe because foreign PVP-holding licensees did not want these plantlets to compete with plants already produced in Europe.

IV. INSTITUTIONAL ASPECTS

UPOV is legally separate from WIPO, and is not part of the United Nations. Despite UPOV's formal distance from WIPO, the two have a close relationship. The UPOV Office is located in the WIPO building in Geneva, where UPOV meetings are also held. WIPO services the Office. And by formal agreement, the Director-General is the Secretary-General of UPOV with the power to approve the appointment of the Vice Secretary-General. The latter oversees the day-to-day operations of UPOV. It seems worthwhile, and arguably necessary, to open a debate as to the appropriateness of the head of a United Nations agency at the same time also leading a non-UN agency operating in such a commercially sensitive and strategic area.

The present relationship between WIPO and UPOV is defined by the 1982 WIPO/UPOV Agreement (UPOV, 1982a). Much of the Agreement concerns the various administrative and practical tasks that WIPO must undertake for UPOV. These are not free of charge: UPOV is required to pay WIPO 'for any service rendered to, and any expenditure incurred on behalf of, UPOV'. Article 3 affirms the 'complete independence' of WIPO's International Bureau and the UPOV Office in respect of the exercise of their functions. What is behind this legal independence from WIPO despite their having such a close and *practically dependent* relationship? Going back in time, UPOV was not unanimously welcomed. AIPPI, though by no means opposed to PVP, was especially firm in its criticisms of the Convention and the formation of UPOV, and expressed a preference for incorporating PVP rules within the Paris Convention for the Protection of Industrial Property, now administered by WIPO and previously by BIRPI (UPOV, 1974).

The Office of UPOV is very small with a current full-time staff of 11 people of whom about half are involved in the substantive technical work of the Union. This small group consists of people with backgrounds in such fields as agricultural economics, agronomy, plant breeding and law. The highest body within the UPOV system is the Council, which comprises one representative of each of the Member states and has an elected President and Vice-President. Regular sessions of the Council take place once a year, but in recent years the Council has tended to meet twice, once in October and then again in March or April. Countries that have signed but not ratified the Convention can send observers. The Council is subject to rules of procedure of which the latest version was adopted in 1982 (UPOV, 1982b). Below the Council is the Consultative Committee. Since 1988, this committee has been delegated decision-making powers 'concerning the granting of observer status to non-governmental organizations' (UPOV, 2005b). The Consultative Committee normally holds closed sessions restricted to members of the Union. Next on the hierarchy are two committees: the Legal and Administrative Committee and the Technical Committee.[6]

UPOV membership has expanded rapidly since the establishment of the WTO and the proliferation of bilateral trade agreements: 39 of its 68 current members joined after 1995. UPOV can no longer be seen as a European 'club' if the membership is anything to go by. However, active participation is another matter. For example, at the March session of the Consultative Committee 49 countries were represented. Out of these, 31 were developed countries plus the European Union and 18 were developing countries. And yet UPOV does not appear at all open to those who are not members of the 'PVP community'. The most obvious barrier to entry is that PVP is a highly technical and scientific area of intellectual property law involving specialised field testing procedures and requiring a knowledge of biological and agricultural sciences including genetics and agronomy. *But PVP is not a uniquely complex area of intellectual property law.* Interestingly, neither the 1978 or 1991 revisions contain any provisions concerning the settlement of disputes between UPOV Members about the application or interpretation of the Convention.

As already mentioned, the Consultative Committee has the power to decide on granting observer status to international NGOs and intergovernmental organizations in accordance with rules adopted by the Council. Paragraph 2 of the relevant document on the rules is of special importance in this regard (UPOV, 2005b). Accordingly, such granting 'is reserved to those organizations *with competence in areas of direct relevance in matters governed by the UPOV Convention.* The constituent treaty for intergovernmental organizations and the statutes for intergovernmental organizations will form the basis to determine that competence'. However, both the President of the Council and the UPOV Office may grant *ad hoc* invitations to an IGO or an NGO to attend a particular Council session. Authorisation may be granted to observe sessions of the Council, the Administrative and Legal Committee (CAJ), the Technical Committee (TC), and the Technical Working Parties (TWPs). However, the Consultative Committee's sessions are normally closed to all except Members of the Union. An organization seeking observer status must do the following:

> In the first instance, the head of the organization should send a letter to the Secretary-General of UPOV requesting the granting of observer status to the Council and, if appropriate, to the CAJ, the TC and/or the TWPs. The letter should contain a brief description of the organization's objectives, activities, structure and membership and: for intergovernmental organizations, a copy of the constituent treaty; and for international non-governmental organizations a copy of the statutes. Organizations which have been granted observer status to the Council may subsequently request, by means of a letter from the head of the organization, observer status to the CAJ, the TC and/or the TWPs, if this was not initially requested. (UPOV, 2005b: para 3)

Observer status in the various UPOV bodies is granted for an unspecified duration. It 'consists almost entirely of plant-breeding or biotechnology companies, associations of such companies, and intellectual property protection groups' (Mara, 2009). It includes organizations like the International Chamber of Commerce which, despite its long involvement in international intellectual property rulemaking, has no particular reputation for 'technical competence' in a field as specialised as PVP. And yet public interest NGOs – including farmers' groups – find themselves being refused such status for allegedly lacking such competence (see below). It is worth pointing out that until recently WIPO had a similar kind of observership profile. This has changed, undeniably for the benefit of WIPO as it seeks to evolve intellectual property to reflect the needs of a rapidly changing world and the interests of all stakeholders. UPOV should follow suit.

In late 2009, two public interest NGOs were denied observer status at UPOV: the Association of Plant Breeding for the Benefit of Society (APREBES), comprising various organizations from the North and South, and the European Farmers Coordination (now known as the European Coordination of Via Campesina, or ECVC). According to the *IP Watch* report, UPOV informed them 'that their applications for observer status "could not be considered further" until they demonstrate "competence in areas of direct relevance in respect of matters governed by the UPOV Convention"'. However, while a lack of competence was the official justification for the refusal as per paragraph 2 of the relevant rules, the decision was evidently politically motivated and the UPOV Office appears to have been directly involved (Mara, 2009). But in a face-to-face interview with the current Vice Secretary-General of UPOV on 20 July 2010, he denied that any applications for observer status had been refused. Of course a refusal is only one way; simply taking a unilateral position that an applicant organization is not technically competent and disqualifying it on that basis may not constitute a 'refusal' as such but it still amounts to keeping it out of the club. In October 2010, the UPOV Council reconsidered the applications of APREBES and ECVC who had attracted the support of Germany, Norway and Switzerland. On this occasion the decision was made to admit them. Whether this indicates a shift towards greater inclusiveness remains to be seen (Mara, 2010).

One key point to be made here is that the inclusion of such organizations at UPOV meetings in the long term would be beneficial for all concerned. 'Technical competence' in areas directly relevant to matters governed by the Convention is a subjective matter that can easily be applied arbitrarily. It should not be used as a pretext to keep out important stakeholders just because they have a sceptical or critical perspective on PVP, or at least on the UPOV PVP model. The PVP community would be well advised to welcome such organizations into the 'fold' and encourage them to engage constructively. Second, the UPOV Office must not behave in a way that leads others reasonably to perceive that it is playing a 'gatekeeper' role in the sense of influencing the process by which observer applications are being considered.

V. UPOV IN THE WORLD

UPOV's initially gradual expansion may have served a useful purpose for the older (i.e. European) Members of the Union. An attempt to expand more rapidly in its first two decades might have led to the entry of 'outsiders' who may then have worked to change the culture in certain ways, such as by pushing UPOV to accept national PVP regimes that were not fully consistent with UPOV's rules. This view may be somewhat cynical. But it is quite plausible that such a long consolidation period helped make it easier to absorb the recent membership expansion without threatening the leadership of the established custodians. Prospective UPOV Members, whether states or intergovernmental organizations of which the European Union is the only one, are required to request an analysis of their law or draft law from the UPOV Council before they can join. If the law is deemed compliant with UPOV and has entered into force (but not necessarily been technically implemented), the government or intergovernmental organization can proceed to ratify the Convention, thereby becoming an UPOV Member. If modifications are deemed by the Council or Office as necessary for compliance, these must be effected before ratification is allowed (UPOV, 2009). Obviously, this enables existing Members of UPOV (and the UPOV Office) to impose a fairly strict conformity requirement upon new ones and may quite possibly give those Members able and willing to be assertive a degree of leverage over the legislatures of applicant countries. Indeed, the UPOV Office plays an essential role in 'guiding' the aspiring Member through the membership procedure including the assessment of 'conformity' of its law with the UPOV Convention and prepares the recommendation on this matter to the Council. Comments made on the laws of prospective Members are not publicly available.

So why do countries join UPOV and what role does the Office of UPOV and the Council play in shaping countries' views on PVP that dispose them to seek UPOV membership? One obvious factor is Article 27.3(b) of TRIPS, which requires WTO Members to 'provide for the protection of plant varieties either by patents or by an effective *sui generis* system or by any combination thereof'. TRIPS does not specify UPOV as providing the *'sui generis'* alternative to patents. Any 'effective' PVP regime is possible. But the UPOV Office has been actively discouraging deviations from the UPOV norms. Thus, in a position statement based on an intervention by UPOV before the WTO's Council for TRIPS, it is stated that 'the plant variety protection system established on the UPOV Convention meets the requirements of Article 27.3(b) of the TRIPS Agreement' (UPOV, 2002). So far this is perfectly reasonable. But the statement goes on to state this: 'the introduction of a system which differs significantly from the harmonized approach based on the UPOV Convention will raise questions with regard to the implementation of the TRIPS Agreement'. For countries unsure of where their interests lie with respect to intellectual property protection in the field of plant breeding but anxious to avoid being criticized by the US and EU for failing to meet their TRIPS commitments, this is quite a powerful statement.

UPOV's mission receives a great deal of support from powerful nations. Nowadays, both the United States through its free trade agreements and the European Union by way of its economic partnership agreements are pressing developing country parties to these agreements to commit themselves to applying for UPOV membership, or if they are already UPOV Members to provide patent protection for plants. Moreover, technical assistance programmes sometimes stress UPOV-conformity with no proper evaluation of how PVP should benefit the country as a whole. To make matters worse, such programmes may be carried out without in any way consulting local stakeholders such as farmers' groups, public sector breeding institutions and local seed companies. It should be borne in mind that some technical assistance coming from the developed world is intended to serve primarily the interests of businesses in those same parts of the world. To express this plainly, *the intent is mostly about protecting the PVP rights of developed country businesses in the developing world rather than about helping the developing countries to produce their own varieties to protect.*

Being ostensibly a member-driven intergovernmental organization, there is a line to be drawn between advocacy and legitimate outreach activities. The UPOV Office does have views on such issues as access to genetic resources and benefit sharing, the disclosure of origin in intellectual property, and the human right to food, despite claiming that it has no mandate beyond ensuring effective PVP systems. Concerning these issues, the Office has proved to be very efficient in responding to public criticisms of PVP implied or otherwise. Despite the fact that the outgoing Vice Secretary-General of UPOV professed not to know the meaning of 'farmers' rights', the UPOV Office presumes itself to have sufficient technical competence on such matters as the above issues to send position statements to the relevant forums. For example, whereas the Peruvian PVP regime provides for a disclosure of origin requirement and despite the enthusiasm of many developing countries for including this measure in their intellectual property regimes, the Office has declared that such a mandatory disclosure of origin requirements is not allowed as these form 'an additional condition of protection' (UPOV, 2002). It is noteworthy that in at least one case a UPOV Member has criticized the UPOV Office for adopting a line that it disagreed with. This is Brazil, which disagreed with a submission made by the UPOV Office to the Working Group on Access and Benefit Sharing of the Convention on Biological Diversity.

Another good example of this is UPOV's response to the United Nations Special Rapporteur on the Right to Food, which was somewhat critical of the way that developing countries have been 'led to' adopt UPOV standards (UNGA, 2009). *As with other responses (and submissions to other international forums and processes), it would be interesting to know how much input the UPOV Council put into drafting and approving this response, or whether it was entirely an initiative of the Office.* It does not always appear to be the case that the UPOV Office has kept to the side of the line where it is supposed to remain. It may or may not be sound policy for countries to counter the harmonisation trend being actively promoted by the UPOV Office with their own PVP laws. But there is no legal basis for implying that a non UPOV-compliant PVP law is contrary to TRIPS simply for being inconsistent with UPOV.

International harmonisation based on UPOV's standards, whether in terms of statutory law, implementation rules or of testing procedures, is something that the UPOV community is very keen on, and the UPOV Office has been more than willing to play its part *as an advocate*. Sometimes this has provoked controversy. A good example here is the PVP section of the 1999 Revised Bangui Agreement[7] of the 16 member state-strong *Organisation Africaine de la Propriété Intellectuelle* (OAPI). WIPO, the UPOV Office and the French intellectual property office (INPI) played key roles in the preparation, adoption and ratification of this instrument, which came into force in 2002 and 'applies automatically as national law in each of the OAPI member states that ratifies the agreement', and was intended to be fully TRIPS compliant (Deere, 2009: 253). And yet most OAPI members are least-developed countries that did not have to fully implement TRIPS until 1 January 2006 (and now are not required to until 1 July 2013). It provides for PVP in Annex 10, which came into force in January 2006 though has not yet been implemented. It is entirely consistent with the 1991 Act of UPOV.

WIPO, UPOV and INPI all had input into draft texts, but 'at no point in the Bangui revision process was there any formal interstate negotiation of the draft text' (Deere, 2009: 261). Moreover:

> ... neither the OAPI Secretariat, member states, or international donors undertook any substantive empirical assessments to substantiate expectations about the prospective gains or to identify the distribution of potential losses from the revised Agreement. While it is true that the OAPI Secretariat forwarded the draft text to national intellectual property offices, there is no record of any substantive written comments from member states to the OAPI Secretariat ... (Deere, 2009: 261)

UPOV 1991 was deemed a politically convenient model for the OAPI Secretariat to get its member states to adopt whether or not it was beneficial for them in any other ways: 'the OAPI Secretariat advised its members that UPOV offered a law that member states could take "off the shelf" and that the development of an alternative *sui generis* law, would be a time-consuming and impractical endeavour'. It is worth noting in this context that not one developing country UPOV Member that joined under the 1978 Act has elected to 'upgrade' to UPOV 1991.

In contrast to its enthusiasm for the Revised Bangui Agreement, the UPOV Office was hardly reticent in its criticism of an alternative model regime that had been adopted in draft form by the Organization of African Unity Council of Ministers in 1998, and which was being actively promoted throughout Africa by the Organization (Ekpere, 2000). The 'African Model Legislation for the Protection of the Rights of Local Communities, Farmers and Breeders, and for the Regulation of Access to Biological Resources', developed by the Scientific, Technical and Research Commission of the OAU with some international NGO input from organizations including Third World Network, GRAIN, Rural Advancement Foundation International (now named ETC Group) and the Gaia Foundation, was finalised in 2000. It provides relatively weak PVP rights as compared to UPOV. In 2001, the OAU hosted a conference to discuss the model: UPOV and WIPO were invited to give their comments. UPOV Office representatives also provided a 10-page critique. This included the redrafting of more than 30 of the model's articles, allegedly to turn the Model Legislation into UPOV 1991. This highly critical stance did not sit well with those concerned about its enthusiastic promotion of the UPOV Convention at the OAPI. It also offended the conference's hosts. Taken together, the behaviour in Africa of the UPOV Office at that time does seem to cross over into advocacy work.

VI. ARE THERE ALTERNATIVES?

A critical discussion on UPOV is inadequate and futile if alternative property systems for plant varieties are precluded. The obvious alternative to the UPOV system is simply to eschew any special regime and extend the scope of patentable subject matter to include plants and plant varieties, an option that TRIPS permits. There are a number of reasons why this is probably inadvisable for most countries. For one thing, the normal extent of the private and experimental use exemptions in patent law is extremely and inappropriately narrow for plant breeding and would stifle innovation and create excessively strong monopolies.

Given the specificities of plant breeding and innovation in this field, it makes much sense to provide a special regime. UPOV has some advantages over patents. It provides some legal clarity where patents do not: whereas a single product may be protected by numerous patents, any plant variety is covered by a single PVP certificate. Unsurprisingly there is far less litigation than with patents. That the UPOV system was designed with and for the European plant breeding community does not automatically make it unsuitable for use elsewhere, but adaptations to what may be very different economic, social and agricultural and environmental conditions are probably necessary. Interestingly, India, Thailand and Peru, all UPOV non-members, have PVP systems based on the 1978 Act but which arguably diverge in certain ways, such as by conditionally allowing farmers' sale of seed.

Plant breeding has not been made obsolete by biotechnology, it is just as vital as ever, and as long as there is some private investment in breeding there will be interest in intellectual property protection. Admittedly, intellectual property may also be useful for the public sector as it seeks to protect its own innovations for the public good and to generate research income through licensing. Nonetheless, most of the interest in securing protection comes from the business sector. But what if there is not much private investment in the first place? Will the availability of PVP make a difference? There is no compelling evidence that the existence of PVP alone will stimulate the establishment of private sector plant breeding enterprises, though it may well encourage the growth of an industry that already exists (World Bank, 2006). What the empirical evidence does lead us to expect is that the vast majority of PVP applications in developing countries will come from foreigners, at least in the early years.

Creating institutions that in the short term at least are primarily occupied in protecting developed world assets in the developing world is not inherently a bad thing for the latter countries if that is the price to be paid for the transfer of valuable improved genetic material and associated technology to the developing countries *and the price is not unduly exorbitant.* Local stakeholders' respect for the PVP system in place will undoubtedly be influenced by the effectiveness of enforcement and the maintenance of reasonable limitations and exceptions to the fullest extent allowed by UPOV. But in the longer term the image of PVP will be enhanced when they have intellectual property of their own to defend. As long as PVP is about protecting the rights of foreigners alone one cannot assume that local firms, breeders and farmers will feel any compelling moral reasons for observing the intellectual property rights for the varieties they use.

UPOV statistics show a steady global growth in applications alongside a proportionate overall increase in foreign applications. There is also clear evidence of developed country-based seed companies becoming more interested in developing country markets, sometimes taking over domestic firms (as in Argentina), or using foreign territories for producing their plants for exportation. Often such plants are ornamentals or out-of-season vegetables for the European and North American markets. For example, out of 482 PVP applications in Kenya from 1997 to 2003, 247 were for roses, all of which were foreign bred (UPOV, 2005a: 55). Whether foreign applicants are shifting breeding operations to developing countries in order to adapt their varieties to local conditions, which might be a very good thing for these countries, cannot be revealed by these statistics. But this does not appear to be very common yet.

While some developed countries, of which New Zealand is a good example, may have a large proportion of non-resident applications the higher cost of protected seed and the need to pay royalties and licensing fees is unlikely to impose such heavy burdens on the national economy, local seed suppliers or commercial farmers as compared to poorer nations. *For developing countries, which are more likely than developed countries to have a big shortfall in resident applications as compared to non-resident ones, such additional costs may be quite burdensome.* This matter does require case-by-case analysis: much depends on the kinds of plant for which foreign applications are most common (see Table 5.1).

Even if those developing countries with an established domestic private sector experience a growth in investment thanks to PVP, public sector breeding is still likely to be of vital importance. It is not a realistic or sensible policy to depend on the private sector to do all the work. Public sector crop improvement is the norm in most parts of the world. Private investment in breeding is less ubiquitous although still important, especially in North America and Western Europe. In a great many developing countries hardly any seed companies exist to carry out in-country breeding. Many low income farmers may not even benefit from such breeding if it is targeted purely at commercial sectors. Nonetheless, cash crops can be an important source of income for farming communities and the national economy. Public sector breeding may be highly relevant here also. While private investment may be useful in making up for cuts in government spending on crop improvement programmes, it does not automatically make sense for public breeders to be kept away from commercially oriented breeding as a matter of policy. There is no guarantee that the private sector will step into the breach to take advantage of the elimination of public sector competition even with the availability of PVP.

Table 5.1 PVP application statistics of selected countries

	Applications by residents			Applications by non-residents			Total		
	1999	2004	2008	1999	2004	2008	1999	2004	2008
Argentina	85	123	263	122	88	79	207	222	342
Kenya	16	16	28*	45	45	64*	61	61	92*
Netherlands	757	337	490	143	124	261	900	461	751
New Zealand	57	53	69	112	96	88	169	149	157
South Africa	53	86	103	153	226	192	206	312	295
USA (PVPA)	400	291	366	30	36	59	430	327	425
Global total	6,689	7,875	8,253	3,312	4,161	4,379	10,001	12,036	12,632

Source: Based on official UPOV statistics (*2007 figures)

VII. OPTIONS AND STRATEGIES FOR PRO-DEVELOPMENT APPROACHES TO PVP GOVERNANCE

Arguably, the UPOV Convention is insufficiently sensitive to the specific needs of a diverse range of countries, in large part because it is a one-size-fits-all system that was not designed with the developing world in mind. The assumption that it can function effectively in all countries of the world is an example of 'faith-based policymaking', not an empirically tested truth. It is, however, true that the Convention contains some vague language that could be used to better balance the interests of PVP holders and small farmers in favour of the latter. For example, the relatively generous scope for replanting saved seed as in the United States, whose UPOV compliance has never been officially challenged, may be a suitable example to follow as against the more pro-breeder measures under European PVP law which generally require that breeders be remunerated. The Union has expanded considerably in recent years, yet the majority of countries in the world remain outside. One likely reason that so many have not joined is that they remain sceptical about the merits of PVP and are unwilling to commit to an agreement that provides so little leeway for adaptations to local conditions. Pro- and anti-UPOV views tend to be propagated in completely separate forums with very little substantive debate. This is unfortunate. Some criticisms and concerns about UPOV are increasingly well-reasoned and should be debated openly. The UPOV Council and the other UPOV bodies can also do much more in this regard. It might well be that 'clubbishness' is part of the problem. To address this UPOV needs to open up.

PVP is not a uniquely complicated area of intellectual property law. One may compare the situation to WIPO, an institution which has been criticized in the past for a lack of openness and for being too influenced by 'expert' associations like AIPPI while excluding public interest-oriented NGOs that some might, perhaps conveniently, have deemed as unfit to offer constructive input due to an alleged political bias or else to possessing insufficient technical competence. The technical competence of NGOs has improved considerably in recent years and their enhanced involvement as observers in WIPO forums is likely to have contributed to this. Consequently, greater NGO engagement in WIPO meetings has not 'dumbed down' the substantive deliberations going on in WIPO committees; on the contrary, as evidenced for example by the work of the Intergovernmental Committee on Intellectual Property and Genetic Resources, Traditional Knowledge and Folklore, NGO input has been constructive and resulted in mutual learning and a far more sophisticated level of discussion than would otherwise have been the case. It is no longer justifiable for the official discussion on PVP to be the exclusive domain of plant breeders and their legal representatives as well as Ministry of Agriculture and PVP office functionaries.

An interesting, but admittedly rather old, example of this comes from the records of a symposium that was held during a session of the UPOV Council in 1980. Some of the presentations and discussions referred to a recent and highly influential publication by activist Pat Mooney called 'Seeds of the Earth', which had taken a critical stance on intellectual property in agriculture. Mooney's report was almost unanimously dismissed as ill-informed, subversive and destructive. But given the amount of attention paid to it, a tacit acknowledgement of its importance to the speakers and delegates, one wonders why they could not have invited him to the symposium to debate his work with them. Perhaps everybody would have ended up the wiser for it (UPOV, 1981).

PVP and its design have important implications for crop improvement, agricultural and food policy, food security, rural development, biodiversity and genetic resource conservation, and human rights. Despite this, there is a huge lack of awareness about PVP, especially in developing countries (including UPOV members) concerning the flexibilities, limitations and exceptions allowable under UPOV. These are highly restricted but they are not insignificant. For example, the United States, an UPOV member, does not require that breeders be remunerated when their protected seeds are harvested and replanted by farmers on their own fields. Whether this is allowable under UPOV is a matter for some controversy. Institutions responsible for administering PVP rules must be transparent in how they operate and democratically accountable. A diversity of views should be encouraged and all stakeholders and interested parties are entitled to have a say in how the relevant institutions are run, including UPOV. This inevitably entails institutional reforms. First, the UPOV Council and committees should accept interested NGOs as observers whatever their stance *vis-à-vis* the UPOV Convention. As observers they should be allowed to speak on matters relating to the agenda. The technical competence criterion should not be applied strictly or selectively. Second, the UPOV Office should scrupulously limit its activities to those technical and advisory roles it is mandated to perform, while avoiding activities that could be construed as advocacy. Third, the relationship between WIPO and the UPOV Office, including the dual role of the Director-General of WIPO as Secretary-General of UPOV, should be reconsidered in light of WIPO's status as a specialised agency of the United Nations. Finally, developing countries, whether or not they are UPOV members, should be encouraged to protect farmers' rights for small farmers and in the interests of food security *including when this affects the scope of the breeders' rights.*

NOTES

In addition to the two editors of this volume, the author is grateful to the following people for their helpful comments on versions of what became this chapter: Caroline

Dommen, Carlos Correa, Johannes Kotschi, Ahmed Abdul Latif, Niels Louwaars, François Meienberg, Pedro Roffe, Charlotte Seymour-Smith, Geoff Tansey and two anonymous reviewers. He would also like to thank Rolf Jördens and Peter Button of UPOV for agreeing to be interviewed and those government representatives who agreed to talk to him.

1. This is a common assumption, but one should not overstate the case. Open access did prevail but it was not universally applied and at all times, even at the local level (Kingsbury, 2009: 65–66).
2. Some genetic technologies might in fact counteract this trend.
3. FIS later merged with ASSINSEL to form the International Seed Federation.
4. 'Homogeneous' instead of 'uniform', in UPOV 1978.
5. Art. 17(2), UPOV 1991.
6. The work of the latter is assisted by several Technical Working Parties and a Working Group: Technical Working Party for Agricultural Crops (TWA); Technical Working Party for Fruit Crops (TWF); Technical Working Party for Ornamental Plants and Forest Trees (TWO); Technical Working Party for Vegetables (TWV); Technical Working Party on Automation and Computer Programs (TWC); and Working Group on Biochemical and Molecular Techniques, and DNA-Profiling in Particular (BMT).
7. Formally, the *Accord Portant Revision de l'Accord de Bangui du 2 Mars 1977 Instituant une Organisation Africaine de la Propriété Intellectuelle.*

BIBLIOGRAPHY

Brokensha, D. (1999) 'What African farmers know', in D. Posey (ed), *Cultural and Spiritual Values of Biodiversity.* Nairobi and London: UNEP and IT Publications.

Cruz, J.-F. (2004) 'Fonio: A small grain with potential', *LEISA Magazine,* March: 16–17.

Deere, C. (2009) *The Implementation Game: The TRIPS Agreement and the Global Politics of Intellectual Property Reform in Developing Countries.* Cambridge: Cambridge University Press.

Dutfield, G. (2008) 'The UPOV Convention', in G. Tansey and T. Rajotte (eds), *The Future Control of Food: A Guide to International Negotiations and Rules on Intellectual Property, Biodiversity and Food Security.* London: Earthscan, pp. 27–47.

Dutfield G. and Suthersanen, U. (2005) 'Harmonisation or Differentiation in Intellectual Property Protection? The lessons of history', *Prometheus,* **23**(2): 131–147.

Dutfield, G., Muraguri, L. and Leverve, F. (2010) 'Exploring the Flexibilities of TRIPS to Promote Biotechnology in Developing Countries', in C. Correa (ed), *Research Handbook on Intellectual Property under WTO Rules.* Cheltenham, UK and Northampton, MA, USA: Edward Elgar, pp. 540–588.

Ekpere, J. (2010) *The OAU's Model Law: The Protection of the Rights of Local Communities, Farmers and Breeders and for the Regulation of Access to Biological Resources: An Explanatory Booklet.* Organisation of African Unity.

Heitz, A. (1987) 'The History of Plant Variety Protection', in *UPOV: The First Twenty-Five Years of the International Convention for the Protection of New Varieties of Plants.* Geneva: UPOV.

Jaffé, W. and van Wijk, J. (1995) *The Impact of Plant Breeders' Rights in Developing Countries.* The Hague: Directorate General International Cooperation, Ministry of Foreign Affairs.

Kingsbury, N. (2009) *Hybrid: The History and Science of Plant Breeding.* Chicago: University of Chicago Press.

Louwaars, N. (2006) 'Policy and institutions for intellectual property rights for seed system development: comparing industrialised and developing countries'. Paper presented at the Seminar on Intellectual Property Rights in Agriculture, Faisalabad, Pakistan, 3–7 April.

Louwaars, N. P., Tripp, R., Eaton, D., Henson-Apollonio, V., Hu, R., Mendoza, M., Muhhuku, F., Pal, S. and Wekundah, J. (2005) *Impacts of Strengthened Intellectual Property Regimes on the Plant Breeding Industry in Developing Countries: A Synthesis of Five Case Studies.* Study commissioned by the Bank, Wageningen: Wageningen UR.

Louwaars N., Dons, H., van Overwalle, G., Raven, H., Arundel, A., Eaton, D. and Nelis, A. (2009) *Breeding Business: The Future of Plant Breeding in the light of Development in Patent Rights and Plant Breeder's Rights.* Wageningen: Wagingen UR Centre for Genetic Resources.

Mara, K. (2009) 'Farmers' Advocacy Groups Rejected as Observers in Plant Rights Organisation', *IP Watch* 10 November, available at   http://www.ip-watch.org/weblog/2009/11/10/farmers%E2%80%99-advocacy-groups-rejected-as-observers-in-plant-rights-organisation/

Mara, K. (2010) 'Change Coming to Quiet UN Plant Variety Protection Agency', *IP Watch,* 26 October, available at http://www.ip-watch.org/weblog/2010/10/26/change-coming-for-quiet-un-plant-variety-protection-agency/

Mooney, P. (1979) *Seeds of the Earth: Private or Public Resource?* Ottawa: Canadian Council for International Cooperation and International Coalition for Development Action.

Richards, P. (1999) 'Casting Seeds to the Four Winds: A Modest Proposal for Plant Genetic Diversity Management', in D. Posey (ed), *Cultural and Spiritual Values of Biodiversity* (UNEP & IT).

Sage, G. (2002) 'Intellectual Property, Agriculture and Genetic Resources', Commission on Intellectual Property Rights (on file with the author).

United Nations General Assembly (UNGA) (2009) 'The Right to Food: Seed Policies and the Right to Food; Enhancing Agro-biodiversity and Encouraging Innovation'. *Interim Report of the Special Rapporteur on the Right to Food* (A/64/170).

UPOV (1974) 'Actes des Conférences Internationales pour la Protection des Obtentions Végétales' (1957–61). Geneva: UPOV.

UPOV (1981) 'Records of a Symposium (October 15, 1981)'. Geneva: UPOV.

UPOV (1982a) 'Agreement between the World Intellectual Property Organization and the International Union for the Protection of New Varieties of Plants, November 26, 1982' (UPOV/INF/80). Geneva: UPOV.

UPOV (1982b) 'Rules of procedure of the Council (October 15, 1982)' (UPOV/INF/7). Geneva: UPOV.

UPOV (2002) 'International harmonization is essential for effective plant variety protection, trade and transfer of technology. UPOV position based on an intervention in the TRIPs Council September 19, 2002'. Geneva: UPOV.

UPOV (2005a) *UPOV Report on the Impact of Plant Variety Protection.* Geneva: UPOV.

UPOV (2005b) 'Rules governing the granting of observer status to states, international organizations and international non-governmental organizations in UPOV and access to UPOV document (October 27, 2005)' (UPOV C/39/13). Geneva: UPOV.

UPOV (2009) 'Guidance on how to become a member of UPOV (October 22, 2009) (UPOV/INF/13/1)'. Geneva: UPOV.

World Bank (2006) *Intellectual Property Rights: Designing Regimes to Support Plant Breeding in Developing Countries.* Washington, DC: World Bank Agriculture and Rural Development Department.

6 GMOs: trade and welfare impacts of current policies and prospects for reform
Kym Anderson and Lee Ann Jackson

I. INTRODUCTION

The agricultural biotechnology revolution of the past two decades has provided the world with an opportunity to rapidly accelerate growth in the production of food, feed, fibre and biofuel crops as well as livestock. Beginning in 1996, the area sown to crops with genetically modified organisms (GMOs) grew to 148 million hectares by 2010, currently spread over 29 countries but expected to involve 40 countries by 2015 (James, 2009). This uptake is rapid even by the standards of the last century, when hybrid varieties dramatically increased average corn yields during the 1940s (Griliches, 1958) and dwarf varieties of high-yielding wheat and rice caused what became known as the Green Revolution in Asia and elsewhere from the 1960s onwards (Evenson and Gollin, 2003). Yet this new technology's reach has been limited to date by the reluctance of many countries to embrace it, ostensibly for fear of its possible effects on the environment, on food safety, or on access to markets in countries not yet at ease with GMOs.

Uncertainty about market access occurs due to the diverse regulatory response countries have had to the environmental and food safety aspects of these products. In the United States (US), GM crop varieties were introduced to the food system in the mid-1990s without any requirements for identifying their GMO content, allowing their rapid adoption. By contrast in the 1990s the EC instituted a requirement that the GM content in food be disclosed on food labels. These policies constrained widespread adoption initially to just three GM food/feed crops (maize, soybean and canola) plus cotton in the three countries where production had already taken off by 1998, namely the US, Argentina and Canada. Imports into the EC of GM products were also required to undergo a regulatory approval process and in the late 1990s these approval processes for import of GM products often experienced protracted delays. Exporters of GM products (US, Canada and Argentina) initiated a dispute at the World Trade Organization (WTO), arguing that these delays constituted a *de facto* moratorium on the production and importation of food products that might contain GMOs. By the time the Panel had ruled that the EC approval delays constituted a *de facto* moratorium, the EC had replaced its moratorium with new regulatory arrangements involving complicated segregation, identity preservation and labelling requirements, thereby introducing new challenges for the exporters of GM products.

This chapter first examines the economic consequences of those diverse policy approaches by the main adopters and sceptics of GMOs. In particular, it summarizes recent empirical estimates of the impacts on developing country welfare of the limited adoption of GM varieties and of trade-distorting policies, based on simulations using the GTAP model of the global economy. The chapter then examines the evolving policy landscape in Europe with respect to GMs, beginning with the WTO dispute case and following this with the regulatory developments since then. The concluding section speculates on how policies might develop in the future.

II. ECONOMIC EFFECTS OF POLICIES AFFECTING GM CROPS

What have been the impacts on high-income and developing country welfare of the limited adoption of GM varieties so far and of the EC's reaction to that, and what would be the impacts of a wider adoption of GM crop technologies? These questions are addressed by considering first-generation corn and oilseed GM crops and then the prospective adoption of first or second generation (nutritionally enhanced) rice and wheat.[1] In a recent study we employed a model of the world economy known as GTAP (Hertel, 1997) and reported several sets of simulation results (Anderson and Jackson, 2005). The impacts of GM food crop adoption by the US, Canada and Argentina alone are considered first, without and then with policy reactions by the EC. The simulation is then re-run with the EC added to the list of adopters to explore the trade-offs for the EC between productivity growth via GM adoption and the benefits of remaining GM-free given the prior move to adopt in the Americas. A change of heart in the EC would reduce the reticence of the rest of the world to adopt GM food crop varieties, so the effects on all other countries then adopting are explored as well.

The base case in the GTAP model, which is calibrated to 1997 just prior to the EC moratorium being imposed, is compared with an alternative set of simulations whereby the effects of adoption of currently available GM varieties of maize, soybean and canola by the first adopters (Argentina, Canada and the US) are explored without and then with the EC *de facto* moratorium on the GMOs in place.[2] Plausible assumptions about the farm productivity effects of these new varieties and the likely percentage of each crop area that converts to GM varieties are taken from the available literature, including Marra, Pardey and Alston (2002), Qaim and Zilberman (2003) and Huang *et al.* (2004).3

Table 6.1 Estimated economic welfare effects of GM coarse grain and oilseed adoption by various countries (equivalent variation in income, 1997 US$ million per year)

| | US, CAN and ARG adopt | | All countries adopt | |
	Without policy response	With EC moratorium	Without policy response	
	Sim 1a	Sim 1b	Sim 1c	EV as % of GDP (sim 1c)
Argentina	312	247	287	0.11
Canada	72	7	65	0.01
US	939	628	897	0.01
EC-15	267	−3145	595	0.01
Sthn African Customs Union	3	7	9	0.01
Rest of Sub-Saharan Africa	−2	14	60	0.03
Rest of the world	700	1027	2204	0.02
World	2290	−1243	4047	0.013

Source: Anderson and Jackson (2005)

The estimated national economic welfare effects of the first set of these shocks are summarized in Table 6.1. Assuming no adverse reaction by consumers or trade policy responses by governments, the first column shows that the adoption of GM varieties of coarse grains and oilseeds by the US, Canada and Argentina would have benefited the world by almost US$2.3 billion per year, of which $1.3 billion is reaped into the adopting countries while Asia and the EC enjoy most of the rest (through an improvement in their terms of trade, as net importers of those two sets of farm products). The only losers in that scenario are countries that export those or related competing products. Australia and New Zealand lose slightly (not shown in Table 6.1) because their exports of grass-fed livestock products are less competitive with now-cheaper grain-fed livestock products in GM-adopting countries. The non-South African Customs Union (SACU) countries of Sub-Saharan Africa (SSA) as a group also lose, although again only slightly. South Africa gains slightly as a net importer of coarse grains and oilseeds, while the net welfare effect on the rest of the South African Development Community is negligible.

Column 2 of Table 6.1 shows the effects when the EC's moratorium is taken into account. The gains for the adopting countries are one-third less, the EC loses instead of gains (not accounting for the value EC consumers place on being certain they are not consuming food containing GMOs), and the world as a whole would be worse off (by $1.2 billion per year, instead of better off by $2.3 billion, a difference of $3.5 billion) because the gains from the new technology would be more than offset by the massive increase in agricultural protectionism in the EC due to its import restrictions on those crops from GM-adopting American countries. For SSA other than SACU, however, welfare would be $46 million per year greater than in Sim 1b because in Sim 1c African farmers are able to sell into the EC with less competition from the Western Hemisphere. As a proportion of GDP, those economies gain three times as much as SACU (see the final column in Table 6.1).

However, if by adopting the technology in the EC the rest of the world also became uninhibited about adopting GM varieties of these crops, global welfare would be increased by nearly twice as much as it would when just North America and Argentina adopt, and almost all of the extra global gains would be enjoyed by developing countries. If one believes the EC's policy stance is determining the rest of the world's reluctance to adopt GM varieties of these crops, then the cost of the EC's moratorium to people outside the EC15 has been up to $0.4 billion per year for the three GM-adopting countries (compare columns 2 and 3 of Table 6.1) and $1.1 billion per year for other developing countries.

Those estimates understate the global welfare cost of the EC's policy in at least four respects. First, the fact that the EC's stance has induced some other countries to also impose similar moratoria on GM food crops (if not cotton) has not been taken into account. Sri Lanka was perhaps the first developing country to ban the production and importation of GM foods. In 2001 China did the same (with some relaxation in 2002), having been denied access to the EC for some soy sauce exports because they may have been produced using GM

Table 6.2 Estimated economic welfare effects of GM coarse grain, oilseed, rice and wheat adoption by various countries (equivalent variation in income, 1997 US\$ million per year)

	US, CAN, ARG, CHN and IND adopt		All countries adopt	
	Without policy response	With EC moratorium	Without policy response	
	Sim 2a	Sim 2b	Sim 2c	EV as % of GDP (sim 2c)
Argentina	350	285	312	0.12
Canada	83	− 23	63	0.01
US	1045	754	1041	0.01
China	841	833	899	0.25
India	669	654	669	0.14
EC-15	355	−4717	810	0.01
Sthn African Customs Union	7	11	15	0.01
Rest of Sub-Saharan Africa	5	27	187	0.11
Rest of the world	964	1322	3509	0.03
World	4308	−892	7506	0.024

Source: Anderson and Jackson (2005)

soybeans imported by China from the US. Second, these are comparative static simulations which ignore that fact that GM food research and development is on-going and that investment in this area has been reduced considerably because of the EC's extreme policy stance as biotech firms redirect their investments towards pharmaceuticals and industrial crops instead of food crops. Third, the gains to the biotech firms that produce GM seeds are ignored in these results (and in subsequent simulations reported below). And fourth, the above results refer to GM adoption of coarse grains and oilseeds only. The world's other two major food crops are rice and wheat, for which GM varieties have been developed and are close to being ready for commercial release.

a. How might GM Rice and Wheat Adoption affect Developing Countries?

The above numbers only refer to the adoption of GM foodcrop

varieties currently in production. If first generation (that is, farm productivity-enhancing) GM rice and wheat adoption was also to be allowed at the rates assumed in endnote 3, global welfare would be increased by nearly twice as much (compare the bottom row of column 3 of Tables 6.1 and 6.2: $7.5 versus $4.0 billion), because the market for those two crops is even larger than for coarse grains and oilseeds. Again, however, SSA economies would gain little if they did not participate, with the benefit in terms of enhanced competitiveness from abstaining in the presence of the EC moratorium being very minor relative to the foregone productivity benefits available from adopting the new technology. Comparing columns 2 and 3 of Table 6.2, these results suggest SSA would be better off by more than $130 million per year if the world were to embrace first generation GM technology for all four groups of food crops rather than for just coarse grains and oilseeds.

While second generation (nutritionally enhanced) GM rice and wheat have not yet been commercialised, several varieties have been approved for field trials and environmental release in various parts of the world. An early study found that, even under conservative adoption and consumption assumptions, introducing Golden Rice in the Philippines could decrease the number of disability-adjusted life years lost due to Vitamin A deficiency by between 6 and 47 per cent (Zimmermann and Qaim, 2004). That is equivalent to an increase in unskilled labour productivity of up to 0.53 per cent. Based on those findings, Anderson, Jackson and Nielsen (2005) represent these health impacts with an assumed 0.5 per cent improvement in unskilled labour productivity in all sectors of Golden Rice-adopting Asian developing economies. Given the low nutrition levels of poor workers in Africa, and the fact that if Golden Rice were to be adopted in Asia and Africa then nutritionally enhanced GM varieties of wheat and other foods would soon follow, we assume the productivity of unskilled labour would rise by 2 per cent following the adoption of second generation GM crops. We also assume there would be no direct impact on the productivity of skilled labourers who were rich enough to already enjoy a nutritious diet.[4] And to continue to err on the conservative side, we assume second generation GM crop varieties are no more productive in the use of factors and inputs than traditional varieties net of segregation and identity preservation costs, even though there is evidence to suggest they may indeed be input-saving.[5]

Table 6.3 suggests this second generation GM technology could have a major impact on poor people's welfare: if it were to be adopted in SSA, for example, its estimated gain is 18 times as great as it would

Table 6.3 Estimated economic welfare effects of GM crop adoption with Sub-Saharan Africa's being 2nd generation, nutritionally enhanced rice and wheat (equivalent variation in income, 1997 US$ million per year)

	US, CAN, ARG, CHN and IND adopt first-generation GM coarse grains, oilseeds, rice and wheat and SSA adopts 2nd generation rice and wheat	
	Without EC moratorium Sim 3a	With EC moratorium Sim 3b
Sthn African Customs Union	1786	1789
Rest of Sub-Saharan Africa	1824	1846
All Sub-Saharan Africa	3610	3635

Source: Anderson and Jackson (2005)

be if the GM varieties were just farm productivity enhancing (compare Sims 2c and 3a). And again, this startling result is independent of whether the EC maintains its current approach (compare Sims 3a and 3b). Needless to say, adopting these second generation GM varieties in the developing countries of Asia would add far more, given the large population of rice and wheat consumers in Asia. Anderson *et al.* (2005) show that even Golden Rice on its own could add $3.2 billion per year to developing country economic welfare.

b. Caveats

As with all CGE modelling results, the above are subject to a number of qualifications. Of obvious importance is the assumption that we have no satisfactory way of valuing any loss of welfare for consumers who would like to avoid consuming foods containing GMOs but cannot if such foods are introduced into their marketplace without credible labelling. Since we have assumed that loss to be zero (following WHO, 2005), we are overstating the gains from adopting this technology to that extent. An alternative way to cope with this issue is to introduce a cost of segregation and identity preservation. We did that implicitly by choosing conservative cost savings due to the new technology, stating they were net of any fees charged for segregation and identity preservation. If such fees were a high share of the farm gate price, it would be unprofitable to market many GM varieties if that was a required condition of sale. But some would suggest those costs could prove to be minuscule – at least in developed economies –

on the grounds that such segregation is increasingly being demanded by consumers of many conventional foods anyway (e.g., different grades or varieties or attributes of each crop) so the marginal cost of expanding such systems to handle GM-ness would not be great, at least in those countries that have already shown a willingness to pay for product differentiation.

In all these simulations we assume for simplicity's sake that there are no negative environmental risks net of the positive environmental benefits associated with producing GM crops, and that there is no discounting and/or loss of market access abroad for other food products because of what GM adoption does for a country's generic reputation as a producer of 'clean, green, safe food'. In fact some GM crops (e.g., cotton) will reduce not only negative environmental externalities but also farmers' health risks that are associated with spraying pesticides (see Hossain *et al.,* 2004).

It is difficult to know how close to the mark our assumed boost to unskilled labour productivity is following the adoption of second generation GM varieties (see Stein, Sachdev and Qaim, 2008). But even if it is a gross exaggeration, discounting heavily the massive magnitude of the estimated welfare gain from adopting such varieties would still allow for a large benefit – particularly bearing in mind that developing countries are being offered this technology at no cost by its private sector developers, and that we have included no valuation of the non-pecuniary gain in well-being for sufferers of malnutrition. The cost of adapting off-the-shelf technology to local conditions in Africa may well be non-trivial, however, and perhaps require a better-functioning agricultural research system than has operated in the past four decades (as evidenced by Africa's relatively poor take-up of the previous green revolution – see Evenson and Gollin, 2003).

Finally, and perhaps most importantly, the above comparative static modelling assumes first generation GM technology delivers just a one-off increase in total factor productivity for that portion of a crop's area planted with the GM varieties. But what is more likely is that if/when the principle of GM crop production is accepted there would be an increase in the *rate* of agricultural factor productivity growth into the future. Similarly, second generation GM varieties with additional health attributes such as those associated with Golden Rice would be quicker in coming on stream the more countries embraced the technology. And biotech firms would be encouraged to invest more in non-food GM crop varieties too (adding to the success already achieved with GM cotton) if there was an embracing of currently developed GM crop varieties by Sub-Saharan African and other developing countries. Hence the present value of future returns from GM adoption may be many times the numbers shown above. For that reason, care is needed in interpreting cases where our results suggest that when rich countries introduce trade barriers against GM products, food-importing developing countries benefit. This is because our analysis does not take into account that these barriers have slowed the investment in agricultural biotechnology, and so have also reduced future market and technological spill-overs to developing countries from that prospective research and development.

III. THE WTO DISPUTE

With the above as background, we turn now to summarize the WTO dispute between the initial GM-adopting countries and the EC before reviewing regulatory developments since that dispute.[6]

In 2006 the WTO dispute panel of *European Communities – Measures Affecting the Approval and Marketing of Biotech Products (EC–Biotech)* issued a report (WTO, 2006). This case clearly highlights the differences in regulatory approaches taken by WTO Members related to food safety and environmental risk. The three complaining parties (the US, Canada and Argentina) raised the dispute against the EC, emphasizing the ways in which delays in the implementation of regulations concerning GM products could create barriers to trade. The relevant legal instruments to this dispute included the approval requirements and administrative procedures for a deliberate release of GMOs into the environment (Directive 90/220/EEC and Directive 2001/18), as well as the marketing requirements for novel foods and food ingredients (Regulation 258/97). The complainants focused their claims on the operation and application of the EC approval regime for biotech products, rather than criticizing the approval process itself.

The complaining parties raised three distinct categories of claims. First, they argued that the EC was violating WTO obligations by imposing a *de facto* general moratorium on the approval of biotechnology products for agricultural cultivation. The complainants also argued that a *de facto* moratorium existed at the product level for specific biotechnology products. Thirty products were at issue under this claim including both herbicide tolerant and pesticide-producing crops. Finally, the complainants in the dispute also claimed that EC member states prohibited or restricted the marketing biotech products regardless of the fact that the EC safety assessment, European Food

Safety Authority (EFSA), had found that these products did not pose significant risk. This category of claims concerned nine distinct measures taken by six different EC member states (Austria, France, Germany, Greece, Italy and Luxembourg). According to EC regulations a member state may provisionally restrict or prohibit the use and/or sale of a product in its territory where it has 'justifiable reasons to consider that a product which has been properly notified and has received written consent ... constitutes a risk to human health or the environment'. Article 23 of Directive 2001/18 provides that a safeguard measure may be adopted where, 'as a result of new or additional information made available since the date of the consent and affecting the environmental risk assessment or reassessment of existing information on the basis of new or additional scientific knowledge', a member state has 'detailed grounds for considering that a GMO as or in a product ... constitutes a risk to human health or the environment ... '.

In their submissions to the panel on these issues, the complainants invoked arguments on a range of provisions and agreements in the WTO law, including specific articles included in the Agreement on the Application of Sanitary and Phytosanitary Measures (SPS Agreement), the Agreement on Technical Barriers to Trade (TBT Agreement), the Agreement on Agriculture and the GATT. One of the primary threshold issues for the panellists to decide was whether the SPS Agreement was applicable to the procedures that made up the EC approval process. The SPS Agreement includes the following definition of an SPS measure in Annex A:

Sanitary or phytosanitary measure – Any measure applied:
(a) to protect animal or plant life or health within the territory of the Member from risks arising from the entry, establishment or spread of pests, diseases, disease-carrying organisms or disease-causing organisms;
(b) to protect human or animal life or health within the territory of the Member from risks arising from additives, contaminants, toxins or disease-causing organisms in foods, beverages or feedstuffs;
(c) to protect human life or health within the territory of the Member from risks arising from diseases carried by animals, plants or products thereof, or from the entry, establishment or spread of pests; or
(d) to prevent or limit other damage within the territory of the Member from the entry, establishment or spread of pests.

> Sanitary or phytosanitary measures include all relevant laws, decrees, regulations, requirements and procedures including, *inter alia*, end product criteria; processes and production methods; testing, inspection, certification and approval procedures; quarantine treatments including relevant requirements associated with the transport of animals or plants, or with the materials necessary for their survival during transport; provisions on relevant statistical methods, sampling procedures and methods of risk assessment; and packaging and labelling requirements directly related to food safety.

The EC maintained that the approval procedures did not entirely fall within the scope of the Agreement. In the EC's view the fact that the objective of the regulatory procedures at issue included both SPS and non-SPS objectives and given the formulation of the SPS Agreement those aspects of the EC regulation that were not focused on SPS objectives did not fall under the scope of the Agreement. The complaining parties noted that the EC had acknowledged that the relevant legal instruments were adopted for some of the reasons indicated in the above definition of an SPS measure and that was sufficient to determine that they fell within the scope of the SPS Agreement. The parties to the dispute also considered that the TBT Agreement could be relevant particularly given that under this Agreement governments are entitled to require that imported products comply with the mandatory technical regulations that are necessary to fulfil a legitimate objective. Protection of human, animal, plant and environmental health is among the legitimate objectives for which product requirements may be developed under the TBT Agreement. The panel in this case explicitly considered the possibility that WTO Members might enact a procedure that would incorporate both SPS measures and non-SPS measures. The panel concluded that the relevant EC approval procedures constituted an SPS measure. This determination had crucial significance to the panel's analysis due to the specific obligations laid out in the SPS Agreement requiring WTO Members to ensure that SPS measures would be based on science.

a. Panel's Analysis and Findings

The panel's analysis focused on interpreting the provisions of the SPS Agreement which states that WTO Members were entitled to take measures to protect human, animal or plant life or health, as long as these measures were based on scientific principles and were not maintained without scientific evidence. The SPS Agreement also encourages the use of international standards guidelines and recommendations and states that those measures which conform to these international standards will be presumed to be consistent with relevant provisions of the SPS Agreement. Members have the right to introduce measures that would lead to a higher level of risk protection than that which would be achieved through the application of an international standard, but these more stringent measures must be based on a risk assessment.

With respect to the three claims made by complainants, the panel concluded that the evidence indicated that a *de facto* moratorium had been in place during the period of time in question. At the time that the panel report was issued several biotechnology products had been approved, therefore in light of these approvals no action would be required by the EC to lift the *de facto* moratorium.

The panel also found that member states were not in compliance, noting that 'For each of the products at issue, the European Communities' relevant scientific committee had evaluated the potential risks to human health and/or the environment prior to the granting of Community-wide approval, and had provided a positive opinion. The relevant EC scientific committee subsequently also reviewed the arguments and the evidence submitted by the Member State to justify the prohibition, and did not consider that such information called into question its earlier conclusions' (WTO, 2006: para 8.9). Given the above, the panel concluded that sufficient scientific evidence was available to permit a risk assessment as required by the SPS Agreement and that there was no indication that the relevant scientific evidence was insufficient to perform a risk assessment, such that the member state might have had recourse to a provisional measure under Article 5.7 of the SPS Agreement.

Some commentators have suggested that the panel's explicit discussion of which questions were not at issue in the dispute reflects the panel's recognition of the political nature of the rulings in this dispute (Cheyne, 2008). Among the issues that the panel did not examine were whether biotech products in general were safe or not and whether the biotech products at issue in this dispute were 'like' their conventional counterparts. In addition the panel did not consider whether the EC's approval procedures, as established by Directive 90/220, Directive 2001/18 and Regulation 258/97, were consistent with its obligations under the WTO agreements and these were not raised by the complaining parties.

b. SPS and Science in the Dispute

In *EC–Biotech* the panel explored the relationship between requirements to justify SPS measures with a risk assessment and the right to implement SPS measures provisionally in situations where there was insufficient scientific evidence (Eliason, 2009). The SPS Agreement includes the right for WTO Members to implement SPS measures without scientific justification in the event that there is insufficient scientific evidence. Specifically, Article 5.7 of the SPS Agreement states that:

> In cases where relevant scientific evidence is insufficient, a Member may provisionally adopt sanitary or phytosanitary measures on the basis of available pertinent information, including that from the relevant international organizations as well as from sanitary or phytosanitary measures applied by other Members. In such circumstances, Members shall seek to obtain the additional information necessary for a more objective assessment of risk and review the sanitary or phytosanitary measure accordingly within a reasonable period of time.

The *EC–Biotech* Panel interpreted this article as containing four cumulative requirements (Kogan, 2007). A Member may provisionally adopt an SPS measure in the case of insufficient scientific evidence and these measures should be based on available information. In addition, once the measure is implemented that Member may maintain the measure only if it seeks to obtain additional information and reviews the measure within a reasonable amount of time. The panel noted that scientific uncertainty was not the same thing as insufficient scientific evidence. Some authors argue that implicit to this decision was the recognition of the dynamic nature of science which allows for the possibility that the evaluation of sufficiency of scientific information may need to adapt in situations where new scientific information arises (Kogan, 2007).

c. Follow-up to the Dispute

At the time of the adoption of the Panel Report by the WTO membership, the EC had approved one product in 2004. Thus, the panel found that the general moratorium was no longer in place at the time of issuing the report and did not make recommendations regarding this measure. With respect to the product-specific moratorium and the national safeguard measures, the panel requested the EC to bring the measures 'into conformity with its obligations under the SPS Agreement'. None of the complainants chose to appeal the report, essentially allowing the EC additional time to navigate the complexities of its internal political situation on this issue.

The complaining parties approached panel recommendations on product-specific moratoria and the continued imposition by member states of safeguard measures in different ways. After the 2006 DSB ruling found that the EC was violating obligations under the SPS Agreement, the parties agreed to engage in technical discussions to address the biotech issues and also agreed to a twelve-month reasonable period of time for the implementation of these talks. In 2009 Canada agreed to extend the reasonable period of time twice and eventually the EC approved the marketing and sale of the canola biotech product at issue for Canada (ICTSD, 2009). Similarly, in 2010 Argentina also reached a mutually agreed solution, including continuing bilateral dialogue on agricultural biotechnology products market access issues of mutual interest. On the US side after the initial agreement among the parties that the EC be given a reasonable amount of time to comply with the rulings, the US requested authorization to suspend concessions from the DSB. Arbitration proceedings were requested by the parties but in February 2008 the same parties agreed to suspend these proceedings (Poli, 2010).

IV. DEVELOPMENTS IN THE EC SINCE THE *EC–BIOTECH* DISPUTE

EC policies towards biotechnology have been evolving in the aftermath of the *EC–Biotech* dispute. While the moratorium has been lifted, several other aspects of the regulatory environment in the EC will have potentially continued trade-limiting impacts. The member state issue continues to play a large role in determining the trade in biotechnology products, with some EC member states maintaining an intolerant stance towards these products regardless of the assessments of safety at a Commission level. Labelling and segregation policies act as a technical barrier to trade in such products by requiring that exporters label these to show a particular level of GMO content. Finally, the complexity of the scientific evaluation system within the EC has the possibility to introduce delays to the approval process.

a.   Labelling and Segregation

In May 2004 the EC replaced its moratorium with new regulatory arrangements. These regulatory arrangements involved segregation, identity preservation and labelling requirements, which may increase the costs of exporting to the EC and thus create limitations on access to EC markets for exporters of GM products. Traceability legislation requires business operators to keep track of information with respect to products that contain or are produced by biotechnology. This legislation is intended to provide information that is necessary for labelling claims which will state that GMO content does not surpass a specified threshold. The labelling provides consumers with the necessary information to differentiate across traditional and GM products. However, the tolerance level specified for an 'adventitious presence' of GM content means that, given the processing chain, there can be small amounts of GM material that occur in what would otherwise be considered a non-GM crop. The impact that these regulations have on imports of products potentially containing GM content depends upon these tolerance limits.

In 2010 European Commission documents obtained by Friends of the Earth Europe revealed new proposals that would open Europe's doors to the import of unauthorized GM feed. In November 2010 the European Commission provided to EC member states a new proposal to change the legislation on GM foods and feeds. The proposal, which was discussed in a meeting of member states on 15 November, weakened the EC's zero tolerance policy by allowing traces of non-approved GM crops in imports coming into Europe (with a threshold of 0.1 per cent). Experts consider this proposed threshold value to be the technical limit of detection since, for GMO content less than 0.1 per cent, current detection methods do not deliver unequivocal results (GMO Compass, 2010).

The potential costs of complying with labelling requirements have been examined by various authors (see for example Bonsi, Hammett and Smith, 2008). Producers and exporters face costs associated with translation of foreign requirements, the adjustment of processing facilities to meet labelling requirements, and verification that the exported product will meet the standards of the destination market. Testing costs for GMOs are high, which may limit the market access to countries that can afford to invest in the technology and expertise required to meet these requirements (UNEP/IISD, 2000).

b.   Relationship of Member States to EC policy

More recently the EC has initiated changes in the legal structure relating to the approval of biotechnology products at the EC level and the EC member state levels. These changes will have repercussions on the market for biotechnology products within and outside the EC. In particular, the changes will give member states the ability to restrict cultivation within their borders for socio-economic reasons, notwithstanding whether the EFSA has conducted a risk assessment for these products and determined that they do not pose substantial risks.

The EC in December 2008 adopted a series of measures aimed at overcoming differences and reaching unified decisions (Reuters, 2009). The European Commission has been struggling to find a way to manage the fact that a number of member states have retained bans on the growing of GM crops, despite its best efforts to persuade them to comply. Under EC law, these states can legislate a national ban on GMOs if the government in question can justify the prohibition. On several occasions member states have voted against Commission attempts to force member states to lift bans on GM production.

In July 2010 the European Commission proposed to modify the EC's policy for approving GM crops. The proposed modification would allow countries more freedom to ban cultivation on their territory while retaining an EC-wide authorization system. The changes included a recommendation on coexistence which allowed more flexibility to member states taking into account their local conditions when adopting co-existence measures. The proposed regulation amends Directive 2001/18/EC to allow member states to restrict or prohibit the cultivation of GMOs in their territory. The plans would allow planting in pro-GM countries such as Spain, the Netherlands and the Czech Republic, thus opening up new markets for biotech companies while at the same time legally endorsing existing GM bans in countries like Italy, Austria and Hungary. Due to EC legislative procedures, EC member states in the Council of Ministers were unable to reach a qualified majority for or against GMO authorizations, referring the matter back to the Commission which in turn authorized them *via* a special regulatory procedure (Reuters, 2010). Several member states, including France and Germany, opposed the Commission's July 2010 proposal. Many smaller member states such as Austria, Luxembourg, Bulgaria, and the Baltic states expressed support. Some countries have called for the Commission to allow the unapproved GM crops to be permitted for human consumption as well, pointing out that it would be nearly impossible to distinguish between the world's crop supplies as food and feed. In its comments at the Environmental Council, France made it clear that it wanted to work primarily on strengthening the environmental risk assessment used for GMO approvals.

c.   Risk Assessment in the EC

In response to EC governments' call for stronger EFSA assessment procedures for GMOs, the EFSA strengthened the risk assessment procedure by revising the guidelines for an environmental risk assessment of GMOs. The member states had recommended that EFSA should be Europe's final arbiter on the safety of GM crops, but with input coming from national bodies. They also agreed that decisions should take into account the medium- and long-term environmental impact of any decision and not just the health aspects (DE, 2009). EFSA's new guidelines outlined a detailed assessment approach for evaluating the environmental risks of GMOs. EFSA highlighted several specific areas of concern that should be evaluated including the 'persistence and invasiveness of the GM plant' and the effects on human and animal health. The guidelines also require biotech companies proposing GMOs for human or animal consumption to account for 'intended and unintended effects'. To date, ESFA has approved one variety of corn produced by Monsanto and one strain of potato that will be grown for industrial use alone.

d.   Repercussions of the EU Policy on Developing Countries

A new econometric analysis of the EU moratorium and its product-specific measures and national bans that were at issue in the *EC–Biotech* dispute estimated that US exports to the EC between 2003 and 2005 would have been US$2.0 billion larger without those measures (which represents 26 per cent of total US exports of maize, oilseed rape, cotton and corn gluten) (Disdier and Fontagné, 2010). For Canada and Argentina, those losses were $350 million and $52 million (representing 28 and 4 per cent of their total exports of the affected products, respectively).[7] While the EC has modified policies at the EC level to reduce import barriers to GM products to the Union as a whole, the continuing restrictions by numerous EC member states remain as a deterrent.

For developing countries in Africa and Asia, it has been the fear of such trade losses that has deterred them from approving the adoption of GM technologies. That fear appears to be real and until recently it has also been pervasive. The first signs of it lessening have been with respect to cotton: since China, India and South Africa joined Argentina and Brazil in growing biotech cotton, Columbia, Costa Rica, Mexico and (from 2010) Myanmar and Pakistan have allowed plantings (James, 2009). But far more important in term of trying to achieve the UN Millennium Development Goals of reducing poverty, malnutrition and hunger is the adoption of GM technologies for major food staples in developing countries. While EC restrictions remain, each developing country needs to assess the risk of losing exports to the EC. If that risk is low, adoption could be the best strategy. Even if it is high, and even if there was a sizeable premium on GM-free products over their GM counterparts, the welfare cost of trade losses that might be incurred from adoption needs to be weighed against the potential benefits to domestic consumers and farmers in the developing countries themselves.

There is also the option to produce GM products and to develop segregated GM and non-GM markets. However, this option requires the infrastructure for testing and a comprehensive segregation system throughout the agricultural production system. This has been a challenge even for countries with highly industrialized agriculture and in situations where a GM crop variety is not intended for human consumption. For example, recently the US Department of Agriculture sought to deregulate a variety of corn that had been genetically modified to facilitate ethanol production. That action generated intense public debate about the possibility of a co-mingling of GM and non-GM crops (*New York Times*, 2011). Due to the costs associated with developing a two-track approach and the uncertainty about the sustainability of a segregated agricultural system, this option would not be realistic for most low-income countries.

If developing countries who are WTO Members were to adopt GM products and confronted barriers to importing these into the EC, they would have recourse to the WTO dispute settlement system. The previous GMO dispute argument was based primarily on the obligations and entitlements embedded in the SPS Agreement. This meant that the EC measures were evaluated in relation to whether or not they were based on a scientific assessment of risks. However, GMO policies in the EC are in flux, as noted above, and this means that previous dispute outcomes may not be the only relevant guidance in this area. The current policy debate in the EC emphasizes consumer preferences as much as it emphasizes the potential health and environmental risks associated with these products. This means that other Agreements within the WTO may be relevant in the future. However, as the recent study by Disdier and Fontagné (2010) makes clear, the losses from trade restrictions are roughly proportional to the value of the bilateral trade involved, so a small economy is unlikely to be able to justify the legal cost of WTO dispute settlement unless it can persuade enough other economies to become parties in the case.

V. CONCLUSIONS

The outcome of the *EC–Biotech* dispute and ensuing regulatory developments will have far-reaching implications for the international trade in biotechnology products. On-going uncertainty about the regulatory environment in the EC, a major importer of agricultural products, will continue to create disincentives for the adoption of these crops in many food-exporting countries. Thus the costs and distributional consequences within and between countries of foregone production of GM varieties, explored earlier in this chapter, will also continue.

The regulatory environment for biotech products in the EC also continues to dampen incentives for research and development for new GM crop varieties. With a number of other countries also imposing strict labelling regulations on GM foods (Carter and Gruère, 2006), and even private importing firms seeking GM-free foods (Gruère and Sangupta, 2009), biotech firms are diverting more of their research and development investments away from food. At the same time, the public agricultural research system has been shy about investing heavily in this technology – including the CGIAR which depends heavily on rich-country grants from EC member states. This type of systemic impact on investment incentives will have a lasting impact on potential innovation, given the lengthy amount of time required to develop new products and technologies.

The modelling results presented above make it clear that the new agricultural biotechnologies promise much to the non-adopting countries should they choose to allow the adoption of GM crop varieties. The gains from farm-productivity enhancing GM varieties could be multiplied – perhaps many fold – if second generation bio-fortified GM varieties such as Golden Rice were also to be embraced. Moreover, the estimated gains to developing countries are only slightly lower if the EC's policies continue to effectively restrict imports of affected crop products from adopting countries. Importantly, developing countries may not gain if they impose bans on GM crop imports even with the continued presence of policies restricting imports from GM-adopting countries: the estimated consumer loss net of that protectionism boost to Asian and Sub-Saharan African farmers is far more than the small gain in terms of greater market access to the EC.[8]

The stakes in this issue are thus very high, with prospective welfare gains that could alleviate poverty directly and substantially in those countries willing and able to adopt this new biotechnology. Developing countries need to assess whether they share the food safety and environmental concerns of Europeans regarding GMOs. If not, their citizens in general, and their poor in particular, have much to gain from adopting GM crop varieties – and those gains will increase as climate change proceeds and requires adaptation by farmers to changes in weather patterns and in particular to increased weather volatility and the higher costs of water for irrigation (Tester and Langridge, 2010). Unlike for North America and Argentina, who are heavily dependent on exports of maize and oilseeds, the welfare gains from GM crop adoption by Asian and Sub-Saharan African countries would not be greatly jeopardized by rich countries maintaining effective bans on imports of those GM crop products from adopting countries.

NOTES

This chapter has benefited from the authors' earlier work with Chantal Pohl Nielsen and Ernesto Valenzuela, and from comments by participants in the Study Week on Transgenic Plants for Food Security in the Context of Development, Vatican City, 15-19 May 2009. The views are the authors' own, however. Thanks are due to the Australian Research Council for financial assistance.

1. The potential benefits of wider adoption of GM cotton are omitted here, but comparable results are available, using the same global model, in Anderson, *et al.* (2008).
2. This has to be done in a slightly inflating way in that the GTAP model is not disaggregated below 'coarse grains' and 'oilseeds'. However, in the current adopting countries (Argentina, Canada and the US), maize, soybean and canola *are* the dominant coarse grains and oilseed crops.
3. We assume 45 per cent of US and Canadian coarse grain production is GM and, when they adopt, all Latin American countries and Australia are assumed to adopt GM coarse grains at two-thirds the level of the US while all other countries are assumed to adopt GM coarse grains at one-third the level of US adoption. For oilseeds, we assume that 75 per cent of oilseed production in the US, Canada and Argentina (and Brazil when we allow it) is GM. Again other Latin American countries and Australia are assumed to adopt at two-thirds the extent of the major adopters and the remaining regions adopt at one-third the extent of the major adopters. For the prospective rice scenarios, major assumed adopters, including the US, Canada, China, India, and all other Asian countries, are assumed to produce 45 per cent of their crop using GM varieties. All other regions adopt at two-thirds this rate. Prospective GM wheat adoption is assumed to occur to the same extent as coarse grain adoption for all regions. The GM varieties are assumed to enjoy higher total factor productivity than conventional varieties to the extent of 7.5 per cent for coarse grains, 6 per cent for oilseeds and 5 per cent for wheat and rice. The simulations are able to estimate the equivalent variations in income, measured in 1997 US dollars, that would result from these assumed degrees of adoption and productivity growth for the GM portion of each crop and its consequent effect on markets.
4. There would also be non-pecuniary benefits of people feeling healthier and less expenditure on health care, but these too are ignored so as to continue to err on the conservative side.
5. Bouis (2002, 2007) and Welch (2002) suggest nutritionally enhanced rice and

wheat cultivars are more resistant to disease, their roots extend more deeply into the soil so they require less irrigation and are more drought resistant, they release chemical compounds that unbind trace elements in the soil and thus require fewer chemical inputs, and their seeds have higher survival rates.

6. For more on the EU dispute, see the (2007) Special GMO Symposium in Volume 6, No. 2, of the journal *World Trade Review*.

7. Certainly some of those potential exports went to other countries so that the total trade loss was less than these bilateral trade losses (and hence the estimated net welfare losses reported in Table 6.1 are only a fraction of the trade losses estimated by Disdier and Fontagné, 2010).

8. This is consistent with the finding by Paarlberg (2006, 2009) that African exports of food crops in general to the EU that might be affected adversely by GM adoption represent a very small share of the region's exports. See also Karembu *et al.* (2009).

BIBLIOGRAPHY

Alston, J., Marra, M. Pardey, P. and Wyatt, T. (2000) 'A Meta Analysis of Rates of Return to *Agricultural R&D: Ex Pede Herculum?*', *IFPRI Research Report 113.* Washington, DC: International Food Policy Research Institute.

Anderson, K. and Jackson, L. A. (2005) 'Some Implications of GM Food Technology Policies for Sub-Saharan Africa', *Journal of African Economies,* **14** (3): 385–410.

Anderson, K., Jackson, L. A. and Nielsen, C. P. (2005) 'GM Rice Adoption: Implications for Welfare and Poverty Alleviation', *Journal of Economic Integration,* **20** (4): 771–788.

Anderson, K., Valenzuela, E. and Jackson, L. A. (2008) 'Recent and Prospective Adoption of Genetically Modified Cotton: A global CGE analysis of economic impacts', *Economic Development and Cultural Change,* **56** (2): 265–296.

Bonsi, R., Hammett, A. L. and Smith, B. (2008) 'Eco-labels and International Trade: Problems and solutions', *Journal of World Trade,* **42** (3): 407–432.

Bouis, H. E. (2002) 'Plant Breeding: A new tool to fight micronutrient malnutrition', *Journal of Nutrition,* **132**: 491S–494S.

Bouis, H. E. (2007) 'The Potential of Genetically Modified Food Crops to Improve Human Nutrition in Developing Countries', *Journal of Development Studies,* **43** (1): 79–96.

Carter, C. and Gruère, G. (2006) 'International Approval and Labeling Regulations of Genetically Modified Food in Major Trading Countries', in R. Just, J. Alston, and D. Zilberman (eds), *Economics of Regulation of Agricultural Biotechnologies.* New York: Springer, Chapter 21.

Cheyne, I. (2008) 'Life after the Biotech Products Dispute', *Environmental Law Review,* **10**: 52–71.

DE (2009) 'How EU Member States approach GMOs', available at http://www.reuters.com/article/idUSLDE6120K120100204?pageNumber = 1

Disdier, A. and Fontagne, L. (2010) 'Trade Impact of European Measure on GMOs Condemned by the WTO Panel', *Review of World Economics,* **146** (3) September: 495–514.

Eliason, A. (2009) 'Science versus law in WTO jurisprudence: The (mis)interpretation of the scientific process and the (in)sufficiency of scientific evidence in *EC-Biotech*', *NYU Journal of International Law and Politics,* **41**: 341–406.

Evenson, R. and Gollin, D. (2003) 'Assessing the Impact of the Green Revolution, 1960–2000', *Science,* **300***:* 758–762.

GMO Compass (2010) 'Biotechnology: EU Commission for 0.1 per cent tolerance in feed imports', 29 October. Available at http://www.gmo-compass.org/eng/news/

544.biotechnology_eu_commission_01_per_cent_tolerance_feed.html
Griliches, Z. (1958) 'Research Costs and Social Returns: Hybrid Corn and Related Technologies', *Journal of Political Economy*, **66** (5): 419–431.
Gruère, G. and Sengupta, D. (2009) 'GM-free Private Standards and their Effects on Biosafety Decision-Making in Developing Countries' , *Food Policy*, **34** (5): 399–406.
Hertel, T. W. (ed.) (1997) *Global Trade Analysis: Modeling and Applications*. Cambridge and New York: Cambridge University Press.
Hossain, F., Pray, C., Lu, Y., Huang, J., Fan, C. and Hu, R. (2004) 'Genetically Modified Cotton and Farmers' Health in China', *International Journal of Occupational and Environmental Health*, **10**: 307–14.
Huang, J., Hu, R., van Meijl, H. and van Tongeren, F. (2004) 'Biotechnology Boosts to Crop Productivity in China: Trade and Welfare Implications', *Journal of Development Economics*, **75**(1): 27–54.
ICTSD (2009) 'Canada and EU Resolve Trade Dispute on GMOs', 22 July.
James, C. (2009) *Global Status of Commercialized Biotech/GM Crops: 2009*, Brief 41, (International Service for the Acquisition of Agri-biotech Applications, Ithaca NY).
Karembu, M., Nguthi, F. and Ismail, H. (2009) *Biotech Crops in Africa: The Final Frontier*. Nairobi: ISAAA AfriCenter (available at www.isaaa.org).
Kogan, L. (2007) 'World Trade Organization Biotech Decision Clarifies Central Role of Science in Evaluating Health and Environmental Risks for Regulation Purposes', *Global Trade and Customs Journal*, **2** (3): 149–155.
Marra, M., Pardey, P. and Alston, J. (2002) 'The Payoffs to Agricultural Biotechnology: An Assessment of the Evidence', *AgBioForum*, **5** (2): 43–50. Available at http://www.agbioforum.org/v5n2/v5n2a02-marra.pdf
Paarlberg, R. (2006) 'Are Genetically Modified (GM) Crops a Commercial Risk for Africa?', *International Journal of Technology and Globalization*, **2** (1/2): 81–92.
Paarlberg, R. (2009) *Starved for Science: How Biotechnology is Being Kept Out of Africa*. Cambridge MA: Harvard University Press.
Poli, S. (2010) 'Continuity and Change in the EU Regulatory Framework on GMOs, After the WTO Dispute on "Biotech Products"', *Legal Issues of Economic Integration*, **37** (2): 133–148.
Qaim, M. and Zilberman, D. (2003) 'Yield Effects of Genetically Modified Crops in Developing Countries', *Science*, **299**: 900–902.
Reuters (2010) 'EU wants to put GMO dispute to an end', 12 July, updated 13 July.
Stein, A., Sachdev, H. and Qaim, M. (2008) 'Genetic Engineering for the Poor: Golden rice and public health in India', *World Development*, **36** (1): 144–158.
Tester, M. and Langridge, P. (2010) 'Breeding Technologies to Increase Crop Production in a Changing World', *Science*, **327**: 818–822.
UNEP/IISD (2000) *Environment and Trade: A Handbook*, United Nations Environment Program Division of Technology, Industry, and Economics, Economics and Trade Unit and the International Institute for Sustainable Development. Available at http://www.iisd.org/pdf/envirotrade_handbook.pdf
Welch, R. M. (2002) 'Breeding Strategies for Biofortified Staple Plant Foods to Reduce Micronutrient Malnutrition Globally', *Journal of Nutrition*, **132**: 495S–499S.
WHO (2005), *Modern Food Biotechnology, Human Health and Development: An Evidence-based Study*. Geneva: World Health Organization.
World Trade Online (2010) 'Commission GMO Proposal Faces Uphill Battle Among Member States', 21 October.
WTO (2006) WT/DS 291, WT/DS292 and WT/DS293, *European Communities – Measures Affecting the Approval and Marketing of Biotech Products*. Geneva: World Trade Organization.
Zimmermann, R. and Qaim, M. (2004) 'Potential Health Benefits of Golden Rice: A Philippines case study', *Food Policy*, **29** (2): 147–168.

7 Addressing the solution of SPS and TBT matters through trade negotiations
Eugenia Laurenza and Ignacio Carreño

I. INTRODUCTION

International trade in agricultural products is increasingly being affected by the adoption and maintenance of regulations, standards and requirements intended to ensure that food which is imported, manufactured and consumed is safe; aimed at protecting the health and life of animals and plants; and directed at the pursuit of important policy objectives such as, *inter alia*, human health or safety, animal or plant life or health, and the environment. Although the objectives that these measures intend to pursue are, in principle, legitimate, measures of this kind may result in barriers to trade to the extent that: (i) they discriminate against imports; and (ii) there are concrete difficulties associated with complying with such standards. These difficulties may be increased by the differences in the way in which each importing country implements the legitimate objectives, and this may significantly impair the ability of exporters to gain access to third country markets.

Within the WTO framework, the General Agreement on Tariffs and Trade (GATT) and, to a greater extent, the Agreement on the Application of Sanitary and Phytosanitary Measures (SPS Agreement) and the Agreement on Technical Barriers to Trade (TBT Agreement) attempt to regulate the trade-related aspects of such measures. This legal framework rests, *inter alia*, on the following pillars: the non-discrimination and the least-trade restrictive measure principles; harmonisation of international standards; and transparency. The TBT Agreement, which covers technical regulations, standards and conformity assessment procedures, requires that technical regulations and conformity assessment procedures be no more trade restrictive than necessary to fulfil a legitimate objective, such as the protection of human health or safety, animal or plant life or health, or the environment.[1] The main difference between technical regulations and standards is that the latter are non-binding instruments, in most cases not governmental but rather industry-driven (McGovern, 2008: 7.21–2). The SPS Agreement, which is relevant to sanitary and phytosanitary measures (SPS measures), elaborates on the notion of risk and requires that all SPS measures adopted by a WTO Member be based on an assessment of the risks.[2]

Although the existing WTO framework sets out clear principles to avoid discrimination and minimise trade distortions, it does not prevent TBT or SPS measures from reducing and affecting market access opportunities for exporters of agricultural products and rendering void, in many cases, the commercial concessions and the benefits of tariff liberalisation in agricultural products. Difficulties and restrictions encountered in connection with access to third-country markets are continuously raised by exporters of agricultural products.

The instruments available under WTO law to attempt to find a solution to trade concerns arising from the application of SPS and TBT measures are currently limited to the review and technical discussions taking place within the SPS and TBT Committees, and the WTO dispute settlement process, which is invoked when there is an allegation of inconsistency with WTO rules. Developing countries have faced difficulties in 'forcing' discussions towards a solution of trade concerns, and the WTO dispute settlement process has been an expensive and unwieldy mechanism for developing countries to utilise in seeking a solution to SPS and TBT disputes. Between these two possibilities – informal discussions and formal dispute settlement – no viable mechanisms to assist developing countries in seeking solutions to SPS and TBT concerns have yet appeared.

This chapter argues that in order to ensure that the benefits of tariff liberalisation and commercial concessions on agricultural products are not impaired by trade concerns arising from the application of SPS and TBT measures, negotiations and commercially meaningful results on regulations, standards and requirements affecting agricultural trade and falling within the scope of the SPS and TBT Agreements should be factored into the ongoing multilateral trade negotiations, and accompany negotiations on agricultural tariff liberalisation and market access concessions. In particular, it is suggested that the solution of SPS and TBT concerns be systematically addressed in the context of trade negotiations, just as tariff reduction and multilateral rules are, so that tariff liberalisation is coupled with effective and increased market access opportunities and not impaired by restrictive domestic regulations. Specific market access problems regarding SPS and TBT measures need to be identified, negotiated and addressed within the framework of cyclical multilateral trade negotiations, as it is increasingly happening at the regional and bilateral level. The concluding section of this paper offers practical proposals for possible reform within the current or future multilateral negotiations.

Part II provides a brief overview on where SPS and TBT issues affecting agricultural products currently stand in the WTO Doha Round, and shows how discussions on non-tariff measures affecting agricultural products, initially taking place (albeit marginally) within the agricultural negotiations, have progressively been dropped. Part III identifies specific problems and legal shortcomings, as the existing instruments and mechanisms currently available within the WTO to counter SPS and TBT concerns do not appear to be sufficient to solve practical market access issues. Part IV provides some proposals on how to ensure that SPS and TBT types of non-tariff measures are properly taken into account in the context of (current or future) market access negotiations. The chapter suggests that WTO Members propose, negotiate and adopt new instruments that can either better delineate the functioning of existing instruments, or equip WTO Members with new tools to address specific market access issues and focus their attention during the negotiations and subsequent implementation.

II. WTO NEGOTIATIONS AND SPS AND TBT ISSUES

1   The Launch of Negotiations on Agriculture

Following the conclusion of the Uruguay Round and the entry into force of (*inter alia*) the WTO Agreement on Agriculture (AoA) and the SPS and TBT Agreements, WTO Members launched multilateral negotiations in early 2000 under Article 20 of the AoA to carry out reforms towards a further liberalisation of the trade in agricultural products. A number of negotiating proposals submitted following the official launch of the agricultural negotiations addressed the impact of several non-tariff measures in various ways. These negotiating proposals were tabled by a number of developing countries as well as developed countries. Issues debated in the early phases of the negotiations included, in particular, the relationship between agricultural trade and the protection of the environment; mandatory labelling requirements; food safety and the application of the precautionary principle; animal welfare; the effect of SPS and TBT requirements on market access; and the need for technical assistance and special and differential treatment on SPS and TBT matters.

A group of developing countries tabled a submission explicitly recognising the impact of SPS measures on market access. In this submission, these WTO Members argued that the lack of mutual recognition of inspections and standards was causing major problems for developing countries' exports, as several major importing countries were asking developing countries to adopt the same standards and procedures rather than standards and procedures which are simply '*equivalent*' as required by Article 4.1 of the SPS Agreement.[3] These WTO Members argued that a lack of financial or technical resources presented a huge obstacle for developing countries in implementing these stringent requirements, or even taking a significant role in the standards-setting process (WTO, 2000a). Another group of developing countries considered food safety issues as market access issues and argued that technical assistance and special and differential treatment in the SPS and the TBT Agreements should be given more prominence within the framework of the AoA and be addressed in the context of the agricultural negotiations (WTO, 2001a). Other WTO Members recognised the importance of complying with certain societal goals, reflected in a number of so-called '*non-trade concerns*' and the impact that these have on agricultural trade. These concerns included the protection of the environment, food safety considerations (including the application of the precautionary principle), mandatory labelling, and animal welfare. On these bases a number of WTO Members tabled proposals suggesting links between agricultural trade and the SPS and TBT measures applied by WTO Members (WTO, 2000b, 2000c, 2000d).

With respect to food safety, WTO Members seemed to agree that consumers must be protected and that there was an equal need to avoid protectionism in disguise. The discussion was about whether or not the SPS Agreement (in particular, Article 5.7 on the precautionary principle) was clear enough to maintain that balance in an appropriate manner. The European Union (EU) supported clarifying this through an understanding that would also send the right signals to consumers. The question was whether this should be discussed within the SPS and TBT Committees, rather than in the context of the agriculture negotiations. In relation to consumer labelling, some WTO Members suggested that voluntary or mandatory labelling would be a way to deal with non-trade concerns such as animal welfare and genetically modified organisms without distorting trade. In addition, whereas some WTO Members linked such discussions to parallel discussions within the TBT Committee, other WTO Members considered that this subject should not be dealt with in the context of the agricultural negotiations. Developing countries emphasised the effect on trade of non-tariff measures and the need for technical assistance, *inter alia* in relation to the implementation of the SPS and TBT Agreements and for the purposes of special and differential treatment.

2 The Negotiations in the Doha Round

With the 2001 Doha Ministerial Declaration (WTO, 2001b) WTO Members launched multilateral trade negotiations on a range of subjects. The Ministerial Declaration did not provide a specific mandate to negotiate new or improved disciplines within the SPS and TBT Agreements, nor did it address the relationship between the disciplines covered by these agreements and market access for agricultural products. On the other hand, certain difficulties faced by developing countries in connection with the implementation of the SPS and TBT Agreements were recognised and addressed by the Doha Decision on Implementation-related Issues and Concerns (the Doha Implementing Decision) (WTO, 2001c).

Under this decision, Members agreed that the 'longer time-frame' for developing countries to comply with other countries' new SPS measures referred to in Article 10.2 of the SPS Agreement should be normally understood to mean a period of not less than six months. In addition, the Doha Implementing Decision provided that where the appropriate level of sanitary and phytosanitary protection did not allow scope for the phased introduction of a new measure, but specific problems had been identified by a Member, the Member applying the measure would have to, upon request, enter into consultations with a view to finding a mutually satisfactory solution to the problem. Further, it provided that the 'reasonable interval' between the publication of a country's new SPS measure and its entry into force should be normally understood to mean a period of not less than six months. It also instructed the SPS Committee to develop expeditiously the specific programme to further the implementation of the equivalence provisions. As to developing countries' participation in setting international SPS standards, the Doha Implementing Decision noted the actions taken by the WTO Director-General to help developing-country Members participate more effectively, including efforts to coordinate with the relevant organisations and to identify needs for technical assistance in the field. It also called for Members to provide assistance to least-developed countries in order that they could respond adequately to new SPS measures that might obstruct their trade and for assistance to help them implement the agreement as a whole. Further to the Doha Implementing Decision, the SPS Committee adopted a procedure to enhance the transparency of special and differential treatment in favour of developing country Members (see Part III.2 below) and the Standards and Trade Development Facility was established.

Further to including the negotiations already ongoing in agricultural trade, the Doha Ministerial Declaration did provide for a new negotiating mandate. In addition to reductions of (with a view to phasing out) all forms of export subsidies and substantial reductions in trade-distorting domestic support, substantial improvements in market access were included in the negotiating mandate, whereby special and differential treatment for developing countries was to be an integral part of all elements of the negotiations. A specific reference to food safety matters and other non-tariff measures was not included in the mandate. It did, however, confirm that 'non-trade concerns' would be taken into account in line with the AoA.

Paragraph 14 of the Doha Ministerial Declaration concerns the establishment of 'Modalities' for the agricultural negotiations. 'Modalities' (i.e., formulas, flexibilities, disciplines) are targets (including numerical targets) for achieving the objectives of the negotiations, as well as issues related to rules. The 'Modalities', which included provisions for special and differential treatment, were initially to be agreed by no later than 31 March 2003, and negotiations were to be concluded by 1 January 2005. In the phase of 'preparation for Modalities', positions on food safety and mandatory labelling were still being discussed. Positions tabled at this stage of the negotiations could be summarised as follows:

- In relation to food safety, certain WTO Members considered that their specific proposals regarding the clarification of issues linked to the precautionary principle related to Article 5.7 of the SPS Agreement should be dealt with in the framework of the negotiations on agriculture (WTO, 2000c). WTO Members in favour of including food safety issues in the negotiations believed that, rather than relying on the rulings of the WTO Dispute Settlement Body, WTO Members should aim at clarifying aspects of food safety through the negotiations. These aspects were: the proportionality of the measures to the food safety target; non-discrimination; a consistent application of the measures; a comparison of the costs and benefits of alternative measures; a re-evaluation of scientific data as new information emerged; and that measures should be based on science. Some WTO Members believed that such aspects should not be part of the agricultural negotiations (WTO, 2000e: 1). Other WTO Members stated that SPS measures were already replacing tariffs and were resulting in trade barriers.

- Similarly, the debate in relation to mandatory labelling in the 'preparation for Modalities' phase was centred on whether mandatory labelling should be covered in the context of the agricultural negotiations. While some WTO Members considered that their specific proposals regarding improved consumer information, criteria and guidelines for the implementation of mandatory labelling for food and agricultural products should be dealt with in the framework of the negotiations on agriculture, other WTO Members insisted that such issues should be addressed within the TBT Committee, which was considered to be the appropriate *forum* (WTO, 2000f: 2).

- Lastly, a group of developing countries put forward a proposal for a commitment by developed countries to earmark their technical and financial assistance, either in their Schedules or by pooling resources, for the improvement of developing countries' capacity in the areas of, *inter alia*, SPS and TBT, in cooperation with the relevant standards-setting organisations and other agencies involved in trade-related capacity building (WTO, 2002).

Almost one year after the deadlock in the negotiations that followed the Cancun Ministerial meeting, WTO Members agreed on a 'framework' to be used in order to agree on 'Modalities'. Annex A of the Decision Adopted by the General Council on 1 August 2004 does not mention food safety and food labelling as issues affecting market access (WTO, 2004b). It does, however, confirm that non-trade concerns, as referred to in Paragraph 13 of the Doha Declaration, will be taken into account. Food safety and labelling, as well as environment and animal welfare, are not included within the 'issues of interest but not agreed' (which comprise sectoral initiatives, geographical indications, and differential export taxes). Similarly, the Hong Kong Ministerial Declaration does not provide a reference to food safety and labelling, and Annex A to the Hong Kong Ministerial Declaration containing the '*Report by the Chairman of the Special Session of the Committee on Agriculture to the TNC*' is silent on the subject of non-trade concerns. The Hong Kong Ministerial Declaration does refer to non-tariff measures solely in the context of the commodities trade (WTO, 2005: para 55). In practice, due to the lack of political support (and perhaps interest) in pursuing further these issues within the context of agricultural negotiations, discussions on food safety, food labelling, as well as the impact of measures aimed at protecting animal welfare and the environment, were dropped from the negotiations as separate non-market access issues, except in connection with the commodities trade.

The impact of non-tariff measures on agricultural commodities trade was mentioned again in subsequent submissions and in the texts of the Chairpersons of the Special Sessions of the Committee on Agriculture. In its proposal of 8 June 2006, for instance, the African Group advocated that '*modalities shall provide for the adoption of the suitable procedures for negotiations on the elimination of non-tariff measures affecting trade in commodities*' (WTO, 2006a: 4). On 17 July 2006, the agriculture negotiations' Chairperson's report to the Trade Negotiations Committee was circulated to WTO Members (WTO, 2006b). At its heart were 'draft modalities for preparing the schedules (of commitments) for the agriculture negotiations'. Paragraph 16 of the report (on market access for commodity products) provided that '*[p]rovision shall be made for suitable procedures for negotiations on the elimination of non-tariff measures affecting trade in commodities*'. The text, which was initially bracketed, was then agreed upon by WTO Members and confirmed in the subsequent revisions of the Draft Modalities for agriculture of 1 August 2007 (corrected on 16 August 2007) and of 6 December 2008, confirming the commitment (WTO, 2007; WTO, 2008a: para 93).

Nine years since the launch of the Doha Round, WTO Members have still not reached an agreement on the 'Modalities' for undertaking commitments in agriculture. On 22 March 2010, the Chairman of the Negotiating Group on Agriculture issued his report to the Trade Negotiations Committee for the Purpose of the Trade Negotiations Committee Stocktaking Exercise (WTO, 2010a). This stocktaking exercise does not refer to food safety and food labelling, or to non-tariff measures in general.

3   Doha Negotiations on Non-agricultural Market Access

In parallel to agricultural trade, WTO Members are negotiating on a range of issues that, once they are agreed upon, will form part of the 'single undertaking'. These include tariff liberalisation on non-agricultural market access (so-called 'NAMA negotiations'). In the context of the NAMA negotiations, the debate on the impact of non-tariff measures on the trade in non-agricultural products has been far more fruitful and is leading WTO Members to reach an agreement on a set of horizontal and vertical mechanisms to address non-tariff measures. The reduction or elimination of non-tariff measures was explicitly recognised as part of the objectives of NAMA negotiations in paragraph 16 of the Doha Declaration. In the current stage of the negotiations, Members have agreed that initiatives in this area must aim at reducing or eliminating, as appropriate, non-tariff measures, particularly on products that are of export interest to developing country Members, and at enhancing market access opportunities. To this end, a number of proposals on horizontal and vertical (i.e., sectoral) instruments dealing with non-tariff measures are being considered (WTO, 2008b). Of particular relevance is the horizontal mechanism crafted in the draft Ministerial Decision on Procedures for the Facilitation of Solutions to Non-Tariff Barriers. This mechanism consists of a procedure for the resolution of matters arising in connection to non-tariff barriers. It includes two stages (the request for information stage and the procedures for the resolution of the concern) and is aimed, through the work of a Facilitator (the Chairperson of the relevant WTO Committee or the Chairperson of the Council for Trade in Goods), at achieving a mutually-agreed solution. Under its current proposal, the mechanism does not consider non-tariff barriers (i.e., SPS and TBT measures) affecting agricultural products as being beyond its scope. In fact, WTO Members have not yet agreed on whether this mechanism should also cover SPS measures.

4   Conclusions

WTO Members recognised the links between agricultural liberalisation and SPS/TBT types of non-tariff measures in the early stages of the agricultural negotiations. However, the work on the linkages between SPS and TBT measures and agricultural trade was progressively abandoned over the course of the Doha agricultural negotiations, and SPS/TBT types of non-tariff barriers affecting agricultural products were dropped from the negotiations. On the other hand, in the context of the NAMA negotiations, the debate on the impact of non-tariff measures on trade in non-agricultural products has been far more fruitful, leading to discussions and the finalisation of proposals for the solution of matters arising in connection with non-tariff barriers. Yet this cleavage in the negotiations creates a risk that commitments on agricultural tariff liberalisation may become ineffective (or even commercially void) if these are not coupled with effective mechanisms that will address the adoption and implementation of non-tariff measures affecting trade in agricultural products. These two fronts of international trade regulation and negotiation must be better synchronised and should, ideally, progress in parallel.

III.   WHY SHOULD ADDRESSING SPS AND TBT MEASURES BE PART OF NEGOTIATIONS?

1   Problems Connected with SPS and TBT Measures

The SPS and TBT Agreements recognise that there are legitimate objectives that justify the adoption of technical regulations or SPS measures. However, the principles of proportionality and least trade restrictiveness, or the extent to which a measure must be based on science, are often interpreted and implemented differently by WTO Members, giving rise to trade irritants and trade frictions. Food safety, environmental and labelling standards are domestic in nature. In principle, each WTO Member reserves the right to adopt the level of SPS protection that it deems appropriate, as well as technical regulations to fulfil legitimate objectives. The level of SPS protection or the means through which the legitimate objectives are being pursued often results in overly-restrictive regulations. In other instances, regrettably, such measures are simply aimed at pursuing protectionist intents. In fact, SPS and TBT types of regulations involve a continuous balancing exercise between legitimate objectives and trade concerns in which domestic pressures, voiced not only by producers but also by consumers and other stakeholders, will in many cases play a role. It is argued that although there is little evidence as to what extent governments set overly trade-restrictive SPS measures in order to protect domestic producers from competition or to avoid political pressure from other stakeholders, the view broadly shared is that such political considerations do play a role in countries' choices of SPS measures (Zahrnt, 2009: 4). Even where they do not carry an element of WTO inconsistency and trade discrimination, they result in trade distortions or cause increased market access costs.

Practical examples of restrictions to trade in agricultural products, in particular from developing countries, arising from the application and interpretation of SPS measures, include issues related to the maximum residue levels (MRLs) for pesticides (i.e., the setting of MRLs for pesticides at the 'limit of detection' or at levels much lower than the levels set by Codex and use of 'temporary' MRLs, which were neither based on scientific evidence nor risk assessments) in different agricultural commodities; measures related to food additives (i.e., bans on certain food additives or mandatory warning statements on food products that contain certain colour additives); and animal welfare requirements in relation to the humane treatment of animals at the time of slaughter. More recently, concerns have been expressed in relation to the EU Regulation on novel foods (EU, 1997). There are also examples of TBT measures which restrict the trade in agricultural products, in particular from developing countries, such as unnecessary trade restrictions without scientific bases (i.e., the 30-year/15-year-prior-use time-frames necessary to apply for exemptions to the standard authorisation procedure in place for all medicinal products) in EU requirements on traditional herbal medicinal products, or US requirements for country of origin labelling for meat and dairy products and agricultural commodities for consumer information purposes.

Developing countries are particularly affected by the imposition of SPS and TBT measures, which impact on a high proportion of their exports (i.e., agricultural products). These requirements also often prevent developing and least-developed countries from enjoying unilateral trade preferences granted by other WTO Members under the Enabling Clause. The types of problems faced by developing countries currently impairing the enjoyment of market access opportunities appear to reside particularly in the difficulties connected with compliance with strict, complex and diverse SPS and TBT requirements. Compliance with third countries' standards requires know-how, capital and investment (e.g., Manarungsan *et al.*, 2005). In addition, there are difficulties and uncertainties related to the possibility of challenging SPS and TBT measures through the available WTO instruments, where it is believed that SPS and TBT measures are being applied inconsistently with the provisions of the SPS and TBT Agreements.

Difficulties connected with compliance consist of a shortfall in the financial and technical resources that are necessary to meet developed countries' stricter standards, which are increased by a lack of substantial harmonisation of the SPS and TBT measures between countries. In addition, developing countries scarcely benefit from the existing trade facilitation tools currently available under the SPS and TBT Agreements. The promotion of a harmonisation of technical regulations and SPS measures and the conclusion of mutual recognition and equivalency agreements, envisaged under the SPS and TBT Agreements, constitute trade-facilitation instruments aimed at minimising the distortions caused by SPS and TBT measures. However, the experience so far shows that these mechanisms have been infrequently used. In particular, Article 3 of the SPS Agreement encourages Members to base their measures on international standards, guidelines and recommendations, where these exist. Article 2.4 of the TBT Agreement also contains a similar provision. However, the implementation and use of harmonisation under the SPS and TBT Agreements pose important problems to developing countries. The agreements are based on a modern understanding of standards and quality issues mainly targeting OECD country problems, while many developing countries are marred by problems of human, technological, and financial resource scarcity that are unknown to most OECD countries. Developing countries face different problems and are often seeking different solutions due to the various characteristics of their private sectors and public health systems. In addition, the process of harmonisation of national standards with international standards, to be universally acceptable to all WTO Members, must ensure that in the formulation of international standards the basic principles of the SPS and TBT Agreements, such as the minimisation of negative trade effects and proportionality, are not lost sight of and are integrated into the process of standards formulation by the international standardising bodies if the standards formulated by them are to prove acceptable to the majority of WTO Members (Vergano, 2009). This also implies that developing countries have the necessary resources to actively and effectively participate in the activities of the international standards-setting organisations. Furthermore, the trend towards increasingly higher and stricter levels of standardisation and technical regulation in developed countries seems problematic. Lastly, the existence of international standards does not prevent countries from adopting stricter SPS and TBT regulations, where there is a scientific justification and provided that such measures are based on an assessment of the risks. On the other hand, the negotiation and conclusion of equivalency and mutual recognition agreements face a number of constraints which are difficult to overcome, especially for countries with low capacity (in terms of resources, negotiating skills, technical and scientific know-how, facilities, laboratories, control systems, etc.). These constraints appear to have prevented a larger recourse to such instruments, even among OECD countries. Technical assistance on SPS and TBT issues has been delivered through a number of projects and facilities and has worked with some success towards supporting developing countries in their efforts to comply with export markets' standards. However, the delivery of financial and technical aid depends on developed countries' donors' interest and the will to make such resources available. To the extent that it is not translated into enforceable commitments, it cannot be systematically relied upon.

The WTO dispute settlement system allows Members the possibility to seek redress for alleged violations where a Member considers that its rights have been violated. In addition, the review mechanisms within the SPS and TBT Committees provide them with the opportunity to discuss trade concerns arising in connection with SPS and TBT measures and to solve trade irritants through consultations. However, as discussed in more detail below, these tools are either not easily accessible to developing countries, or are currently incapable of delivering substantial results and solving the practical trade problems that are constantly faced by operators.

2 The Difficulties of Challenging Overly-restrictive SPS and TBT Measures

2.1 WTO dispute settlement
The WTO dispute settlement mechanism is available to WTO Members seeking to preserve their rights under the covered agreements where a violation is presumed. If a measure adopted by a WTO Member is found to be inconsistent with the provisions of any of the WTO Agreements, the rulings of the Dispute Settlement Body will request the non-compliant WTO Member to bring its legislation into conformity with its obligations and commitments. Should that WTO Member refuse to do so, compensation and/or countermeasures in the form of a suspension of trade concessions are available to WTO Members to redress the damage suffered.

However, the WTO dispute settlement mechanism involves costs that many WTO Members are not willing or able to pay. First, there may be political costs connected to bringing another WTO Member before WTO panels (and eventually the WTO Appellate Body), and certain WTO Members (especially smaller and less-developed countries, as well as countries that benefit from significant quantities of foreign aid) may not be willing to jeopardise their political and diplomatic capital with selected trading partners. Second, there are costs that are strictly connected to the dispute, which involve lawyers' fees (in the vast majority of cases, WTO Members will seek external advice) and, *inter alia*, costs related to attending meetings before a panel and/or the Appellate Body. WTO Members which do not have the capacity to shoulder these costs, and/or are unable to mobilise private resources, are thus severely deterred from using this tool. Third, both TBT and SPS disputes will often involve specific knowledge and complex analyses and assessments. WTO panels and the Appellate Body may be overwhelmed with the technical complexity of SPS cases (Zahrnt, 2009).

In addition, except perhaps where a solution is found through the initial phase of mandatory consultations, the WTO dispute settlement system will not deliver a prompt resolution of the dispute. Panel proceedings last, on average, 14 months, on top of which a reasonable period of time (on average 15 months) for the Member to comply must be added where the report is not appealed. Where the WTO dispute settlement mechanism is used and Dispute Settlement Body rulings establish that, for example, SPS procedures or environmental protection measures are contrary to WTO law, they tend to be perceived as an infringement of State sovereignty and an unbalanced prioritisation of trade over non-trade values. In addition, governments face difficulties in complying with those rulings on SPS or TBT measures that enjoy strong public support. This has been the case, for example, regarding the EU measures on genetically modified food or the use of hormones in cattle growth. On the other hand, delayed compliance or non-compliance, such as in the *EU – Hormones* dispute, are seen as undermining the authority of the WTO dispute settlement system and its ability to resolve trade disputes effectively (WTO, 1998).

These factors may help to explain the relatively scarce use that WTO Members have made of the WTO dispute settlement proceedings in relation to SPS and TBT measures and disputes. In fact, of 419 disputes referred to date to the WTO, only 37 requests for consultations mentioned the SPS Agreement and 41 the TBT Agreement. WTO panels have issued ten reports regarding SPS disputes, and three reports relating to TBT disputes. Similarly, only seven Appellate Body reports have been issued relating to SPS disputes and two Appellate Body reports have been issued concerning TBT disputes. This is a minuscule portion of the overall trade disputes referred to the WTO and cannot be solely attributed to chance or to the inherent difficulty of SPS and TBT matters. There seems to be an absolute disproportion between the amount of trade distortions attributed by traders and governments to SPS and TBT regulation and the number of disputes that actually find their way to Geneva.

2.2 Review and Consultations at the SPS and TBT Committees
The SPS and TBT Agreements include comprehensive transparency provisions and review mechanisms administered by the SPS and TBT Committees. Meetings of the SPS and TBT Committees provide WTO Members with the opportunity to discuss trade concerns arising in connection with SPS and TBT measures and to solve trade irritants through consultations. The SPS Committee reports that 290 specific trade concerns (in relation to food safety, plant health, animal health and zoonoses, which are diseases or infections naturally transmissible from animals to humans), and control, inspection and approval

procedures were raised within the SPS Committee from 1995 through 2009 (WTO, 2010b). Of these, 79 have reportedly been resolved and 18 partially solved (i.e., trade has been allowed for selected products or by some importing WTO Members). No solutions were reported for the remaining 193 concerns (although it is also possible that they were solved without the Committee being informed).

In relation to TBT measures, the fifth triennial review of the operation and implementation of the TBT Agreement reports that the number of specific trade concerns raised in the TBT Committee is significantly increasing (WTO, 2009b: paras 65, 66). The TBT Committee notes that the most frequently invoked reason for raising a concern is the need for more information or clarification about the measure at issue. Two-thirds of the specific trade concerns raised in the TBT Committee are only raised once or twice. A few, however, have been raised during the course of at least five meetings of the Committee, and some have remained on the Committee's agenda for several years. Since 1995, a total of 258 concerns have been raised for discussion within the TBT Committee.

Although the review mechanisms within the SPS and TBT Committees provide *fora* for consultations which have had some success in facilitating the solution of trade concerns (e.g., the information submitted by WTO Members to the SPS Committee suggests that only approximately one-third of the concerns brought to the SPS Committee were resolved, totally or partially), the review mechanisms lack binding rules to enable agenda items to be definitively processed. In other words, items may linger on the agenda for many months if not years. WTO Members are not obliged to modify their measures as a result of the debates taking place at the Committee and trade concerns may remain on the Committee's agenda for years, without Members getting any closer to a solution. In addition, the Committees meet approximately once every three months, and this dilutes the timeframe for a possible solution of the matter and may discourage Members who are seeking to discuss or even solve a trade concern in short measure.[4] In addition, by the time a trade concern is discussed the financial losses may already be significant.

In essence, the review mechanisms administered by the SPS and TBT Committees seem to be in principle a good *forum* to discuss trade concerns arising in connection with SPS and TBT measures. Putting pressure on Members within the Committees upgrades the matter and may help the solution of trade concerns through consultations. However, the current system lacks binding procedures to ensure that matters are actually dealt with in a given timeframe.

Under the SPS Agreement, WTO Members dispose of other tools for the resolution of SPS matters. The SPS Agreement envisages *ad hoc* consultations or negotiations on SPS issues, for example in Article 12.2. The *ad hoc* consultations, also referred to as the 'good offices' of the Chairperson, have been used on only three occasions up to 2010. The mechanism basically provides that if an exporting developing country Member identifies significant difficulties with a proposed measure that has been notified, that Member may, in the comments it submits in writing to the notifying Member, request an opportunity to discuss the issue of concern with the notifying Member, identifying the specific problems that the proposed measure may create for its exports, or the specific reasons why it is unable to comply with the notified measure by the implementation date. In response to such request, where the appropriate level of sanitary and phytosanitary protection gives scope for the phased introduction of the new measure, a longer time-frame for compliance should be accorded to developing country Members, which shall normally be understood to mean a period of not less than six months. To enhance the use of this instrument, WTO Members are currently negotiating, within the SPS Committee, new procedures aimed at further encouraging *ad hoc* consultations or negotiations on specific SPS matters arising between WTO Members (WTO, 2011). Moreover, further to the Doha Implementing Decision, the SPS Committee adopted the Procedure to Enhance the Transparency of Special and Differential Treatment in Favour of Developing Country Members (WTO, 2004a). As this mechanism was hardly used, it was revised in 2009 (WTO, 2009c).

3   Negotiations as the Preferred Forum for the Solution of SPS and TBT Matters

Developing countries' difficulties with complying with developed countries' regulations, and challenging developed countries' implementation of SPS or TBT measures where they are perceived contrary to the obligations of the WTO, significantly impact on trade in the products concerned by the measures, and ensure that the gains that stand to be achieved from tariff concessions negotiated within rounds of trade negotiations, as well as other tariff preferences or previous multilateral concessions, are significantly impaired. A shortcoming of the current system is that it does not cater for a negotiated solution of SPS and TBT types of trade concerns, leaving WTO Members with no tools other than technical discussions at the SPS and TBT Committees level, and WTO dispute settlement, in addition to voluntary technical assistance to enhance compliance.

WTO rounds of negotiations, including those currently taking place under the Doha Declaration, have traditionally focused on securing greater market access through tariff reduction as well as on the establishment, or revision, of multilateral trade rules. However, the solution of concrete impediments arising from the adoption of SPS and TBT measures on agricultural products is not subject to negotiations. SPS and TBT measures are simply 'imposed' on trading partners, without being subject to any multilateral mechanism that would set the framework for a negotiated solution of the matter. Instead, the lack of capacity for complying with SPS and TBT regulations and the ineffectiveness, relative inaccessibility and uncertainty linked to existing tools suggest that there should be a clear preference for using the negotiating *forum* to address those issues that are of key commercial relevance to exporting countries (especially least-developed countries) and 'force' a solution of these matters.

What is being suggested, therefore, is that there should be a specific dedicated negotiating space where the tabling, discussion and solution through commitments and binding instruments of trade concerns arising from the imposition of SPS and TBT measures can systematically take place and become part of the single undertaking. Negotiations and commercially meaningful results on the regulations, standards and requirements affecting agricultural trade, and falling within the scope of the SPS and TBT Agreements, should be systematically factored into cyclical rounds of trade negotiations and translated into commercial concessions or improved instruments to solve trade concerns, just as the reduction of tariffs and the establishment of multilateral rules are subject to negotiations. This is what is currently happening in NAMA negotiations, as well as in the context of free trade agreement negotiations.

It is not proposed here that negotiations on the solution of SPS and TBT concerns be aimed at changing SPS and TBT regulations to meet the exporting Member's demands. Negotiations should be used as a *forum* to discuss specific and identified trade concerns and find a solution through the achievement of enforceable commitments that would, for example, secure the use of existing trade facilitation tools (where the conditions would allow) or facilitate compliance (for example in the case of developing countries) with SPS and TBT requirements through tailored-made technical assistance packages, or set specific roadmaps, with defined deadlines, mandating the adoption of decisions or the establishment of dialogues and enhanced cooperation between the Members concerned.

IV. SOLVING TRADE CONCERNS THROUGH NEGOTIATIONS

Specific market access concerns currently affecting the trade in agricultural products should be identified, negotiated and addressed within the framework of cyclical multilateral trade negotiations on agriculture, SPS and TBT issues. In particular, trade negotiations should be systematically used as a venue and a *forum* to discuss specific trade concerns and 'force' the solution of the matter. The assumption of this mechanism is that specific market access problems could be identified and tabled for solution as a specific 'request' within the negotiations.

There are a number of ways in which trade negotiations may deliver commercially meaningful results. Trade negotiations might allow WTO Members to assess and discuss specific trade concerns, resolving technical problems through the setting of roadmaps with defined deadlines, mandating the adoption of decisions or the establishment of dialogues and enhanced cooperation between the Members concerned, and finding a solution through the achievement of enforceable commitments that could, for example, secure the use of existing trade facilitation tools (where the conditions would allow) or facilitate compliance (for example in the case of developing countries) with SPS and TBT requirements through tailor-made technical assistance packages. In addition, negotiations may result in elaboration and agreement on instruments that could better spell-out the functioning of existing provisions. This chapter highlights a few possible options for commercially meaningful results on SPS and TBT concerns that could be delivered through negotiations.

Trade negotiations would be able, for example, to allow Members to discuss a specific procedural concern (be it a decision regarding the relevant regulatory authority on an SPS or TBT matter or the provision of scientific evidence) and deliver a commitment through the setting of specific deadlines for the decision and roadmaps for compliance.

In addition, where a WTO Member demonstrates that its measures meet the importing Member's level of SPS protection in relation to a particular agricultural product, a commitment to engage in negotiations of an *ad hoc* equivalency and mutual recognition agreements, with the indication of a clear timeframe for the opening and conclusion of the negotiations, could be raised and facilitated through trade negotiations.

Developing countries may request that commitments be undertaken for the provision of tailored technical assistance programmes aimed at fostering compliance with SPS and TBT measures in selected export markets, in order to overcome their lack of financial and technical resources. International donor-financed technical assistance packages could be designed for specific needs to ensure compliance with SPS and TBT standards and technical regulations in relation to products that were of particular interest to developing countries. The novelty of this approach would reside in ensuring that technical assistance packages be tied to trade negotiations and result in enforceable commitments. This possibility would also appear to give effect to Article 9.2 of the SPS Agreement which provides that '*[w]here substantial investments are required in order for an exporting developing country Member to fulfil the sanitary and phytosanitary requirements of an importing Member, the latter shall consider providing such technical assistance as will permit the developing country Member to maintain and expand its market access opportunities for the products involved*'.

Another important result that trade negotiations may deliver in the area of non-tariff measures affecting the trade in foodstuffs is the possibility of providing an opportunity to conceptualise and agree on sectoral approaches that would tackle shared trade concerns. An example of this approach is the use of sectoral instruments, such as understandings, protocols, decisions and agreements, which WTO Members are currently discussing under NAMA negotiations to address specific non-tariff barriers arising in connection with the trade in specific products (*inter alia*: fireworks, lighters, certain forestry products or electronics) or issues (such as labelling requirements on textile and clothing) (e.g., WTO, 2008b: Annex 5). Some of these proposed instruments contain, for example, an agreement to harmonise TBT measures to international standards; the commitment to give positive consideration to recognition; and a commitment to take positive measures to harmonise the related labelling requirements. Another sectoral instrument clarifies the interpretation of the TBT Agreement in relation to the labelling of textiles, clothing, footwear and travel goods. The proposed instrument establishes a number of rebuttable presumptions (on the application of the trade-restrictiveness principle) that would apply to specific labelling requirements affecting the goods in question.

Similar approaches could perhaps be attempted in relation to specific agricultural products or specific measures that were found to affect products of interest (for example, measures establishing the maximum residue levels for pesticides). New areas where sectoral approaches and multilateral convergence may be reached include animal welfare requirements and process and production methods aimed at achieving environmental protection. Sectoral approaches, multilateral convergence in these (and other) areas would allow countries to overcome more easily the trade barriers arising from differences among regulations, enhancing dialogue and, to a lesser extent, encouraging harmonisation.

Along the same lines, WTO Members could consider developing understandings or clarifications in relation to the application of specific principles of the SPS or TBT Agreements. Under the SPS Agreement, WTO Members shall ensure that any SPS measure is applied only to the extent necessary to protect human, animal or plant life or health; that it is based on scientific principles; and that it is not maintained without sufficient scientific evidence. Procedural requirements could be established to increase transparency in the risk assessment process or to ensure that the views of all stakeholders, including importers and foreign producers, are taken into consideration. In addition, the principles guiding WTO Member compliance with the principle of the 'least-trade restrictive measure', or addressing a comparison of costs and benefits of alternative measures, could be elaborated. Understandings and clarifications have worked well in the framework of a number of provisions of the GATT, and could also be effective tools in the context of SPS and TBT measures.

Progress in the solution of SPS and TBT problems is also taking place in the context of regional and bilateral negotiations of free trade agreements. In these frameworks negotiations are conducted amongst two or a handful of countries, with a view to abolishing tariffs and to maximising trade gains. In such *fora*, the higher flexibility of the negotiating setting, and the possibility of reaching a greater regulatory convergence with a chosen trading partner(s), increase the likelihood of finding solutions to specific SPS and TBT problems. As a result, the solution of SPS and TBT issues is systematically factored into the negotiations through, *inter alia*, the development of specific chapters setting out the basis for greater cooperation and the creation of mechanisms promoting convergence. For example, in the free trade agreement recently concluded between the EU and Korea, both parties' dedicated specific chapters on SPS and TBT measures with enhanced cooperation provisions and WTO-plus commitments. It appears that a similar approach is also being followed by the EU in the context of the ongoing free trade agreement negotiations with Canada. Regulatory convergence achieved by fewer WTO Members in the bilateral/regional contexts could be attempted at the multilateral or plurilateral level. Although this could result in a further tightening of

SPS and TBT requirements, it also increases the likelihood that harmonised standards will be agreed upon, which is certainly preferable to the imposition of unilateral measures that developing countries will find difficult to challenge in the first place.

There are many ways in which trade negotiations may deliver significant results regarding SPS and TBT measures, and there appears to be no concrete objection that would prevent the adoption of similar negotiating approaches in the multilateral arena and in relation to agricultural trade. The adoption of these approaches should also be coupled with the agreement on new or enhanced mechanisms for the solution of SPS and TBT matters that are currently being discussed within NAMA negotiations and the SPS Committee. Indeed, this is already being attempted in relation to TBT measures affecting industrial products. Where there is lack of political will from some WTO Members to commit to such new instruments, initial convergence may be sought and developed by smaller groups of WTO Members through instruments that are granted plurilateral effect.

NOTES

1.   Annex 1 to the TBT Agreement defines technical regulations as a 'document which lays down product characteristics or their related processes and production methods, including the applicable administrative provisions, with which compliance is mandatory. It may also include or deal exclusively with terminology, symbols, packaging, marking or labelling requirements as they apply to a product, process or production method.' A standard is a 'document approved by a recognized body, that provides, for common and repeated use, rules, guidelines or characteristics for products or related processes and production methods, with which compliance is not mandatory. It may also include or deal exclusively with terminology, symbols, packaging, marking or labelling requirements as they apply to a product, process or production method.' Conformity assessment procedures are procedures used to determine that the relevant requirements in technical regulations or standards are fulfilled.

2.   Annex A to the SPS Agreement defines sanitary or phytosanitary measure as 'any measure applied: (a) to protect animal or plant life or health within the territory of the Member from risks arising from the entry, establishment or spread of pests, diseases, disease-carrying organisms or disease-causing organisms; (b) to protect human or animal life or health within the territory of the Member from risks arising from additives, contaminants, toxins or disease-causing organisms in foods, beverages or feedstuffs; (c) to protect human life or health within the territory of the Member from risks arising from diseases carried by animals, plants or products thereof, or from the entry, establishment or spread of pests; or (d) to prevent or limit other damage within the territory of the Member from the entry, establishment or spread of pests. Sanitary or phytosanitary measures include all relevant laws, decrees, regulations, requirements and procedures including, *inter alia*, end product criteria; processes and production methods;

testing, inspection, certification and approval procedures; quarantine treatments including relevant requirements associated with the transport of animals or plants, or with the materials necessary for their survival during transport; provisions on relevant statistical methods, sampling procedures and methods of risk assessment; and packaging and labelling requirements directly related to food safety.'

3.　Article 4.1 of the SPS Agreement requires Members to accept the SPS measures of other Members as equivalent, even if these measures differ from their own or from those used by other Members trading in the same product, if the exporting Member objectively demonstrates to the importing Member that its measures achieve the importing Member's appropriate level of sanitary or phytosanitary protection.

4.　The Working Procedures of the Committee on Sanitary and Phytosanitary Measures provide that the Committee shall hold at least two meetings per year. The Rules of Procedure for the meetings of the WTO Committee on Technical Barriers to Trade provide that the Committee shall meet as necessary, but not less than once a year. In practice, SPS and TBT Committees meet every three months.

BIBLIOGRAPHY

EU (1997) Regulation (EC) No 258/97 of the European Parliament and of the Council of 27 January 1997 concerning novel foods and novel food ingredients, as amended, OJ [1997] L 43/1.

Manarungsan, S., Naewbanij, J. O. and Rerngjakrabhet, T. (2005) 'Costs of Compliance with SPS Standards: Thailand Case Studies of Shrimp, Fresh Asparagus, and Frozen Green Soybeans', *World Bank Agriculture and Rural Development Discussion Paper*. Washington, DC: World Bank.

McGovern, E. (2008) *International Trade Regulation*. Exeter: Globefield Press.

Pollack, A. (2001) 'U.S. approves corn modified for ethanol', *New York Times*, 11 February.

Vergano, P. (2009) *Legal Interpretation of the WTO SPS and TBT Agreements and Key Issues of Development and Trade Concern*, Study for the World Bank. Washington, DC: World Bank.

WTO (1998) *European Communities – Measures Concerning Meat and Meat Products*, WT/DS26.

WTO (2000a) *Joint Submission on Market Access tabled by Cuba, Dominican Republic, El Salvador, Honduras, Kenya, India, Nigeria, Pakistan, Sri Lanka, Uganda and Zimbabwe*, G/AG/NG/W/37.

WTO (2000b) *EU's Comprehensive Negotiating Proposal*, G/AG/NG/W/90.

WTO (2000c) *Communication from Switzerland*, G/AG/NG/W/94.

WTO (2000d) *Communication from Japan*, G/AG/NG/W/91.

WTO (2000e) *Statement by India*, G/AG/NG/W/114.

WTO (2000f) *Statement of Australia*, G/AG/NG/W/41.

WTO (2001a) *Submission by the African Group*, G/AG/NG/W/142.

WTO (2001b) *Doha Ministerial Declaration*, WT/MIN(01)/DEC/1.

WTO (2001c) *Doha Implementation Decision*, WT/MIN(01)/17.

WTO (2002) *Common Position of the Member States of the West African Economic and Monetary Union (WAEMU) in the Multilateral Trade Negotiations on Agriculture* (G/AG/NG/W/188).

WTO (2004a) *Procedure to Enhance the Transparency of Special and Differential Treatment in Favour of Developing Country Members*, G/SPS/33.

WTO (2004b) *August Framework Decision*, WT/L/579.

WTO (2005) *Hong Kong Declaration*, WT/MIN(05)/DEC.
WTO (2006a) *Report of Special Session of the Committee on Agriculture*, TN/AG/GEN/ 18.
WTO (2006b) *Report to Trade Negotiations* Committee, TN/AG/W/3.
WTO (2007) *Draft Modalities on Agriculture*, TN/AG/W/4 (and TN/AG/W/4/Corr.1).
WTO (2008a) *Fourth Draft Modalities on Agriculture*, TN/AG/W/4/Rev.4.
WTO (2008b) *Fourth Draft Modalities on NAMA*, TN/MA/W/103/Rev.3.
WTO (2009b) *Fifth Triennial Review of the Operation and Implementation of the TBT Agreement*, G/TBT/26.
WTO (2009c) *Procedure to Enhance the Transparency of Special and Differential Treatment in Favour of Developing Country Members*, G/SPS/33/Rev.1.
WTO (2010a) *Report to Trade Negotiations Committee*, TN/AG/25.
WTO (2010b) *Report on the Activities of the Committee on Sanitary and Phytosanitary Measures*, G/L/943.
WTO (2011) *Proposed Recommended Procedure to Encourage and Facilitate Ad Hoc Consultations or Negotiations among Members Under the SPS Agreement*, G/SPS/W/ 243/Rev.4.
Zahrnt, V. (2009) 'Transparency of Complex Regulation: How Should WTO Trade Policy Reviews Deal with Sanitary and Phytosanitary Policies?', *ECIPE Working Paper No. 06/2009*.

8 Private standards and trade
Tim Josling

I. INTRODUCTION

Among the more intriguing developments in international agricultural and food trade over the past decade has been the rapid growth in the number and scope of private standards. These standards have arisen as a result of developments in the markets for and the marketing of foods, as described below. But they have also been a response to the evolution of public standards, notably those regulating health and safety. This apparent overlap between the public and the private sector standards adds both to the complexity of the issue and to the amount of interest shown in the subject by students of trade law and economics.

Along with the proliferation of the standards themselves has been a minor boom in the literature on the subject.[1] However, empirical studies that enable one to generalize on the impacts of standards on trade are still relatively rare.[2] As with most issues related to qualitative regulations, finding a basis for the measurement of market impacts is challenging. This chapter will therefore focus on the issue of the impact of private standards on the governance of the international food system rather than attempts to assess the quantitative effects on particular stakeholders.

II. WHAT ARE PRIVATE STANDARDS?

Standards for products sold on domestic or international markets provide information. Depending on the reliability of the information and conformity with the standard, buyers are given an assurance that the product meets certain requirements and possesses certain attributes. This information is of value to the buyer, particularly in cases where there is no previous history on which to base a judgment. But providing that assurance is also useful to the seller who might otherwise have to find alternative ways to reassure the buyer. And standards can be used for product differentiation, useful in monopolistic industries and with the potential to develop specialized market segments.

Food standards are one particular type of standard, notable for the dominance of issues related to health and safety and those concerned with the method of production and its impact on the environment. Public standards in agricultural and food trade have tended to focus on health and safety issues, as there is a near universal obligation by public authorities to prevent where possible the importation of substances that present a risk for human, animal and plant health. To be effective, such health and safety standards need to be mandatory. One might assume, therefore, that private standards deal with attributes other than health and safety, such as the method of production and the environmental impact. These are more subjective qualities that can be appreciated by consumers but are usually deemed to lie outside the scope of government regulations. Such standards would by their nature be voluntary, and their use would be part of a marketing decision by the firms concerned. In this case one could make a clear distinction between mandatory public standards and voluntary private standards. The marketplace would determine what attributes were desired and how the consumer was to be signalled. The government would make sure that all such products were safe.

Whilst it is useful to keep in mind this simple paradigm of the relationship between public and private standards the most interesting issues arise when it breaks down. Private standards are often related to health and safety issues over and above those established by public authorities. Private standards can even be mandatory if the public agencies choose to adopt such standards *de facto* by requiring compliance for (say) imports. Public authorities may also rely on the private sector for monitoring compliance with public standards, thus giving the appearance of more private sector responsibility in standard setting. Public standards can likewise relate to other attributes where risk is not involved, and can even be voluntary on occasions where no public threat is involved. Moreover, the public and private sector will sometimes cooperate in the setting and the administration of standards, thereby adding more ambiguity to the public/private dichotomy.[3]

This apparent overlap has raised the issue of the definition of private standards from a semantic to a substantive matter. Not least among these questions is the nature of the rules that are supposed to guide the use of standards in international trade. Standards introduced to assure health and safety are governed by the provisions of the Agreement on the application of Sanitary and Phytosanitary Measures (the SPS Agreement), while the standards that are not put in place for such purposes are covered in the broader Technical Barriers to Trade

Agreement (the TBT Agreement). Private standards are not primarily addressed in the SPS Agreement, as this focuses on the obligations that governments undertake to ensure there is no avoidable harm to the trade system. Private standards are more naturally at home in the TBT Agreement, which covers all other such potential trade impediments from labelling to quality specifications whether these are of a public or private nature. As the obligations differ significantly between the SPS and TBT Agreements, defining the appropriate set of WTO rules to be applied to any particular standards is important.

In the literature, the distinction between public and private standards has been handled in various ways. Henson and Humphries (2010), in a useful discussion of this topic, point out that making this distinction is rendered more difficult by the various aspects of the standards themselves: the process of standard setting; the adoption of that standard by an entity; the implementation of the standard and the assessment of conformity to that standard. Both the public and the private sector can undertake these functions. There are examples of 'pure' private food standards, where no government entity is involved. These would include those which had been established by private actors in the market, adopted voluntarily, implemented without government intervention, and assessed by private agencies. Single-firm arrangements for quality control would usually fall into this category. But there are many other schemes that constitute a mix of public and private actions, making the definition a matter of choice depending on the context. As the focus of this chapter is on private standards and the WTO, an inclusive definition of private standards will be used that includes any standards where there has been significant participation (other than lobbying) by private firms and bodies in the setting, adopting and implementation processes.[4] The use of private certification firms to monitor compliance to mandatory public standards is mentioned only briefly.

III. WHY ARE PRIVATE STANDARDS PROLIFERATING?

Though there are examples of private food standards earlier in the last century, today's current flurry of activity can be traced to the 1990s. There are probably over 500 private standards in operation at present (UNCTAD, 2007). A 'perfect storm' of events has left the food production and marketing landscape littered with a complex mix of public regulations and private standards. Such proliferation has been attributed to a convergence of events both in the marketplace and in the regulatory arena.

Perhaps the most basic of such events has been the rise in consumer concerns about the safety of the food they purchase. These have arisen in past decades and resulted in tighter government regulations. In the 1990s these concerns were aligned with a distrust among consumers (or bodies claiming to represent them) of the regulatory mechanism itself. The credibility of food safety agencies (particularly in Europe) had indeed been weakened by some unfortunate lapses and it became fashionable to suspect that the administration of public standards was driven by the needs of the industries concerned rather than by the consumers. This tapped into a parallel concern that corporate interests were beginning to dominate the food chain and promote the products of chemical agriculture at the expense of more healthy and tasty foods.

The rise of this consumer interest in food coincided with the concentration of the food retailing sector and its growing international reach, leading to a period of intense competition among a small number of large firms (Swinnen, 2007). Appealing to consumer concerns about food safety provided retailers with a golden opportunity to position themselves as guardians of the health of their customers, even though they were essentially operating under the umbrella of public food safety laws. By expanding the meaning of 'safety' from its traditional context of the avoidance of illness to include healthy dietary practices and particular production methods, it was not difficult to set up firm-level standards that promised the consumer more assurance than just knowing that the food that retailers sold had been approved by the government as safe.

This concentration of the retail sector contributed to the lengthening of supply chains. Large firms were able to take advantage of lower trade barriers to source foodstuffs from abroad, including from countries that had not been seen as traditional suppliers. Once again Europe took the lead in this development, with foodstuffs arriving daily from Africa and Latin America for sale in the supermarkets. Thus private standards that were aimed at providing assurance for business-to-business transactions became necessary and in turn accelerated the global reach of the food firms. And as supermarkets became established in developing countries the adoption of private standards allowed for improvements in the control of quality and reliability in the sourcing of foodstuffs.

As these trends were unfolding, public food safety agencies were being reorganized to take into account the new realities of consumer activism. Attempts to build a wall between food standards and the special interests of the food producers and manufacturers resulted in the establishment of a new set of agencies with broader accountability. The tension between scientific and political considerations remained but the agencies themselves adopted at least a part of the agenda of the critics of the food safety system. However, these agencies had to live under new trade rules (from the SPS Agreement) that required stricter adherence to scientific evidence and the process of risk management. In this environment the rise of private standards, with their ambiguous relationship to science, helped the public agencies to deflect some of what would otherwise have been a much greater pressure to bend scientific risk assessment to address consumer concerns.

One further change in recent years has accelerated the development of private standards. The trend in several countries has been to extend the legal obligation for maintaining safety in the food chain to the private sector, and to add to that obligation the correct labelling of foods sold with quality attributes. In the UK the Food Safety Act defined offences applying to all stages of the food chain (including farmers) of 'rendering food injurious to health (section 7 of the Act); selling, to the purchaser's prejudice, food which is not of the nature or substance or quality demanded (section 14); and falsely or misleadingly describing or presenting food (section 15)'. The Food Safety Act is one example of national legislation coexisting with the General Food Law Regulation of the European Union, adopted in 2002, which requires the traceability of food products and ingredients and covers recalls. The reaction of private sector entities in the food sector in setting up standards was in part a way of ensuring compliance, in effect collectivizing the process of 'due diligence' in improving information from raw material and ingredient suppliers.

IV. TYPES OF PRIVATE STANDARDS

The standards themselves can be categorized along several lines. This section attempts a characterization of some examples of the more visible of the private standards that impinge on trade in food and agricultural products. Some private standards relate to the production of farm products ('pre-farm gate'), others to the handling and processing of these products after they have entered the chain ('post-farm gate'). Some of the latter apply to the retail firms while others may be more related to processing; some are limited to individual firms and some are collectively set and administered; some are specifically tied to public standards while others can have more strict provisions; some are 'business-to-business' standards and as a consequence are generally invisible to the consumer, others are 'business-to-consumer' standards, usually with an identifying label and accompanying information through promotions. From a more analytical perspective, a further distinction can be made between those that are intended as risk management standards and those whose primary function is product differentiation (Henson and Humphries, 2010: 10). But in practice retailers have an incentive to confuse these two categories, as they would prefer that they are seen as providing information through the standards that both reduces the risk (of buying an inappropriate product) and distinguishes the product (from inferior substitutes sold by competitors).

One ubiquitous pre-farm gate standard of a collective nature is known as GlobalGAP (sometimes written as GlobalG.A.P.) that was developed from the EurepGAP standard adopted by several European firms in 1997. The GlobalGAP standard is a code of Good Agricultural Practice that covers a range of factors, including food safety, animal welfare, environmental impacts and worker health and safety.[5] It was originally retailer-driven, but has now broadened to include other parts of the food industry. It remains in the realm of business-to-business standards and is not identified by a label at the consumer level. It also relies on independent certification bodies in several countries. GlobalGAP has clearly filled a need for the food sector and undoubtedly facilitated a growth in the use of imported foods in major markets. It has attracted the participation of such market players as Walmart and McDonalds. The increase in exports of fruit and vegetables to the European market has demonstrated the usefulness of recognized standards in expanding trade to developing countries. But GlobalGAP has not been without its critics. Some cite the cost of meeting the standards as a block to the participation of small farmers in international trade. Others have noted an overlap with other private standards such as those relating to organic foods.

Following a somewhat different path but to the same end are a set of voluntary collective private standards that have their origins in the International Standards Organization (ISO). The ISO is a private sector standard-setting organization with participation from national standards institutes and private sector standards bodies from 157 countries. The ISO seeks to promote a 'free and fair global trading system' by 'providing the management control underpinnings for quality, technical procedural, safety, management, and environmental process standards' (Knudsen and Josling, 2009). In some respects it effectively bridges the space between private and public agencies. Many key ISO standards are contained in ISO 9000, which has become an international reference for meeting generic quality management requirements in business-to-business dealings. Certification under ISO 9000 has thus become a common management tool for companies wishing to participate in international trade. In addition, ISO 22000 relates specifically to the management of food safety in the food industry and includes more detailed standards such as ISO 22005 which relates to the traceability of foodstuffs. The use of such standards can help in achieving increased uniformity in meeting the customer's quality requirements, in meeting applicable regulatory requirements, in enhancing customer satisfaction, and in ensuring food safety. But the focus of such certification requirements on management systems rather than on the content of specific procedures makes them live more easily with public health and safety regulations.

In contrast to such collective schemes, several pre-farm gate standards are confined to single firms. One early example was the Nature's Choice standard of Tesco PLC, a UK-based retailer. Introduced in 1991, it was developed to assure consumers of the quality of fresh produce sold in the retail store and to impose a code of good practice on growers. The standard covers input use, pollution prevention, wildlife conservation and the protection of worker health. Compliance is independently audited. There is even competition among suppliers to reach the Gold Standard of best practices. In the US market the largest retailer of natural and organic products, Whole Foods Market, has established its own individual sets of standards for fresh produce and for meats, with the latter including acceptable animal husbandry practices. In France the retailer Carrefour has established its own *Filière Qualité* (Quality Chain) to provide assurance to consumers. Such firm-level schemes rarely cross the line between public and private functions when it comes to health and safety: they build on existing public standards rather than attempting to supplant them. But they are also willing to take credit for the existence of public standards even if they have no choice but to accept them.

Of a more ambiguous status are the collective standards that attempt to link quality with national or regional production characteristics. Two such schemes that have had some success include the Red Tractor Assured Food Standards in the UK and the *Label Rouge* standards in France.[6] The *Label Rouge* standards for poultry have their origin in the 1960s as a reaction to the spread of intensive broiler production. *Label Rouge* poultry have secured about one third of the French poultry market with high cost pasture based chicken

(Westgren, 1999). The cachet has spread to other foods where HACCP-based quality control combines with regional tradition. *Label Rouge* supply chains (*filières*) have been established in many regions in France and the concept has even been exported to other countries. One key feature of the *Label Rouge* has been the enthusiasm with which the French government has greeted this private venture. The public authorities are a major player in both advocating and protecting the label.[7] The UK Red Tractor Assurance scheme is only ten years old but has struck a similar chord with UK consumers. Some $15 billion of retail sales in the nation's largest supermarkets carry the Red Tractor logo. It has specifically promoted local food production and probably helped UK agriculture to claim a quality premium over imported products. Such discriminatory practices would not be possible with public sector standards.

Other examples of the spread of private standards include initiatives by the US Food Marketing Institute (FMI) and the British Retail Consortium (BRC). The FMI established a Safe Quality Food (SQF) Institute that introduced a certification programme and management system which covers both primary producers (SQF 1000) and processors (SQF 2000) (Knudsen and Josling, 2009). These standards have now been adopted by a number of firms in several countries. In keeping with its roots, the SQF focuses on the nature of the food and its quality rather than on its method of production. The BRC standard was established in 1998 by UK food retailers as a set of guidelines for food production, processing and handling. These standards are now being used in 100 countries and have been renamed Global Standards. Indeed certification by the BRC has been incorporated into several other private standards.

One German example of a retailer-based quality standard is the *Qualitatsicherung* (QS) certification system that started with meat quality certification in 2001 and expanded to include fruit and vegetables in 2004. German and French retail federations (joined later by the Italian federation) initiated a food certification scheme in 2003 (International Featured Standards or IFS) that attracted support from many of the largest retailers in Europe. Meanwhile a parallel activity aimed at reducing the number of audits required by food firms was started in 2000 and by 2007 had attracted several of the major retailers (including some of those associated with the IFS). Some rationalization of these various schemes appears to be under way to deal with the alphabet soup of standards bodies.

V. DO PRIVATE STANDARDS FACILITATE OR RESTRICT TRADE?

Risk management standards tend to be cost reducing and hence they encourage trade. Firms have more information about their supplies and can avoid costly errors. Consumers may also gain from the reduced asymmetry of information and be encouraged to buy more foreign products than otherwise would be the case. Product differentiation will also tend to generate trade, as countries will vary with regard to the cost of producing to different specifications. Whether that trade creation is the main effect will depend on the content of the standard. If the standard is truly global then there should be a positive impact on reliable suppliers who can meet the standards. But if the standards only apply to a sub-group of countries then there could be some 'trade diversion' away from suppliers who otherwise would be able to compete. This could happen in cases where the standards are developed within a free trade area or another such grouping.[8] Thus, as with preferential tariff reductions, the net impact on trade will depend on the balance between the positive impact of cost reduction and the negative effect of diverting trade away from the most efficient supplier.[9]

The notion that standards may be trade-creating is in interesting contrast to the lengthy literature on 'non-tariff barriers' which are taken to include health and safety regulations and other non-fiscal conditions for market access. Indeed early commentators on private standards did tend to approach them as non-tariff barriers. But the general argument that import regulations impede trade is based on the possibility of their being used as 'hidden protection' by favouring domestic suppliers. Too close a relationship between regulators and domestic industries can indeed give rise to such trade restrictions. But the development of private standards that have as their main aim the assurance that imported (and domestic) products meet some desirable criteria does not seem to fall under the heading of disguised trade barriers. In that they counter problems of asymmetric information the introduction of private standards could be one step in the direction of efficient markets, even if some 'undesirable' trade is excluded. In fact, to push the argument further along, one could make a case that such private standards are the more effective approach to open markets as they do not require complex negotiations on tariff levels. Private firms can sign up to join the supply chain and be granted immediate access rather than wait for governments to reduce tariff barriers. And, as noted above, trade expansion as a result of cost reductions is more beneficial to the economy than the equivalent trade that results from the removal of tariffs.

The first-order effect of the increased trade is to benefit those exporters that can meet the private standards. The gain may come in the form of higher prices or more secure outlets. The issue of the excluded exporters is of course important from an economic as well as a political point of view. If private standards were disguised trade barriers then the excluded suppliers would all be foreign sources of the product. However, as informal trade liberalization the excluded suppliers would be those unable or unwilling to meet the standards. Two separate categories of such excluded suppliers need to be identified: those able to supply goods of the required quality if they were able to secure contracts would suffer most and their existence would reduce the potential benefit of the standards themselves. However, there will often be an excess of willing suppliers when lucrative markets open up and one assumes that the terms of any contracts would adjust rapidly so that no such excess supply is available. It would be in the interest of the buyer (acting as the chain 'captain') to restrict demand and make suppliers compete for contracts, but adequate competition in the retail market should limit this tendency. Excluded suppliers that could not meet the required standards are unequivocally hurt in the short run, though some may do well by keeping up their volume in less differentiated markets while others could revamp their production practices.

One would expect that those excluded suppliers unable to meet the importers' private standards would tend to be in developing countries. Hence the international community may take steps to assist such suppliers. But unless the nature of the private standards themselves had some built-in bias it would seem harsh (and counterproductive) to blame the distributional impact of the standards for the unevenness of quality controls and productive capacity in developing countries. The reaction of countries has been to target assistance towards developing countries in order to help them meet the standards that are required for entry into developed country markets.

Even those producers that gain access to developed country markets may not be the only beneficiaries. How much of the benefits will accrue to the producer of these foods as opposed to the processing, distribution and marketing stages in the chain will depend on individual circumstances. Those producers that cannot meet the private standards will correspondingly lose, though they might be able to shift to supplying other, less demanding, markets. If the consumer has to pay a higher price for attributes that are expressed by the private standards then their benefit will crucially depend on whether other options exist for those consumers who are unwilling to pay for those attributes. 'Over-protection' of consumers who may want nothing more than a safe and inexpensive product regardless of its method of production can be a real if hidden cost (Josling *et al.*, 2004).

Less easy to pin down is the distribution of benefits from standards that allow for increased product differentiation. At a fundamental level, artificial product differentiation in the market for an homogeneous product will be to the advantage of the seller and the disadvantage of the consumer. But helpful product differentiation, based on actual differences in taste, is generally beneficial to consumers. Those who can buy the non-preferred product for a lower price will gain and those who have to pay a higher price for the preferred product can at least be assured that they are not unknowingly consuming an inferior product. However, if consumers rely on marketing information provided by the retailer to define the quality attributes and stimulate the demand for them then some of the benefits to the consumer may be illusory.

VI.   DO PRIVATE STANDARDS CONFLICT WITH PUBLIC STANDARDS?

There would seem to be relatively few cases where conflicts have arisen between public and private standards. Private standards, when they address similar issues to public standards, are by their nature more stringent: there would be little point in developing a standard that is less restrictive than a public standard. They are also in essence voluntary, otherwise they would in effect merely replace the public standard. The voluntary nature of these standards reduces the scope for tensions with multilateral trade rules. Therefore conflicts will tend to occur in areas where public standards do not exist but where market participants consider that a standard is needed to assure health and safety for consumers. If the private sector steps in to develop a standard in these cases, the nature of the private standard can indeed be potentially controversial.

One area that has particular potential for a divergence between public and private standards is in the marketing and labelling of organic foods. Private standards were a reaction to the rapid growth, at least until the 2008–9 recession, in the demand for organic produce. Private retailers rushed to expand their organic food offerings as it became clear that some consumers were prepared to pay substantial premia for organic produce, ranging from strawberries and milk to bread and dog food. Indeed the favourable market reaction to foods that had been raised without synthetic chemicals encouraged producers to add biodiversity and animal welfare attributes under the heading of 'organic' in order to pick up on a wider range of concerns that were being expressed through purchase decisions. In particular, the regulations for organic certification usually included the prohibition of the use of Genetically Modified Organisms – though one could make a case that genetically manipulating a plant to produce its own insecticide was a boon to organic farming.

Government involvement in the development of standards for organic foods was a response to the proliferation of private standards. The first regulations relating to organic foods were formulated to give credibility and cohesion to the growing number of standards being introduced by private organizations and retail outlets. The Soil Association in the UK, for example, which dates back to 1946, became one of the earliest organic certification bodies to be approved by the UK government. The first European Union regulations on organic production appeared in 1991 (Regulation 2092/91) (Josling, 2009; Tilman, 2009). This regulation defined a framework for organic food marketing, including the labelling, processing, inspection, and trading of such products. In 1999 the scope of the legislation was extended to include livestock products. This new legislation firmed up the legal framework for organic production and made mandatory (from July 2010) use of the EU organic logo. The enthusiasm with which the EU Commission has taken up the question of organic food certification matches its support for the spread of such farming practices within the EU.

Though support for organic farming by government agencies in the US has lagged behind that in Europe, the establishment of federal standards for organic foods dates back to the 1990 US Organic Foods Production Act (Josling *et al.*, 2004: 172). The National Standards on Organic Agricultural Production and Handling were introduced in 2000.[10] Other countries followed a similar path, defining national standards or, in several cases, adopting standards that were consistent with those in use in major markets. Thus trade-facilitating developments such as mutual recognition and equivalence have allowed the trade in organic produce to grow. So far governments have been able to avoid the pitfalls of linking organic production with human health. This would undoubtedly antagonize producers of conventional produce and lead to serious trade conflicts. Leaving the private sector to play on the ambiguity of consumer perceptions on this issue has thus far proved to be a winning strategy.

The questions surrounding the standards established for organic foods have their counterparts in other areas. One such standard enjoyed a burst of popularity in the UK in the 1990s. The concept of 'food miles' was promoted as a way of making consumers aware of the increased distances over which food often travels as a part of extended supply chains. Though it never reached the status of a widely adopted private standard it has led to some labels indicating, for instance, whether the food has been air-freighted. Food miles came under criticism from distant suppliers, such as New Zealand, who believed that their own efficiency and low carbon use made up for the extra energy needed for transportation. Pressures for similar types of sustainability certification are also gaining ground, for example, with respect to forest products, fish and biofuels. The import of such products may not be prohibited, but eventually the network of standards both public and private linked to sustainability could effectively result in the same outcome.

VII. DO PRIVATE STANDARDS POSE PROBLEMS FOR THE WTO?

The extent to which private standards are covered by the SPS Agreement is still a matter of some discussion among governments. Though the Agreement mainly applies to measures put in place by governments there is a reference to non-governmental entities in Article 13, which (in part) states that: 'Members shall take such reasonable measures as may be available to them to ensure that non-governmental entities within their territories ... comply with the relevant provisions of this Agreement' (WTO, 1995). This would appear to imply that private sector entities have an obligation to comply and that governments should monitor this compliance. But this implication is not entirely convincing. First, there is no place in the Agreement where the obligations of non-governmental entities are spelt out and as a result the 'relevant provisions' are not specified. One can speculate as to how much of the Agreement might be relevant to the private bodies (such as by ruling out those that require governmental action), but the fact that it is not made clear would always render such speculation groundless. Second, the obligation on governments to take reasonable measures when available to them represents the weakest form of 'best endeavours' commitment. It is not clear what would constitute a reasonable measure to ensure compliance when the obligation on the private sector is itself imprecise. And to make even that commitment subject to the availability of appropriate measures (rather than obliging governments to set up such monitoring) compounds the problem. It is difficult to see how that part of Article 13 would be interpreted by a panel if the challenge was that a government had failed to enforce the provisions of the SPS Agreement on a private sector standard-setting body.

Somewhat more precise is the final sentence of Article 13, which states that: 'Members shall ensure that they rely only on the services of non-governmental entities for implementing sanitary and phytosanitary measures only if these entities comply with the provisions of this Agreement' (WTO, 1995). This sentence has a much more direct application. Governments cannot evade their own responsibilities by handing the implementation (including accreditation) of their health and safety regulations to private bodies. All the provisions of the Agreement would seem to apply to those private sector entities that are entrusted with the task of implementation. So far the question of the use of private firms for certification related to public standards has not posed any significant trade problems.

So in what connection has this issue been raised? The SPS Committee has been discussing the question of private standards for some time. In 2005 there was a request by the government of St Vincent and the Grenadines to consider the implication of standards relating to banana imports in the EU on small farmers in that country (G/SPS/GEN/766). The claim was that the restrictions on pesticide use under a private standard (EurepGAP) adopted by the importers were more stringent than those under EU import rules. The EU indicated not only that EurepGAP standards were voluntary and not required by EU legislation, but also that the higher private standards were not inconsistent with EU rules. As the importers concerned accounted for a large share of the exports from St Vincent, they *de facto* constituted mandatory standards. By imposing high costs on their producers the private sector standards were in effect limiting the participation of small farmers in profitable trade: 'Thus the choice of whether or not to comply with a voluntary standard becomes a choice between compliance or exit from the market. In this way, the distinction between private voluntary standards and mandatory 'official' or 'public' requirements can blur' (Wolff and Scannell, 2008).

By 2007 the question of private standards had been elevated to a separate agenda item and in turn has been discussed extensively at SPS

Committee meetings. Information sessions were held to discuss the problem and suggest strategies that could be used by developing countries (G/SPS/GEN/746). Concerns focused on the linked issues of the extent to which private standards constituted a barrier to market access; the burden of the costs of meeting these standards on developing countries; and the extent to which WTO agreements covered such private standards. Despite the fact that meeting private standards undoubtedly adds to the costs of developing country exporters, it is not clear whether the WTO can do much through the SPS Committee to alleviate such burdens. Other multilateral bodies, namely those with the funds available to strengthen the capacity to meet developed country standards, have begun to take up this issue. But the question of whether private standards are subject to some of the disciplines of the SPS Agreement is still a matter for resolution.[11]

So what about the TBT Agreement? Article 3 of the Agreement specifically covers the 'preparation, adoption and application of technical regulations by local government bodies and non-governmental bodies'. The provisions of this article match those in the SPS Agreement: Members 'shall take such reasonable measures as may be available to them to ensure compliance with the same provisions as apply to central governmental bodies', except that of notification. Moreover, central government bodies shall not 'require or encourage non-governmental bodies to act in a way inconsistent' with TBT obligations, and they should 'formulate and implement positive measures and mechanisms in support of the observance of the provisions' by non-governmental bodies. A similar obligation is imposed on governments with respect to non-governmental conformity assessment entities. The implication of these obligations on Members is that discrimination and other practices that are not allowed by government entities should not be adopted by the private sector while public authorities look the other way.

The TBT Agreement also sets out a Code of Good Practice (Annex 3) for non-governmental or industry bodies to prepare, adopt and apply voluntary or private standards. The Code is extensive and includes fundamental provisions for non-discrimination and avoiding standards that impede trade unnecessarily. Over 250 standard-setting bodies apply this code. On paper it would seem to address many of the concerns of developing countries. But Häberli (2008), in a study of market access into the EU and Switzerland of products from developing countries, concludes that 'in practice, however, there is little evidence of such private standard-setters actually having considered the concerns of exporting countries and operators, especially in developing countries. On the contrary, in quite a few cases developing country operators have to meet requirements which exceed production standards in [the developed] country'.

Private standards are also potentially subject to the provisions of the Agreement on Pre-shipment Inspection (API). The API addresses the practice of inspecting traded goods in the territory of the exporter before those goods are shipped to the importer. Such inspection has often been introduced to make it easier to import from developing countries. But the problems relating to discrimination, unnecessary delays and other cost-raising practices led to the adoption in the Uruguay Round of new rules to facilitate such arrangements. A 'pre-shipment entity' in the context of the API is one that is 'contracted or mandated by a Member to carry out pre-shipment inspection activities' (Article 1:4 of the API), so if a private firm arranges for the pre-shipment inspection the constraints in the API (non-discrimination, etc.) will not apply. However, developing countries may on some occasions become involved in such practices as a way of building up exports. In that case the API could become relevant to the standards.

Occupying a position somewhere between a private sector organization and a public body is the International Standards Organization. In the case of ISO standards there has been a more conscious attempt to avoid conflicts with the WTO bodies. Such standards are designed 'to be consistent with and to facilitate compliance with multilateral rules in the Agreement on the Application of Sanitary and Phytosantitary Standards (SPS) and the Agreement on Technical Barriers to Trade (TBT) within the World Trade Organization (WTO)'. But in contrast to the multilateral standard-setting bodies mentioned in the SPS Agreement, the ISO has no special relationship with the WTO's SPS provisions. However, with widespread acceptance of ISO quality management standards the ISO has become an important part of the global standards environment.

VIII. HOW MIGHT PRIVATE STANDARDS BE IMPROVED?

The proliferation of private standards in food and agricultural trade channels has not (yet) produced any major conflict either with multilateral trade rules or with public health and safety standards. Evidence that trade has been impeded is more anecdotal than overwhelming. Some exporters have benefited while others have had to struggle to meet the strict requirements of retail-led supply chains. But there is an underlying inconsistency that is likely to emerge at some stage. Governments have committed themselves (in the SPS Agreement) to adopt regulations based on science and risk assessment in matters of animal, plant and human health. Quality standards are not so constrained (and hence are covered by the TBT Agreement). Private firms, in particular retailers, have no interest in maintaining this firewall between risk-management and quality attributes. They sell a bundle of attributes tailored to consumer demands and ambiguity on such matters as the health claims for organic produce is part of their strategy. Governments appear content to let such matters be handled by the private sector and so may be reluctant to step in to clarify matters.

This apparent stasis does not mean that the situation could not be improved. Several suggestions have been made that might defuse future conflicts. These fall under three heads: the clarification of the place of the private standards in the SPS agreement; the use of codes of best practice for private standard-setting bodies; and the simplification of the task facing producers to comply with multiple standards.

The need for a clarification of the extent to which private standards are covered by the SPS Agreement is widely acknowledged. Constructive ambiguity can help in reaching an agreement but this becomes an impediment when that agreement must be interpreted. The SPS Committee could develop guidelines on the implementation of Article 13. This would avoid the need to amend the text, which could lead to demands to introduce other amendments. The problem is that WTO members may find it difficult to agree on those guidelines. There is a divide between those that are unwilling to extend the reach of the SPS rules to health-related claims by private standard-setting bodies and those who see such an extension as desirable to avoid costly confusion. As a result the matter may have to be clarified by legal rather than political interpretation. A conflict that had resulted in a report from a dispute settlement panel would perhaps clarify the meaning of Article 13. So far no issue has arisen that has been commercially significant enough to spark a dispute.

There also appears to be room for improvement in the way in which private standards are set and in their relation to public standards (regardless of the import of Article 13). The TBT Agreement obliges non-governmental standard-setting bodies to adhere to a Code of Good Practice. It seems odd that these bodies are less constrained when they are considering standards in the area covered by the SPS

Agreement. Many of the private standards schemes already profess adherence to the TBT Code, as mentioned above, and so it would seem relatively uncontroversial to require this of all such standards in the food area. The Code deals with matters of non-discrimination, harmonization and the avoidance of unnecessary restrictions on trade, but it also obliges standards bodies to avoid an overlap with other standards. It may be somewhat easier for governments concerned about excessive costs in meeting standards to be able to address the bodies concerned in the context of an obligation to follow a code.

Some of this is already taking place for reasons not connected to international pressures. Those using private standards have an interest in avoiding costly duplication and confusion among suppliers. The process of 'benchmarking' is being adopted increasingly to relate different standards to some base or benchmark. In this way standards in use in different countries can be evaluated in terms of their relation to the base standard. This does not imply harmonization around one standard (though that could be the outcome in some instances) but it does facilitate mutual recognition. It also provides a possibility of tracking the progress over time of improvements in standards. And, for better or worse, it gives governments additional scope for requiring adherence to 'voluntary' private standards as an alternative to developing mandatory public standards.

Assuming that the use of private standards continues to increase, we may eventually see a time when these standards largely crowd out those that are promulgated by public bodies. Not that the government agencies will lose interest in health and safety but the private standards and the certifications that underpin them may take over many of the functions currently performed by the public sector. In this case one might expect to see more attempts by governments to extend at least some minimal discipline over private standards. To the extent that governments will retain ultimate responsibility in matters of health and safety it is not unreasonable to expect that private standards in that area will become more consistent with the obligations undertaken by governments. Progress in this direction will not come easily if the private sector considers that risk assessment and the use of scientific evidence are too difficult to sell to consumers. As a result this development may have to wait until consumers regain their trust in the scientific establishment and their role in government. Until then the tension remains between public food standards based on acceptable levels of risk consistent with the SPS Agreement and private standards aimed at reassuring consumers that good agricultural practices accompanied by traceability are their best way of regulating the food chain.

NOTES

1.   Seminal contributions include Henson and Reardon (2005) and Fulponi (2006). These articles include references to the earlier literature on standards and trade and to the structural changes in the food industry that have been in part a cause of the proliferation of private standards.

2.   One group of studies has shed light on the practical impact of standards for Africa and other developing regions (Jaffee and Henson, 2005; OECD, 2006a; Fulponi, 2007; Haberli, 2008; World Bank, 2005; Anders and Caswell, 2009; Swinnen and Maertens, 2007).

3.   Overlaying these issues is that of the definition of 'private' in those cases where the government maintains a hand in the private sector activity. This question is not addressed here.

4.   Public standards generally involve public sector participation in the setting of standards, by means of comments. To be a private standard under this definition, the private sector should have participated in the adoption and implementation as well as the setting of the standard.

5.   Though many of these private standards focus on the production of agricultural crops and livestock products, similar 'Good Practice' standards are found at other levels of the supply chain. Examples include Good handling practices (GHP), Good processing practices (GPP) and Good management practices (GMP) (Knudsen and Josling, 2009).

6.   The use of the word 'red' in both these schemes is puzzling, as it is usually taken as a warning: green tractors and labels might seem to provide more comfort to the consumer.

7.   In addition, the *Label Rouge* is registered as a Protected Geographical Indication (PGI) under EU law.

8.   Though the same can be said about public standards, at least there is a multilateral framework (the SPS Agreement) under which such standards are regulated. There is still a chance of an efficient supplier being excluded from a market because its government has not adopted the appropriate standard. But the mechanism exists for such trade diversion to be minimized, such as through the adoption of international standards or the negotiation of equivalence agreements.

9.   It should be pointed out that the economic gains from 'new' trade as a result of cost reductions are greater than those associated with a tariff reduction that generates the equivalent volume of trade. A portion of the impact of the tariff cut is a transfer from government to consumer in the importing country. The reduction in transactions cost adds to consumer welfare but has no corresponding taxpayer loss.

10. Following an extraordinary response to the request for public comment, the USDA agreed to ban the use of GM ingredients and radiation in the production of organic foods.

11. A submission by the UK government on this question (G/SPS/GEN/802) addresses some of these legal issues.

BIBLIOGRAPHY

Anders, S. and Caswell, J. (2009) 'Standards as Barriers versus Standards as Catalyst: Assessing the impact of HACCP Implementation on U.S. Seafood Imports', *American Journal of Agricultural Economics*, **91**: 310–321.

Fulponi, L. (2006) 'Private Voluntary Standards in the Food System: The perspective of major food retailers in OECD countries', *Food Policy,* **31** (1): 1–13.

Fulponi, L. (2007) 'Private Voluntary Standards and Developing Country Market Access: Preliminary results', communication from OECD to WTO SPS Committee, G/SPS/GEN/763, 27 February.

Gascoine, D. (2007) 'PVS within the WTO Multilateral Framework'. Report for DFID.

Häberli, C. (2008) 'Market Access in Switzerland and in the European Union for Agricultural Products from Least Developed Countries,' *NCCR Working Paper No 2008/5*, Bern.

Henson, S. (2007) 'The Role of Public and Private Standards in Regulating International Food Markets', *Journal of International Agricultural Trade and Development,* **4** (1): 52–66.

Henson, S. and Humphries, J. (2010) 'Understanding the Complexities of Private Standards in Global Agri-Food Chains' (manuscript).

Henson, S. and Reardon, T. (2005) 'Private Agri-food Standards: Implications for food policy and the agri-food system', *Food Policy,* **30** (3): 241–253.

Jaffee, S. and Henson, S. (2005) 'Agro-Food Exports from Developing Countries: The challenges posed by standards', in *Global Agricultural Trade and Developing Countries*. Washington, DC: World Bank.

Josling, T. (2009) 'EU Food Quality and Food Labeling Policies: Burden or opportunity for developing countries?' (contribution to GMF study on the impact of EU policies on Developing Countries).

Josling, T., Roberts, D. and Orden, D. (2004) *Food Regulation and Trade: Toward a Safe and Open Global System*. Washington, DC: Institute for International Economics.

Knudsen, R. and Josling, T. (2009) 'A New Generation of Standards: Implications for the Caribbean and Latin America', Economic Commission for Latin America and the Caribbean, Project Document.

OECD (2006a) *Private Standard Schemes and Developing Country Access to Global Value Chains: Challenges and Opportunities Emerging from Four Case Studies*. Paris: OECD.

OECD (2006b) 'Private Standards and the Shaping of the Agro-Food System', AGR/CA/APM(2006)9/FINAL. Paris: OECD.

St Vincent and the Grenadines (2007) 'Private Industry Standards', G/SPS/GEN/766, Geneva.

Swinnen, J. (ed) (2007) *Global Supply Chains: Standards and the Poor*. Wallingford: CABI.

Swinnen, J. and Maertens, M. (2007) 'Globalization, Agri-food Standards and Development', *Rivista di Economia Agraria,* **62** (3): 413–421.

Tilman, B. (2009) 'European Food Quality Policy: The importance of geographical indications, organic certification and food quality assurance schemes in European countries', *Estey Centre Journal of International Law and Trade Policy,* **10** (1): 111–130.

UNCTAD (2007) 'Typology of Global Standards', published as WTO Document G/SPS/GEN/760, 26 February, Geneva.

Westgren, R. (1999) 'Delivering Food Safety, Food Quality, and Sustainable Production Practices: The Label Rouge poultry system in France', *American Journal of Agricultural Economics*: 1107–1111.

Wolff, C. and Scannell, M. (2008) 'Implication of Private Standards in International Trade of Animals and Animal Products', 76th General Session of the International Committee of the World Organization for Animal Health (OIE, Paris).

World Bank (2005) 'Food Safety and Agricultural Health Standards: Challenges and opportunities for developing country exports', Report no. 31207. Washington, DC: World Bank.

WTO (1995) *The Results of the Uruguay Round of Multilateral Trade Negotiations: The Legal Texts*. Geneva: WTO.

WTO (2007) 'Private Standards and the SPS Agreement: Note by the Secretariat', G/SPS/GEN/746. Geneva: WTO.

WEBSITES FOR INFORMATION ON SELECTED PRIVATE STANDARDS:

British Retail Consortium Global Standard: www.brc.org.uk/standards/about_food.htm

Carrefour Filière Qualité: www.carrefour.fr/etmoi/fqc/

EurepGAP: www.eurepgap.org

Global Food Safety Initiative: www.ciesnet.com/2-wwedo/2.2-programmes/2.2.food safety.gfsi.asp

International Featured Standards: www.food-care.info

ISO 22000 (Food safety management systems) and ISO 22005 (Traceability in the feed and food chain): www.iso.org

Label Rouge: www.label-rouge.org

Qualitat und Sicherheit GmbH QS: www.q-s.info/index.php?id=92&L=1

Red Tractor Assured Food Standards: www.redtractor.org.uk

Safe Quality Food (SQF) 1000 and 2000: www.sqfi.com

Tesco Nature's Choice: www.tescocorporate.com

9 Climate change policies for agriculture and WTO agreements

David Blandford

I. INTRODUCTION

Since the General Agreement on Tariffs and Trade (GATT) was drafted in 1947 the policy agenda for international trade has expanded enormously. The primary concern in the immediate post-war period was to impose greater discipline on trade policies by promoting transparency and non-discrimination through the application of tariffs on the most-favoured-nation (MFN) principle, and to provide a framework for negotiated reductions in those tariffs. The trade agenda expanded during the 1960s when the interests of developing countries came to greater prominence, culminating in waivers to allow rich countries to offer tariff preferences to poorer countries. Exceptions were also made for the reduction in tariffs among members of trading blocs, such as the European Union (EU), providing that there was non-discrimination among WTO members outside the bloc (through a common tariff applied by each country or a common external tariff applied by all countries). The Uruguay Round agreement of 1994, establishing the World Trade Organization (WTO), reflected a further major expansion in the trade agenda by effectively including agriculture under GATT disciplines for the first time through a specific Agreement on Agriculture (the AoA). The provisions of a number of other Uruguay Round agreements are also of significance for the sector. These include those on sanitary and phyto-sanitary measures (SPS) and technical barriers to trade (TBT), and a strengthened approach to subsidies through the Agreement on Subsidies and Countervailing Measures (SCM). A much improved dispute settlement procedure was also an important development for trade issues that could be contentious, and this often applies to agriculture.

More recently, the WTO framework has been confronted by an expanding range of global issues, which although not limited to international trade have implications for existing agreements and for the future direction of world trade law. Environmental issues in general and those associated with climate change fall into this category.

II. NEW POLICY ISSUES AND THE GATT/WTO FRAMEWORK

The central purpose of the GATT/WTO framework is to impose disciplines on trade and related policies and to facilitate trade liberalization. The framework was founded on the presumption that government policies affecting trade were aimed either at protecting domestic industries from international competition (through measures to restrict imports) or at providing domestic industries with a competitive advantage in international markets (through various forms of export subsidies). Both types of measures led to international market 'distortions' that are reflected in lower prices to the detriment of non-subsidizing exporters. The interests of importers, who might benefit from lower prices, were not taken into account. The belief was that trade liberalization through multilateral negotiations would reduce distortions by opening up markets to greater competition. The logic of this approach finds its foundation in classical and neo-classical economic theory, which demonstrates that under certain assumptions, such as the existence of competitive markets, free trade will result in the maximization of global economic welfare; by contrast, protective trade policies will result in a reduction in global welfare.[1]

By the time the Uruguay Round of GATT negotiations were launched in 1986 this purist view of the gains from international trade had begun to be questioned. It had long been realized that markets might not result in the most efficient allocation of resources because of the existence of externalities. Unpriced 'goods', such as positive or negative environmental effects, might be generated by economic activity. The emission of greenhouse gases (GHG) is a clear example of an unpriced good that can have a negative impact on economic welfare. Producers who generate such emissions do not face a cost in contributing to the damage associated with global warming and consequently fail to take emissions into account in deciding how much to produce.[2] Consumers will face a lower price for the good since the full production costs (including the costs of any damage) are not reflected in the price. Taken together, these effects will result in the over-production and over-consumption of a good that creates a negative externality.

Land-use management practices resulting in the sequestration of atmospheric carbon in the soil are also an example of an unpriced good since producers are unlikely to be rewarded for the positive contribution made to reducing global warming. There are also some goods (so-called public goods) whose production costs are difficult to recover through the market; an example here might be the preservation of natural habitats that contribute to the removal of carbon from the atmosphere. Economic welfare may be reduced if the value of preserving such natural habitats is not taken into account. The inability of markets, when left to their own devices, to generate an efficient allocation of resources in the presence of externalities or public goods is termed 'market failure'.

Three main approaches have been suggested to deal with the problem. One is to impose regulations on producers that will have the effect of internalizing the costs of pollution. An example of this is the imposition of a limit on GHG emissions for each emitter. Providing that the permitted amount of emissions is less than would otherwise be generated under existing prices and that the regulation is enforced, the resulting reduction in total profit would reflect the implicit internalization of the costs of pollution.[3] If the total supply of the product is reduced its price will rise and at least part of the pollution cost will be passed on to consumers. A second approach is to create property rights, that is, to provide control over the allocation of an unpriced good so that its providers can recoup the full costs of its provision. An example here would be to limit the total quantity of emissions and to create tradable emission permits. High emitters will need to purchase permits from low emitters in order to maintain a given level of output and this will cause the costs of emissions to be reflected in product prices. Again, for this approach to be effective the total amount of permitted emissions must be less than would otherwise be generated under existing prices, emissions must be monitored, and sufficiently high penalties imposed for non-compliance. A third approach is to use taxes and subsidies to internalize the costs of externalities or public goods. An example of this would be to impose a carbon tax equivalent to the cost of the environmental damage generated by the release of atmospheric carbon in the production of goods to internalize the costs of that damage. Similarly, a subsidy could be paid to those who generated positive externalities or provided public goods to ensure that there was a sufficient supply of these. Many economists tend to have a preference for the 'market-based' approaches of property right creation and taxes/subsidies and to be suspicious of regulation due to the inflexibility that this may create. However, regulation can be an efficient (and essential) approach to correcting some market failure problems if designed and implemented appropriately (see Blandford, 2010, for a further discussion of these issues).

The internalization of the costs of externalities will affect the distribution of economic welfare among producers and consumers, as well as between the two groups. In the context of negative externalities, all of the approaches suggested above are founded on the polluter-pays principle (i.e., that the party responsible for generating pollution should bear the responsibility for correcting the resulting distortion in markets).[4] This can be difficult to implement in practice. For example, while it may be fairly straightforward to determine emissions of greenhouse gases from plants that burn coal to produce electricity, it may be much more difficult to determine emissions from growing crops or producing livestock because of the geographically dispersed nature of farming activities. The former point-source pollution is far easier to address than the latter non-point-source pollution.

There has been an extreme reluctance to apply the polluter-pays approach to agriculture, even in the face of considerable problems in such areas as water quality. Instead, countries have often adopted a pay-the-polluter approach, namely by using subsidies and other incentives to induce farmers to reduce the negative externalities generated by their activities. The redistributive implications of the pay-the-polluter approach are more attractive to farmers than the polluter-pays approach and the former tends to be more acceptable politically. Unfortunately, paying the polluter has often proven to be expensive and inefficient in reducing agricultural externalities. In addition, since it involves subsidies rather than taxes, producers who are not eligible to receive payments (particularly those in other countries) are often sceptical about its use. They view it as a way of maintaining production at a higher level than would otherwise be the case and hence being equivalent to a production subsidy.

In an international context the pay-the-polluter approach is even more problematic to implement since it can involve a redistribution between nations, between high polluting versus low polluting countries, and between rich and poor.

III. CLIMATE CHANGE POLICIES AND AGRICULTURE

It is now widely accepted that the world's climate is changing and that we are in a period of global warming. The earth's climate has gone through various phases of warming and cooling even within the span of human history, and there is some disagreement about how much of the current warming is due to human activity. Many compounds found in the Earth's atmosphere act as 'greenhouse gases' in that they allow sunlight to pass through the atmosphere but absorb reflected infrared radiation from the earth's surface – essentially trapping heat in the atmosphere and contributing to global warming. The concentration of these gases (primarily water vapour, carbon dioxide, methane and nitrous oxide) has increased substantially since the beginning of the Industrial Revolution in the eighteenth century. In 2005 the atmospheric concentration of carbon dioxide (CO_2) was 379 parts per million (ppm) compared to a range of 275 to 285 ppm in the pre-industrial era (AD 1000–1750) (Solomon *et al.*, 2007).

Agriculture is unusual in that it is one of a small number of industries that can contribute positively and negatively to climate change – negatively, by generating greenhouse gas emissions, and positively, by removing carbon from the atmosphere (sequestration). Agriculture is a major source of global GHG emissions, accounting for at least 10–12 per cent of total anthropogenic emissions in 2005 (Wreford *et al.*, 2010). That may be compared to the estimated contribution of agriculture to world GDP of roughly 6 per cent (CIA, 2011). Methane (CH_4) produced by animals through enteric fermentation or manure and from rice cultivation accounts for roughly 54 per cent of agriculture's total emissions (CO_2 equivalent), with the balance in the form of nitrous oxide (N_2O) released as a result of a range of soil and land management practices. Agriculture accounts for roughly 60 per cent of global emissions of nitrous oxide and roughly 50 per cent of total methane emissions. In addition, agriculture is a significant user of energy through the energy content of agro-chemicals and other purchased inputs, on-farm energy consumption and the use of transportation services. While on-farm energy use in OECD agriculture is roughly in-line with its contribution to GDP at around 2 per cent of total energy consumption (OECD, 2008), energy usage in a range of closely related sectors – including those that supply farm inputs and transportation services, process food and deliver it to consumers – is far higher. A recent analysis for the food system as a whole in the United States concluded that the total food-related share of the national energy budget was roughly 16 per cent in 2007 (Canning *et al.*, 2010).

Analysis suggests that changes in technology and management practices could substantially reduce GHG emissions from agriculture. A study of UK land use by agriculture and forestry in 2008, for example, estimated that under a policy environment that promotes mitigation, GHG emissions from UK agriculture could be reduced by 6 per cent in 2012 and close to 25 per cent in 2022 (a study by DEFRA quoted by Wreford *et al.*, 2010). A study of carbon sequestration potential in US agriculture concluded that with a sufficiently high level of economic incentives (price for carbon) an amount of carbon equivalent to 4–8 per cent of total US GHG emissions in 2001 could be sequestered by agriculture through changes in land use and management practices (Lewandrowski *et al.*, 2004).

IV. POLICY APPROACHES TO CLIMATE CHANGE IN AGRICULTURE AND WTO AGREEMENTS

In line with many other sectors of the economy, agriculture is likely to be affected by economy-wide policies that attempt to reduce GHG emissions. Such policies include the regulation of emissions, carbon taxes and cap-and-trade schemes. Trade policies might be influenced by the use of such policies and this could have implications for obligations and rights under existing WTO agreements. There is a possibility that differential treatment might be applied to agriculture under some of these policies and that this might have WTO implications. Finally, specific sectoral policies might be used to promote the positive contribution of agriculture to GHG mitigation, which may also affect WTO rights and obligations.

a.   Economy-wide Climate Change Policies

The internalization of GHG emission costs through regulation, the imposition of taxes on fossil-fuel energy sources (coal, natural gas, oil), or the use of cap-and-trade schemes would all affect profitability in the agricultural sector. Agriculture is a significant user of fossil-fuels, not least through the natural gas which is the principal feedstock for fertilizer, but also through direct energy consumption in agricultural production. Without changes in input use, either through gains in efficiency in the use of fossil fuels or the substitution of 'green' alternatives for fossil-fuel inputs, agriculture's costs would rise as a result of higher energy prices. Cost increases would be felt by farmers through lower profits and by consumers through higher food prices. Given the price inelasticity of food demand the burden would be primarily borne by consumers over the long-run, but there could be important redistributive impacts within the agricultural sector. High fossil-fuel-using products that are prone to substitution effects in consumption would likely experience a decline in demand and become less profitable.

The use of regulations to limit GHG emissions or cap-and-trade schemes to internalize emission costs is less likely to impose additional direct costs on agriculture because of the challenges, both political and practical, of including the sector in such policies. As noted earlier, it is difficult to regulate agricultural emissions because of the non-point-pollution issue. By extension, it is also difficult to impose an effective cap on those emissions. Nevertheless, efforts could be made to include agriculture in cap-and-trade (CT) schemes. GHG emission standards could be specified for agricultural production processes, similar to the emission standards that target phosphorous, nitrogen or organic material in order to improve water quality.[5] As with other forms of regulation, the effectiveness of this approach depends on the ability to monitor GHG emissions in agriculture and to impose penalty costs on those who exceed allowable standards. It is easier to achieve this for concentrated production operations, such as animal feedlots that are point sources of pollution rather than more diversified farming operations, which are non-point sources. As a result, this approach is likely to have a limited application in agriculture.

There has been considerable political interest in using CT schemes rather than carbon taxes, not least because the potential for changes in agricultural activities to reduce emissions or to sequester carbon opens up the possibility of creating an additional revenue stream for farmers. It is also viewed as more politically expedient to establish emission limits than to impose new taxes. CT schemes require that a limit be placed on the total volume of GHG emissions. Firms can then buy and sell permits to emit. Initial emission allowances can be distributed to firms without cost or auctioned off to the highest bidder (or a combination of these methods can be used). Providing that the cap is binding, the former yields a windfall gain to firms while the latter results in revenue for taxpayers. To be effective, CT schemes require that the compliance with emission permits be monitored and that there are sanctions which will make it unprofitable not to comply.

There are several possible implications of a government-established CT system for agriculture. A key issue is whether agriculture's GHG emissions are included in the cap and whether they would be subject to limitations. If that is the case, farmers might be subject to the same windfall gain from an initial allocation of GHG entitlements as other firms. Farmers are provided with an additional asset (the emission permit) that has a market value. If they are able to reduce their emissions below the allowable limit the sale of unused permits yields additional income. If they are not able to do this, the need to obtain additional permits turns CT into an additional cost of production as CT acts to internalize the external costs of emissions (providing that compliance with the cap can be monitored effectively). As with carbon taxes, CT can also impose additional costs on agriculture indirectly. For example, emissions from industries supplying agriculture with inputs (energy, chemicals, and machinery) or services, such as transportation, might be constrained through CT. In that case, the cost of agricultural inputs and marketing services will rise. If farmers or those that provide them with marketing services are not able to realize offsetting productivity gains, such that the use of inputs and services per unit of output falls, costs will increase and their profits will decline. Internalizing the costs of emissions in this way leads to an economy-wide restructuring of production costs.

Agriculture can benefit from CT even if its emissions are not included in the cap. Agricultural producers may be allowed to offer carbon credits (offsets) resulting from carbon sequestration or other GHG reduction activities to firms that are subject to emission constraints. Firms could meet their requirements in part by purchasing such agricultural offsets. Farmers might be able to realize revenues from producing biomass (e.g., planting trees) or reducing methane emissions from livestock by using manure digesters to generate biogas for electricity production. In such cases there can be two revenue streams: one from selling the initial GHG reduction credit and a second from the sale of related products (e.g., wood or energy). In addition to policies that attempt to internalize the costs of GHG emissions, governments may introduce measures to stimulate the development of new technologies ('green' technologies), either through providing funding for public research and development or tax credits and other financial incentives for private firms to develop and adopt such technologies.

b.   Economy-wide Climate Change Policies and WTO Agreements

Policies that impose explicit or implicit taxes on domestic producers rarely provoke challenges in the WTO, since they are likely to reduce exports, rather than increase them. Although importers may be negatively affected by higher world prices, their opportunities to complain are few. In general, this accentuates the asymmetry of current trade rules, which constrain the behaviour of governments of importing countries to a much greater extent than that of exporting countries (Mitra and Josling, 2009).

Taxes on domestic producers can pose a challenge to trade rules if they are accompanied by adjustments in tariffs or border taxes or other devices to offset their apparent competitive impacts. If the domestic industry is being taxed to reduce the use of fossil fuels or the emission of GHG then imports of competing goods from other countries using similar technologies will not help to achieve those objectives; this is often called 'carbon leakage'. It could be argued that the tax merely redistributes production of the good in question and does not achieve the broader global aim of GHG reduction or fossil fuel replacement. On the other hand producers in other countries may also be applying measures to reduce emissions, or might be able to produce goods using lower-emission technologies.[6] In agriculture, for example, less intensive production of crops and livestock in some countries that have a comparative advantage in agriculture could generate lower emissions. In that case the use of a border tax will act against the tax policy by reducing its effectiveness. Indeed one could argue for an import subsidy as a complement to the domestic producer tax if lower emission foreign sources of products are available. The essential issue here is that the GATT/WTO framework is based on the assumption that any differential treatment of trading partners is discriminatory, rather than a necessary requirement to eliminate the distortions created by market failure.

If countries are to meet their existing obligations under WTO agreements they have only limited ability to address the problems created by carbon leakage through the use of existing tariffs. A major success of the GATT has been to reduce the tariffs on many goods progressively and through the AoA some limited progress has been achieved in agriculture. Some countries apply tariffs below the bound rates that resulted from the Agreement and they would be able to increase those without violating their commitments. However, since the MFN principle would still apply, it would not be possible to use differential tariffs to address the issue of varying carbon leakage as the result of differing climate change policies in trading partners. If sufficient 'headroom' existed between an existing applied tariff and the bound rate, the applied tariff could be increased to offset a cost advantage created by lower emission standards in another country, but in applying the MFN principle the rate would have to be set at a level to offset the cost advantage of the highest polluter. While this would not be discriminatory in WTO terms, it would be in economic terms, since a trading partner with the strictest climate change standards and hence the highest increase in costs would face the greatest challenge in overcoming the effects of the MFN tariff.

The basic issue here is that the GATT/WTO framework is based on the assumption that any differential treatment of trading partners is likely to be designed to alter the balance of competition to the advantage of the discriminating party. The possibility that differential treatment might be required in order to address externalities was not considered. The AoA through its Green Box provisions does admit to the existence of externalities but limits the treatment of these to domestic support measures, rather than extending this to trade measures. The relevance of the AoA in this respect is addressed below.

A carbon tax is a broad-based tax and it raises issues similar to sales taxes or value added taxes. Under such conditions 'border tax adjustments' are justified to prevent distortions to international trade as a result of the incidence of these taxes. If industries are taxed at the point of production (the origin principle) then a country's exports will be burdened and imports encouraged unless imports face the same tax and exports are taxed in the country of destination.[7] Border tax adjustments (BTAs) are consistent with WTO rules (Article III of the GATT), though their implementation could cause problems.[8] The US administration has indicated that it wishes to avoid potential clashes with trade rules in developing US climate change legislation. Retaliation by other countries would be virtually assured if border tax adjustments were to be applied, particularly since it is almost inevitable that these would differ by country of origin of the products concerned and would likely be considered discriminatory under the provisions of the GATT. Whether the US Congress will actually follow a cautious path in terms of international obligations if it eventually addresses climate change policies remains to be seen, since the application of border tax adjustments in order to create a 'level playing field' (i.e., to correct any perceived competitive advantage created for competitors) could have considerable domestic appeal. When trade policies are determined largely on the basis of domestic political considerations the scope for conflicts is enlarged.

The link between cap-and-trade systems and trade rules is of particular relevance. Emissions trading systems are already in place in Europe and Australia and are being discussed in many other countries. It is not the imposition of the cap on emissions, which would normally give foreign competitors an advantage, that causes trade problems, but the response of the government to requests by domestic producers for a level playing field. There are two key aspects of the administration of a CT policy that can adversely influence trade partners. The first is the allocation of permits: free distribution of a portion of the permits could be considered by competitors to be a subsidy to the firms that receive them. The second issue is whether firms exporting to the country operating a CT scheme themselves require permits.

Several of the bills that were under consideration by the US Congress in 2009 specifically called for firms supplying imports to the

US to have permits (issued in their own countries) to avoid undercutting US firms (Hufbauer *et al.,* 2009). A bill approved by the House Energy and Commerce Committee (the American Clean Energy and Security Act of 2009) allowed for the possibility of border taxes at a later date (after 2020), but called for the negotiation of binding emission reductions with other countries before that time. It also provided for International Reserve Allowances (to begin after 2025) that would be required for imported inputs of raw materials (agriculture is not specifically mentioned) to avoid carbon leakage. The degree to which such requirements could be subject to challenges in the WTO is unclear. To the extent that requirements are imposed unilaterally and are viewed to be discriminatory in terms of their impact on trading partners, the likelihood of a challenge is increased. On the other hand, if the measures taken are related to a multilateral agreement on climate change mitigation, such as that being pursued through the United Nations Framework Convention on Climate Change, the likelihood of a challenge is probably reduced.

CT schemes also raise subsidy concerns. A free allocation of permits could be considered a subsidy and subject to an evaluation as such under the Subsidies and Countervailing Measures (SCM) Agreement, negotiated in the Uruguay Round, although it is less clear whether funds from the sale of offsets from a carbon sequestration activity would be considered a subsidy. The logic for viewing free allocation as a subsidy is that the aim of permitting is to impose additional costs on polluting firms, but the fact that firms do not have to pay for the right to pollute (up to a certain level) means that the allocation contains an element of subsidy. Admittedly, high polluting firms may need to purchase additional permits to enable them to increase their polluting activity, but the average cost of pollution will be much lower than the marginal cost due to the fact that those firms have already been awarded a certain pollution entitlement. In the case where a low polluting firm is able to sell or rent some of its entitlement to high polluting firms, the subsidy element is even more apparent since the government has created an asset that the firm can use to realize additional revenue through the sale or rental of surplus emission permits.

The treatment of subsidies in the WTO has a complex legal history built on the experience of the GATT. Subsidies are not necessarily inconsistent with the articles of the GATT/WTO, but they are closely circumscribed. In so far as climate change policy involves actions at the border, the provisions of the GATT are relevant, particularly those that guard against discrimination among suppliers or counter actions against imports in general. In addition to the provisions of the SCM, for agricultural products there are further disciplines in the AoA (these are discussed below in the context of sector-specific climate measures).

The SCM Agreement contains a legal definition of the term 'subsidy'. According to Article 1 of the Agreement, a subsidy has to have three basic elements: it must entail a financial contribution; it must be made by a government or any public body within the territory of a Member; and it must confer a benefit. Even if a measure qualifies as a subsidy under the SCM Agreement, it is not subject to the full disciplines of that Agreement unless it is a *specific* subsidy under Article 2 (Howse *et al.*, 2006). Specific subsidies are further divided into two categories: those that are prohibited and those that are allowed, subject to constraints. Two types of subsidies are prohibited: export incentive subsidies that are contingent on export performance, and local content subsidies that are granted for the use of domestic inputs over imported goods. In the context of the latter provision it is worth noting that the United States has recently (22 December, 2010 – DS419) filed a case at the WTO alleging that some of China's green energy policies, specifically government support for the development of wind power equipment, are in violation of the SCM because support appears to be contingent on Chinese manufacturers using parts and components made in China. To the extent that domestic policies that are designed to promote the development and adoption of green technologies embody a domestic content provision, they may be subject to challenge. Other subsidies are deemed 'actionable' in that they are potentially subject to challenge. The SCM Agreement provides a clear process through which actionable subsidies are identified. A WTO Member can initiate remedial measures if it can prove that non-prohibited actionable subsidies caused serious prejudice to its interests. Serious prejudice may arise where one or more of the following apply: displaced imports into the market of the subsidizing country; displaced exports to third country markets as a result of the subsidy; significant price suppression as a result of the subsidy; and an increase in world market share by the subsidizing country (Article 6.3 of the SCM).

As mentioned above, the WTO's SCM Agreement defines a subsidy as a financial benefit that comes from a governmental or public entity; whether the fact that a government can leave the operation of the carbon market to the private sector makes the offset mechanism less of a subsidy remains to be resolved. In this context, WTO rulings in the Canada-Dairy case (DS103/113) may have some bearing (WTO, 1999a, 1999b). Canada was held to be granting a subsidy to cheese producers for export by maintaining a high price for milk through the regulation of sales on the domestic market, while providing a discounted price to processors of dairy products for export. Through this mechanism farmers could sell milk to cheese producers at below their (average) cost of production. There was no export subsidy, as such, given to cheese producers but the fact that they could obtain milk at below the costs of production was sufficient to judge that Canada was not meeting its commitments under the AoA. In the context of sequestration offsets the question would therefore arise as to whether the government through its actions had created the value of the offsets and that payment for these through a private carbon market constituted a subsidy.

Finally, with respect to the SCM there is the issue of research and development expenditures and subsidies for the development and adoption of climate-friendly technologies. Such measures could run afoul of WTO agreements if they are judged to provide a benefit to domestic industries. Article 8 of the SCM identifies three types of specific subsidies that were non-actionable for a period of five years following the adoption of the Agreement (i.e., until the end of 1999) providing that they met certain conditions. Two of these relate to support for applied research and development and for assistance to firms in disadvantaged regions as part of regional development policies. The third, which is particularly relevant to the climate policy case, is for assistance to firms to promote the adaptation of existing facilities to new environmental requirements. Subsidies under this category were non-actionable if they promoted the adaptation of facilities that had been in operation for at least two years, covered no more than 20 per cent of the cost of adaptation, and did not cover the cost of replacing and operating the assisted investment, which must be borne by the firm. It is clear that the environmental assistance conditions in the SCM Agreement were designed for industrial firms that were required to introduce such things as pollution abatement technologies and the exemption has now lapsed. However, its mere existence indicates that support for environmentally-enhancing expenditures has been acknowledged as being legitimate in the WTO. However, with the expiry of the provision in the SCM such support could be actionable.

Several other WTO agreements (GATS, SPS, TBT, TRIPS) may be of relevance to climate change policies. All of these specify that no country should be prevented from taking measures that are necessary to ensure the protection of human, animal or plant life or health. The TBT Agreement extends this principle to protection of the environment. However, all the agreements indicate that such measures should not be discriminatory or constitute a disguised restriction on international trade. The TBT Agreement is particularly relevant with respect to the product standards that countries might seek to impose in the context of climate change policies, e.g., whether requirements can be imposed on suppliers for low carbon production systems or whether labelling is required if imports do not conform to domestic standards.

Article III of the GATT and the TBT Agreement focus on ensuring equality of treatment in technical regulations for imported products and 'like products' of national origin (TBT Article 2:1). An important issue here is whether the environmental provision would permit countries to impose the technical regulations associated with GHG policies. In particular, would products derived from production methods with low emissions and those under other methods be 'like products'? Since the emissions difference between them is not actually embodied in the products but is an offshoot of the techniques used in production they would certainly seem to be 'like products'. Thus if a country decided to require its farmers to use production practices that it viewed to be more sustainable than existing practices, could it then require that imports be produced using the same or comparable practices? *A priori*, the answer would seem to be no. The TBT Agreement does not allow countries to impose their production regulations or standards on other countries nor does it allow prohibitions on the imports produced using a lower standard.

Article XX of the GATT provides some exceptions for measures that are inconsistent with GATT principles. Exception (b) covers measures 'necessary to protect human, animal or plant life or health' and exception (g) covers measures 'relating to the conservation of exhaustible natural resources if such measures are made effective in conjunction with restrictions on domestic production or consumption'. The use of measures that relate to these exceptions has generated a limited number of dispute settlement cases. Perhaps of greatest interest is the ruling in the *Shrimp-Turtle* case brought against the US by India, Malaysia, Pakistan and Thailand. The issue in the case was the US prohibition on imports of shrimp and shrimp products caught in ways that could cause injury or death to sea turtles. The restriction was ruled to be justified, although not the way in which it had been applied (i.e., solely to imports from certain countries). The ruling seems to open the possibility that import restrictions could be imposed in a non-discriminatory manner on imports of products generated by high GHG-emitting production systems, particularly in terms of exception (g) above. A case would have to be made that domestic measures taken to limit GHG emissions relate to the conservation of exhaustible natural resources and that these measures were made in conjunction with the restrictions on domestic production or consumption. It would not necessarily be easy to satisfy those requirements, but it would probably be easier than to make the case for exception (b) that the products themselves posed a direct threat to human health, even if the production methods that generated them might ultimately do so through their effect on the climate.

Suppose instead a country required that all domestic products from climate-unfriendly production systems be labelled, could it require the same for imported products? The answer to this is unclear. To the extent that labelling is required for both domestic and imported products this would seem to be permitted under the TBT Agreement. However, since that agreement requires equal treatment for imports of 'like' products, it does not appear that imports alone could be required to be labelled. Again there might be a case for an exemption under Article XX (g).

c. Sectoral Climate Change Policies

In addition to the possibility of preferential treatment for agriculture in the application of economy-wide policies that are designed to reduce GHG emissions, there is also the possibility that governments will use specific policies that are targeted at agriculture either to reduce its emissions or to promote carbon sequestration activities.

As noted earlier it is difficult to regulate GHG emissions in agriculture because of the non-point-source issue. However, rather than attempting to do this directly limitations could be imposed on the size of operations (for example, the number of animals in a feedlot) or there could be particular production requirements (for example, the methods for handling animal waste). These types of restrictions (process standards) can be easier to enforce than emission reduction requirements. It is simpler to verify that process standards are being applied than to monitor the outputs from those processes. Consequently, process standards can be applied both to concentrated and more diversified forms of production. In each case, however, regulation is only likely to be effective if there are sanctions (costs) for those producers who do not conform. In agriculture, it is often administratively (and politically) difficult to design regulatory systems that include adequate inspection requirements and sanctions for non-compliance. International competitors are also unlikely to protest if process standards are imposed on producers in another country since this is likely to increase their costs. However, they might want to seek some redress if a country failed to enforce such standards as part of an international agreement to limit emissions.

Because of the challenges of using a regulatory approach in agriculture, the focus has often been on providing direct or indirect incentives for farmers to adopt changes in production practices that will result in improved environmental outcomes. This has been the principal approach adopted in agri-environmental schemes in Europe and North America with respect to such aims as reducing water pollution or maintaining bio-diversity. With respect to GHG emissions, this approach could be used to:

- change production practices in order to reduce agricultural GHG emissions through the adoption of lower emission methods of crop or livestock production, for example, by encouraging conversion from conventional to conservation tillage;[9]
- keep land out of agricultural production in order to avoid carbon emissions (e.g., through enrolling land in the Conservation Reserve Programme in the United States);
- enhance carbon storage in trees and soils through tree planting.

Indirect incentives might be provided for these changes in that they would be a condition for receiving other government benefits, for example 'cross-compliance' (the imposition of environmental or other standards) can be used as a condition for receiving income support. Alternatively, specific financial incentives may be offered that are designed to promote the adoption of those requirements (e.g., payments under agri-environmental programmes or investment subsidies for equipment that reduces GHG emissions). Payments might also be made to compensate producers for the additional costs of adopting a practice or to provide an additional incentive (a return above costs) to promote adoption. Incentive payments are likely to be needed if there are limited private benefits from adoption (e.g., the practice requirements do not result in a reduction in the production costs or an increase in the value of products in the market).

Rather than providing incentives for changes in existing production practices, payments may be made to increase the output of products that are viewed as contributing to lower GHG emissions in the economy as a whole. Two examples of this are the production of existing crops or alternative cellulosic feedstocks for the production of biofuels and the development of on-farm sources of alternative energy (e.g., co-generation from biomass). The emphasis in this case is on promoting the expansion of specific outputs rather than a change in input use or production methods. Incentives can be provided through output subsidies (for example, a subsidy per acre or per ton for the production of feedstock) or through investment subsidies (for example, in co-generation equipment). Subsidies can also be provided indirectly through energy use mandates, such as those applying to renewable energy or through consumption or blending mandates for biofuels.[10] In markets where electricity prices are regulated, the price paid for farm-generated bio-energy could be set at a rate that provides an incentive to invest in on-farm generation and supply.

Public research and extension can also be used to enhance agriculture's contribution to addressing climate change. Public funds could be directed towards research on improving animal feed use, nutrient digestion, carbon sequestration and other approaches to GHG reduction and remediation. Research can increase the supply of new technologies that could be adopted by farmers with the aim of reducing GHG emissions from agriculture or enhancing its role in carbon capture. However, it is important to note that research which is not directly targeted towards these aims but which results in productivity gains (a higher output per unit of input) can also result in a relative, if not an absolute, reduction in GHG emissions. Research that results in the more efficient use of inputs whose production involves significant emissions (e.g., fertilizer, agro-chemicals or energy) can have a particularly significant impact. Indeed, to focus on absolute reductions in GHG emissions from agriculture runs the risk of conflict with food security goals. The more useful metric in this case may be GHG emissions per unit of food output: reductions in that measure would avoid such a clash of objectives. Productivity gains on existing arable land also contribute to climate change mitigation, since they reduce the pressure to convert land from other uses, for example, forests.

Public support for research and training in connection with GHG emissions rests on the same premise that underlies using public funds to enhance investment in activities that are viewed to have a significant public good dimension. In this case the perceived gains to society extend beyond the impact of productivity improvements on the cost of food, to cover the perceived social benefits from reductions in GHG emissions through reduced global warming and less disruptive changes in climate.

d. Sectoral Policies and WTO Agreements

When specific policies are focused on agriculture and provide support to the sector, their use may be covered by the terms of the AoA in addition to the SCM. One of the major aims of the AoA was to impose discipline on those forms of domestic support for agriculture that were judged to be most trade distorting. Countries are required to notify their domestic support for agriculture, although the timeliness of notifications has varied across WTO members (Orden *et al.*, 2011). Market price support and support provided by non-exempt direct payments are calculated through the aggregate measurement of support (AMS). There is a limitation (binding) on the maximum total AMS for countries that included this in their Uruguay Round Agreement schedules. Other countries are limited to providing support below applicable *de minimis* levels.[11] Climate change polices are not explicitly addressed in the AoA since they were not on the international agenda at the time of Uruguay Round. However, the AoA reflects externality and public good issues in the context of agriculture to a limited extent through the exemption of certain measures under Annex 2 (the Green Box). Direct payments under production limiting programmes (Blue Box) are also exempt from limitations, as are certain payments made by developing countries under development programmes.

The Green Box provisions provide some possibilities for the inclusion of policies designed to encourage climate change mitigation in agriculture.[12] Research and development expenditures for climate change technologies or for the diffusion of these technologies to farmers could be notified under such provisions. Policies that provide financial compensation for farmers for the adoption of production methods that promote GHG reduction could also be notified under these provisions. The required conditions are that any support measures should be a part of a clearly defined environmental programme and that the amount of compensation should be equal to the income foregone or to the additional costs incurred in the adoption of required measures. Meeting the latter requirement can be problematic in practice, and particularly for the operation of voluntary programmes such as those in the United States, since the apparent inability to reward producers for their participation might limit farmers' willingness to participate. Consequently, programmes that embody incentive payments could be subject to challenge.[13] This would, however, be more likely if the programme was judged by other countries to be output enhancing.

Income support payments that are not linked to current production can also be notified under the Green Box, but it might be difficult to argue that payments which have production conditions, albeit environmental ones, are fully decoupled. Consequently, such measures might be subject to challenge, particularly if they were held to be production-enhancing.[14] On the other hand if payments were made to farmers that required production limitations in order to reduce emissions, such payments might be notified under the Blue Box provisions. Whether such payments would be challenged would probably depend on whether the production limitation was judged to have offset the potential output-enhancing effect of the subsidy.

In addition to the measures taken to reduce GHG emissions from agriculture, a range of other measures is being used to promote the production of farm outputs with a smaller environmental footprint. It is often argued that biofuels fall into this category, although there is a divergence of opinion on the net contribution of various types of biofuels to the reduction in GHG emissions. A range of policy measures can be used to promote the domestic production of biofuels, including consumption or blending mandates, tax credits and direct subsidies, in addition to import protection.[15] Subsidies for the production of biofuels and their incorporation into gasoline and diesel appear to pose various challenges for the WTO rules on agricultural trade and policy. Symptomatic of the uncertainty is a lack of agreement on whether or not biofuels are covered by the rules relating to agricultural products or whether they are industrial products and thus covered by other rules. If biofuels are to be considered agricultural in nature then the subsidies designed to promote their production should be notified to the WTO as such and may thus be subject to limitations under the terms of the AoA. If not they would still have to be notified, but would be subject to the SCM.

If biofuel subsidies are counted as agricultural subsidies, the issue arises as to whether they should be notified as trade distorting (under the 'Amber Box' category) or trade-neutral (under the 'Green Box'). Some biofuel subsidies could be considered as providing indirect support to the producers of feedstock, mainly corn and oilseeds, and as such would be 'coupled' to production. This would place the subsidies in the trade-distorting category and they would then fall under the disciplines of the AoA. But others might be consistent with those classified as minimally trade-distorting (for example, if the feedstock was a waste product or cellulosic material that is not a 'marketable agricultural product'). In that case biofuel subsidies could fit within the Green Box as currently defined, or one that might emerge from a negotiated modification.

Subsidies can be countervailed if they are shown to cause injury to domestic producers in competing countries. This provides a targeted way to offset such subsidies. European biodiesel makers have for instance attempted to show that US producers were causing them harm through allegedly subsidized exports of B99 fuel that were eligible for a $1 per gallon domestic tax credit (the so-called 'splash and dash' trade). The possibility of a similar challenge to US exports of gasoline-ethanol blends has also been identified (Yano *et al.*, 2010). Safeguard actions under Article XIX of the GATT could also be used to increase tariffs or to impose quotas in the event of injury created by surges in the imports of biofuels, but unlike countervailing measures these are supposed to be applied on an MFN basis. Less likely, though still plausible, is the possibility of a challenge under the 'nullification or impairment' conditions (Article XXIII): for example, a country could argue that ethanol subsidies were unexpected at the time when tariff schedules were agreed and that benefits accruing to it directly or indirectly under WTO agreements are being nullified or impaired by such subsidies. This could form the basis for a non-violation complaint under Article XXIII (i.e., one made on the basis that although the measure does not conflict with the GATT, it results in the nullification or impairment of a benefit). To date, however, there have been only a few complaints made on these broad grounds and even fewer on the basis of an even broader 'situation complaint'; the majority of successful complaints under Article XXIII have centred on 'violation complaints', in which nullification and impairment are presumed through a failure to carry out specific obligations under the GATT.

V.   THE DOHA ROUND AND CLIMATE CHANGE ISSUES

A 1994 Ministerial Decision created a Committee on Trade and Environment (CTE) in the WTO. The 2001 Doha mandate included a section dealing with the Committee's work, but climate change issues have not been a significant part of the Doha Round. There have been some negotiations on liberalizing trade in environmental goods and services by reducing or eliminating tariffs and non-tariff barriers. However, it has been difficult to reach agreement on what to include in the category of environmental goods. For example, Brazil has proposed that biofuels be recognized as an environmental good but it seems unlikely that this will be accepted. Even if it were, it is unclear which tariff reductions would actually apply. The US, for example, has a relatively low regular tariff on ethanol of 2.5 per cent, but most of the protection for domestic producers is created through an additional special duty of 54 cents per gallon. The US entered the additional duty in its Uruguay Round schedule of bound tariffs under the heading of 'other duties and levies' and treats it as an autonomous measure that is not subject to negotiation. Consequently, it is unclear whether this special duty will be included in any agreed tariff reduction if a final Doha agreement is reached.

The US has notified some subsidies for biofuels to the Committee on Subsidies and Countervailing Measures. In a recent submission, it notified the USDA Direct Payments and Bioenergy programme (G/SCM/N/155/USA, 20 May 2009) together with a number of energy and fuel-related programmes as of 2005 and 2006 (before the subsequent increase in support to biofuels) (Annex B). The volumetric ethanol excise tax credit (VEETC) of 51 cents (as it was at that time) was notified, along with an additional 10 cents per gallon income tax credit for small producers. The $1.01 per gallon federal production tax credit for cellulosic ethanol was notified, and the revenue foregone is shown as $1,540 million for 2005 and $2,620 million for 2006. For biodiesel, the US notification mentions the $1.00 per gallon tax credit and an additional 10 cents for small producers, and identifies the costs of these programmes (revenue foregone) as $30 million for 2005 and $90 million for 2006. The 2006 total for biofuels is thus $2.7 billion, or less than one-half of the $5.9 – $7.1 billion subsidy for liquid biofuels calculated by Koplow (2007) for the Global Subsidies Initiative, which also included some (but not all) of the subsidies provided by individual states and also subsidies to support the consumption of biofuels. In the most recent US submission under the SCM (G/SCM/N/186/USA) additional information is supplied on various subsidies, including $198 million for research and development into biomass and bio-refinery development in the fiscal year (FY) 2008. The submission demonstrates the rapid rise in the implicit subsidy provided to biofuels through excise tax credits; this had reached $4,460 million for ethanol and $1,218 million for biodiesel in FY2008.

The latest EU subsidies notification (G/SCM/N/186/EEC) was submitted on 23 December 2009 and covered 2007-2008, with some additional coverage of programmes that were not addressed in 2005 and 2006. The notification covers regional development and programmes under the Common Agricultural Policy (CAP): it presumably includes some elements of biofuels-related support under the CAP's Pillar II. However, the nature of the notification is not such as to make a full accounting possible. The only specific notification that relates to biofuels is the Energy Crops Scheme. Expenditure under the scheme was notified as €13.5 million in 2004 and €54 million in 2006.

The subsequent notification mentions the amount (€45 per hectare) in 2007 and 2008 but not the total cost. The payments under the energy crops scheme are also reported in the agricultural notification for those years.

As noted above, the treatment of ethanol under the AoA is complex. The Annex to the Agreement indicates that it covers HS Chapters 1 to 24 less fish and fish products, plus some other products. There is no specific entry for bioethanol for fuel under the harmonized system. However, ethanol is traded under HS 2207, which includes both undenatured (HS 220710) and denatured alcohol (HS 220720). Biodiesel is covered by HS 382490. Consequently there would seem to be a *prima facie* case that ethanol would be a covered product under the AoA, whereas biodiesel would not. This would imply that ethanol would be covered by the particular conditions applying to agricultural products in terms of market access, export competition and domestic support in a Doha agreement. Biodiesel would be covered by whatever final agreement is reached on non-agricultural products.

Article 1a of the AoA indicates that 'all support *provided for an agricultural product in favour of the producers of (a) basic agricultural product* or non-product-specific support provided for agricultural producers in general, other than support provided under programmes that qualify as exempt from reduction under Annex 2 (Green Box)' (emphasis added) should be included in a country's aggregate measurement of support (AMS). This is subject to each country's commitment on the final bound total AMS agreed in the Uruguay Round. A 'basic agricultural product' in relation to domestic support commitments is defined as the product as close as practicable to the point of first sale as specified in a Member's Schedule and related supporting material (Article 1b). The AoA goes on to state that 'Any domestic support measure in favour of agricultural producers, including any modification to such measure, and any measure that is subsequently introduced that cannot be shown to (be exempt from reduction) ... shall be included in the Member's calculation of its Current Total AMS' (Article 7:2a). So a key issue would seem to be this: if ethanol is judged to be an agricultural product, do any of the measures used to promote the production of ethanol constitute support for the producers of a basic agricultural product (e.g., corn or sugar)? Alternatively, if it cannot be shown that the support is specific to a particular basic agricultural product (for example, due to the possibility of using various feedstocks to produce ethanol) would it fall under the heading of non-product-specific support and as such also have to be included in the calculation of the current AMS? Certain direct support provided to US producers for use of agricultural products in the production of bioenergy and biodiesel has already been notified to the WTO for 2002–2005 by the US under the other product-specific category of support.[16]

If the enhanced disciplines on domestic support embodied in the draft agricultural agreement (WTO, 2008) are implemented, this would reduce the ability of the EU and the US to provide trade-distorting support to their farmers and stay within the terms of the agreement (Blandford and Josling, 2011; Orden *et al.*, 2011). There is some flexibility in how policies are notified to the WTO, particularly in terms of the notification of the market price support component of the AMS, but successful challenges to what support is notified or how much support is notified could create problems for some countries under a future agreement.[17] Josling and Blandford (2010), for example, estimate that if the price-enhancing effect of ethanol programmes for US corn were to be taken into account, this could increase the notified total AMS by roughly $3 billion. That is a significant amount in the context of the substantial reduction in the binding for the total AMS from roughly $19.1 billion under the existing Agreement to $7.6 billion in the Doha proposals. In addition, the proposed product-specific binding for corn under a new agreement would almost certainly be violated if the effects of ethanol policies on corn prices were taken into account.[18] More generally, climate change policies that were judged to provide a specific subsidy to particular agricultural crops (product-specific support), or to agriculture more generally (non-product-specific support), would be subject to tighter disciplines through the overall package of restrictions on domestic support proposed in the Doha Round: tighter limitations on the total AMS and new ceilings on the AMS for individual products; reductions in *de minimis* for product-specific and non-product-specific AMS; a cap on Blue Box support and individual caps on Blue Box measures or support by commodity; and a cap on the overall trade-distorting support (OTDS) calculated as the sum of the total AMS, *de minimis* and Blue Box.

Finally, although some modest proposals have been made to expand the Green Box, primarily to take into account the interests of developing countries, it seems unlikely that there will be major changes to Green Box provisions in a final Doha agreement and little attempt to expand the categories to include climate change policies (Blandford and Josling, 2007). Hence, to the extent that countries decide to notify expenditures relating to climate change policies for agriculture under the Green Box, this may generate greater scrutiny of whether such policies actually qualify under the provisions of a revised AoA.

VI. CONCLUSIONS

The WTO framework was not set up to deal with issues that have broad international implications such as climate change. While no attempt is being made to address such policies in a comprehensive manner in the WTO, to the extent that policies have implications for international trade they may impinge on existing or future WTO agreements. Climate change and the policies adopted to address this will have implications for international trade law and how it is applied. The promotion of trade will need to be consistent with other objectives, such as mitigating climate change. Freer trade may be complementary to achieving objectives such as the reduction of greenhouse gas emissions, but this is not necessarily the case. Domestic policies adopted to deal with climate change might conflict with international obligations under the WTO.

Agriculture may be particularly prone to such potential conflict because it is a sector that often receives preferential treatment in the domestic policy arena. There has been a reluctance to address the negative environmental externalities generated by agriculture by internalizing their costs, and there is a predilection for providing subsidies to the sector. The fact that agriculture is a significant contributor to global greenhouse gas emissions but also has the potential to contribute positively to mitigation activities further complicates the picture. The application of climate change policies in agriculture may not only impinge on provisions in the current or potential future agreement on agriculture in the WTO, but also on other agreements.

NOTES

The material presented in this chapter has benefited from a close collaboration with Tim Josling of Stanford University on a number of research projects. Tim should be accorded a share of the credit for any useful contribution, while being held blameless for any errors of fact or interpretation.

1. Trade theorists also demonstrated that a large country could exploit its market power to increase its domestic economic welfare at the expense of the 'rest of the world.' Although this may not be the explicit objective of large trading countries, such as the EU and the US, the spill-over effects of their domestic agricultural trade policies on international markets have frequently been a major source of tension in international relations.
2. They may ultimately face costs imposed by climate change in common with others in society, but these are not apparent when the decision is made on how much of a polluting good to produce.

3. This requires that the penalty for non-compliance exceeds any additional potential profit from failing to comply.

4. The approach might be characterized more accurately as the 'polluter initially pays' principle. The internalization of the costs of pollution across the economy will result on these ultimately being passed on to consumers through higher product prices.

5. The tight regulation of the application of livestock manure by farmers in the Netherlands, which has involved the monitoring of data on nutrient balances at the level of each farm, is one example of such an approach.

6. This argument has been made for lamb and dairy products produced under pasture-based systems in New Zealand in comparison with more intensive feeding systems used in the Europe (see Saunders *et al.*, 2006).

7. Taxation at the point of consumption, in principle, also requires border tax adjustments in order not to favour export sectors.

8. BTAs are allowed if the additional tax levied on imports matches any indirect tax that has been paid on the domestic production of similar products. They should not be applied so as to afford protection to domestic production (GATT, Article III.1). A regulation is not a tax, so an import levy designed to match the cost of compliance with domestic rules is not strictly a BTA (see Hufbauer *et al.*, 2009: 66).

9. The process of tilling the soil releases carbon dioxide into the atmosphere. Minimum tillage aims to limit this process by only turning the soil enough for planting.

10. Some economists have argued that subsidies and mandates are alternative policies: that if blending is mandated one does not need a subsidy. Politically, the subsidy may be necessary to be able to get agreement on the mandate.

11. The *de minimis* levels for developed countries are 5 per cent for the product-specific AMS applied to the value of production for each commodity and 5 per cent for the non-product-specific AMS applied to the total value of agricultural production. The corresponding figure is 10 per cent for developing countries. Countries that have acceded to the WTO may have a lower *de minimis*, for example, the figure applicable to China is 8 per cent.

12. Developing countries could have a wider range of options by taking advantage of special and differential treatment under Article 6.2 through the development programme box.

13. Whether or not payments are defined as being above and beyond the costs of complying with an existing government programme depends on the way they are formulated. If a farmer has a choice between joining an environmental stewardship programme or keeping eligibility for current farm income payments (direct payments, counter-cyclicals, etc.) then income forgone includes the amount of those payments. And if the payments are calculated with the cost to the farmer in mind, it would be difficult to argue that they are not equivalent to the 'extra costs' involved in complying with the programme. Therefore all, or most, of the stewardship payments might actually qualify as Green Box payments.

14. The legal interpretation of a production linkage can differ from an economic one. In the *US–Brazil* cotton case (DS267) US direct payments to cotton producers were judged not to be decoupled not because they increased cotton production (i.e., created a distortion in the cotton market), but because of a prohibition of the planting of certain crops (primarily fruit and vegetables) on programme acreage. Recent analysis for Norway suggests that the provision of carbon sequestration payments could increase agricultural output as producers intensify production on land remaining in production (Blandford *et al.*, 2011). If such effects are shown to apply elsewhere it is interesting to speculate on whether payments linked to sequestration activities could actually be notified as Green Box.

15. For an extensive discussion of biofuels policies and their relationship to WTO rules, see Josling and Blandford (2009).
16. The programme concerned is the Bioenergy Program administered by the Commodity Credit Corporation of the US Department of Agriculture. This involved corn and sorghum (entire period) and wheat (2002-03 only) for bioenergy and livestock and soybeans for biodiesel. Note that this notification appears to accept a broad definition of biofuels as agricultural products.
17. The US has already taken advantage of this flexibility to reduce its notified support for dairy products (see Orden *et al.*, 2011). While it applies to a limited range of products (dairy and sugar) in the US case, this flexibility could be extremely important for some other high support countries with extensive price support schemes. Blandford *et al.* (2010) examined the implications for Norway. They showed that the ability to redefine existing price support policies for major commodities in such a way as to reduce the notified amount of support, without fundamentally affecting the domestic market situation, could be extremely significant for that country.
18. See the chapter on the United States by Blandford and Orden in Orden *et al.* (2011).

BIBLIOGRAPHY

Blandford, D. (2010) 'The Visible or Invisible Hand? The balance between markets and regulation in agricultural policy', *Journal of Agricultural Economics*, **61**(3): 459–479.
Blandford, D. and Josling, T. (2007) 'Should the Green Box be Modified?', *IPC Discussion Paper*. Washington, DC: International Food and Agricultural Trade Policy Council.
Blandford, D. and Josling, T. (2009) 'Greenhouse Gas Reduction Policies and Agriculture: Implications for production incentives and international trade disciplines', *Issue Brief No. 1*, ITCSD-IPC Platform on Climate Change, Agriculture and Trade. Geneva/Washington, DC: International Centre for Trade and Sustainable Development and International Food and Agricultural Trade Policy Council.
Blandford, D. and Josling, T. (2011) 'The WTO Agricultural Modalities Proposals and their Impact on Domestic Support in the EU and the US', in W. Martin and A. Mattoo (eds), *The Doha Development Agenda*. Washington, DC: World Bank.
Blandford D, Gaasland, I. and Vårdal, E. (2011) 'Interaction between Trade Liberalization and Climate Change Policy: An application to Norwegian agriculture'. Paper prepared for the XIIIth Congress of the European Association of Agricultural Economists, Zurich, Switzerland, 30 August–2 September.
Blandford, D., Gaasland, I., Garcia, R. and Vårdal, E. (2010) 'How Effective are WTO Disciplines on Domestic Support and Market Access for Agriculture?', *The World Economy* **33** (11): 1470–1485.
Canning, P., Charles, A., Huang, S., Polenske, K. R. and Waters, A. (2010) 'Energy Use in the US Food System', *Economic Research Report Number 94*, Economic Research Service. Washington, DC: US Department of Agriculture.
Central Intelligence Agency (2011) *The World Factbook*. Available at https://www.cia.gov/library/publications/the-world-factbook (accessed 5 February 2011).
Howse, R., Van Bork, P. and Hebebrand, C. (2006) *WTO Disciplines and Biofuels: Opportunities and constraints in the creation of a global marketplace* (IPC Discussion Paper, Washington).
Hufbauer, G., Charnovitz, S. and Kim, J. (2009) *Global Warming and the World Trade System*. Washington, DC: Peterson Institute for International Economics.
Josling, T. and Blandford, D. (2009) 'Biofuels Subsidies and the Green Box', in R.

Meléndez-Ortiz, C. Bellmann and J. Hepburn (eds), *Agricultural Subsidies in the WTO Green Box: Ensuring Coherence with Sustainable Development Goals.* Cambridge: Cambridge University Press.

Koplow, D. (2007) *Biofuels – At What Cost? Government Support for Ethanol and Biodiesel in the United States: 2007 Update.* Geneva: Global Subsidies Initiative.

Lewandrowski, J., Jones, C., House, R., Sperow, M., Eve, M. and Paustian, K. (2004) 'Economics of Sequestering Carbon in the US Agricultural Sector', *Technical Bulletin 1909.* Washington, DC: Economic Research Service, US Department of Agriculture.

Mitra, S. and Josling, T. (2009) 'Agricultural Export Restrictions: Welfare Implications and Trade Disciplines', *IPC Position Paper Agricultural and Rural Development Policy Series.* Washington, DC: International Food & Agricultural Trade Policy Council.

OECD (2008) *Environmental Performance of Agriculture in OECD Countries since 1990.* Paris: OECD.

Orden, D., Blandford, D. and Josling, T. (eds) (2011) *WTO Disciplines on Agricultural Support: Seeking a fair basis for trade.* Cambridge: Cambridge University Press.

Saunders, C., Barber, A. and Taylor, G. (2006) 'Food Miles – Comparative Energy/ Emissions Performance of New Zealand's Agriculture Industry', *Research Report No. 285.* Christchurch, New Zealand: Agricultural Economics Research Unit, Lincoln University.

Solomon, S., Qin, D., Manning, M., Chen, Z., Marquis, M., Averyt, K. B., Tignor, M. and Miller, H. L. (eds) (2007) *Contribution of Working Group I to the Fourth Assessment Report on Climate Change, 2007.* Cambridge and New York: Cambridge University Press.

Wreford, A., Moran, D. and Adger, N. (2010) *Climate Change and Agriculture: Impacts, adaptation and mitigation.* Paris: OECD.

WTO (1999a) *Canada – Measures Affecting the Importation of Milk and the Exportation of Dairy Products,* Report of the Panel, WT/DS103/R, WT/DS113/R, 17 May.

WTO (1999b) *Canada – Measures Affecting the Importation of Milk and the Exportation of Dairy Products,* AB-1999-4 – Report of the Appellate Body, 13 October.

WTO (2008) *Revised Draft Modalities for Agriculture,* TN/AG/W/4/Rev.4, 6 December.

Yano, Y., Blandford, D. and Surry, Y. (2010) 'Do Current US Ethanol Policies Make Sense?', *Policy Issues* PI10, Agricultural and Applied Economics Association, August. Available at: www.aaea.org/publications/policy-issues/

10 Biofuels, food security and the WTO Agreement on Agriculture

Stephanie Switzer

I. INTRODUCTION

The past ten years have witnessed a flurry of interest in the promotion of biofuels as an alternative to conventional fossil fuels. Biofuels may be defined as 'liquid or gaseous fuels produced from biomass that can be used to replace petrol, diesel and other transport fuels' (Keam and McCormick, 2008: 8). At present, biofuels are commercially available in two forms: bioethanol and biodiesel. Bioethanol is suitable for blending with conventional petrol and is produced from crops containing starch or sugar such as sugar cane, sugar beet and corn. Biodiesel, the term given to 'fatty acid methyl ester' (FAME), has been touted as a replacement for conventional diesel and is produced in large part from plant oils such as palm oil and rapeseed (Kojima *et al.*, 2007: 29; Petillion, 2005). Both ethanol and biodiesel may be processed at a range of scales, from a subsistence level to large-scale industrial production intended for international markets.

Biofuels produced from food crops such as corn, sugar and vegetable oils are generally referred to as 'first generation' biofuels. There is, however, growing interest in so-called 'second generation' biofuels derived from lignin, cellulose and hemi-cellulose, although such fuels are not currently in commercial production and are unlikely to be for a number of years (Howse *et al.*, 2006: 7). It is anticipated that when production of second-generation biofuels becomes commercially viable, they will be able to garner larger yields than their first generation counterparts. Perhaps of greatest significance is the potential to produce biofuels from non-food agricultural feedstocks such as miscanthus and the non-edible portions of food crops, as well as allow a larger range of waste materials to be transformed into fuels (Legge, 2008: 7).

A number of countries have introduced legislation to promote the use of biofuels in the transport sector. At United States' federal level, the Energy Independence and Security Act of 2007 amending the Clean Air Act has established an annual target volume by 2022 of 36 billion gallons of renewable fuel for fuel sold or introduced into commerce in the United States. In the European Union (EU), the 2009 Renewable Energy Directive, Directive 2009/28, mandates that a 10 per cent share for renewables in the transport sector be achieved by 2020, with considerable emphasis placed upon the role of biofuels in meeting this target (Switzer and McMahon, 2011). In addition, while the turn to biofuels is often portrayed as a developed country issue, Brazil has a highly developed ethanol industry and has assisted countries such as Jamaica to develop an ethanol processing capacity (Steenblick, 2006: 10; WTO, 2011). Indeed, as reported in Jamaica's recent trade policy review, it was the first English-speaking Caribbean country to introduce a 10 per cent ethanol blending mandate for gasoline (WTO, 2011).

A number of concerns exist regarding the promotion of biofuels as an alternative to conventional fossil fuels. Such concerns include the potential impact that the use of agricultural products as feedstocks for biofuels could have upon the availability and price of food (Rudaheranwa, 2009). Similarly, the prospective conversion of certain areas such as high-value forests or peatlands to grow feedstocks raises issues pertaining to environmental protection (Keam and McCormick, 2008: 6). This chapter will look at the way in which the trade regime constructs such concerns. It will be contended that while food security and environmental protection are recognised under the Agreement on Agriculture (AoA) as legitimate non-trade concerns, their construction under it represents what may be referred to as an 'incompletely theorised agreement.' In essence, agreement was secured that such concerns may be taken into account in the liberalisation process but the question of 'how' and moreover 'why' was left incompletely theorised and within the competence of Members. The argument will be put forward that while leaving certain issues incompletely theorised may at times be both necessary and desirable, there will arise occasions when a more complete theorisation may be required so as to guard against the risk of inconsistency. In essence, to the extent that incomplete theorisation may 'hide' inconsistency, more complete theorisation may be necessary to throw light on the potential for such inconsistency as well offer new ways of thinking about a particular issue. In this regard, particular attention will be paid to the conceptualisation of food security which exists under the AoA with it being argued that the arrangement therein not only produces an overtly narrow approach but is also productive of inconsistency.

Using the example provided by the rise in international trade in biofuels, it will be argued that communicative space is required within the trade regime to allow for the articulation of a wider conception of food security than currently exists under the AoA. The purpose of seeking to identify communicative opportunities through which a broader reading of food security can be advanced is not to expound upon a definitive account of food security or the particular actions which should be taken in that regard. Rather, by seeking to draw attention to the broader elements of food security which are at present little addressed within the trade regime, the inadequacy of the incompletely theorised agreement will become more evident. It will be concluded that there is 'space' within the trade regime to begin to offer new understandings of non-trade concerns such as food security but that such space needs to be utilised.

II.   BIOFUELS – THE WHY, THE HOW AND THE RISKS

As iterated above, the central goal of this contribution is to utilise the lens provided by the rise in trade in biofuels to elucidate upon the need for a wider articulation of non-trade concerns such as food security. However, as a first step in this analysis, it is necessary to establish why the 'flurry' of interest in biofuels has occurred as well as delineate in more detail why an increased recourse to biofuels may raise particular concerns.

One of the more explicit aims behind the recent promotion of biofuels as an alternative to fossil fuels stems from their alleged potential to reduce the greenhouse gas emissions associated with climate change (Zah *et al.*, 2007). However, it is also clear that biofuels have been touted as a tool to promote rural development as well as to enhance energy security (Legge, 2008: 6; WTO, 2011: 25–26). Indeed, these latter goals, while seemingly subsidiary to the central aim of climate change mitigation, should not automatically be conceived of in this way. This is because while concern for the effects of climate change is a relatively recent development, it is to be noted that governmental intervention in the biofuel sector is by no means a new phenomenon with past interventions motivated largely by a concern for the rural sector (Steenblick, 2007: 1).

Leading on from the above analysis, while biofuels have been promoted as a 'climate friendly' alternative to conventional fossil fuels, their ability to reduce greenhouse gas (GHG) emissions varies greatly depending upon the feedstock as well as the method used to convert the feedstock into fuel for transport (Tilman *et al.,* 2009). Further emissions may be produced if certain types of land such as peatlands, wetlands and high-value forests are used to cultivate biofuel feedstocks. This is because of the stored carbon which would be released if the land was cultivated for biofuel production (Commission, 2006: 24). The impact of such land-use change is far from negligible, with recent studies positing that the promotion of certain biofuels such as corn-based ethanol could lead to an increase in the GHG emissions associated with climate change if forests and grasslands are turned over to the cultivation of feedstocks (Searchinger, 2008). Similar concerns also arise to the extent that the cultivation of biofuel feedstocks may displace food production onto land that was not previously in use for agricultural purposes. Accordingly, indirect land-use change is very much the other side of the coin to direct land-use change. Furthermore, to the extent that biofuel feedstocks are grown on set-aside land, this could result in a biodiversity loss to the extent that such lands have become 'havens' of biodiversity (Legge, 2008: 14).

In addition to the environmental concerns raised by increased production of biofuels, it is also clear that policies encouraging their use as an alternative to fossil fuels could have a detrimental effect upon food availability as well as the price of food. Such impacts may result from the displacement of land usually used to grow food to instead grow energy crops. Similarly, crops such as corn may be diverted for use as fuel rather than food. The consequence of both of these trends could be less by way of food supply, thereby resulting in higher food prices. While predictions as to the impact of biofuel policies upon the availability and price of certain commodities vary, it is generally accepted that the 'prices for most crop products would develop much more strongly than without this source of additional demand, with the markets for sugar and vegetable oils affected most significantly' (OECD, 2006: 26). In addition, as a consequence of the strong link between individual agricultural commodities, an increase in the use of one agricultural commodity for biofuel production is likely to have an impact upon a large range of agricultural commodities (Kojima *et al.,* 2007: 31). In essence, therefore, the potential impact of increased biofuel production is unlikely to be confined to those commodities used as feedstocks but instead could affect commodities prices as a whole.[1]

While agricultural producers may benefit from price rises, higher agricultural commodity prices could potentially have a negative effect upon the food security of individual households, particularly with respect to urban consumers and net food buyers in rural communities (FAO, 2008: 85). By extension, higher import bills are likely to be faced at country level, imposing a particularly heavy burden upon net-food importing developing and least-developed countries. Fears as to the possible impact of the increased use of biofuels in the transport sector appear to have been borne out by the food price crisis which occurred in 2007/2008. Analysts have posited that while the rise in food prices during the crisis had a range of causes (including high oil prices, rising input costs to farmers, depreciation of the US dollar, rising demand for meat, adverse weather conditions as well as chronic underinvestment in the agricultural sector), the conversion of food stocks and land previously utilised to grow food to produce biofuels was also partly responsible (Rudaheranwa, 2009: 2).

There is debate as to the exact nature of the impact of increased biofuel production upon food prices. Mitchell (2008: 17), for example, posits that between 70 and 75 per cent of the recent rise in the price of food commodities was attributable to biofuels and the 'related consequences' of increased biofuel production, such as low stocks of grain, speculation on commodities markets and prohibitions on exports. Similarly, Abbott *et al.* (2009) identify biofuel production as a 'significant' – but by no means the sole – factor in the food price crisis, while Rosegrant (2008) attributes 30 per cent of the rise in food prices during the 2007 to 2008 crisis to biofuel production. Regardless of the debate which exists as to the precise role played by biofuel production in the recent food price crisis, it is clear that it has had at least some impact upon food prices (Kojima *et al.*, 2007: 36; Rudaheranwa, 2009: 5). This causal link has prompted calls for a fundamental rethink of the use of subsidies and associated biofuel mandates which have the potential to distort the market for such fuels by preventing the most efficient producers from benefiting from the opportunity presented by biofuels as well as undermining the food security of certain consumers. In regard to such calls, it is necessary to consider how they link in with the conceptualisation of food security which currently exists in the multilateral trade regime.

III. FOOD SECURITY AND THE WTO AGREEMENT ON AGRICULTURE

The central objective of the AoA is, according to the Preamble, to 'establish a fair and market-oriented agricultural trading system', to be achieved, at least in part, through 'substantial progressive reductions in agricultural support and protection'. It has been argued that an implicit aim behind the reduction in agricultural support and protection was to arrest the dampening effect that policies of subsidisation typically had on food prices. (Matthews, 2010: 4). Hence, at least in part, it may be contended that one goal of the Agreement was 'to correct a situation of mounting surpluses in a number of products produced in a number of developed countries through rising levels of budgetary support and protection' (Zhang, 2004: 578).

Food security may be defined as existing, 'when all people, at all times, have physical, social and economic access to sufficient, safe and nutritious food which meets their dietary needs and food preferences for an active and healthy life' (FAO, 2010: 1). Food security is given overt recognition in the AoA with, for example, paragraph 6 of the Preamble noting that regard should be had for the non-trade concerns of Members such as food security and environmental protection. Similarly, while avoiding explicit reference to the phrase food security, the Decision on least-developed countries and net-food importing developing countries (NFIDC Decision) recognised that these countries may experience difficulties as a result of the process of liberalisation initiated under the AoA. To address these concerns, developing Members likely to experience difficulties in this regard were permitted under paragraph 3 of the Decision to adopt less by way of liberalisation commitments, and a pledge was made to establish rules to ensure the 'availability of food aid at a level which is sufficient to continue to provide assistance in meeting the needs of developing countries'. Members were also tasked to give full consideration to requests for technical assistance to boost agricultural productivity in NFIDCs and there was an agreement to review the terms of the Food Aid Convention 1986.

Earlier in this volume Smith opines that while food security is recognised as a relevant non-trade concern to be taken into account within the regulation of agricultural trade, neither the Agreement nor the NFIDC Decision seek to define food security or identify food security as an end in itself. Rather, what the applicable provisions do is to grant Members a form of 'policy space' to identify their food security needs and address them as required, with the proviso that the discipline provided by the AoA is adhered to. While the 2008 Draft Modalities serve to reflect that countries may experience food security/insecurity in different ways, Smith argues that the Modalities are still largely constructed upon the existing view that such issues are within the policy space of the Member to respond to. As such, these issues are regulated in a manner which is in some respects distinct to the articulation of food security advocated by proponents of, for example, the right to food (ILA, 2010: 13).

In seeking to understand more fully the 'distinctness' of the articulation of food security as a non-trade concern within the WTO legal framework, it may be useful to utilise the lens provided by Cass Sunstein's notion of the incompletely theorised agreement. To expand, Sunstein (1996: 4) posits that 'well functioning' systems of law have a tendency to adopt certain tools or techniques in order to ensure stability. One mechanism he proposed which may be utilised to promote agreement in diverse societies is the incompletely theorised agreement. As he contended (1995: 1379) 'incompletely theorised agreements play a pervasive role in law and society. It is rare for a person, and especially a group, to theorise any subject completely – that is, to accept both a highly abstract theory and a series of steps that relate the theory to a concrete conclusion. In fact, people often reach incompletely theorised agreements on a general principle. Such agreements are incompletely theorised in the sense that people who accept the principle need not agree on what it entails in particular cases'. Hence, people may agree upon the 'correctness' of a particular rule but not upon why there is a need for such a rule or what principles or theories account for it.

Sunstein (2007: 2–3) articulates that an incompletely theorised agreement may arise at various levels of meaning. First, such agreements may arise where there is agreement upon a general principle but no consensus upon how the principle applies in particular situations. Second, agreement may be secured on a so-called mid-level principle but not on the theory which informs the principle or what it entails in individual cases. Finally, on other occasions, a 'conceptual descent' may be necessary whereby discussions are moved to a more precise level of particularity. Sunstein, while employing the concept of the incompletely theorised agreement in a largely descriptive sense, notes that in a diverse constitutional setting, there may be some merit in avoiding theoretical or practical conflicts. Thus the incompletely theorised agreement is at times a useful tool in that it makes cooperative enterprises possible. Silence on a controversial issue may, for example, help to ease potential conflict. Indeed, one common conception of the 'purpose' of law is to either provide for or create the conditions necessary for stability (Post, 2009). However, it is also clear that short-term stability is not an all-encompassing goal to be striven for at the expense of other values. In this regard, Sunstein (1995: 1750) recognised that the benefits of an incompletely theorised agreement will at times be limited and as such, he contended that 'fuller theorisation' of an issue may be of benefit so as to promote a 'wider and deeper inquiry into the grounds for judgment' and prevent 'inconsistency, bias, or self-interest'.

Linking to the above exposition of the incompletely theorised agreement, it is inarguable that there is agreement under the AoA on the mid-level principle of food security as a 'legitimate' non-trade concern. However, it is also clear that details as to its operationalisation were left incompletely theorised and within the competence – or, in the words of Smith, the policy space – of the Member to both define and, moreover, deal with. As such, the commonly used articulation of food security noted in this section of the discussion is not referred to under the AoA. Accordingly, we may posit that that Agreement sets out the mid-level principle of concern for food security but leaves the implementation and indeed the 'meaning' of it incompletely theorised and within the competence of the Member.

Continuing with the above conceptualisation of the implementation and meaning of food security under the Agreement as within the competence or policy 'space' of the Member, it has been argued that the existence of 'exogenous' and 'endogenous' factors can potentially limit a country's policy space and that together these two factors define the size of a country's 'effective national policy space' (Hamwey, 2005: 4). Endogenous factors are 'internal' and include aspects such as resource constraints which may impact upon a country's domestic policy-making capacity. On the other hand, exogenous factors are external limiting factors to domestic policy-making discretion. With regard to the first factor relating to endogeneity, it is arguable that leaving 'space' for Members to define and address food security concerns may be good policy if they have the ability to respond to such needs in an appropriate way. Accordingly, understanding the rules in this way, as Smith has argued above, countries are given 'more power ... to address food security rather than less'. However, it is arguable that this arrangement could result in suboptimal policy making if such 'space' is allowed to stagnate due, for example, to a lack of capacity or a lack of funding (Mechlem, 2006: 153). In this regard, it is notable that while recognition of the need for funding was made pursuant to the NFIDC Decision, the volume of aid directed towards agricultural productivity has fallen since the 1980s (Mechlem, 2006: 159). Furthermore, until recently, the agricultural sector has been marred by a pattern of chronic underinvestment (WTO, 2010b).

The implication of the above is *not* that countries with limited capacity should be granted less by way of policy space to tackle food security concerns, but rather that the grant of 'legal freedom' will rarely be sufficient *on its own* to address issues of food security given the capacity constraints of the countries involved. In a similar vein, the grant of legal freedom to developing countries under the provisions of special and differential treatment has been criticised as not doing enough to promote developing countries' relevant financial, development and trade needs. Hence, in the words of Hudec describing the ineffectiveness of certain of the provisions of special and differential treatment, 'once it had been conceded, as a matter of principle that legal freedom constitutes "help" to developing countries, the future was virtually fixed' (1987: 18). It is contended that a similar argument may be applied to the treatment of food security under WTO legal disciplines.

The creation of domestic policy space through the incomplete theorisation of food security also implies that that the 'appropriate' response will be largely endogenous, that is, mainly within the competence – as opposed to capacity – of the relevant Member to orientate. At first glance, this seems 'correct' given that countries with similar levels of agricultural trade may often incur very different patterns of hunger and food insecurity, indicating that 'the impact of food security is mediated by factors such as markets, natural resource endowments, human capacity, institutions and policies, and the degree of equity with which benefits are distributed' (Mechlem, 2006: 132). However, to the extent that exogenous – that is, external limiting factors may result in a limitation of the policy space of Members to take measures to ensure food security, this is largely unaddressed, except through provisions such as that under the NFIDC Decision tasking Members to focus upon making the grant of food aid more effective and the more general task of the AoA to reduce the level of trade distorting subsidisation.

An example of one of the more contentious exogenous factors which may impact upon the policy space of Members to take action for food security purposes relates to the relatively permissive regime which exists in relation to export restrictions which have the capacity to reduce the availability of food (WTO, 2010g: 11–12). To expand, the recent increase in food prices prompted countries to adopt a range of responses such as reducing exports and building up domestic stocks of foodstuffs. In certain instances, such policies have actually had a detrimental impact by producing a 'feed-back' loop whereby prices were driven up further by a lack of supply and the associated fear of a reduced supply (Evans, 2006: 1; Rudaheranwa, 2009: 5). While certain of these measures such as an increase in export taxes do not fall to be considered under WTO legal disciplines, others such as the imposition of export restraints are subject to lax regulation under Article 12 of the AoA and Article XI of the GATT (Rudaheranwa, 2009: 5; Diaz-Bonilla and Fransisco-Bonilla, 2010). While the 2008 Draft Modalities proposed some tightening up of the discipline applicable to export restraints, it is unlikely that these will have any significant effect upon the practice. Hence, the argument being advanced is not that issues pertaining to food security should not be dealt with at the national level or that international approaches to such issues are always somehow 'better' but rather that the scope to address certain concerns at a domestic or regional level may be limited by exogenous factors (Jackson, 2008: 3–5).

A mix of endogenous and exogenous limitations on Members' policy space to deal with the issue of food security is apparent in relation to the spectre of 'land grabbing'. The term has become common parlance for the giving over of agricultural land, particularly in Africa, to the production of agricultural products for export. Action Aid reports that in five African countries, an area the size of Belgium has become dedicated to the production of industrial biofuels, all of which are for export (Rice, 2010: 3). At country – endogenous – level, land grabs may arise as a consequence of inadequate systems of land tenure, while at an exogenous level such 'grabs' are in part the consequence of the policies of other Members which provide incentives to promote the use of biofuels as an alternative to fossil fuels, although it must be noted that the cultivation of biofuel feedstocks is not the sole reason for land grabs.

Land grabs may be characterised as exogenous to the extent that the policies of external actors create the incentives for such land grabs to occur. While the particular conditions for investment in the agricultural sector will very much depend upon the contract at issue, it is also clear that the practice of land grabbing can undermine the food security of particular societal sectors. Hence, to the extent that this practice is not accompanied by consultations to ensure that local people benefit through employment opportunities as well as access to technology and other benefits, it may have a detrimental impact upon the food security of individual households – and in particular, of women – due to the loss of access to land and other associated natural resources (Deininger *et al.*, 2010: 70). Land grabbing does not directly fall within the legal competence of the AoA and hence, to the extent that food security has an investment dimension, as Häberli has argued earlier in this volume, the 'space' left for the development of these rules must be effectively utilised for such incomplete theorisation not to result in inconsistency.

Applying the lessons garnered from the above analysis of how endogenous as well as exogenous variables may impact upon the policy space of Members, it is clear that how food security is approached within the WTO is necessarily 'different' from, for example, a 'rights'-based account of food security (ILA, 2010: 13–14). To the extent that the 'narrow' conceptualisation of food security within the trade regime represents an example of the use of the incompletely theorised agreement, it is contended that this is an example of incomplete theorisation resulting in inconsistency. Recalling that one of the advantages of the incompletely theorised agreement is that it may promote stability, it is axiomatic that such stability will be undermined to the extent that it is productive of inconsistency.

It is arguable that the constricted reading of food security means that it may be difficult to raise certain issues within the trade regime, such as the distributional elements of food security and the impact of trade policies upon the food security of individual households (Diaz-Bonilla *et al.*, 2002: 4–5). This is because discussion of distributional impacts does not comport with the narrow construction of food security found within the trade regime and so such concerns do not easily find a 'fit' therein. This trend is apparent not only in relation to the issue of food security. In a similar vein, Lang (2005: 414) cites the example of water privatisation under the GATS in regard to which the trade regime provides an institutional space for a discussion of the issues arising therein, but not one under which arguments relating to the individual and distributional outcomes of such privatization have any 'obvious entry point'. Indeed, the trade regime has no 'obvious language in which such discussion might occur, and (importantly) there is a strong sense that such scrutiny would be unjustified and illegitimate and a matter better left for authorities at the national level'.[2]

Linking in with the above commentary on how Members may not have the competence or capacity to deal with certain issues pertaining to food security, the extent to which these issues are excluded due to a lack of 'fit' may result in inconsistency in the construction of the incompletely theorised agreement. It is therefore worthwhile highlighting that while the AoA seeks to strike a balance between trade and non-trade concerns (Smith, 2007: 91) and seemingly provides the necessary communicative space for this to be achieved, it is apparent that the arrangement whereby food security is primarily constructed as a domestic issue within the policy space of the Member concerned has undermined the efficacy of such a space.

IV. THE NEED FOR SPACE

The central goal of this chapter is to utilise the lens provided by the trade in biofuels to shed light upon the consistency – or otherwise – of the construction of non-trade concerns such as food security under the AoA. In this regard, it may be noted that many of the policies which have been implemented to promote the use of biofuels as an alternative to fossil fuels have been advanced in large part for national purposes. As such, 'biofuel development polices have a direct impact on these triple challenges [of climate, food security and energy security] and yet it is national polices with national interests that have been the driving force of setting biofuel targets' (Fischer *et al.*, 2009: 39). It is also evident, however, that these national policies may have spill-over effects, as exemplified previously in regard to the role played by biofuels in the 2007/2008 food price crisis. In this regard, attention may be turned to the EU Renewable Energy Directive which seeks to encourage the use of biofuels as an alternative to fossil fuels in transport through the establishment of a 10 per cent renewables target. What the EU regime does not do is make any real attempt to deal with the potential impact of its biofuels policy on food security. Hence, while the EU appears cognisant of the link between biofuel production and food [in]security, the Directive contains no formal commitments in regard to how to tackle the potential impact of biofuels upon food prices.

Such spill-over effects arise not only in respect of food security, but also, as indicated previously, in the effect that policies promoting biofuels may have on hastening direct as well as indirect land-use change in areas outside the national 'policy space' of the relevant Member. In this regard, a recent analysis of the indirect-land use change impacts of the 2009 EU Renewable Energy Directive found that an area of land slightly smaller than the Republic of Ireland could be required to meet the extra demand for biofuels established under it and that a significant amount of such land would need to be found from outside the EU (Bowyer, 2010: 12). The analysis is based upon the National Renewable Action Plans of 23 Member States and is therefore perhaps a slightly better indicator of such impacts than a report commissioned by the EU Commission which was based upon assumptions as to the action plans of the Member States and posited a much lower figure (Al-Riffia *et al.*, 2010).

Pursuant to Article 19(6) of the EU Renewable Energy Directive, the Commission was directed to report on the issue of indirect land-use by December 2010 and this was to be accompanied by a proposal, if appropriate, for a concrete methodology for climate change emissions caused by indirect land-use change. However, due to the difficulties and uncertainties of modelling indirect land-use change, the date for the

Commission's report has been changed to July 2011 (Commission, 2010). In the interim, the EU has attempted to deal with direct land-use change through the introduction of various incentives for both domestic and imported biofuels which meet certain designated 'sustainability' criteria, including avoiding the conversion of certain high-carbon stock land (Switzer and McMahon, 2011). While indirect land-use change is hard to model, it is underscored that the occurrence of indirect land-use change in respect of the production of biofuels feedstocks is the 'direct effects of changes in agriculture ... and forestry' (Fritsche *et al.*, 2009: 4). Hence, issues pertaining to food security and environmental protection, at least in respect of land-use change, are closely linked.

Concerns such as land-use change find little by way of expression in WTO debates. Where these issues are raised, they are normally presented through the 'barrier to trade' lens whereby processes such as certification are raised as potential restrictions to imports (WTO, 2009: 7). Without commenting upon the efficacy or otherwise of the employment of such a lens, there appears to be little by way of 'entry points' for an engaged discussion as to how to tackle such issues. Seemingly, in line with the 'domestic' orientation of food security under the AoA, issues pertaining to the non-trade concern of environmental protection are also conceptualised in much the same way. This is inherently problematic given that it is clear that the capacity and competence to deal with non-trade concerns are not always within the domestic policy space of Members to address. In this regard, to the extent that Members may wish to take action within their *own* national policy space to promote sustainable forms of agriculture and incentivise practices which avoid land-use change and are conducive of domestic food security, these may have to 'swim against the tide' of exogenous factors such as the mandates and blending requirements introduced by other countries to encourage bioenergy use (IBRD, 2008: 66; WTO, 2010f: 12).

Linked to the above discussion, attention has recently been drawn to the need to promote more 'sustainable' agricultural practices, both in respect of the promotion of biofuels as well as in the broader context of agricultural production as a whole. Such efforts are called for pursuant to the Rome Declaration on Food Security, which under Commitment Three calls for efforts to ensure the 'productive capacity [and] sustainable management of natural resources and protection of the environment' (FAO, 1996). This is pertinent to the biofuels debate in that it may be contended that the promotion of 'good' biofuels in a manner which takes account of concerns such as food security and environmental protection 'can only be dealt with in an overall framework of sustainable land use, and in the context of overall food and fibre policies and respective markets' (Fritsche *et al.,* 2009). In essence, stemming from the interconnectedness of environmental protection and food security as non-trade concerns, a coordinated response based upon sustainable land-use may be required so as to deal coherently with the challenge posed by biofuels. By extension, this also draws attention to the notion that such coordination is unlikely to be achieved through domestic policy mandates to promote biofuel use which are designed primarily to promote national level policies. As such, it is necessary not only to draw attention to the inconsistency of the incompletely theorised agreement through which such concerns are addressed, but also to begin to think about the 'space' within the trade regime to approach issues such as the sustainable management of land and natural resources.

It may, of course, be contended that the WTO has a scant role to play in encouraging sustainable practices in the management of land and other natural resources. However, in response, it is to be noted that the rules on domestic support under the AoA's Green Box allow for support to be granted for environmental programmes. Furthermore, outside of the context of the AoA, the trade regime has recently sought to introduce greater discipline to curtail unsustainable practices in relation to another natural resource, that of fish. In this regard, pursuant to paragraph 28 of the Doha Declaration, negotiators are mandated to 'clarify and improve WTO Disciplines on Fisheries Subsidies' (WTO, 2001). Furthermore, under paragraph 9 of the 2005 Hong Kong Ministerial Declaration, Members committed to the strengthening of disciplines on fisheries subsidies, including through the 'prohibition of certain forms of fisheries subsidies that contribute to overcapacity and over-fishing' (WTO, 2005). While the process of such clarification has been difficult and is not yet complete, it has been argued that such discussions represent, at least in part, an attempt not only to implement specific obligations in the fisheries sector but also to protect a particular resource (Chang, 2003: 882). Moreover, the disciplining of fisheries subsidies to ensure that they do not result in overfishing or overcapacity is reducible to an effort to marry an environmental with a trade approach. As such, it is clear that in respect of fisheries communicative space has been made available in which to raise issues of sustainable resource management. The lessons from this are an important retort to those who would argue that the trade regime does not typically involve itself in sustainable land or resource management issues.

It is, however, vital to recognise the argument that disciplines in the fisheries sector are required because they pertain to a shared resource and that the sector is too 'unique' to be governed by existing disciplines. Given that fisheries are a shared resource, it is clear that the effectiveness of any action taken by individual Members in respect of these will be limited to the extent that such efforts can be undermined by the practices of others. This rationale for action can be applied to agriculture more generally in that the incentivising practices of one Member to promote sustainable practices may be undermined by the practices of others. We can see this, for example, in relation to the use of biofuel mandates which may directly contradict the attempts of others to promote more sustainable forms of agriculture in a manner that is conducive to the achievement of environmental goals and food security (IBRD, 2008: 66). Hence, while fish are a 'shared resource' which are necessarily different from biofuels, it is also clear that an analogy may be offered with biofuels to the extent that the practices of one Member may undermine the policy space of another Member to promote sustainable approaches. The point being made here is not that the approach to the issues raised by the increase in biofuels trade must be the same as that found under the fisheries example, but rather that attempts to marry a trade and sustainable resource management approach are not 'alien' to the trade regime even if the rationale for such an approach stems from a different context.

It is thus established that the promotion of more sustainable forms of resource management is not *necessarily* outside of the competence of the trade regime. As a result, to the extent that raising issues of sustainable resource management in the agricultural/biofuels sector may allow for a wider reading of food security to be introduced, such conversations are not *necessarily* outside the competence of the trade regime. As will be explored in more detail below, the value of introducing a wider reading of non-trade concerns such as food security into the trade regime is that it may allow for an arrangement whereby food security is constructed as an incompletely theorised agreement to be challenged. The next section will elucidate further upon the notion of such communicative space and the 'access routes' which can be utilised to promote a wider articulation of food security. In this regard, while the focus of the rest of discussion will be upon food security, given the connection advanced previously between food security and other goals such as environmental protection, the opening up of communicative access routes in order to advance a wider articulation of one non-trade concern by necessity has implications for other non-trade concerns.

V. ELUCIDATING UPON COMMUNICATIVE 'SPACE'

As established above, the increased use of biofuels exemplifies that the construction of food security as a non-trade concern within the policy space of Members to both define and react to is potentially conducive of inconsistency. Moreover, while it is important to be cognisant of the notion that positioning responses to particular concerns such as food security on multilateral level will not always be optimal, the reading given to non-trade concerns under the AoA may be insufficient to deal with the challenge posed by the increased resort to biofuels. Indeed, the recent food price crisis and the effects of climate change upon agricultural production are likely to challenge further the 'set-up' which exists under the AoA to deal with food security concerns. In this regard, recent figures as to the effects of climate change estimate that certain of the economies most dependent upon agriculture face a loss of up to 50 per cent of output by 2080 (Keane *et al.*, 2010: 1).

The overarching aim of this chapter is not to seek to articulate a 'new' definition for food security for the WTO or indeed to expound upon a prescriptive account of the kind of regulation necessary to achieve food security, however this is defined. In addition, the task is not to elucidate upon what a completely theorised account of food security under the Agreement on Agriculture would look like. Rather, the challenge has been to demonstrate that the arrangement pursuant to which the 'why' and 'how' of food security under the AoA has been left incompletely theorised may be suboptimal to the extent that it results in inconsistency. It is argued that communicative 'space' is required to begin to more fully theorise food security so as to broaden our understanding of the dynamics of food security. As such, it is to be underlined that there is a distinction to be made between a complete theorisation of food security under the auspices of the WTO and a *more* – but not fully – complete theorisation. This work seeks to elucidate upon opportunities to provide for communicative space so as to more fully – but not completely – theorise the concern of food security. It does not attempt to completely theorise food security since it would be normatively improper to do so. It is, however, to be recognised that the possibility exists for a complete theorisation of food security under the WTO which in itself provides for communicative space. While this is not considered further, it is contended that a necessary step to any such arrangement is the destabilisation of the present incompletely theorised agreement which represents food security under the WTO. Hence, in seeking to advance upon the possibilities for the creation and moreover utilisation of communicative space, it is intended that the inconsistency which exists in regard to the current arrangement may be challenged and destabilised. By challenging and destabilising the present construction, it is hoped that the way may be paved for more coordinated responses between Members on how to tackle concerns such as food security. However, as a preliminary step, it is necessary to identify to what extent potential access routes exist to allow for such a wider, and by extension destabilising, reading to be advanced.

It is contended that one potential communicative access route which could be utilised to advance a wider reading of food security is to be found under the Aid for Trade process. At its most basic, the Aid for Trade initiative creates opportunities for communication about the particular needs of developing countries and the kind of resources required to meet those needs (Cai, 2009: 296). Additionally, each Aid for Trade project also permits the various parties involved to learn about each other. This is particularly significant given that Aid for Trade projects typically involve a multitude of actors such as non-governmental groups with whom the WTO has struggled to enter into dialogue.

Mainstreaming 'food security' within national poverty reduction and development strategies as part of the Aid for Trade process may help to address certain of the endogenous constraints Members might face in tackling food security. Indeed, recent conversations within the WTO under the Aid for Trade banner have underlined a need to address the investment aspects of food security as well as remedy the chronic pattern of underinvestment which has plagued the agricultural sector in developing countries (WTO, 2010a; 2010b). Addressing food security concerns under the Aid for Trade mandate is also likely to allow a wider conceptualisation of food security to be advanced within the trade regime given the focus under it upon monitoring, impact and evaluation. In essence, it may allow for a discussion on the distributional consequences of certain policies and thereby might address, to a certain degree, the criticism outlined previously that the typical reading of food security does not address such concerns. In this regard, much attention has been paid to issues of gender under the Aid for Trade process. An additional 'access route' that is being increasingly utilised to draw attention to issues such as land tenure and the associated spectre of land-grabbing is the Trade Policy Review Process (WTO, 2010d; 2010e). While the length of time between reviews may reduce the efficacy of the process, it is arguable that as a communicative access route it may help to throw some light on certain dimensions of food security which do not find expression in other WTO forums (Ghosh, 2010: 446).

VI. CONCLUSIONS

It is to be underlined that in identifying possible communicative access routes, the goal has not been to advance a particular ideal reading for food security within the trade regime. In addition, given that the aim of introducing a wider conception of food security is *not* to articulate a prescriptive set of arrangements to achieve a certain ideal, little by way of comment has been passed upon what, from a normative perspective, the WTO 'should' do to better address the concern of food security. While this latter statement may seem to undermine the substance of the discussion so far, it is to be noted that a central tranche of the criticism advanced in respect of the incompletely theorised agreement was that it cannot take sufficient account of the exogenous and endogenous factors which may limit a country's policy space to take certain actions. By bringing communication on concerns such as land grabbing and land tenure into the trade regime, greater attention may be given to the inadequacies of the current construction of food security. In this regard, the discussion on sustainable land/resource management was advanced to demonstrate that a coordinated response to such issues does not necessarily fall outside of the remit of the trade regime. To the extent that increased promotion of biofuels as an alternative to fossil fuels may exacerbate the instability of the incompletely theorised agreement, articulating a wider conception of food security may prove a useful starting point for commencing a discussion on promoting greater coherence in national policy making and ensuring that sustainable practices in the agricultural sector may be encouraged and not undermined by country-level blending and consumption mandates for the use of biofuels. Hence, the argument is not that the WTO should 'do it all' but rather that the current approach to food security is inadequate.

The underlying aim of this chapter was to review how the non-trade concerns of food security and to a lesser extent environmental protection are constructed under the WTO's AoA. In this regard, the argument was advanced that while agreement has been secured on the mid-level principle of food security as a legitimate concern to be taken into account during the liberalisation process, the question of 'how' and moreover 'why' was left incompletely theorised and within the competence of Members. It was articulated that while leaving certain issues incompletely theorised will at times be both necessary and desirable, on other occasions a more complete theorisation will be required so as to guard against risks such as bias or inconsistency. In this regard, the argument was advanced that leaving the 'how' and the 'why' of food security incompletely theorised did in fact lead to inconsistency.

The example provided by increasing trade in the international trade in biofuels was utilised to bolster the contention that communicative 'space' is required within the trade regime to help articulate a wider conception of food security. Various communicative access routes were identified as suitable avenues through which to challenge the current construction of food security. It is contended that the offering of alternative, broader accounts of food security could form an important starting point in discussions on how to promote more sustainable forms of agriculture with biofuels a central element of this.

NOTES

1. Note, however, that the price impact of biofuel production may be ameliorated through the production of by-products as well as more land being brought into food production in response to higher prices; see Matthews (2010: 4). The main by-products in this regard are dried distillers' grains and solubles (DDGS) from the production of ethanol and meals and oil cakes from biodiesel; see Al-Riffia *et al.* (2010: 55).
2. The failure of the WTO to provide a forum for 'purposeful deliberation and consultation between its members on matters of common interest' has been described as in essence the 'missing middle' of the trade regime; see generally Evenett (2009).

BIBLIOGRAPHY

Abbott, P., Hunt, C. and Tyner, W. E. (2009) 'What's Driving Food Prices – March 2009 Update', *Farm Foundation Issue Report*, available at http://ageconsearch.umn.edu/bitstream/48495/2/FINAL%203-10-09%20-%20Food%20Prices%20Update.pdf (accessed 25 February 2011).
Al-Riffia, P., Dimaranan, B. and Laboral, D. (2010) 'Global Trade and Environmental Impact Study of the EU Biofuels Mandate', available at http://www.ifpri.org/sites/default/files/publications/biofuelsreportec.pdf (accessed 25 February 2011).
Bowyer, C. (2010) 'Anticipated Indirect Land Use Change Associated with Expanded Use of Biofuels and Bioliquids in the EU – An Analysis of the National Renewable Action Plans', Institute of European Environmental Policy, available at http://www.ieeplondon.org.uk/publications/pdfs/2010/iluc_analysis.pdf, (accessed 25 February 2011).
Cai, P. (2009) 'Sutton Colloquium Article: Aid for trade – a roadmap for success', *Denver Journal of International Law and Policy*, **36**: 283.

Chang, S. (2003) 'WTO Disciplines on Fisheries Subsidies: A historic step towards sustainability?', *Journal of International Economic Law*, **6** (4): 879.

Commission (2006) Staff Working Document accompanying document to the Communication from the Commission to the Council and the European Parliament: *Biofuels Progress Report* SEC (2006) 1721 (10 January 2007).

Commission (2010) 'Report from the Commission on indirect land-use change related to biofuels and bioliquids', COM(2010)811 final.

Deininger, K. *et al.* (2010) *Rising Global Interest in Farmlands: Can it yield sustainable and equitable benefits?* Washington, DC: World Bank.

Diaz-Bonilla, E. and Francisco-Bonilla, J. (2010) 'Food Security, Price Volatility and Trade: Some reflections for developing countries', ICTSD Programme on Agricultural Trade and Sustainable Development, Issue Paper No. 28.

Díaz-Bonilla, E., Thomas, M. and Robinson, S. (2002) 'On Boxes, Contents and Users; Food Security and the WTO Negotiations', *TMD Discussion Paper*, available at http://ageconsearch.umn.edu/bitstream/16266/1/tm020082.pdf

Evans, A. (2006) *Rising Food Prices: Drivers and Implications for Development*. London: Chatham House.

Evenett, S. (2009), 'Aid for Trade and the 'Missing Middle' of the World Trade Organisation', *Global Governance*, **15**: 359.

FAO (1996) 'The Rome Declaration on Food Security', available at http://www.fao.org/docrep/003/w3613e/w3613e00.HTM

FAO (2008) *The State of Food and Agriculture – Biofuels: Prospects, Risks and Opportunities*. Rome, Italy: United Nations.

FAO (2010) High Level Task Force on the Food Security Crisis, *Updated Comprehensive Framework for Action*. Rome: FAO.

Fischer, G. *et al.* (2009) *Biofuels and Food Security: Implications of an Accelerated Biofuel Production*. Vienna: OFID.

Fritsche, U., Kampmani, B. and Bergsma, G. (2009) 'Better use of Biomass for Energy – Position Paper of IEA RETD and IEA Bioenergy', available at http://www.oeko.de/service/bio/dateien/iea_bubeposition_paper_final.pdf (accessed 25 February 2011).

Ghosh, A. (2010) 'Developing Countries in the WTO Trade Policy Review Mechanism', *World Trade Review*, **9** (3): 419.

Hamwey, R. (2005) 'Expanding National Policy Space for Development: Why the multilateral trading system must change', *South Centre Working Paper*, available at http://www.southcentre.org/index.php?option = com_content&task = view&id = 336 (accessed 22 February 2011).

Harmer, T. (2009) 'Biofuels Subsidies and the Law of the WTO', ICTSD Programme on Agricultural Trade and Sustainable Development, *Issue Paper 20*.

Howse, R. *et al.* (2006) *WTO Disciplines and Biofuels: Opportunities and Constraints in the Creation of a Global Marketplace*, International Food and Agricultural Trade IPC Discussion Paper, available at http://www.tradeobservatory.org/library.cfm?refID = 96515 (accessed 25 February 2011).

Hudec, R. (1987) *Developing Countries in the GATT Legal* System. London: TPRC.

IBRD (2008) *Sustainable Land Management Sourcebook*. Washington, DC: World Bank.

International Law Association (ILA) (2010) 'The Hague Conference (2010): International Trade Law', available at http://www.ila-hq.org/download.cfm/docid/177B9AF7-E32B-4BE2-8836FA3A655C3482

Jackson, J. (2008) 'Sovereignty: Outdated concept or new approaches?', in W. Shan, P. Simons and D. Singh (eds), *Redefining Sovereignty in International Economic Law*. Oxford: Hart.

Keam, S. and McCormick, N. (2008) *Implementing Sustainable Bioenergy Production: A Compilation of Tools and Approaches*. Switzerland: IUCN.

Keane, J., MacGregor, J., Page, S., Peskett, L. and Thorstensen, V. (2010) 'Development, Trade and Carbon Reduction: Designing coexistence to promote development', *ODI Working Paper* 315.

Kojima, M., Mitchell, D. and Ward, W. (2007) 'Considering Trade Policies for Liquid Biofuels', ESMAP, World Bank, *Renewable Energy Special Report 004/07*, available at http://siteresources.worldbank.org/INTOGMC/Resources/Considering_trade_policies_for_liquid_biofuels.pdf (accessed 22 February 2011).

Lang, A. (2005) 'Beyond Formal Obligation: The trade regime and the making of political priorities', *Leiden Journal of International Law*, **18**: 403.

Legge, T. (2008) 'The Potential Contribution of Biofuels to Sustainable Development and a Low Carbon Future,' *Chatham House Programme Paper*, available at http://www.chathamhouse.org.uk/files/12492_biofuelspp1008.pdf (accessed 22 February 2011).

Matthews, A. (2010) *How Might the EU's Common Agricultural Policy Affect Trade and Development Post 2013? An Analysis of the European Commission's November 2010 Communication*. Geneva: ICTSD.

Mechlem, K. (2006) 'Harmonising Trade in Agriculture and Human Rights: Options for the integration of the right to food into the Agreement on Agriculture', *Max Planck Yearbook of United Nations Law*, **10**: 127.

Mitchell, D. (2008) 'A Note on Rising Food Prices', *World Bank Development Prospects Group Policy Research Working Paper 4682*, available at http://www-wds.world bank.org/external/default/WDSContentServer/IW3P/IB/2008/07/28/000020439_20080728103002/Rendered/PDF/WP4682.pdf (accessed 25 February 2011).

OECD Directorate for Food, Agriculture and Fisheries Committee for Agriculture (2006) 'Agricultural Market Impacts of Future Growth in the Production of Biofuels', Working Party on Agricultural Policies and Markets AGR/CA/APM (2005) 24/FINAL.

Petillion, K. (2005) 'Report on the Legal Issues Regarding Biofuels in Transport', VIEWLS Project, available at http://ec.europa.eu/energy/res/sectors/doc/bioenergy/legal_issues_biofuels.pdf (accessed 22 February 2011).

Post, R. (2009) 'Theorising Disagreement: Re-conceiving the relationship between law and politics', Yale Law School, *Public Law Working Paper* No. 145, http://papers.ssrn.com/sol3/papers.cfm?abstract_id=1434103

Rice, T. (2010) *Meals Per Gallon: The Impact of Industrial Biofuels on People and Global Hunger*. London: Action Aid.

Rosegrant, M. (2008), 'Biofuels and Grain Prices – Impacts and Policy Responses', Testimony for the U.S. Senate Committee on Homeland Security and Governmental Affairs on 7 May 2008, available at http://www.ifpri.org/blog/biofuels-and-grain-prices-impacts-and-policy-responses (accessed 21 December 2010).

Rudaheranwa, N. (2009) *Biofuel Subsidies and Food Prices in the Context of WTO Agreements*. London: Commonwealth Secretariat.

Searchinger, T. (2008) 'Use of U.S. Croplands for Biofuels Increases Greenhouse Gases Through Emissions from Land-Use Change', *Science*, **39**: 1238.

Smith, F. (2007) 'Thinking Outside the Green Box: Non-trade concerns in a post-Doha environment', *Environmental Law Review*, **9** (2): 89–115.

Steenblick, S. (2006) 'Liberalisation of Trade in Renewable Energy and Associated Technologies: Biodiesel, solar thermal and geothermal energy', *OECD Trade and Environment Working Paper* 2006 – 0, COM/ENV/TD (2005)78/FINAL.

Sunstein, C. (1995) 'Incompletely Theorised Agreements', *Harvard Law Review*, **108** (7): 1733.

Sunstein, C. (1996) *Legal Reasoning and Political Conflict*. Oxford: OUP.

Sunstein, C. (2007) 'Incompletely Theorised Agreements in Constitutional Law', *John M. Olin Law and Economics Working Paper* No. 322 (2D Series), *Public Law and Legal Theory Working Paper* No 147.

Switzer, S. and McMahon, J. (2011) 'EU Biofuels Policy – Raising the Question of WTO Compatibility', *International and Comparative Law Quarterly*, 60: 713–736.

Tilman, D. *et al.* (2009) 'Beneficial Biofuels – The Food, Energy and Environment

Trilemma', *Science,* **325**: 270.
von Braun, J. (2008) *Food and Financial Crisis: Implications for Agriculture and the Poor.* Washington, DC: IFPRI.
WTO (2001) *Doha WTO Ministerial Declaration*, WT/MIN(01)/DEC/1.
WTO (2005) *Doha Work Programme Ministerial Declaration*, WT/MIN(05)/DEC.
WTO (2009) Committee on Trade and Environment, 'Report of Meeting held on 10 July 2009' (31 August) WT/CTE/M/47.
WTO (2010a) Committee on Trade and Development Aid for Trade, 'Mainstreaming Aid for Trade at a Thematic Level – Workshop on Aid for Trade and Agriculture: Background Note by the Secretariat' (18 February) COMTD, AFT/W/17.
WTO (2010b) Committee on Trade and Development, 'Note on the Meeting of 17 March 2010' (30 April) WTO/COMTD/A4T/M/14.
WTO (2010c) Committee on Trade and Environment, 'Environmental Database 2007 – Note by the Secretariat' (17 May) WTO/CTD/EDB/7.
WTO (2010d) Trade Policy Review Body, 'Report by the Secretariat – Benin, Burkina Faso and Mali' (30 August) WT/TPR/S/236.
WTO (2010e) Trade Policy Review Body, 'Report by the Secretariat – Papua New Guinea' (12 October) WT/TPR/S/239.
WTO (2010f) Trade Policy Review Body, 'Trade Policy Review – Report of the Democratic Republic of Congo' (20 October) WT/TPR/G/240.
WTO (2010g) Committee on Agriculture, 'Annual Monitoring Exercise in respect of the Follow-up to the Ministerial Decision on Measures Concerning the Possible Negative Effects of the Reform Programme on Least-Developed and Net Food-Importing Developing Countries' (20 December) G/AG/GEN/94.
WTO (2011) Trade Policy Review Body, 'Jamaica – Record of Meeting' (23 February) WT/TPR/M/242.
Zah, R., Böni, H., Gauch, M., Hischier, R., Lehmann, M. and Wäger, P. (2007) *Life Cycle Assessment of Energy Products: Environmental Assessment of Biofuels.* St. Gallen, Switzerland: Empa.
Zhang, R. (2004) 'Food Security: Food trade regime and food aid regime', *Journal of International Economic Law,* **7** (3): 565.

11 Stretching the boundaries of multifunctionality? An evolving Common Agricultural Policy within the world trade legal order
Michael Cardwell

I. INTRODUCTION

When the European Union (EU) commenced reform of the Common Agricultural Policy (CAP) for the period post-2013, it became immediately apparent that multifunctionality remained a part of the 'European Model of Agriculture': as stated by Commissioner Cioloş in Dublin on 1 October 2010, 'a fundamental element' is that 'agriculture has a crucial multifunctional role for our territories' (Commission, 2010a). And when shortly thereafter the Commission issued its key Communication, *The CAP Towards 2020: Meeting the Food, Natural Resources and Territorial Challenges of the Future* (2010 Communication), there could be no doubt that the post-reform role for agriculture would be far broader than the mere production of food and fibre (Commission, 2010b). That said, while multifunctionality has arguably remained a constant feature of EU agriculture, the importance attached to it in policy terms would seem to vary and, moreover, its precise attributes may be regarded as somewhat protean. For example, the 2010 Communication highlights new, 'non-productivist' challenges, not least of these being climate change;[1] yet, significantly, in light of the further new challenge of ensuring food security, renewed emphasis is accorded to the core activity of production itself. Moreover, it is unequivocally declared that 'the primary role of agriculture is to supply food' (Commission, 2010b: 4).

This state of affairs may not perhaps be surprising, in light of frequent reiteration by the EU institutions that the CAP is an evolving policy. For example, such characterisation was prominent in the policy document which initiated the Mid-term Review (Commission, 2002: 4, 5) and the 2010 Communication itself stated that 'the CAP has evolved, but further changes are necessary in order to respond to the new challenges' (Commission, 2010b: 5). Inevitably, these developments have the capacity to generate interesting legal issues, including: (i) the current nature and role of multifunctionality (and, not least, whether it is susceptible of legal definition or serves a wider purpose in policy development); and (ii) the extent to which EU agricultural reform may be reconfiguring the relationship between multifunctionality and non-trade concerns in the world trade context.

However, before turning to examine such issues, two preliminary matters of substance may be considered. First, some assessment is required as to what are the conventional boundaries of multifunctional agriculture, a question which itself continues to be fiercely contested, not least in the context of the World Trade Organization (WTO). Indeed, as indicated, no examination of multifunctional agriculture within the EU can ignore the influence of world trade (O'Neill, 2002). In carrying out this assessment, frequent reference will be made to the analytical work undertaken by the Organisation for Economic Co-operation and Development (OECD). Although much of this work was completed a decade ago, it would still seem to have a strong contemporary resonance. Firstly, as shall be seen, there was already an awareness of the difficulties in locating food security within standard interpretations of multifunctionality. Secondly, the early role of multifunctionality within EU agricultural policy may be traced from the time of the Agenda 2000 reforms. This should have the benefit of determining the extent to which EU interpretation of the concept could already be considered fluid, while at the same time providing some benchmark to test the extent to which the 2007–2009 Health Check and the proposed further reform have yet further stretched existing boundaries.

II. THE BOUNDARIES OF MULTIFUNCTIONALITY

As indicated, the preliminary question is to determine what are the conventional boundaries of multifunctional agriculture; an expression that is considered 'barbarous' (House of Lords Select Committee on the EU, 1999: para 139). Early in its genesis, the concept was theoretically grounded (Pisani, 1994), but for some time there has been criticism that it lacks rigour (Wilson, 2007: 6–8). In addition, over the last decade the argument has been advanced that emphasis should rather be accorded to a multifunctional countryside, on the basis that production agriculture has lost much of its primacy. This argument, which sees multifunctionality as an attribute of rural space, also highlights the countryside as a place of consumption, with such consumption extending well beyond agricultural products to include, for example, tourism and other forms of amenity (Potter, 2004: 15–35; Slee, 2005; Marsden and Sonnino, 2008). A broader vision would, besides, seem consistent with the economic reality in at least some parts of the EU. For example, during the closure of much of the United Kingdom countryside at the time of the 2001 foot-and-mouth crisis, the financial shock sustained by the tourist industry was apprehended to be considerably greater than that sustained by agriculture (Countryside Agency, 2001: 23–42). On the other hand, it must also be recognized that there are those who consider that multifunctional agriculture retains a degree of integrity within a wider and less clearly delineated 'multifunctional rurality' (Wilson, 2007: 223–227). And, as already seen and will be considered again later, it may be premature to discount the importance of agricultural production in a world seeking to meet the imperative of food security.

While such debate continues, reasonable certainty would yet seem achievable on three points. Firstly, an express reference to multifunctionality in the agricultural context would appear to be relatively recent. For example, it was not a well-established concept when referred to in the Agenda 21 documentation at the time of the Rio Earth Summit; Chapter 14 included as one of its programme areas 'agricultural policy review, planning and integrated programming in the light of the multifunctional aspect of agriculture, particularly with regard to food security and sustainable development' (UN, 1992). Moreover, only at the time of its 1998 Communiqué was real impetus given to OECD policy initiatives in this area (OECD, 1998). Nonetheless, it must also be emphasized that agriculture has long been regarded as more than the provision of food and fibre. Thus, under Article 39(2) of the EC Treaty as originally enacted (now Article 39(2) of the Treaty on the Functioning of the European Union), implementation of the CAP was to take account of, *inter alia*, 'the particular nature of agricultural activity, which results from the social structure of agriculture and from the structural and natural disparities between the various agricultural regions' and 'the fact that in the Member States agriculture constitutes a sector closely linked with the economy as a whole'. In a similar vein, Commissioner Fischer Boel asserted in 2006 that the 'multifunctional' model was a feature of the 1958 Stresa Conference, with developments in the late 1990s being characterized as 'defining – or should I say "redefining" – our agricultural model' (Commission, 2006b). Accordingly, while it would be difficult to detect specific use of the expression multifunctionality in agricultural policy circles for much longer than two decades, a vision of agriculture which extends beyond production enjoys a far more extended history (Daugbjerg and Swinbank, 2009: 159).

Secondly, multifunctionality has traditionally been associated with the 'European Model of Agriculture' (Cardwell, 2004; Greer, 2005). Without doubt, both terms began to enjoy wider currency at approximately the same time, there being only a few months difference between the 1998 OECD Communiqué already noted and the declaration at the Presidency Council, held in Luxembourg on 12–13 December 1997, that the European Union would 'continue developing the present European model of agriculture'. Notably, this declaration implied that the multifunctional model itself was not new; but Commissioner Fischer Boel has observed that, since that Council, the clear vision offered has become 'explicitly known as the European Model of Agriculture' (Commission, 2006b). In any event, a full (and classic) description of the European Model of Agriculture may be found in the policy document which initiated the Mid-term Review (Commission, 2002: 2):

- a competitive agricultural sector;
- production methods that support environmentally friendly, quality products that the public wants;
- a fair standard of living and income stability for the agricultural community;
- diversity in forms of agriculture, maintaining visual amenities and supporting rural communities;
- simplicity in agricultural policy and the sharing of responsibilities among the Commission and member-states;
- justification of support through the provision of services that the public expects farmers to provide.

Likewise, in a 2006 background paper, the Finnish Presidency could still affirm that 'multi-functionality is at the heart of the European Model of Agriculture' (Finland, 2006). Consequently, the focus continued to be directed towards the protection of the environment, food quality, visual amenity and the maintenance of vibrant rural communities; and these would appear relatively uncontroversial 'joint products' of agricultural production, falling within conventional boundaries of multifunctionality (OECD, 2001). The more complex question, to be discussed later in greater detail, is whether the same could be said following the shift in focus that is now so evident in the 2010 Communication.

Thirdly, this model has consistently been held up by the EU as worthy of defence in the Doha Round negotiations. Indeed, even before the formal commencement of the Doha Round Commissioner Fischler had stated 'that the European model of agriculture, which is based on competitive, multifunctional and sustainable farming throughout Europe is not for negotiation' (Commission, 1999). When the *EC Comprehensive Negotiating Proposal* was issued towards the close of 2000, there was express assertion that, if there were to be further trade liberalization and expansion, it would be 'vital to muster strong public support, which can only be achieved if other concerns are met, in particular the multifunctional role of agriculture, which covers the protection of the environment and the sustained vitality of rural communities, food safety and other consumer concerns including animal welfare' (WTO, 2000b). Further, and more recently, Commissioner Fischer Boel confirmed that 'agriculture provides essential things for society which are not sold in packets on the supermarket shelf' (Commission, 2007a).

On the other hand, there is also certainty that the attribution of such a role to the European Model of Agriculture has been fiercely debated by certain WTO members and, not least, the Cairns Group: for example, as early as 1999 an Australian report concluded that 'the spillover benefits from agriculture are being put forward as a reason to maintain or even increase agricultural protection' (ABARE, 1999: 5). Moreover, in the United States, *The Use and Abuse of Multifunctionality*, prepared by the Economic Research Service of the USDA, noted that the degree of enthusiasm for the 'multifunctional' agenda could be related to the extent to which the member concerned was facing an obligation to reduce domestic support (Bohman *et al.*, 1999: 6). That said, it must also be acknowledged that criticism of multifunctionality in the world trade context is far from unknown in the EU (Swinbank, 2001). Besides, even the sternest critics outside the EU accept that 'non-trade concerns' should be taken into account in the agriculture negotiations: rather, the issue remains whether they are taken into account by policies which only minimally distort trade (Smith, 2000; WTO, 2001a). Similarly, *The Use and Abuse of Multifunctionality* took a decidedly balanced approach, accepting that 'the non-food outputs of agriculture represent legitimate domestic policy objectives' and reserving its criticism for any distortions in international trade which might result (Bohman *et al.*, 1999: 22). There is also considerable evidence that the USDA continues to promote an agricultural policy which shares many of the characteristics of the European Model of Agriculture. Thus, in *Food and Agricultural Policy: Taking Stock for the New Century* there was an assertion that 'Americans consider environmental quality as a kind of "nonmarket good" that is extremely important in consumer choices' (USDA, 2001: 2). Illustrating this policy in action, the flagship Conservation Reserve Program provides for maximum enrolment of some 32 million acres up to 2012 (Williams, 2005).[2] More generally, there is increasing advocacy of an agriculture which embraces food, farming and sustainability (Schneider, 2010).

Accordingly, while multifunctionality continues to be contested in the WTO, there can perhaps be detected greater harmony than is popularly imagined. Yet it remains impossible to deny that any assessment of whether recent EU policy developments seek to extend the boundaries of multifunctionality comes up against the problem that those boundaries are far from clear. Further, most attempts at definition tend to appear in research reports and policy documents rather than legal texts. Very useful guidance may be provided by the former category and, not least, the 'working definition' put forward in 2001 by the OECD in their report, *Multifunctionality: Towards an Analytical Framework*, which identified key elements as being '*i)* the existence of multiple commodity and non-commodity outputs that are jointly produced by agriculture; and *ii)* the fact that some of the non-commodity outputs exhibit the characteristics of externalities or public goods, with the result that markets for these goods do not exist or function poorly' (OECD, 2001: 13; Durand and Van Huylenbroeck, 2003). However, not only does this lack legal status, but the report also expressly stated that its primary purpose was not to develop a precise definition. Likewise, in an earlier OECD report, *Multifunctionality: A Framework for Policy Analysis*, no detailed investigation was attempted into 'what should or should not be included in multifunctionality in the various OECD Member countries' (OECD, 1998: 6). And, with regard to relevant legal texts, it may be highlighted that the term multifunctionality is not to be found among the objectives of the CAP in the Treaty on the Functioning of the European Union (notwithstanding the opportunity for amendment at the time of the Lisbon Treaty); and, while the 'multifunctional aspect of agriculture' does receive reference in the Agenda 21 documentation, there is no such reference in the Agreement on Agriculture. Besides, it is not even to be found in the Cork Declaration, which has guided EU rural development initiatives for over a decade (Commission, 1996). On the other hand, both the Agenda 2000 document and the key communication which initiated the Mid-term Review do employ the word 'multifunctional', although, interestingly, they do so with regard to 'multifunctional rural areas' (as opposed to 'multifunctional agriculture') (Commission, 1997: Part One, III, 3; Commission, 2002:

9). More recently, in the Preamble to the strategic guidelines for rural development issued in 2006, it was recited that these 'should reflect the multifunctional role farming plays in the richness and diversity of landscapes, food products and cultural and natural heritage throughout the Community'; and the guidelines themselves affirmed that the European Model of Agriculture reflects such a role.[3] It may be noted, however, that this wording was to be found in the guidelines (as opposed to the implementing regulation), while even more recently there was no express mention of multifunctionality in the 2010 Communication.

Accordingly, even in the EU context, there would appear to be no serious attempt to develop a definition of multifunctionality in the legal texts. Rather, the term is more likely to be employed in policy documents or in guidance. Indeed, it may readily be associated with 'soft' (as opposed to 'hard') law. There would seem to be clear several advantages in such approach. The direction of policy can be signalled without becoming bound up by detail; and, as has been seen, the somewhat protean nature of the term allows for policy to evolve within the same conceptual framework. Further, a 'negotiating space' is generated, with particular reference to the Doha Round. Yet, at the same time, it must also be recognized that the Agreement on Agriculture has attracted cogent criticism for the very reason that it lacks the clarity of expression that is required for effective regulation of international trade (O'Connor, 2003; Smith, 2009, 2010).

III. MULTIFUNCTIONALITY AND THE COMMON AGRICULTURAL POLICY: AGENDA 2000 TO THE 2007–2009 HEALTH CHECK

Nevertheless, there can be little doubt that, when multifunctional attributes were first expressly accorded to the CAP, they fell within boundaries that were widely accepted in the international debate. In particular, the imposition of environmental protection requirements upon receipt of numerous direct payments under the Agenda 2000 reforms would seem to conform well to the criteria for multifunctionality as suggested by the OECD (Court of Auditors, 2000; Jack, 2009: 57–58). There was a high level of 'jointness' between the act of production and the 'public good' which it generated (in the form of an enhanced environment); and, in the words of the OECD, 'the key issues on the production side of multifunctionality are related to the nature and degree of jointness of the multiple outputs of agriculture' (OECD, 2001: 4). At the same time, it may be noted that in the agricultural context the European Court of Justice has also adopted a determinedly multifunctional interpretation of environmental protection requirements, specifically re-affirming that such measures, although enacted under the Agriculture Title of the EC Treaty, have not been restricted to pursuing agricultural objectives.[4] That said, the picture would appear somewhat more nuanced in the case of payments for land set-aside. Such land had been subject to environmental protection requirements for a good while before the Agenda 2000 reforms;[5] but the measures had been primarily designed to secure a better market balance through supply control (as opposed to securing an enhanced environment), with the result that the general prohibition on production sat far less easily with notions of multifunctional jointness. This position was further complicated by the fact that production on set-aside land was not absolutely prohibited, it being possible to grow non-food crops in specifically defined circumstances.[6] Yet, whatever the policy motivations, the absence of production on land set-aside has *de facto* been found to generate environmental benefits (IEEP, 2008a). Accordingly, it can be said with some certainty that in this instance the linkages between production and environmental benefits were not straightforward. At the same time, it may be emphasized that the Agenda 2000 reforms saw rural development constituted as Pillar II of the CAP under Council Regulation 1257/1999 on support for rural development, with the broader rural economy as supported by that Regulation having long been internationally accepted as a feature of 'multifunctional' agriculture (OECD, 1998: 4).

In any event, the extension of cross compliance beyond environmental protection requirements at the time of the Mid-term Review of the CAP formed part of a wider 'multifunctional' vision for the European Model of Agriculture, with the range of public goods being substantially extended (Daugbjerg and Swinbank, 2009: 141). The receipt of most support under Pillar I of the CAP (comprising market management measures and direct payments) became dependent upon the observation of statutory management requirements which embraced not just environmental protection, but also public, animal and plant health and animal welfare; and, in addition, there was a general obligation to maintain all agricultural land in a good agricultural and environmental condition (Cardwell, 2005). While *prima facie* this legislative initiative promoted and broadened the degree of multifunctional jointness, on closer analysis the position would again appear to be more complex. Since the Mid-term Review, the bulk of Pillar I support has been bundled together into the Single Farm Payment and, critically, its receipt is not dependent upon the production of a particular crop or, indeed, production at all. It is sufficient for the farmer to engage in an 'agricultural activity' and 'agricultural activity' includes simply maintaining the land in a good agricultural and environmental condition, without any requirement to grow crops or raise livestock.[7] Such provisions may strengthen the compatibility of the Single Farm Payment with the criteria for Green Box exemption as decoupled income support within Annex 2.6 to the Agreement on Agriculture (Commission, 2002: 19; Swinbank and Tranter, 2005; Cardwell and Rodgers, 2006; Swinbank, 2009a).[8] Yet arguably these have the concomitant effect of weakening the linkage with production which is so central to the multifunctional agenda. Further, as indicated, the multifunctional credentials of the Single Farm Payment would appear the less by reason that, if a Green Box exemption is to be secured, it is on the basis of qualifying as decoupled income support as opposed to, for example, a payment under an environmental programme within Annex 2.12 to the Agreement on Agriculture.

It may also be observed that these wider public goods such as animal welfare did not bulk large in early OECD analysis of the scope of multifunctionality as found, for example, in *Multifunctionality: A Framework for Policy Analysis* where the emphasis was placed on environmental protection, the rural economy and food security (OECD, 1998: 3). On the other hand, Norway had responded to that document by advocating that zoo-sanitary and public health considerations were also functions of agriculture as a 'multifunctional' activity (OECD, 1999) and, from the start of the Mid-term Review reform process, the Commission consistently regarded the imposition of such obligations as necessary to address the expectations of civil society. Indeed, Commissioner Fischler stated it to be 'the only mechanism that allows us to meet the demands that the European public has of its agricultural policy' (Commission, 2004). However, while a multifunctional discourse was adopted towards the domestic audience, it may also be observed that in the world trade context the language of multifunctionality was largely replaced by reference to 'non-trade concerns' (Daugbjerg and Swinbank, 2009: 161). For example, the *European Communities Proposal: Animal Welfare and Trade in Agriculture* announced that 'the EC wishes to raise animal welfare as an important non-trade concern in the current negotiations'; and the main thrust of the argument was shifted from 'jointness' to ensuring that high animal welfare standards should not impact negatively on European Community competitiveness (WTO, 2000a). That said, in this context also great weight was placed upon meeting the demands made by the public upon agriculture: in the words of *The EC's Proposal for Modalities in the WTO Agriculture Negotiations*, for support for trade reform to be maintained, 'society needs to be reassured that certain societal goals such as the specific domestic support needs of developing countries, the protection of the environment, rural development and animal welfare may be achieved without obstacles created by the WTO' (McMahon, 2005). A matter of interest is that, at this juncture, the European Community would seem to have interpreted food security as being largely a matter for developing countries. Thus, *The EC's Proposal for Modalities in the WTO Agriculture Negotiations* advocated a 'food security box' to tackle this imperative and in 2006 Commissioner Fischer Boel could affirm that 'the challenge of producing enough food is no longer an issue' (Commission, 2006a).

Following the Mid-term Review, a further shift in policy focus could again be detected, in that there was increased emphasis on food quality, linked to competitiveness in world trade (Erjavec and Erjavec, 2009). Thus, soon after her appointment, Commissioner Fischer Boel advocated 'an agriculture that seeks its opportunities on the market and that operates in a competitive and sustainable way' (Commission, 2005b). Importantly, such competitiveness was increasingly cast in terms of food quality, which related not just to the end product but also to the method of production (including organic production) and association with a particular region (Commission, 2009a; McMahon, 2002). On the other hand, the 'multifunctional' agenda is also evident, for in the same speech she added that 'Europe also needs a policy for its rural areas that supports structural adjustments, helps to maintain cultivated landscapes and the quality of life in rural areas, as well as enabling new sources of income and job opportunities to be developed'.

IV. MULTIFUNCTIONALITY AND THE COMMON AGRICULTURAL POLICY: THE 2007–2009 HEALTH CHECK AND THE 2010 COMMUNICATION

1. Introduction

Soon after her appointment, Commissioner Fischer Boel had also signalled that mitigating the effects of climate change would be a policy objective of her term of office. Indeed, already by January 2005 she saw agriculture as contributing to meeting the Kyoto objectives (Commission, 2005c). Moreover, by the time when the Health Check was announced in November 2007, there could be no doubt that the role of the CAP was being reconfigured to meet 'crucial new challenges', identified as climate change, bio-energy and water management (Commission, 2007b: 9). Such proposals subsequently found their way into an amended legislative framework for rural development, under which Member States were obliged, as from 1 January 2010, to provide in their rural development programmes, in accordance with their specific needs, for types of operations having as their priorities, *inter alia*, climate change and renewable energies.[9] Amended strategic guidelines for rural development adopted the same terminology, expressly referring to climate change and renewable energy as two of the 'new challenges' of the CAP.[10]

Importantly, in response to the food crisis of 2008, food security emerged during the Health Check reform process as a further imperative for the CAP. There were immediate and practical steps which could be taken, such as the abolition of compulsory set-aside for 2008, but a broader policy response was also deemed necessary (Commission, 2008). Accordingly, by the time of the 2010 Communication the three key challenges for the CAP were formally identified as food security, the environment and climate change, and territorial balance (Commission, 2010b: 4–5). Besides, as has been already noted, there was no hesitation in asserting that the primary role of agriculture was to supply food; and in this regard the vision has become far more 'productivist', with the 2010 Communication declaring that 'it is essential that EU agriculture maintains its production capacity and improves it' (while also acknowledging that EU international trade commitments will need to be respected) (Commission, 2010b: 4). The focus on competitiveness in terms of quality is, however, retained, with it being highlighted that the EU is the largest exporter of mostly processed and high value-added agricultural products (O'Connor, 2010).

A major question, therefore, is the extent to which this reformulation of policy objectives takes the CAP outside conventional boundaries of multifunctionality. It has already been observed that the word multifunctional does not as such appear in the 2010 Communication and neither food security nor climate change featured large in the early EU discourse on multifunctionality. On the other hand, it may be reiterated that Commissioner Cioloş believed it to be fundamental that agriculture retain 'a crucial multifunctional role for our territories' (Commission, 2010a) and while the 2010 Communication would seem to have thrown the emphasis back on production there is still ample evidence of the language of multifunctionality, with this being especially so in the case of 'territorial balance'. Thus the roles attributed to agriculture include its potential to promote tourism and there is an affirmation that 'in many regions agriculture is the basis of local traditions and of the social identity' (Commission, 2010b: 5). Further, the 2010 Communication retained a reference to the 'public goods' conferred by agriculture, using terminology that was familiar from a decade earlier: by way of illustration, an objective for the future CAP will be to 'secure the enhanced provision of environmental public goods as many of the public benefits generated through agriculture are not remunerated through the normal functioning of markets' (Commission, 2010b: 7).

2. Food Security

Turning first to food security, it has already been seen that this was identified by the OECD as a 'multifunctional' element of agriculture in *Multifunctionality: A Framework for Policy Analysis*, and there is also much support for such a proposition both institutionally and in the academic literature (FAO, 1999; Vatn, 2002). However, at the same time there must be recognition that the issue is not free from doubt: in the words of Bohman *et al.* (1999: 16), 'while countries generally agree that food security is a legitimate objective, they do not agree on the public good aspect of food security, nor on how it is related to domestic agriculture'. In this context, therefore, a key question which remains to be answered definitively is the extent to which food security may rather be subsumed into the primary role of agriculture, namely the production of food and fibre (Mann, 2008). As already noted, this is arguably the approach adopted by the Commission in the 2010 Communication, with its emphasis on addressing the global food demand by boosting production within the EU. Moreover, the concrete expression of such an approach may be found in the abolition of compulsory set-aside in face of the 2008 food crisis: as enunciated in the policy document initiating the Health Check, 'the foreseeable demand and supply situation for cereals, including the demand linked to the fulfilment of the biofuel target set by the EU, argues for mobilising land which is presently kept out of production through the compulsory set aside scheme' (Commission, 2007b: 7). By contrast, elsewhere food security is characterized as a 'non-commodity output', while the OECD highlights that the concept fits uneasily within the accepted criteria for assessing what constitutes multifunctionality and, in particular, the criterion of 'jointness': as subsequently stated in *Multifunctionality: Towards an Analytical Framework*, 'the linkage is with the food itself, which is a primary output, and a tradable good, whereas other multifunctional outputs are non-tradable' (OECD, 2001: 16). Further, the OECD has also consistently characterized food security as being more complex than simply a matter of 'to produce or not to produce': for example, in this context a major role is ascribed to public stock-holding and food imports (OECD, 1998: 16). Likewise, when the United Kingdom government addressed the question of food security in 2009, the policy choice was not simply whether to boost domestic production so as to promote national self-sufficiency: rather, a key factor was considered to be the ability to assure imports (DEFRA, 2009). Nonetheless, it should also be mentioned that the OECD considered that there could be some merit in unlocking the production potential of land idled or set-aside, which chimes better with the drive to increase output as articulated in the 2010 Communication.

What is more certain is that whether or not food security qualifies as a multifunctional element of agriculture it is generally accepted as a legitimate non-trade concern for the purposes of the Agreement on Agriculture, with the Preamble expressly reciting that 'commitments under the reform programme should be made in an equitable way among all Members, having regard to non-trade concerns, including food security and the need to protect the environment' (see Chapter 2 in this volume). The Doha Declaration has confirmed that 'non-trade concerns will be taken into account in the negotiations as provided for in the Agreement on Agriculture' (WTO, 2001b: para 13). Consistent with such an approach, measures to address food security have been found *ab initio* among the Green Box exemptions from domestic support reduction commitments, as set out in Annex 2 to the Agreement on Agriculture. For example, exemption has been conferred for public stockholding for food security purposes under Annex 2.3 and this provision may be expanded in the Doha Development Round, so as to provide a blanket exemption in the case of the acquisition of stocks of foodstuffs by developing countries with the objective of supporting low-income or resource-poor producers (WTO, 2008: Annex B; Desta, 2001). However, it would seem to be beyond any doubt that measures to address food security are not confined to Annex 2 since food security also inevitably raises trade concerns and perhaps the clearest illustration of this over recent years has been members resorting to export restrictions (Häberli, 2010; Siddhartha and Josling, 2009). Thus, according to a report emanating from the International Food Policy Research Institute, in 2007–2008 'export restrictions played a dominant role in turning a critical situation into a full-blown crisis' (Headey and Fan, 2010: 96). In particular, when one key exporting member implemented a ban or restrictions the pressure was increased upon other exporting members, thereby creating a 'contagion effect': thus the Ukrainian ban (later converted into a restriction) on grain exports was considered to have been a significant factor in generating similar restrictions imposed by Russia and Kazakhstan. In any event, these issues persist (WTO, 2011b) and it may be highlighted that an additional, unfortunate feature of the 2007–2008 food crisis was that, even as prices soared, levels of food aid fell, indicating that one of the key tools in the Green Box would not be likely to provide anything close to a full and permanent solution (WFP, 2008).

The Doha Round negotiations have throughout addressed the issue of food security and the Revised Draft Modalities of December 2008 include, for example, the provision that any new export prohibitions and restrictions in foodstuffs and feed under GATT 1994 Article XI(2)(a) should not normally last any longer than a year (WTO, 2008: para 179). Again, this would tend to confirm that measures addressing levels of imports and exports may be at least equally vital in this context and indeed the crucial role of trade in maintaining supplies was expressly highlighted for WTO agriculture delegates in November 2010 by the Special Representative of the United Nations Secretary-General (WTO, 2010). At the same time, a new and much expanded Article 10.4 of the Agreement on Agriculture would recast the provisions on international food aid so as to increase the focus on the needs of the recipients, including a provision (in defined circumstances) for the food aid to be targeted to meet the nutritional requirements of identified food insecure groups (WTO, 2008: Annex L). In many ways, these developments in the negotiations could be regarded as highlighting the multifunctional nature of food security, in that it is only ever likely to be realized by a combination of trade/production and non-trade/non-production measures (OECD, 1998: 18). Moreover, as indicated, this is but one instance under the Agreement on Agriculture where it may be difficult to establish a bright-line distinction between trade and non-trade concerns (Smith, 2007).

That said, it may also be reiterated that there remains no international consensus that food security is truly a multifunctional attribute of agriculture: as graphically stated by New Zealand in response to *Multifunctionality: A Framework for Policy Analysis*, 'food security *is* an important non-trade concern, but it is *not* part of multifunctionality ... If anything, food security is a joint product with *trade* not agricultural production' (OECD, 1999: 31). In addition, it is generally accepted that, for a proper accommodation of 'multi-functional' objectives within the agricultural world trade regime, a key criterion is the ability to value the 'positive externality' which is the joint product of agriculture (Paarlberg *et al.*, 2002). Yet, while this may be a sufficiently difficult exercise in the case of, for example, amenity landscape, that exercise becomes almost impossible when seeking to value food security both at the level of the nation state and at the level of the individual (Fleischer and Tsur, 2000). Further, at a conceptual level, it is arguable that food security is not a 'function' of agriculture, but rather an end in itself.

3. Climate Change

Likewise, it is no simple exercise to assess the extent to which mitigating climate change may be characterized as a multifunctional attribute of agriculture. There are definitely voices which assert that the growing of biofuels satisfies the necessary criteria: for example, in 2007 the President of the European Council of Young Farmers declared that 'multifunctionality needs to be extended to take account of new emerging uses of farm activities such as non-food production and advances in bio-energy. It is a fundamental concept of the future CAP' (Ballari, 2007). Besides, as long ago as 1999 there was wider articulation of the 'energy function' of agriculture (FAO, 1999). On the other hand, there can be few who would argue that agriculture generates purely 'positive externalities' in relation to climate change, since there is ample evidence that it is a major contributor to greenhouse gas emissions. Perhaps most notably, the FAO report, *Livestock's Long Shadow: Environmental Issues and Options*, found that livestock accounted for 18 per cent of greenhouse gas emissions, a greater proportion even than transport (FAO, 2006: xxi). Such effects have been contested (Pitesky *et al.*, 2009). Yet there remain genuine concerns over the extent to which agriculture gives rise to 'negative externalities', with the OECD by 2001 already characterizing greenhouse gas emissions as one of the 'negative side-effects' of commodity production (OECD, 2001: 30). Further, there is the difficulty that many of the measures designed to boost food security may have the concomitant effect of impacting adversely on climate change, a tension openly accepted at the heart of EU policy-making.

Not least, the European Parliament Resolution of 13 January 2009 warned that efforts to promote renewable energy through biofuel production could be prejudicial to biodiversity, raise food prices, and damage land-use patterns (European Parliament, 2009). As a consequence, one function of agriculture could be directly straining against another; and the European Parliament called for the striking of an appropriate balance. This interconnectedness was likewise accorded prominence in the recent United Kingdom Foresight Report, *The Future of Food and Farming*, which emphasized that global food security could only be achieved through sustainable agriculture and that in order to achieve this end addressing climate change had become imperative (Foresight, 2011).

In this context may be examined the multifunctional credentials of two prominent features of EU climate change policy: firstly, land management; and secondly, the production of feedstock for bio-energy (on the former see Chapter 9 this volume, and on the latter see Chapter 9 and Chapter 10 this volume). The EU has promoted the former as central to its policy agenda of reducing greenhouse gas emissions and the role of agriculture in terms of carbon sequestration and the protection of carbon in soils receive an express mention in the 2010 Communication (Commission, 2010b: 5). For such a purpose, it is understood that a major contribution can be made by further enhancement of the cross-compliance rules under Pillar I, as well as by specific actions under Pillar II which go beyond cross-compliance, yet remain 'linked to agriculture', such as permanent pasture and ecological set-aside. This approach would seem to be well captured by the expression 'green productivity', as employed with reference to climate change mitigation by Commissioner Fischer Boel (Commission, 2009b).

There is definitely compelling evidence that agricultural land management practices can both reduce greenhouse gas and promote carbon sequestration. For example, in the 2010 Communication it was claimed greenhouse gas emissions from agriculture had fallen by 20 per cent since 1990 (Commission, 2010b: 5). Similarly, a United Kingdom study in 2010 found a fall of 21 per cent between 1990 and 2008, this being 'largely due to less fertiliser use and reduced livestock numbers as a result of CAP reform' (UK Committee on Climate Change, 2010: 231). That said, while some praise is accorded to the CAP, in the language of multifunctionality such developments in fertiliser use and more extensive livestock production could perhaps be better characterized as the reduction of a negative externality than the creation of a positive externality (although it may also be recognized that the reduction of some negative externalities can at the same time give rise to a positive externality, an example of this being the positive effect on water quality of lower fertiliser and pesticide applications).

In consequence, it might be expected that specific land management measures under Pillar II could perform a more overtly positive function. In particular, research has indicated that placing land into permanent set-aside has major benefits in terms of carbon storage, being nearly as effective as forestry, and permanent set-aside is expressly enumerated in the revised EU rural development legislation as an operation which addresses the priority of climate change adaptation and mitigation (IEEP, 2008b: 73–76). Further, for the purposes of the Agreement on Agriculture, support provided by such resource retirement programmes may qualify for the Green Box within Annex 2.10, with the emphasis being laid, in terminology redolent of non-trade concerns, upon the absence of marketable agricultural production. On the other hand, where *no* agricultural activity takes place there may be significant difficulty in meeting the requirement of jointness as emphasized by the OECD.

Faced with this potential difficulty, a clearer multifunctional role for agriculture may arguably be sought in measures that are more closely linked to production, such as cross-compliance obligations attached to direct payments. That said, it has already been noted that there is no specific requirement to undertake production in order to qualify for the Single Farm Payment. Further, it may be argued that the focus for many of these obligations is instead to limit externalities and that nearly all the current obligations pre-date the present priority granted to the mitigation of climate change (although it should also be noted that, at the time of the Health Check, the opportunity was taken to reinforce the protection and management of water in the context of agricultural activity).[11] Against such a background, if the cross-compliance regime is to perform a significant multifunctional role in mitigating greenhouse gas emissions, there is sound logic in its further enhancement as proposed by the 2010 Communication.

The climate change credentials of bio-energy and in particular biofuels have been even more hotly contested and the extent to which the production of feedstock for bio-energy forms part of multi-functional agriculture likewise gives rise to complex issues, three of which may be considered (House of Commons Environmental Audit Committee, 2008: para 34). Firstly, there is the question of the extent to which such an activity should be considered purely agricultural (rather than multifunctional). This question is not made easier by the fact that, under the Agreement on Agriculture, bioethanol is classified as an agricultural product whereas biodiesel is not (WTO, 2006). There must be a respectable argument that, in terms of multifunctionality, the growing of feedstock for bioethanol is to be regarded as no more than another species of agricultural production and such integration would seem to be the closer in that bioethanol can be derived from 'dual use' crops, such as sugar and cereals, which might equally be sold for human consumption (Swinbank, 2009b). However, it should also be noted that this characteristic is shared by certain forms of feedstock for biodiesel, such as oilseed rape, and as already indicated biodiesel is not classified as an agricultural product for WTO purposes (Switzer and McMahon, 2011). That said, for the purposes of the multifunctionality debate, it may be prudent not to rely too heavily on analogies with the legal position adopted within WTO, where the question in terms of production of feedstock begins rather with whether or not there is a subsidy which is captured by the rules governing domestic support reduction commitments, and in this regard subsidies for production of an agricultural product are captured regardless of their ultimate use (Josling and Blandford, 2009).

In the context of multifunctionality, however, some assistance may again be derived from OECD analysis and, in particular, developments in that analysis which took place a decade ago. If the multifunctional element to receive emphasis is the provision of non-food services (this being the case, for example, in *Multifunctionality: A Framework for Policy Analysis*), then the answer would seem to be that growing feedstock for bio-energy does indeed perform a non-food function and this would be the clearer in the case of biomass (as opposed to biofuel) production, where feedstock such as short rotation coppice and miscanthus offer no alternative food use (Commission, 2005a). By contrast, in *Multifunctionality: Towards an Analytical Framework*, the OECD subsequently noted that many products of primary production are non-food outputs and significantly that specific examples of non-food outputs included 'renewable energy or raw materials for industrial production' (OECD, 2001: 10). In consequence, the preferred distinction was not between food and non-food functions, but between commodity and non-commodity outputs and on this interpretation much of the cultivation of feedstock for bio-energy would seem to be subsumed, as the cultivation of commodities, within primary agricultural production.

Secondly, arguments in favour of support for multifunctional agriculture generally highlight the characteristic that it has the ability to generate public goods in circumstances where otherwise there would be 'market failure' (Grossman, 2003). Yet it is not always clear that in the case of bio-energy production there is such market failure. For example, in 2005 the *Biomass Action Plan* could already state that 'biomass in heating is often cost-competitive' (Commission, 2005a: 6). When the legislative framework for direct payments was reformed by the Health Check, specific support for energy crops under Pillar I of the CAP was withdrawn, it being cited that 'due to recent developments in the bio-energy sector and, in particular, to the strong demand for such products on international markets and the introduction of binding targets for the share of bio-energy in total fuel by 2020, there is no longer sufficient reason' for such support.[12] In consequence there is a case that, where such dual use crops are grown without specific support, there should be no WTO difficulties, the only support available would be the Single Farm Payment, which covers, *inter alia*, cereals and sugar beet and which, as has already been seen, is understood to be Green Box exempt as decoupled income support within Annex 2.6 to the Agreement on Agriculture (IPC and RIEL, 2006: 20–21).

That said, the rural development legislation under Pillar II does continue to provide for targeted measures to promote renewable energies, including support for perennial energy crops in the form of short rotation coppice and herbaceous grasses. The Rural Development Programme for England 2007–2013 fully accepted that such targeted measures were necessary to ensure the necessary level of production: perennial energy crops enjoyed a clear advantage in terms of climate change mitigation over annual crops when used as feedstock for transport fuels, but 'without any public support it was unlikely that private investment would take place at the required scale to encourage continuing demand' (DEFRA, 2007). However, although this might indicate market failure there must be some doubt about whether or not such targeted support for perennial energy crops is Green Box compliant (Switzer and McMahon, 2011). In particular, while there is an overarching environmental objective in the mitigation of climate change, this would not in itself seem sufficient to qualify as a 'clearly-defined government environmental or conservation programme environmental programme' under Annex 2.12 to the Agreement on Agriculture (Josling and Blandford, 2009). The Doha Development Round negotiations do offer an opportunity to reform the Green Box criteria (WTO, 2004: Annex A, para 16), but the current amendments proposed for these criteria do not squarely address the Green Box compatibility of biofuel subsidies (WTO, 2004: Annex B; see also Chapter 9 this volume). Further, if the scale of such subsidies is significant, then there is the additional hurdle of the fundamental requirement that the measures should have no, or at most minimal, trade-distorting effects or effects on production. What may be suggested is that, in light of the novelty of the issue, any conferment of Green Box exemption on biofuel production should be specifically crafted to address the known areas of controversy, avoiding the temptation to bring it within (albeit amended) existing criteria.

Thirdly, in view of the extent to which the green credentials of biofuels are contested, it may be suggested that they do not in any event generate 'public goods'. That said, it may be highlighted that, even if they do not give rise to a public good in the form of climate change mitigation as such, the argument has consistently been advanced that they perform other beneficial, non-commodity functions. Thus, for example, when laying down the *EU Strategy for Biofuels*, the European Commission included within the objectives 'new opportunities to diversify income and employment in rural areas', while in the earlier *Biomass Action Plan* direct employment for 250,000–300,000 people was envisaged, mainly in rural areas (Commission, 2006c: 3; Commission, 2005a: 6). A second non-commodity function that is widely articulated has been fuel security, an objective which has had even greater resonance in the United States (House of Lords European Union Committee, 2006: para 14; Gehlhar *et al.*, 2010). Accordingly, when the new EU regulatory framework for renewable energies was issued in 2009, it was perhaps no surprise that Directive 2009/28/EC on the promotion of the use of energy from renewable sources made explicit reference to securing energy supplies and fostering growth and employment.[13] Further, and significantly, environmental priorities have likewise been directly addressed within this new framework. Thus under Articles 17 and 18 of the Directive sustainability criteria have been applied to the production of feedstock (Endres, 2010). Indeed the Preamble, at Recital 69, went so far as to suggest that EU consumers would find it 'morally unacceptable' for increased biofuel and bioliquid use to have the effect of destroying biodiverse lands. Thus, for example, under Article 17(1) protection is accorded to primary forest, areas designated for nature protection purposes (whether by law or the relevant local authority), and wetlands, and notably these sustainability criteria are expressed to apply 'irrespective of whether the raw materials were cultivated inside or outside the territory of the Community'. This requirement may assist in preventing, not least, the destruction of rainforest for the growing of biofuel feedstock (Burrell, 2010). Yet it may also resurrect (to the extent that it was not settled in *Shrimp–Turtle*)[14] the difficult issue of whether or not, for the purposes of WTO law, one Member may condition the production methods of another (IPC and REIL, 2006; Endres, 2010). Besides, as in the case of cross-compliance conditions, such sustainability criteria may perhaps be more accurately characterized as reducing a 'negative externality' than as creating a 'positive externality', with the result that it may be hard to classify unequivocally the growing of feedstock for bio-energy as an environmental 'public good'. The issue becomes even more pertinent in the world trade context by reason that the Doha Declaration expressly includes agreement to negotiations on 'the reduction or, as appropriate, elimination of tariff and non-tariff barriers to environmental goods and services' (WTO, 2001b: para 31(iii)). It has been proposed in the Committee on Trade and Environment that biofuels (including biodiesel) should qualify as 'environmental goods' (WTO, 2007), but consensus on any definition would seem still some distance away (WTO, 2011a). However, notwithstanding this ongoing debate, there remains confidence within the EU that the CAP of the future can address the conflict between climate and environment policy goals (Commission, 2010b: 9).

V.   CONCLUSION

Recent initiatives by the EU institutions would tend to confirm that, although it is less frequently found in policy discourse, a 'multifunctional' model of agriculture remains entrenched at the heart of the CAP. However, the CAP is without doubt subject to ongoing reform and, in the words of Commissioner Fischer Boel, 'the European Model of Agriculture should not be seen as something static, rigid, out of time and reality, but something which is dynamic and evolves over time' (Commission, 2006b). As part of this process, the 2010 Communication confirms that food security and climate change mitigation now feature high up the list of new priorities and in the language of multifunctionality these changing policy objectives bring with them a reconfiguration of the non-commodity outputs generated by agriculture. It may not, however, be correct to regard this as simply extending the range of public goods at the expense of a 'productivist' model. Indeed, there is arguably a renewed focus on the supply of food as constituting the primary role of agriculture and on commodity as opposed to non-commodity outputs. More particularly, the enhanced role of food security reverts back to the original (and still unchanged) objectives of the CAP and to the early analysis of multifunctionality conducted by the OECD (OECD, 1997: 4).

In any event, it is no easy matter to determine the extent to which both food security and the mitigation of climate change comply with conventional notions of multifunctionality. As has been seen, there are good arguments that at least some policy initiatives become submerged in the primary role of production. This would seem especially so where, in the case of food security, the measures adopted focus on boosting commodity production and, in the case of climate change mitigation, the feedstock for renewable energy is provided by 'dual use' crops. By contrast, it is not immediately clear that certain other policy initiatives satisfy the degree of jointness necessary to qualify even as non-commodity outputs of agriculture (despite the fact that they may qualify, for the purposes of the Agreement on Agriculture, as non-trade concerns): examples here might be public stockholding for food security purposes or even permanent set-aside to promote carbon sequestration.

Accordingly it may be concluded that, notwithstanding the renewed focus on production, the present and future direction of EU agricultural policy has the capacity to reconfigure, if not always stretch, the boundaries of multifunctionality. It may also be suggested that this is not necessarily a bad thing. Any attempt to set rigid boundaries to multifunctionality would seem unwise as new demands are placed upon the agricultural sector and significantly the OECD has accepted that 'the links between the commodity and non-commodity outputs have to be seen in a dynamic context' and that 'the public good nature of certain externalities may change over time' (OECD, 2001: 17, 21). Moreover, as this process takes place it would appear wise to recognize that evolving multifunctional 'public goods' may come to compete or even conflict: the simultaneous achievement of food security and climate change mitigation is definitely a major policy challenge for both the present and the future (OECD, 2010; Foresight, 2011).

In conclusion, therefore, perhaps too much is expected of multifunctionality in terms of its precise use as a juridical point of reference and it is probably no coincidence that, as has been witnessed already, the word does not loom large in legal texts. Further, the European Model of Agriculture, with which the term is so frequently associated, has been described by Commissioner Fischer Boel as embodying 'a core set of values that reflects the diversity of European Agriculture' (Commission, 2006b). Against this background, while multifunctionality may not be susceptible to a precise definition, it may yet have a positive role to play in assisting in the identification and discussion of valuable non-commodity outputs, whose potential trade effects may then be addressed.

NOTES

1.   Climate change was earlier identified as a new, 'non-productivist' challenge in the legislation which implemented the 2009 CAP Health Check: Council Regulation 1698/2005 on support for rural development by the European Agricultural Fund for Rural Development (EAFRD) [2005] OJ L277/1, Art. 16*a*, as amended by Council Regulation 74/2009 [2009] OJ L30/100; and Council Decision 2006/144 on the Community strategic guidelines for rural development (programming period 2007 to 2013) [2006] OJ L55/20, Annex, para. 3.4a, as amended by Council Decision 2009/61 [2009] OJ L30/112.
2.   16 USC § 3831(d).
3.   Council Decision 2006/144/EC [2006] OJ L55/20, Preamble (2) and Annex, para. 2.1.
4.   Case C-428/07 *R (on the application of Horvath)* v *Secretary of State for Environment, Food and Rural Affairs* [2009] ECR I-6355, para. 29.
5.   See, in particular, Council Regulation 1765/92 establishing a support system for producers of certain agricultural crops [1992] OJ L181/12, Art. 7(3) (enacted at the time when set-aside became compulsory under the 1992 MacSharry reforms).
6.   See, in particular, Council Regulation 1765/92 [1992] OJ L181/12, Art. 7(4).
7.   See now Council Regulation 73/2009 establishing common rules for direct support schemes for farmers under the common agricultural policy and establishing certain support schemes for farmers [2009] OJ L30/16, Art 2(a) and (c). The difficult question of whether or not a particular land use meets the criteria for the Single Farm Payment was considered by the European Court of Justice in Case C-61/09 *Landkreis Bad Dürkheim* v *Aufsichts- und Dienstleistungsdirektion*, 14 October 2010 (not yet reported). It was held that, even though an area would be eligible where the overriding objective was landscape management and nature conservation, some use for agricultural purposes was also required.
8.   See, in this context, the reports of the Appellate Body and the Panel in *United States – Subsidies on Upland Cotton* (2005) WT/DS267/AB/R and (2004) WT/DS267/R.
9.   Council Regulation 1698/2005 [2005] OJ L277/1, Art 16*a*, as amended by Council Regulation 74/2009 [2009] OJ L30/100.
10.   Council Decision 2006/144 2006 [2006] OJ L55/20, Annex, para. 3.4a, as amended by Council Decision 2009/61[2009] OJ L30/112.
11.   Council Regulation 73/2009 [2009] OJ L30/16, Preamble (6) and Annex III.
12.   Council Regulation 73/2009 [2009] OJ L30/16, Preamble (42).
13.   [2009] OJ L140/16, Preamble (2) and (3).
14.   See the reports of the Appellate Body and the Panel in *United States – Import Prohibition of Certain Shrimp and Shrimp Products* (1998) WT/DS58/AB/R and (1998) WT/DS58/R.

BIBLIOGRAPHY

ABARE (1999) 'Multifunctionality': A pretext for protection?', *Abare Current Issues*, **3**: 1–6.

Ballari, G. (2007) *A Young, Innovative and Modern European Agriculture*, Brussels, 17 April 2007, available at http://ec.europa.eu/agriculture/events/youngfarmers/ballari2_en.pdf (accessed 26 April 2011).

Bohman, M. *et al.* (1999) *The Use and Abuse of Multifunctionality*. Washington, DC: Economic Research Service/USDA.

Burrell, A. (ed) (2010) *Impacts of the EU Biofuel Target on Agricultural Markets and Land Use: A Comparative Modelling Assessment.* Seville: European Commission Joint Research Centre.

Cardwell, M. (2004) *The European Model of Agriculture.* Oxford: OUP.

Cardwell, M. (2005) 'The Place of Multifunctional Agriculture in World Trade', in B. O'Connor (ed), *Agriculture in WTO Law.* London: Cameron May, pp. 379–400.

Cardwell, M. and Rodgers, C. (2006) 'Reforming the WTO Legal Order for Agricultural Trade: Issues for European rural policy in the Doha Round', *International and Comparative Law Quarterly,* **55**: 805–838.

Commission (1996) *The Cork Declaration – A Living Countryside,* available at http://ec.europa.eu/agriculture/rur/cork_en.htm (accessed 26 April 2011).

Commission (1997) *Agenda 2000: For a Stronger and Wider Union,* COM(1997)2000.

Commission (1999) Commissioner Fischler, Speech/99/138, *WTO Negotiations – Agricultural Aspects,* Brussels, 22 October.

Commission (2002) *Mid-term Review of the Common Agricultural Policy,* COM(2002)394.

Commission (2003) *Explanatory Memorandum: A Long-term Policy Perspective for Sustainable Agriculture,* COM(2003)23.

Commission (2004) Commissioner Fischler, Speech/04/08, *Trade, Reform, and the Future of Europe,* Krems, Austria, 9 January.

Commission (2005a) *Communication from the Commission: Biomass Action Plan,* COM(2005)628.

Commission (2005b) Commissioner Fischer Boel, Speech/05/25, *Agriculture and Rural Development in the EU25 – Looking Forward,* Berlin, 20 January.

Commission (2005c) Commissioner Fischer Boel, Speech/05/28, *Sustainable Agriculture and Innovation – Chance and Challenge for Policy and Society,* Berlin, 22 January.

Commission (2006a) Commissioner Fischer Boel, *Full Steam Ahead: a Fresh Approach to European Agricultural Policy,* Canberra, 1 March.

Commission (2006b) Commissioner Fischer Boel, Speech/06/531, *The European Model of Agriculture,* Oulu, Finland, 26 September.

Commission (2006c) *Communication from the Commission: an EU Strategy for Biofuels,* COM(2006)34.

Commission (2006d) Commissioner Fischer Boel, Speech/06/531, *The European Model of Agriculture,* Oulu, Finland, 26 September.

Commission (2007a), Commissioner Fischer Boel, Speech/07/225, *Giving a Voice to the Future of Farming in the EU,* Brussels, 17 April.

Commission (2007b), *Communication from the Commission to the European Parliament and the Council: Preparing for the 'Healthcheck' of CAP Reform,* COM(2007)722.

Commission (2008) Commissioner Fischer Boel, Speech/08/293, *Food Security and the CAP Health Check,* Ljubljana, 2 June.

Commission (2009a) *Communication from the Commission to the European Parliament, the Council, the European Economic and Social Committee and the Committee of the Regions on Agricultural Product Quality Policy,* COM(2009)234.

Commission (2009b) Commissioner Fischer Boel, Speech/09/260, *The Search for Green Productivity,* Beijing, 21 May.

Commission (2010a) Address by Commissioner for Agriculture and Rural Development, Dacian Cioloş, to the Joint Committee on Agriculture, Fisheries and Food, Dublin, 1 October available at http://ec.europa.eu/ireland/press_office/speeches-press_releases/ciolos-dacian-speech-1-oct-2010_en.htm (accessed 26 April 2011).

Commission (2010b) *The CAP Towards 2020: Meeting the Food, Natural Resources and Territorial Challenges of the Future,* COM(2010) 672.

Commission (2010c) IP/10/1692, *An Enhanced EU Policy to Help Better Communicate the Quality of Food Products,* Brussels, 10 December.

Countryside Agency (2001) *Foot and Mouth Disease: The State of the Countryside.* Cheltenham: Countryside Agency.

Court of Auditors (2000) *Special Report No 14/2000 on 'Greening the CAP'.* Luxembourg: Court of Auditors, [2000] OJ C353/1.

Daugbjerg, C. and Swinbank, A. (2009) *Ideas, Institutions, and Trade: The WTO and the Curious Role of EU Farm Policy in Trade Liberalization.* Oxford: OUP.

DEFRA (2007) *The Rural Development Programme for England 2007-2013,* available at http://archive.defra.gov.uk/rural/rdpe/progdoc.htm (accessed 26 April 2011).

DEFRA (2009) *UK Food Security Assessment: Our Approach.* London: DEFRA.

Desta, M. (2001) 'Food Security and International Trade Law – An Appraisal of the WTO Approach', *Journal of World Trade,* **35**: 449–468.

Durand, G. and Van Huylenbroeck, G. (2003) 'Multifunctionality and Rural Development: A general framework', in G. Van Huylenbroeck and G. Durand (eds), *Multifunctional Agriculture: A New Paradigm for European Agriculture and Rural Development.* Aldershot: Ashgate Publishing, pp. 1–16.

Endres, J. (2010) 'Clearing the Air: The meta-standard approach to ensuring biofuels environmental and social sustainability', *Virginia Environmental Law Journal,* **28**: 73–120.

Erjavec, K. and Erjavec, E. (2009) 'Changing EU Agricultural Policy Discourses? The discourse analysis of Commissioners' speeches 2000-2007', *Food Policy,* **34**: 218–226.

European Parliament (2009) *The Common Agricultural Policy and Global Food Security* (2008/2153(INI)).

FAO (1999a) *Rome Declaration on World Food Security,* 13 November 1996.

FAO (1999b) *The Multifunctional Character of Agriculture and Land: The Energy Function – Background Paper 2: Bioenergy.* Rome: FAO.

FAO (2006) *Livestock's Long Shadow: Environmental Issues and Options.* Rome: FAO.

Finland (2006) *The European Model of Agriculture – Challenges Ahead: A Background Paper for the Meeting of Ministers of Agriculture in Oulu 26.9.2006, SN 3098/06,* available at http://www.euroqualityfiles.net/Documents%20EUAM%20and%20 CEECAP/Europe/Future%20policy/oulu_european_model_agriculture_en.pdf (accessed 15 December 2010).

Fleischer, A. and Tsur, Y. (2000) 'Measuring the Recreational Value of Agricultural Landscape', *European Review of Agricultural Economics,* **27**: 385–398.

Foresight (2011) *The Future of Food and Farming: Challenges and Choices for Global Sustainability.* London: The Government Office for Science.

Gehlhar, M. *et al.* (2010) *Effects of Increased Biofuels on the U.S. Economy in 2022: Economic Research Report Number 102.* Washington, DC: USDA/ERS.

Greer, A. (2005) *Agricultural Policy in Europe.* Manchester: Manchester University Press.

Grossman, M. (2003) 'Multifunctionality and Non-trade Concerns', in M. Cardwell *et al.* (eds), *Agriculture and International Trade: Law, Policy and the WTO.* Wallingford: CAB International, pp. 85–129.

Häberli, C. (2010) 'Food Security and WTO rules', in B. Karapinar and C. Häberli (eds), *Food Crises and the WTO.* Cambridge: Cambridge University Press, pp. 297–322.

Headey, D. and Fan, S. (2010) *Reflections on the Global Food Crisis.* Washington, DC: International Food Policy Research Institute.

House of Commons Environment, Food and Rural Affairs Committee (2005) *Eighth Report of Session 2005–06: Climate Change: the Role of Bioenergy,* HC 965-I.

House of Commons Environmental Audit Committee (2008) *Are Biofuels Sustainable? - First Report of Session 2007–08,* HC 76-I and HC 528.

House of Lords European Union Committee (2006) *The EU Strategy on Biofuels: From Field to Fuel – 47th Report of Session 2005-06,* HL 267-I.

House of Lords Select Committee on the European Union (1999) *The World Trade Organisation: the EU Mandate after Seattle – Tenth Report of Session 1999–2000,* HL76-I.

Institute for European Environmental Policy (IEEP) (2008a) *The Environmental Benefits of Set-Aside in the EU: a Summary of Evidence.* London: Institute for

European Environmental Policy.

Institute for European Environmental Policy (IEEP) (2008b) *Reflecting Environmental Land Use Needs into EU Policy: Preserving and Enhancing the Environmental Benefit of Unfarmed Features on EU Farmland – Final Report.* London: Institute for European Environmental Policy.

IPC and Renewable Energy and International Law (2006) *WTO Disciplines and Biofuels: Opportunities and Constraints in the Creation of a Global Marketplace,* Washington, DC: International Food and Trade Policy Council and Renewable Energy and International Law.

Jack, B. (2009) *Agriculture and EU Environmental Law.* Aldershot: Ashgate Publishing.

Josling, T. and Blandford, D. (2009) 'Biofuels Subsidies in the Green Box', in R. Meléndez-Ortiz, C. Bellmann and J. Hepburn (eds), *Agricultural Subsidies in the WTO Green Box.* Cambridge: Cambridge University Press, pp. 530–568.

Korkeaoja, J. (2006) 'Our Common European Model of Agriculture', *EuroChoices,* **5** (3): 6–12.

Mann, S. (2008) 'Degrees of Jointness for Food Security and Agriculture', in *Multifunctionality in Agriculture: Evaluating the Degree of Jointness – Policy Implications.* Paris: OECD, pp. 159–170.

Marsden, T. and Sonnino, R. (2008) 'Rural Development and the Regional State: Denying multifunctional agriculture in the UK', *Journal of Rural Studies,* **24**: 422–431.

McMahon, J. (2002) 'The Common Agricultural Policy: From quantity to quality', *Northern Ireland Legal Quarterly,* **53**: 9–27.

McMahon, J. (2005) 'The Agreement on Agriculture', P. Macrory *et al.* (eds), *The World Trade Organization: Legal, Economic and Political Analysis (Vol. I).* New York: Springer, pp. 187–230.

Mitra, S. and Josling, T. (2009) *Agricultural Export Restrictions: Welfare Implications and Trade Disciplines.* Washington, DC: International Food and Agricultural Trade Policy Council.

Motaal, D. (2008) 'The Biofuels Landscape: Is there a role for the WTO?', *Journal of World Trade,* **42**: 61–86.

O'Connor, B. (2003) 'A Note on the Need for more Clarity in the World Trade Organization Agreement on Agriculture', *Journal of World Trade,* **37**: 839–846.

O'Connor, B. (2010) 'The Food Crisis and the Role of the CAP', in B. Karapinar and C. Häberli (eds), *Food Crises and the WTO.* Cambridge: Cambridge University Press, pp. 187–219.

O'Neill, M. (2002) 'Agriculture, the EC and the WTO: A legal critical analysis of the concepts of sustainability and multifunctionality', *Environmental Law Review,* **4**: 144–155.

OECD (1998) *Multifunctionality: a Framework for Policy Analysis,* AGR/CA(98)9. Paris: OECD.

OECD (1998a) Ministerial Communiqué, available at http://www.oecd.org/document/34/0,3343,en_2649_33727_31852962_1_1_1_1,00.html#mar98 (accessed 26 April 2011).

OECD (1999) *Written Comments on the Document 'Multifunctionality: A Framework for Policy Analysis',* AGR/CA/RD(99)1. Paris: OECD.

OECD (2001) *Multifunctionality: Towards an Analytical Framework.* Paris: OECD.

OECD (2010) Ministerial Communiqué, available at http://www.oecd.org/document/2/0,3746,en_21571361_43893445_44664898_1_1_1_1,00.html (accessed 16 September 2011).

Paarlberg, P., Bredahl, M. and Lee, J. (2002) 'Multifunctionality and Agricultural Trade Negotiations', *Review of Agricultural Economics,* **24**: 322–335.

Pisani, E. (1994). *Pour une Agriculture Marchande et Ménagère.* La Tour d'Aigues: Editions de l'Aube.

Pitesky, M., Stackhouse, K. and Mitloehner, F. (2009) 'Clearing the Air: Livestock's contribution to climate change', *Advances in Agronomy,* **103**: 1–40.

Potter, C. (2004) 'Multifunctionality as an Agricultural and Rural Policy Concept', in F. Brouwer (ed), *Sustaining Agriculture and the Rural Environment: Governance, Policy and Multifunctionality*. Cheltenham, UK and Northampton, MA, USA: Edward Elgar, pp. 15–35.

Schneider, S. (2010) 'A Reconsideration of Agricultural Law: A call for the law of food, farming, and sustainability', *William and Mary Environmental Law and Policy Review*, **34**: 935–963.

Slee, R. (2005) 'From Countrysides of Production to Countrysides of Consumption?', *Journal of Agricultural Science*, **143**: 255–265.

Smith, F. (2000) '"Multifunctionality" and "Non-Trade Concerns" in the Agriculture Negotiations', *Journal of International Economic Law:* 707–713.

Smith, F. (2007) 'Thinking outside the Green Box: Non-trade concerns in a post-Doha environment', *Environmental Law Review*, **9**: 89–115.

Smith, F. (2009) *Agriculture and the WTO: Towards a New Language of International Agricultural Trade Regulation*. Cheltenham, UK and Northampton, MA, USA: Edward Elgar.

Smith, F. (2010) 'Law, Language and International Trade', *Current Legal Problems*, **63**: 448–474.

Swinbank, A. (2001) *Multifunctionality: A European Euphemism for Protectionism?*, FWAG Conference, National Agricultural Centre, Stoneleigh, available at http://www.apd.rdg.ac.uk/AgEcon/research/workingpapers/as1.pdf (accessed 26 April 2011).

Swinbank, A. (2009a) 'The Reform of the EU's Common Agricultural Policy', in R. Meléndez-Ortiz, C. Bellmann and J. Hepburn (eds), *Agricultural Subsidies in the WTO Green Box*. Cambridge: Cambridge University Press, pp. 70–85.

Swinbank, A. (2009b) 'EU Policies on Bioenergy and their Potential Clash with the WTO', *Journal of Agricultural Economics*, **60**: 485–503.

Swinbank, A. and Tranter, R. (2005) 'Decoupling EU Farm Support: Does the new Single Payment Scheme fit within the Green Box?', *Estey Centre Journal of International Law and Trade Policy*, **6**: 47–61.

Switzer, S. and McMahon, J. (2011) 'EU Biofuels Policy – Raising the question of WTO compatibility', *International and Comparative Law Quarterly*, **60**: 713–736.

UK Committee on Climate Change (2010) *Meeting Carbon Budgets – Ensuring a Low-carbon Recovery: Second Report to Parliament*. London: Committee on Climate Change.

UN (1992) *Agenda 21*, available at http://www.un.org/esa/dsd/agenda21/res_agenda21_14.shtml (accessed 26 April 2011).

USDA (2001) *Food and Agricultural Policy: Taking Stock for the New Century*. Washington, DC: USDA.

Vatn, A. (2002) 'Multifunctional Agriculture: Some consequences for international trade', *European Review of Agricultural Economics*, **29**: 309–327.

Williams, E. (2005) 'Green Payments: The next generation of U.S. farm programs?', *Drake Journal of Agricultural Law*, **10**: 173–204.

Wilson, G. (2007) *Multifunctional Agriculture: A Transition Theory Perspective*. Wallingford: CAB International.

World Food Programme (WFP) (2008) *2007: Food Aid Flows*. Rome: World Food Programme.

WTO (1999) WT/GC/W/273, 27 July.

WTO (2000a) G/AG/NG/W/19, 28 June.

WTO (2000b) G/AG/NG/W/90, 14 December.

WTO (2001a) *Seventh Special Session of the Committee on Agriculture, 26–28 March 2001: Statement by Australia*, G/AG/NG/W/167, 6 April.

WTO (2001b) *Ministerial Declaration*, WT/MIN(01)/DEC/W/1, 20 November.

WTO (2004) *Doha Work Programme: Decision Adopted by the General Council on 1 August 2004*, WT/L/579, 2 August.

WTO (2006) *Activities of the WTO and Climate Change*, available at http://

www.wto.org/english/tratop_e/envir_e/climate_challenge_e.htm (accessed 26 April 2011).

WTO (2007) *Biofuels, Organic Food Proposed as Environmental Goods*, 8 November, available at http://www.wto.org/english/news_e/news07_e/envir_nov07_e.htm (accessed 26 April 2011).

WTO (2008) TN/AG/W/4/Rev.4, *Revised Draft Modalities for Agriculture*, 6 December.

WTO (2010) *Trade Important for Food Security, UN Specialist Tells Agriculture Delegations*, 18 November, available at http://www.wto.org/english/news_e/news10_e/agri_18nov10_e.htm (accessed 22 January 2011).

WTO (2011a) *Members Ready to Move Forward on Environment Negotiations*, 10 and 14 January, available at http://www.wto.org/english/news_e/news11_e/envir_10jan 11_e.htm (accessed 26 April 2011).

WTO (2011b) *Agriculture Committee Continues to Discuss Export Restraints*, 31 March, available at http://www.wto.org/english/news_e/news11_e/ag_com_31mar11_e.htm (accessed 22 April 2011).

Index

Abbott, P. 254
access to justice, R2F 74–6
access to markets 6–7, 21–2
  effect of SPS and TBT measures
    180
  excluded suppliers and standards
    211–12
  GM crops and 160–1, 170–1
Adler, M. 128
Africa
  biggest importer of cereals 90
  food exports 79
  GM crops and 162, 164, 173, 175–6
  land grabs 50, 259
Africa Partnership Forum 76
African Model Legislation for the
    Protection of the Rights of
    Local Communities, Farmers
    and Breeders, and for the
    Regulation of Access to
    Biological Resources 149
Aggregate Measurement of Support
    (AMS) 8–10, 11, 12, 29, 31,
    33–5, 240, 244, 245
Agreement on Agriculture *see*
    Uruguay Round Agreement on
    Agriculture
Agreement on Government
    Procurement 75
Agreement on Pre-shipment
    Inspection (API) 217
Agreement on Subsidies and
    Countervailing Measures (SCM)
    12, 15, 223, 233, 234–5, 243
  research and development
    expenditures 235
Agreement on Technical Barriers to
    Trade (TBT) 82, 166, 167,
    179–201
  climate change and 235–6, 237
  GM crops and 167
  standards and 203–4, 216–17,
    218–19, 236

TBT measures restricting trade in
    agricultural products 189
Agreement on the Application of
    Sanitary and Phytosanitary
    Measures (SPS) 82, 179–201
  ad hoc consultations or
    negotiations on SPS 194, 223
  GM crops and 166–70, 179–81
  political considerations play role in
    countries' choices of SPS
    measures 188
  review and consultations at the
    SPS and TBT Committees
    192–4
  standards and 203–4, 214–17, 218
Agreement on Trade-Related Aspects
    of Intellectual Property Rights
    (TRIPS) 41, 134, 136, 142,
    146–7, 148, 150
  access to justice obligations found
    in 75
agri-food imports, figures for 107,
    108(fig)
agricultural trade, definitions 129n2
agriculture
  climate change policies and 226–8
  'energy function' of 286
  major contributor/source of GHG
    emissions 227, 286
'agro-dumping' 76
Aid for Trade 77, 98, 266
AIPPI *see* International Association
    for the Protection of Intellectual
    Property
Al-Riffia, P. 261
Alston, J. 159
Amber Box 7–10, 13, 16, 29, 86, 241
Anderson, K. 52, 76, 87, 88, 92, 109,
    158, 162, 163
animal welfare 182, 188, 280–1
APREBES *see* Association of Plant
    Breeding for the Benefit of
    Society